DEMOGRAPHIC STUDY OF PRIMITIVE TRIBE

DEMOGRAPHIC STUDY OF PRIMITIVE TRIBE

A COMPARATIVE FRAMEWORK

DR. RANJAN KUMAR BISWAS

SAAD PUBLICATIONS

NEW DELHI - 110 053

SAAD PUBLICATIONS
526, Vijay Park, Street No. 5
Maujpur, Delhi - 110 053 (India)
Phones : 22914760 Mob.: 9810154460

Demographic Study of Primitive Tribe

First Published, 2006

ISBN 81-902572-3-4

PRINTED IN INDIA

Published by Mrs. Sunita Sharma for SAAD Publications, Delhi and Printed at Tarun Offset Printers, Delhi.

Dedicated to the Beloved Memory of

My Elder Brother

Late Sh. Khetramohan Biswas

PREFACE

Saharia tribal people are entangled as the autochthonous of Indian sub-continent. Their sporadical dispersions are confined not only in particular area but also amplified overlapping from one political boundary to another. It is substantial that twenty-one century is the era of technological revolution and the people are concerned to the common agenda of globalization. In spite of this, tribes are habituated to inhabit in hilly tracts and forest regions. Forest resources are endeavoured to exist their daily life. Most of them are positioned under the continuum of socio-economic backward condition, unexposed to modern technological devices, isolated from the main stream of national life, etc which help them to preserve the homogeneity of their unifying traditional beliefs, norms and customs. Being undone, they are resorted to the lap of nature for the pass of their materialistic life without having any dream of tranquility. Any collective dogmatic discourse is also not bestowed for the issue of their entire development.

However, in the context of over all tribal development processes, the present study focuses on a strange and ambivalent attitude. For promoting them to the national life, development is essentially required without any bruised of their traditional culture. Keeping in view of their socio-cultural orthodox, an attempt is made to confer an intensive assessment of demographic components with a comparative framework of other tribal and non-tribal people of India. As a distinguished manner, the first introducing chapter of the present book comprises about tribe, primitive tribe, their concentration and socio-cultural life, demography including fertility, mortality and migration, demographic-anthropology, review of literature, aims and objectives, etc. The second chapter is illustrated by relevant methods for data collection, processing and analyzing. Subsequently, the third chapter consists of a complete socio-cultural parameter of Saharia tribe. In the forth chapter, the results of the study related to population composition, various parameters of fertility and mortality, migration, maternal and child health care, health seeking behaviour and family planning are discussed with a comparative framework of other population. The last chapter systematically embodies a brief account of the over all studies and then furnishes a lot of proposals for their entire socio-economic development.

At the end, acknowledgement is dilated to **Prof. A.K. Kapoor** with a deep sense of gratitude. In breathing out my submission, he is highly appreciated for his sympathetical cooperative nature which provides all round helps to me starting from the initial phase upto the final preparation of this book. As a payment of dedication of this great soul, my hearty salute is no more enough.. I have to feel indebted to him throughout my whole life. It is also acknowledged to all Saharia tribal people for contributing their relevant information. Once more, many thanks are imparted to the authors whose books, articles, reports, etc. have been consulted for this extensive work. Further, my special obligation is reflected to the computer operator for incorporating his ideal artistic excellence. It is also consent that I am so grateful to the publishers for enhancing my immense pleasure by publishing this book.

—DR. RANJAN KUMAR BISWAS

CONTENTS

CHAPTER - I

INTRODUCTION

In a very substantive manner, it is emphasisely attributed that introduction chapter is capable to imply the information about the over all subject matter. In this context, this chapter attempts to consist of the descriptive acquaintation of demography and its evolutionary stages, fertility, mortality, migration and demographic-anthropology. Socio-biological characteristics of Indian tribes: an overview and aims and objectives are also embraced in this chapter.

The greater assuming and significance increasing of demographic study are not only confined in India but also effectively dispersed all over the world. A primary concept is astonished that the ever-growing population is sustained as a particular character of developing and under-developing countries whereas developed countries share it in generally. It is a realized vision that after all, ever-growing population of every country is transgressed on own socio-cultural and political systems. In this regard, the ancient period is also concerned with the significance of increasing population study. History witnesses that both India and abroad were assured almost similar form of inadequate population. During those periods, the explosion of population was not considered as a matter of fact because requirements of growing population were retrained in comparison with the availability of resources. So ever-growing population is concerned as one of the reasons, implicated with the adequate resources.

However, in the recent process of demographic discourse, almost the central. place is occupied by several demographic issues. Various issues relating to rapid population growth throughout the Third World consist of continuation of high fertility in various parts, high infant and child mortality, low status of women and their reproductive health, sex-discrimination and sex differential in mortality which are appeared to be the over-riding items, embodied in the global agenda for immediate attention, research and mitigation. The role of culture (including kinship and inheritance), intimated with the literature of relatively fast growing population is conceptualized as the important explanatory component in understanding the variations of demographic behaviour. Indeed, the manifold and fairly well established assessments confer that the quite important role in shaping demographic outcomes are played by the intrinsic socio-cultural traits of a particular society.

DEMOGRAPHY

The term "Demography" is being originated from two Greek words – 'Demas' meaning people and 'Grapho' meaning draw or write. Further, these two words are come into combination which togetherly indicates to draw or write about people. Combining these Greek words, Guillard first introduced this term 'Demography' in his book "Elements De Statistique Humaine on Demographic Camparre", in 1855. But Graunt is honoured as the real founder of demography. In 1662, he published his famous book entitled "Natural and Political Observation Made Upon the Bills of Mortality" where he scientifically described the demography related works. However, for easily comprehending the meaning, a number of demographic definitions have been made by geographers, economists, social scientists and others. Some of the important definitions are referred to make a clear concept about the manner. The Multilingual Demographic Dictionary defines demography as the "Scientific study of human populations primarily with respect to their size, their structure and their development, (U.N.1958: 3)". According to Cox (1970), "Demography is the study of statistical methods of human population involving primarily the measurements of the size, growth and diminution of the number of the people, the proportions of living being born or dying within the same area or origin and the related functions of fertility, mortality and marriage" According to Bogue (1969), "Demography is the mathematical and statistical study of size, compositions and spatial distribution of human population and of change over time in these aspects through the operations of the processes of fertility, mortality, marriage, migration and social mobility. Although it maintains a continuous descriptive and comparative analysis of trends, in each of these processes and their net result, its long run goal is to develop theories to explain the events that it charts and compares". Hauser & Duncan (1959) defined, "Demography is the study of size, territorial distribution and composition of population, changes their in and the components of such changes, which may be defined as natality, mortality, territorial movement (migration) and social mobility (change of status)".

Demography is considered as one of the oldest science. It is actually very difficult to specify the beginning period of demographic studies in the world. But from manifold point of view, a clear postulation confers that demographic studies are too old as like as human society itself. It is behaved that human beings traditionally keep in mind the over all account of total population in the world. For smoothly conducting administrative works and solving all socio-cultural problems, the requirements were made to gather the exact records of human population. During the flourishing period of Egyptian, Chinese, Greek and ancient Indian civilizations, population records were maintained for various purposes. It is defined that in Jeddah, population estimation was begun in 2030 B.C. The famous Greek historian, Herodotous described that before attacking Greece, Zerxes had taken an account his soldiers in almost 480 B.C. It is also comprised that population enumeration was conducted in Babylon before 3800 B.C., in China around 3000 B.C. and in Egypt almost 2500 B.C. The prominent evidences signify that systematic estimation of Roman population was started from 435 B.C.

According to so many religious books, starting of population counting in India was occurred during the era of *Ramayana* and *Mahabharta*. The sufficient references postulate that population enumeration was initiated specially to those persons who dedicated their life through the Great War of Mahabhrata. Later on, evidences on population counting were followed in the Arthashastra of Kautilya during the ruling period of Chandragupta Maurya in the third century B.C. and very recently in Ain-I-Akabari.

Demography in Modern Time

Although Graunt was considered as the father of Demography, yet, for administrative and political purposes, the estimation of human population was realized long time before the birth of Christ. To examine the reality of population in various countries like-Egypt, India, Rome and others, the writings of Plato, Aristottle, Confucious, et al. were helped so much. At early stage, Graunt (1623) started demographic studies and then his works were continuously elaborated by Patty (1690). He wrote a famous treatise entitled 'Essays on Political Arithmetic' where he thoroughly explained about population growth, urbanization, unemployment, national income, etc. These empirical demographic studies were suddenly enabled to spread in England, France and other European countries and even in America, Australia, Asia, Africa and so on. The life table, rate of death and birth-growth of people in Sweden and then Northampton area were also prepared by Price in 1783. After explaining the excellence of population study of knowledge, Lorimer (1959) published his book entitled 'The Development of Demography'. In a chronological order from 1662 to 1750, Lorimer enlisted fourteen articles as an average of one or two per decade. After publishing 'An Essay on Principles of Population' in 1798, Malthus started a controversial but significant phase of demographic history. The important theme of his essay was that "population when unchecked increased in a geometrical ratio whereas food production increased in an arithmetical ratio". He tried to explain that growth of population was, however to be considered as the main cause of poverty. During 20th century, the rapid development of demographic studies was started by implementing the more powerful research tools for analyzing population data. Keeping in view on population problems, German philosopher Marx (1933) defined that over population growth was not considered as the cause of biological factors. It was regarded as human reproduction but reproduction was performed by involving in capitalist mode. It was followed that over population growth was resulted by variable capitalists, source of demand labour, increasing more slowly than the demand of labouring population, etc. From there, the demand of demographic research was increasing all over the world specially in under developed countries. By the efforts of various personnel, Government agencies, associations, councils, etc., this subject was published through standard books and journals for manifold to all. The world conference of demography was organized in 1927 and then various regional Centres were setup in various countries under the supervision of United Nations.

Demography-Before and After Independence of India

Under British rule, the census works were first organized in 1872 throughout India and from there, a programme was framed to conduct such activities at regular intervals. But through census works, population problems were not minutely investigated till 1930. During the period, British rulers tried to convince the Indian people only by expressing the expension of poverty which was transgressed as the result of ever growing population. For discussing about population problems of nation, first All India Population Conference was arranged in 1930. Various great personnel like - Prof. Gian Chand, Dr. Radha Kamal Mukherjee, Dr. N.V. Sowami, Dr. P.C. Jain, Dr. S. Chander Sekher, et al. participated and devoted their common efforts to write a number of useful books and articles for proclaiming the population problems of this country. The British Government first organized a Health Care Committee in 1943 for looking into the population problems. In 1944, the another initiative was emblemed that with the efforts of educationists, health workers, land department and others. 'Population Data Committee' was setup by the chairmanship of Y.M. Yents and this committee was empowered to advise to the Government about the availability of collected data which were linked with the over growth of Indian population.

After independence (1947), various economic development programmes were implemented one after one all over India. The main purposes of these programmes were to reinforce for economic development and to study the various problems of Indian population. For getting the report of population growth and family related problems, planning Commission appointed a committee in 1954. This committee further fixed the Population Planning Committee and Population Research and Programme Committee. The main purpose of these committees were to inform the actual causes of rapid growing of Indian Population. Such way, a 'Family Planning Board' and a 'Sub Committee' on demographic studies were set up (1956) and by the efforts of these two committees, a number of demographic Centres were established in Bombay (1956) and in Calcutta, Madras and Trivandram (1957). Then these types of so many Centres were founded in Dhawar, Lucknow , Poona , Patna, Baroda and other places throughout the nation.

Scope of Demography

The scope of demographic study is very wide. It always discusses the exact causes about slow or swift growth of birth, population growth, sex ratio, health condition, death rate, etc. Beside these, many economic problems like - types of employment, availability of employment, labour force, landed and other properties, sources of income, bonded labour, living standard, food habit, total family expenditure, indebtness, etc. are thoroughly explained by this subject. The various great souls of this discipline believe that this subject helps in studying the different social problems - such as types of family, family structure, marital status, clan, status of woman, succession, property inheritance, political awareness, religious sphere, educational attainment, causes of migration, problems of migrants, etc. In accordance with their statements, demography is considered as the collective study of human life. It is really that in a very sophisticated manner, demography always deals with personal nature, physical characters, birth, family growth, marriage, divorce, dependency, sickness, hereditary, etc.

The other observations reveal that mainly three aspects like- size, composition and distribution are covered under demographic studies. Size always deals with how many people living in a given population group, what types of change taking place in the size and how much effect of these changes. Demographic study is not only limited in particular number of people in a specific area of a decided duration of time but also it covers the point-record of population number and guesses about the future of likely population number. After size, composition is thought as an important component in population study. It includes all measurable characters of a given population. With respect the decided characteristics, composition may differ between two groups and in this context, one group should be smaller or larger than other group. In demographic study, age and sex are considered as most widely used characteristics. According to Thompson & Lewis (1965), "Relationship between composition of a population and its mortality, fertility and net migration is a reciprocal one, *i.e.*, composition affects the demography processes and these processes in turn effect the composition by determining the age and sex structure of a population". After discussion of size and composition, it is a general tendency to come on distribution of demographic study. Distribution always indicates that in which way people are distributed and the changing nature of distribution. Population distribution is basically changed by the effect of cumulative differences in mortality, birth and net migration rate.

In over growing population, the importance of demographic study may not be gauged. As a venture, it is opined that in the gradual growth of social sciences, population study is considered as the milestone. In a systematic manner, the various population data are collected by the study of demography. Generally, the increasing population figures are estimated by conducting such study of several disciplines and then by the help of estimated figures, the various components of demographic study are assessed. Directly or indirectly the different fields are more or less responsible to signify the study. In the context of political field, the authorities are enabled to know about total population, voter, male and female voter, age increasing rate, migration, etc. Keeping in view on economy, demographic study compares between the rate of population growth and the rate of economic development (Sinha & Zacharia, 1986). Obviously, it is followed that population growth is faster than economic development and in this regard, the over population growth is tried to come under control. For planners, it is also required to get an over all idea about population structure in a particular area where they are going to implement the development schemes. With unsystematic population study, their whole plans have the chance to be collapsed. Even by the help of population data, the planners are also enabled to provide more beneficiary schemes relating to better educational institution, hospital facility, suitable transport system, etc. Demography is also closely concerned with the systematic study of organized society. In fact, due to over growing of population, society is aware to know about the essential social needs. As a population factor, it is essential to confer the provision of electricity, road, water, housing, shopping centre, hygienic facility, etc. Population study is very useful to the administrators. With the help of this study, they can understand the reality and concentrate that where they should add more or less stress for over all development. Afterall taking into consideration to the population growth, the whole administrative machinery moves forwardly.

Demography and Its Relation with Other Subjects

Demographic components and its interrelated factors are incorporately associated with the change of population structure. In connection with this, the famous demographers, Hauser & Duncan (1965) conducted the comparative studies between demography and population studies in various manners. Their assessments imply that the different components of population variation and change are studied by only demographic analysis. Whereas population variables and population change are linked with other variables like- social, psychological, economic, biological, genetic, geographical, etc., which are broadly explained by population studies. Similarly, demographic researches are generally sustained within restricted framework of demographic analysis and then these are concerned with population size, composition, change and its components. But population studies are involved in demographic analysis, discovery, explanation of demographic variation and change, etc. However, demographers and others are interested to participate in population studies inter changeably and in this context, they do not give their accepted or established denotation. Further their relevant arguments emphasisely illustrate that the population studies are called as '*investigation*' whereas demographic studies are acquainted as 'science'.

Nowadays, demography is considered as an independent subject. In spite of this, the relationship of demography with other subjects is not totally ignored. But among related subjects, an integration with each other is always set up for maintaining the self-identity. According to Hauser & Duncan (1959), "The disciplines with which demography is closely related are those, which also have concern with aspects of human population directly or as elements of a more broadly defined population". However, demography and other disciplines are briefly stated in the following regards:

Oxford Dictionary defines "Demography is a part of anthropology which treats of statistics of the births, deaths and diseases". Anthropology is concerned to provide a thorough study on a few sections of a particular society whereas demography is externally concerned with world population figure. It is always alerted to the problem related materials which are collected from biological, economic and socio-anthropological fields. As a social animal, human's belief is always concentrated to anthropological studies. But demographic studies indicate that human being is accepted as a unit of society or a group and within this society or group, he is born and also come to loss his existence. In anthropological studies, changes are incorporated in size whereas society or group is almost same. In connection with collection of figures, anthropologists do not take any guidance from demography, but for understanding social reaction and pressure, demographic help is required very much. In fact, this is a cause which provides an important relation between demography and anthropology subjects. So, it is really that the problem of birth, marriage, marriageable age, marriage system, custom and traditions, divorce, death, etc, are studied by both the subjects. Demographers accumulate the information of problem related figures but the importancy of the topic is decided by anthropologists. Beside this, initiating bilateral relation, some of the complicated components linking to inbreeding, assortive mating, breeding, mutuation, gene flow, etc. are studied by both demographers and anthropologists. It is clear that one subject studies the problems which are connected with population and other subject investigates the reasons of problems in view of bio-social parameters. So, it is confirmed that for solving the various population related problems, social interference is not unavoidable, even its adequate requirements in every stage are assumed tremendously. Demography also studies birth and birth rate and such two factors are directly linked with marriage which is considered as social institution and interestingly studied by social anthropologist. It is defined that population growing is not only limited in biological factors, but also an account of social outlook is provided on birth of the children. Infect, social outlook is thought as under the scope of anthropological studies. Except this, various death rates of society people are sincerely studied by demographers. Whereas different situations like-social habits, environments, living condition, etc. are embodied under the study of anthropologists. In the present state, as like as anthropologists, demographers also take an initiative to study the scientific and advancement temperament of society and society approved rules and regulations.

Various impirical studies are assembled for revelation which always helps to make a relation between demography and human ecology. Population is grown through birth but the existence of birth is concerned with human ecology. In fact, number of population of an area is fluctuated by the effect of environment whereas environment is got pure otherwise polluted by the density of population. Population of a given area is how much careful to protect and develop the resources of environment and accordingly environment is also enabled to sacrifice a fresh surrounding for living the population.

Geography is concerned to study the climatic, economic, physical and biotic condition and nowadays, human geography is comparatively more progressed than physical geography. In other side, the modern geographers start to study the population growth and population related problems in different ways and these are thoroughly interpreted in demographic research. Both geographers and demographers conduct the census works in a given geographical area and as an effective manner, they search and recapitulate the reasons of regional imbalances, disparities, local growth, etc. Taking into consideration on area differentiation, present time, the data of population analysis are usually collected by the corroborately initiative of both geographers and demographers. Beside this, birth, death and migration are considered as the important factors in demographic research but nowadays, such factors are deeply studied by most of the geographers. The purposes of the study are to assess the actual aim of achievement of the demographers. In the present era, ethnic concentration of population, races and their concentration in various parts of the country, health, race and sex problems are keenly studied by different geographers. Moreover, urbanization and non-urbanization, financial dynamics, etc. are very difficult to study in geography whereas, these are directly concerned in demographic study. Cultivation and division of labour, Behaviour of society, food habits, span of life, birth and death rates, etc. are much related with geographic computation. Soil and water directly effect fertility and urbanization, ratio of rural-urban population, migration, etc. are depended on geographical resources which are also thoroughly studied in demography. So, it is a very clear assessment that in spite of some fundamental differences, both geography and demography are incorporately related with each other.

There are no any social sciences where the use of statistic is totally ignored. For the ample scope of utilization, the importance of statistic is increasing day to day. Both figures and data collection are regarded as the main aim of statician whereas interpretation of such figures and data are imparted by social scientists. As a result, it is often said that value of statistic is always neutral. Such way, keeping in view on aim, figure, etc., the population related data are also collected by demographers. In generally, it is followed that statistic is concerned with almost all subjects, so it is used as very widely. In this connection, it is somewhat clear statement that demographers are basically restricted to study only the various aspects of population.

Fertility

In every moment, man is experiencing an accelerating growth of population and production of manufactured goods mainly from last quarter of twentieth century. Due to this exponential growth of population, production, consumption, waste and land occupancy are increasing day to day. For studying the actual reasons of such rapid population growth in respecting size, structure and development, 'Demography' has been evolved as tremendous one. The most significant aspects of demographic studies are considered as fertility, morality and migration of human beings and all these are responsible to maintain its size and growth. However, in a very intellectual manner, the term 'fertility' is meant to understand the actual reproductive performance of women. Simply the word 'fertility' is considered as the capacity to produce both living and death offsprings. According to Thompson & Lewis (1965) "Fertility is generally used to indicate the actual reproductive performance of a woman or groups of women. The crude birth rate (number of births per 1000 population per year) is only one measure of fertility". In other words, Benjamin defined (1965), " Fertility measures the rate of which a population adds to itself by births and is normally assessed by relating the number of births to the size of some section of population, such as the number of married couples of the numbers of women of child bearing age, *i.e.*, an appropriate yard-stick of potential fertility".

Before coming in any discussion on fertility, it is much required to acquaint with the term 'fecundity'. The word fecundity deals with the capacity of a man and woman or a couple to take part in reproduction and then produce living offspring. In simple words, it is indicated as the capacity to bear or conceive kid. According to Thompson & Lewis (1965), "Fecundity is a biological potential – the physiological capacity to participate in reproduction. The absence of this potential is known as *fecundity or sterility*". In every society, some proportions of women are estimated under fertile category. In his regard, the main problem is that as like as fertility, fecundity may not be measured. Generally, an aspersion is made about the maximum fertility level which may be attained by fecundity. However, some others define that there is no any significant difference between fertility and fecundity, sometimes these are used as synonymous terms.

In over all demographic studies, fertility occupies the central position. On behalf of the matter, adequate explanations assure that population growth is depended on fertility. Before Second World War, fertility was analyzed in mathematical way. But in early 1930, the dynamic characters of fertility were realized through the rising birth rate instead of declining in North-West Europe and North America. Fertility is basically a biological factor which is governed by so many social rules and regulations. The universal psychological factors are also directly linked with fertility. However, in a statement, it is defined that fertility is bifurcated to confer the dual functions. In one side, through the process of sexual intercourse, both husbands and wives get pleasure and in other side, as a result of this, women begate children and make the generational continuation of progeny. But the rate of fertility is more or less affected and influenced by many biological, social and also some cultural factors. The biological factor yields an aspersion to the good health whereas its related factors indicate diseases, food habits, etc. As good health condition, generally fecundity is improved and death rate is come down. Usually, people do not give any importancy on social factors which have a partial chance to influence or check fertility. The early age at marriage or child marriage always increases fertility rate whereas late age at marriage always comprises reverse character committed in decreasing rate. Polygamy is considered as a vital social factor which also influences fertility rate. The low fertility is not always pertained through separation or divorce. If the separation or divorce is performed during suitable fertile age, then child birth is restricted automatically. Such way, widowhood is also come under estimation as an important factor which controls the fertility rate. After birth of a child, sometimes sexual restriction is imposed by the society and duration of this sexual restriction is depended according to the society-approved rules. In connection with the period of duration of sexual restriction, the fertility may be varied in low or high.

In India as well as abroad, there are so many rules, restrictions, self-responsibility and other factors which influence not to marry in marriageable age of boys or girls. In that condition, they have no any opportunity for mating and thus, fertility is checked automatically. In fact, if frequently mating is initiated between husband and wife, then there is a chance of high fertility (Harrison & Boyce, 1972). Various contraceptives like-oral pills, loop, condom and other unnatural measures like - abortion, infanticide, etc. directly regulate the child birth. In some societies, the handicapped children are not approved to take care and in that condition, they are killed for free from shortage of food problem. There are some remarkable societies where female infanticide is conducted according to the society-approved rules and regulations. In fact, as a result of such infanticide, marriageable female is very rarely available and due to shortage of marriageable female, polyandry marriage is generally held. As a result of polyandry marriage, afterall fertility is come under control. Sometimes, less fertility is estimated in some societies where food supplies are insufficient and in this context, Malthus theory attempts to clarify that through environmental effect, a balance is maintained between food supply and population growth. Rural-urban variation also effects fertility. In rural area, fertility is recorded comparatively higher than urban area and this rural-urban fertility variation is followed in the state of Kerala and Maharashtra of India and also in France. Various economic conditions are directly associated with fertility measures. As an achievement of sound economy in the joint family of agricultural landlord, husband and wife are freely allowed to live together and produce more offsprings. Cultural parameters also imply that due to rule out the religious bar, there is a chance to be conducted a number of marriages and frequently child birth. It is followed that those persons are pressurized by mental works, their offsprings are produced less in number as compared with those who are engaged in some sort of physical works. In some societies, women are involved in different works and as like men, they face various problems which effectively curtail the fertility rate. Beside this, in most of the societies, parental love and old age security are existed and their every attempt is applied to have male children. In this condition, if girls are born then child producing activity is continued till upto the birth of male child. In this process, the ultimate result is converted into high fertility. Economic security and comfortable living standard always influence to perform large number of child births.

Fertility is directly affected by a large number of deaths. Due to the effect of various factors, child morality was very high in the past. But at the present state, child morality is under control and parents may wish their desirable number of children. For checking up the high fertility rate, the role of educated mothers is highly praisable. According to the capacity of better procreation, the educated mothers obviously produce limited number of offsprings. Such type of child birth limitation is not followed among illiterate societies. But for unlimited dispersal of science, fertility controlling contraceptives are so quickly developed and proclaimed all over the world. For limiting the birth rate, incentives as well as disincentives are produced by each political party who are standing inside or outside in Government policy. The sterilization or similar other measures adopted persons are allowed to take more facilities than non-adopted persons. Beside this, all society members are enthusiastic to maintain social status and in this context, all parents desire that their children are to be more capable to get the opportunity of high status. So, for occupying such type of high position, their offsprings have to be born in limited number.

Mortality

In order to understand the matter, only three responsible components are highlighted to change the population structure. Among these, mortality is considered as one of the components whereas the others are being fertility and migration. It is postulated that human beings are mortal. They have to die once upon a time of their life after birth. In other words, after birth, permanent extinction of all signs of life from human body is taken place and it is meant as death. The United Nations and World Health Organization combinely defined (1970), "Death is the permanent disappearance of all evidence of life at any time after birth has taken place (postnatal) cessation of vital functions without capacity of resuscitation". According to this definition, it is a clear understanding that only after live birth, death is occurred. So, a close link is always performed between mortality and live birth. Hauser & Duncan (1959) defined death by saying, "Death prior to complete expulsion or extraction from its mother of a product of conception, irrespecting of the duration of pregnancy, the death is indicated by the fact that after such separation the foetus does not breathe or show any other evidence of life, such as breathing of heat, pulsation of umbilical cord or definite movement of voluntary muscles". Normally a child is to be stayed in the womb of mother during 28 weeks and keeping in view on this matter, the World Health Organization suggests that such remaining 28 weeks should be registered in death records (cf. Raj, 1982).

It is made a very controversial issue connected with the starting period of death related data collection. Some evidences indicate that such data collection practice was begun from very old. Roman History confers that practice of death related information collection was started in third century. In the fourth century, there was lot of evidences of data collection prevailed in ancient Italy. Slowly and gradually, such practice was proclaimed throughout the world. In England, death related eminent information were first collected in 1558, and later on, Thomas (1946) expressed a very systematic manner related to the activity. Grount is regarded as the pioneer of this field. About death, he began the information collection and then in 1662, he published a book, entitled "Natural and Political Observation Mentioned in the Following Index and Made upon the Bills of Mortality". After that, in 1755-57, life table was started to prepare in Sweden. In England, further the information about the various causes of death were started to collect by Farr (1876). In USA, such type concerned data collection was continued at the beginning of 20th century. However, in 1933, under the supervision of USA Census Bureau, information about death and birth were begun to collect from whole country. It is stated that as early as in 1886, the British Government in India realized the need and then they were keenly interested to collect the data about death. At initial phase, it was followed that most of the people of this country did not prefer to get death registered by any competent authorities. They just encouraged the people to come under registration of death. Under the supervision of the Registrar General of India, the death registrations were systematically maintained from 1941. There was a very difficult environment to collect the death related information from all the respondents. In most of the cases, they could not give information about the exact age, occupation, education and reasons of death of deceased persons. Particularly in rural areas, no any such type of register is maintained where death records are easily available of any deceased person. Because there, death certificate is not required in relating to settlement of property or other disputes.

Keeping in view of various demographers, it is proved that comparatively women live longer duration than men. As very authentically, it can be explained that under less strain, normally most of the women are positioned whereas men are always stammered by various undulating forces. Similarly women have enough time to care their health but men are always busy and in this regard, they pay very less attention. As like as, nature gifted physical capacity of women ensures that they are successfully enabled to tolerate the pangs of disease as compared with men. Beside this, most of the women generally stay at home without having any tension which is considered as less exposed to dangers. Side by side, another clarification is made that men are more exposed to dangers because most of the time they tensionally move anywhere outside their home.

All human beings are enthusiastic to live longer duration. In spite of this, they are to be lost their survival power by the occurrence of death. However, various important causes are linked with every death. In some cases, patients are not properly diagnosed by any doctor during the period of their physical problem and as a result, they are incurred to death without identifying the contaminated reason. Due to illiteracy, people are not aware to know the exact cause of death whether they are providing the regulár nursing service to the patient. Within a certain period of time, even the qualified doctors are also unable to identify the exact disease. Sometimes, it is followed that patient is suffering from many diseases and in this condition, a very complexity is arisen to identify the indebted causes of death. Taking into consideration the view of World Health Organization, most of the deaths are occurred by the effect of various diseases.

A lot of evidences defines that in world, various death rates in all countries are not registered in a similar pattern. Always, the diversity in death rates are incorporated by different countries. Even death rates are varied from one to another section of a society and even from one to another state of a country. If some sections of a society are enjoying better medical facilities, their death rates are low as compared with other sections of same society. It is discriminated that mortality may differentiate between time and war, different social classes and within a nation, developed and less developed countries, etc. Mortality differences are also occurred by socio-economic disbalances. In socio-economic advanced nations, death rates are come under control because the people of such nations can easily afford proper medical facility within stipulated period. Beside this, various types of profession also influence death rates. There are many persons who are engaged in vocations, usually their death rates are very less comparatively the other people who are exposed to involve in vocations. Due to loneliness and depressed of widow, divorce and unmarried life, death is more proven as compared with those who lead a happy, affectionate and married (familial) life. Mortality is also influenced by the negative contribution of different environmental effects (Heer & Smith, 1968).

In spite of various merits and demerits realised as the important phenomenon, the rural-urban residential differences also make a great effect to fluctuate the death rates. According to Thompson & Lewis (1965), "The almost complete lack of sanitary measures in nearly all cities until near the end of the 19th century and the crowding of great majority of city dwellers in hovels with no windows, bordering on streets where one could almost touch the structures on both sides by stretching out his arms and where the sewages and drinking water ran down the same, open gutters, ensured contagion and infection almost perfectly." In spite of all these things, different death rates in the village are emblemed obviously high as compared to urban area (Thompson & Lewis, 1965).

It is postulated that married couples live longer life than the widow, widower, divorcee and who are passing isolated life. In this context, Thomas & Lewis defined (1965), "Marriage is selective as regards both physical constitution and social adaptability". Due to physical as well as mental problem, some persons are restricted not to marry and in that condition, they always sick death to die in a shorter period of life. In other side, some particular married couples are understandingly passing the regularity of living and their death rate is very low.

Occupation and mortality are incorporately related with each other. It is evidenced that the underground mining work enforces to high death rate. Marshy and mosquitoes affected working places closing to industrial belt are always infected by malaria germs and in that situation, malaria disease yields an active role to enhance the high death rate. In various cases, statements have been made that due to less opportunity of work, labourers have to engage in hard work but wages are paid as very low, then mortality is influenced. Occupational mobility also increases the death rate. In the context of environment, some workers are interested to change their occupational places but due to various barriers, they are oppressed not to fulfil their desire. In opposite cases, some workers are adjusted with the environment of a particular area and they have no any desire to change their working places. But here also, the crude situation plays a negative role to fail their expectation. So in each condition, there is a higher chance of mortality increasing trend (Thompson & Lewis, 1965).

Infant mortality is considered as serious problem in our country. Whether it is implicated in advanced or backward societies but after all infant mortality is not controlled till now. In infant condition and also above the age of 55 years, generally the death rates are highly observable. But the maximum attention is always provided on infant and in other side, less attention is paid on those persons who attained 55 years age and above. Because in every society, infant mortality is significantly thought as a whole whereas old age mortality is considered as natural death. The available information confer that in developed countries, infant mortality is very low as compared with developing countries. The child of below 4 months of the age is acquainted as Neo-Natal and then upto 12 months is estimated as post Neo-Natal phases. During this period, the various contaminated reasons like—lack of medical facility, unexperienced nurse, congenital, maltransformation, immature birth, temperature variation, illiteracy of parents regarding negligence of child care, pollution, poverty, effected nutritional food, unexpected sex of the child, illed health of mother, shorter birth interval between two children, lack of breast milk, non-availability of nutritional food during pregnancy, system of early age at marriage, etc. are responsible to influence the mortality rate (Thompson & Lewis, 1965).

The permanent extinction of all signs of human life is phenomenon in the context of mortality discussion. But morbidity is different symptoms which indicate that the person is actually alive but due to his mental problem, he is not capable to perform any mental or physical work. Health is considered as the situation of complete physical, mental and social well being. Among all the stated conditions, unluckily the miss of essential one is called *morbidity.* During morbidity condition, person has the chances to be deformed, deficient, mentally depressed and like those. It is defined that in some cases, the disease or physical problem is diagnosed after a long period of time and as an affair of complicated situation, instead of even care, the survival of the patient is considered as under risk. Generally morbid person creates a scene and sense of depression among his closely known persons. In fact, he is regarded as burden to known persons as well as society. In most of the cases, the person who is suffering from long sickness, is going to be isolated by the family as well as by the society. In this condition, the normal persons are irritated and felt burden by affected person. For avoiding such sickness, everybody takes precaution for future.

Migration

Migration means the change of residence from one geographical area to another new area whęre along with the purpose, the new settlement is built up in a permanent or semi-permanent manner. According to Hagerstrand (1957), "We will use the term migration for the change of residence of an individual from one parish or commune to another." Time interval between the date of arrival and the date of departure are usually specified by the migration. Weinberg (1961) defined, "Migration is the changing of the place of abode permanently or, when temporarily for an appreciable duration..... It is used symbolically in the transition from one surrounding to another in the course of human life." However, migration is usually considered as an international phenomenon. At the present situation, the trend of migration of people is increased and it is generally peformed from under developed countries to the developed countries. In this context, this type of migration is thought as brain drainage. For improving the life style, qualified, brilliant, competent and healthy people generally migrate in search of suitable services. In fact, the young generation is usually migrated because they are the over zealousness for hard work. In connection with gender bias, adequate information specify that female migration is always occurred far less common as compared to male migration.

Whether migration is extensive or slow, but there is a clear assessment that migration was started from prehistoric periods. Early migration was generally initiated on the basis of climatic disturbance, social conflict, problem of flora and fauna of various environments. In that time, river or lake valleys were also attracted by the migrants for building up the residences near to its sources. Except the migration from one to another part in the country, migration from one to another country was also taken part. In the context of ancient past, India was a glorified country and for both study and trade purposes, a number of people used to come from foreign countries. In fact, Indian also visited to abroad for spreading the religious activities and trade purposes. So, migration was continued from early stage of Indian history. Later on, the study of Davis (1963) informed that more Indian migrated into foreign countries than those who came in India from abroad.

In fact, tribal as well as local war is also highly indebted to determine the various direction of population dispersion. As a result of war, the potential migrants are usually murdered and in this condition, the new migrants are slowly come from other areas. In the ancient part, migrants came from Aryan to India as the cause of war. In the middle of 5th century, A.D., it was asserted that the invasion of Attila entered into central Europe through a successive achievement of war. Then migration through the reason of war was prescribed as very detrimental because so many potential migrants were to be murdered. Taking into consideration to the whole process of migration, it was a clear view that people shifted from one to another area mentioning relation with each other in their small group.

The collective specification ensures that who transfer their residences from one to another place, they are called as '*migrants*'. 'Place of Origin' is another term and it indicates that the place which is left by migrants. In the context of place of origin, further the persons are regarded as 'out migrants' and the place where migrants resettle is identified as 'immigrants'. In fact, it is clearly known that in respect with place of origin, the persons may be considered as out migrants or in migrants. Thus, persons are regarded as out emigrants and as immigrants for the place of origin and in the place destination respectively. Sometimes migration is performed accrossing the international boundaries, then emigration and immigration terms are used for specifying the matter.

Without any cause, nobody is ready to leave his birth place, friends, kins and neighbours. People migrate from one to another place within same country and also one to another country. In some countries, the rate of migration is very low whereas in some other countries, this rate is very high. However, it is transgressed that so many causes are responsible for the occurrence of migration. Generally a few factors are highly prevalent whereas some other factors collectively enforce the persons to be migrated. All responsible factors are divided into two *i.e.*, pull and push factors. Pull factors indicate better education, health, leisure, etc. whereas push factors indicate loss of job, accommodation, kins, etc. For getting a better economic opportunity, people leave their birth place, area, district, state and even their country. The hill dwellers come to plain land, rural people come to urban area, eastern people come to western side to search the sources of earning. In agricultural society, people leave the uncultivated surplus land to the absolutely landless people and occupy the fertile land for better cultivation. Beside this, the geographical factors are also very much indebted for migration. Generally, people like to migrate to the specific area where comfortable climate and minerals are followed in abundance. As like as, they are not ready to stay in the area where chances of flood, cyclone, fire, earth quake, etc., are occurred quite frequently. Various social factors are also incorporately related with migration. Due to different social barriers, the possibility of over all development approaches are tressed as less whereas the provided social restrictions are unbearable and in such condition, people are enforced to migrate without depending any substitute. Illiterate people are generally followed among various traditional societies. By initiating personal efforts, sometimes the people of these societies are rarely got educated. Even after getting formal education, they normally come to aware to their back dated social rules and regulations and then they also try to add their common voice against child marriage, dowry, drinking habits, wastage of expenditure through social ceremony, etc. In this situation, rarely society approved rules and regulations are changed or modified. Otherwise, they are to be migrated by the pressure of their old orthodox. Various demographic factors are also responsible for the cause of migration. In a residing area where density of population is comparatively very high, people always feel rush and then they incorporate their maximum efforts to go on another area through migration. Beside this, migration is taken place from one area or country where death rate is high due to the effect of diseases, shortage of reasonable materials, etc. as compared with birth rate. Obviously people leave this area and resettle to another area. Migration is also correlated with the pressure of various contaminated political factors. If government recognized political rules are not suited by any groups, normally they migrate to other countries. In some cases, it is also assessed that when people are in suspense of war or other disturbance and Government has no any controlling power, then they normally leave the country for self security. Beside this, people migrate to new places where they are free from religious intoleration. The larger religious groups are always dominant on other groups. There is ample scope to happen the religious conflict. For avoiding such conspiracy, the peaceful minded persons migrate to another place (Thompson & Lewis, 1965). Industrial development is also attracted the migrants. To make investment and ensure of job security, both owner and worker groups respectively leave their native places and settle down the developing industrial towns or cities.

Both in developed and under developed countries, the large number of population growing is considered as an important factor. There, nation is trying to encourage for adopting the family planning programmes. Due to heavy population pressure, poverty and inadequacy of accommodation, indecency and so on, people migrate from one area to another and even from one country to another for getting the better opportunity. In most of the industrilised countries, it is a depiction that they are in a position for considerably controlling the population growth. So in various extents, population pressure can be helped by international migration (Thompson & Lewis, 1965).

Both positive and negative values are hidden in the process of migration. The first, positive value concentrates on a better job. For getting better job opportunity, people are motivated to migrate. Migration is also taken place for achieving favourable climate which is considered as another positive value. Internal migration is sometimes occurred to change particular climate. Beside this, marriage and such type of kin alliance are also regarded as a significant inducement for migration. As like as, so many negative values are also performed through migration. By the process of migration, it is disrupted the international relationship between migrants and kins and also old friends. Migrants are come to new culture, learn new customs discarding old, know sometimes new language, etc. and these are considered as complex process. In this regard, Heer (1967) stated, "Since the cost of migration generally varies in direct proportion to the distance travelled, the member of migrants to a given place tends to very inversely with the distance."

Some expectations are also taken place through migration. In fact, such expectations may be proved as true while in others, these may have a chance to be false. When migrants are in frustration with the context of their expectations, then they think either return to the place of origin or migrate again to the other place. For adjustment to the new environment, generally migrants feel various difficulties. As a pressure of migrated population in a particular area, the price rates of necessary commodities are generally come up. Even fertility and also mortality may be affected by migrated population. Land and real estate-values are come in high price. The new region of migrants is also benefited by availability of low cost labour. Without expensing so much amount, the landlord produce better crops during productive year (Heer & Smith, 1968). Even when migrated area is under populated, then economies of trade are achieved by the help of immigrants and as a result, the cost of goods are deducted by increasing production and marketing. This system also helps to raise living standard of all people of that area.

DEMOGRAPHIC-ANTHROPOLOGY

Demography is regarded as the policy oriented and interdisciplinary science which is concerned with understanding and measuring population change. Fertility, mortality and migration of human beings are the main studied fields of demographic research. In other side, anthropology is considered as the wholistic study of man irrespective of time, space and culture. So, both demography and anthropology are concerned with the study of human beings in the context of various dimensions. Keeping in view of relation, the Euro-American anthropologists practise parallel tracts along which anthropology and demography often run (Bledsoe & Hirschman, 1989). Scholars of both demographic and anthropological fields generally move forward regarding their own agenda, speaking their language and following their suitable method of data collection. Even many anthropologists borrow the research interest from demographers in connection with family formation and dissolution, health, migration and fertility and then phrase these issues as kinship, birth practices, creation of affinal ties, etc. (Greenhalgh, 1989).

Little or even less anthropological attention is generally concentrated on fertility and mortality whereas the demographic attention is always widely focused on mortality and morbidity (Mosley & Chen, 1984). Demography is a professional and global interdisciplinary science during 1930s. The practitioners of demography are generally originated from graduate programmes in sociology, economic and statistic whereas social and economic demography specially confer the practitioners from university level, Governments and Governmental agencies, etc. So, demographic-anthropology is considered as a more recent specialised subject Before 1970s, without taking any training in formal demographic methods, some anthropologists studied the population change. But these studied populations were usually too small for the purpose of formal demographic analysis.

Logically, the collected data of anthropologists are often full of errors and for this, they are not usually very good demographers. As a result, the anthropologists are to be tainted by statistical and demographic methods in university level and such trainings are still far less common in graduate programmes of anthropology. Demographers are generally criticized by anthropologists for their rational economic models of demographic behaviour which emphasize to narrate the cultural differences. Depending on second hand collected data, demographers can come into conclusion but without personal involvement in data collection, anthropologists never can come into same. So, in this field, only demographers as well as anthropologists are not able to develop their adequate and accurate research activities, they co-operatively depend on each other and all these help to originate the new field 'demographic – anthropology'.

Demographers generally adopt large scale and quick data collection methods for completing the national census survey. But as higher qualified anthropologists, they prefer to little scale, slow and intensive data collection field methods for the research of a particular area or community concerning with sample. During long time, anthropological researchers stay among the group or community under study, co-operate with the community members and learn their local language. Spot observation and interview are considered as the main dependable methods of anthropological research. They very much require to learn the native language which tests epistemological fundamental reason in developing qualitative data. In anthropological sense, one type of qualitative data concerns the own ideas of the local respondents and it is referred to as 'emic' data and another type of qualitative data is based on own constructs and categories of researchers and it is also referred to as 'etic' data.(Pike, 1954). Demographers generally follow 'etic' method for data collection.

For avoiding dry discussion, qualitative data offer various ways of acquainting interested anecdotes to make cheerful situation. Most of the demographers may not wish to emulate with energetic field workers. Through data collection and analysis of such data, these field workers show that there is considerable scope for creative combination of anthropological and demographic studies. Beside this, conducting initial qualitative studies of a population, they may lay the ground work for later qualitative surveys, generate hypotheses, target a known location of high mortality among a specific subpopulation and so on. By general information collected on folk classifications, demographers can improve qualitative techniques which ensure that survey data are culturally relevant issues and clearly understood by both researchers and respondents.

The formal surveys generally collect the as usual data whereas qualitative methods specially collect the better qualitative data (Bleek, 1987). Beside this, the researchers allow qualitative methods for probing the different nuances of meaning and solving all evident contradictions in responses. Qualitative data are sometimes used to generate the explanations for quantitative demographic differentials (Ford & Arcury, 1984). To get the reasonable explanations by retrospective as well as time–sequence data, anthropologists always try to combine the qualitative and quantitative methods. But the backgrounds of the event like-illness, deaths, etc. are proved by highly suitable case study and in-depth interview methods.

In summing up, most of the anthropologists in one hand conclude that the first preference should be given on qualitative methods. Because, these methods always collect the view relating to the own problems of respondents, measure thoroughly and cure their melodies. Demographers on the other hand, generally argue that to assess the prevalence of certain problems, the first preference should be given on broad survey and then for checking up the specific issues, anthropological methods may be incorporated. In general view, there is an equal value of both qualitative and quantitative methods. Regarding to the attitudes of the respondents or events, any one of the methods should be applied for the purpose of data collection. Therefore, the best demographic as well as anthropological research work is not only limited between qualitative and quantitative issues but also it is usually moved on capacity of explanation, motivation, categorization, search numerical evidence and so on of the researchers.

A new dimension provides that for mutual understanding and colleagueship with demographers, anthropology has also been changing. In some specific fields of anthropological demography, the various personnel have written the new literatures for guidance and data presentation. For instance in historical demography, the different scholars like – Swedlund & Armelagos (1976), Hassan (1979) and Willigan & Lynch (1982) published so many literatures like – Guide to Methods, Techniques in Archaeological Research, Techniques in Historical Demography respectively, etc. These literatures are very helpful to anthropological research. Beside this, anthropologists are also generating new methods and techniques which are not blamed as 'Home Made' and then these methods and techniques are pretested in the context of particular problems, specially in anthropology, not in demography. In this regard, a series of computer assisted programmes 'KINPROGRAM' was prepared by Collier (1976). In his series, genealogical materials were accepted as input and entire demographic explanations of the population were also produced as output. Dyke & Morrill (1980) conducted a survey on the field of genealogical demography and wrote their report in a volume where both techniques and results were demonstrated skillfully.

All palaeodemographical fields analyse the skeletal remains and archaeologically obtained materials which are almost uncommon field of demography but these are wholly occupied by anthropologists. The different methods of aging and sexing plus, Life Table construction and its explanations, etc. are considered as complicated matters and on the ground, the concerted attacks are continued from various directions. People are always gaining new confidence in their competence. They are involving to read with understanding, plan for study, evaluate the table, develop models of the implications of various findings, etc. Both anthropologists and demographers are also combinely teaching to students about courses in population.

There is identification of many scholars who specially focussed upon the proper units of interpretation in population studies. Bruch (1980) and Netting, *et al.*, (1983) generally targeted to collect household information and in this regard, Skinner (1977) followed that all information were implicated with the various aspects of family norms. However, all these fields are included in genetic demography which shows the breeding group. Depending on these points, the physical anthropologists would formulate the genetic demographic data which helped to correspond in demographic-anthropology as a whole. Palaeodemographic researchers generally study the skeletal remains of prehistoric population. Side by side, palaeo anthropological researchers not only limit their studies in skeletal remains but also they extend their works in associated finds of skeletal remains of prehistoric population and then they also compare these materials with the contemporary people. So, it may be said that in demographic-anthropology, this is the most fascinating and frustrating area.

A very compatible perspective of Malthus (1976) is to reflect on biological orientation to human behaviour. Naturally, the thoughts of Malthus are considered as the important components of Darwin's theory on human evolution. Such way in anthropology, studies of population are very consistent with biological perception. In other side, size and structure of population combinely form a standard set of units and indicators of biological well-being. The views of Wilson (1975), Hastings (1978), Changnon & Irons (1979) and Irons (1979) possess that biological theory in anthropology generates the positive focus upon demographic-anthropology and as a result, this is thriving in large part. To study the formation of social structure in peasant societies, it is required to frequently explore the consequences of population process. In those societies, the interrelation of economy, kinship, family and household are also readily followed but the least escapables relating the consequences are searched by demographic process.

Therefore, it is clear that the field of demographic-anthropology is importantly considered for consisting of the theoretical and methodological advances. The central problem of this field is that the various questions on abilities, models, factual base, etc., may be asked and in replying, the preparation of appropriate answers is too difficult. In this discipline, there is no any standard methodology to continue the research work of population, contemporary or skeletal. The valuable data collection of demographic anthropology is regarded as hard task because there is no any specification of particular methodology for the purpose of particular data collection.

In spite of all these problems, the researchers of this discipline emerge the new consideration of the related literature and apply the suitable method for data collection, proper analysis, interpretation and then prepare the survey report. For establishing a tradition of carefully reviewing and publishing, they continuously circulate the reports and various articles in various journals of demographic-anthropology. During last 20 years, by the positive efforts of researchers, demographic-anthropology has been increasing interest and nowadays, there is an expectation that anthropologists will make a major contribution of demographic process and consequences of humanity. In reverse, demographers will also make a major contribution to comprehend the past and present work of anthropology.

SOCIO-BIOLOGICAL CHARACTERISTICS OF INDIAN TRIBES: AN OVERVIEW

It is a compulsion that all available concerned literatures are required to survey for achieving the general knowledge about the transitional perspective of the research. At this juncture, the researchers generally undertake the extensive literature survey which is connected with their assigned research. For conferring very authentic study, the academic journals, books, government reports, abstracting and index journals and published and unpublished bibliographers, etc. are very much tapped depending on the nature of the research. Generally, the researchers are acquainted to be well-conversant by retrieving the retrospective materials in the field. By devoting sufficient time, they usually review the materials and imaginate about the types of data which may be available for the coming operational research. In this regard, Kothari (1989) defined, "Knowing what data are available often serves to narrow the problem itself as well as the technique that might be used". After all, all available materials help to the researchers to gain sufficient knowledge for taking new strides in concerned research. In this regard, they may enable to move up starting from the existing premise, identify the types of difficulty and take possible encounter for necessary remedies. Such studies assure to bestow the helpful suggestions and promote the new lines which are approachable for the present research.

The review of literatures related to the various components of the Indian people make a very clear assessment to linger the present study in a very sophisticated manner. In accordance with the vogue, people of different social groups are incorroborately implicated as the composers of Indian society. Caste and tribe among all social groups are specified as the dominant unit in forming the ancient Hindu society and later on primitive society. Even prehistoric incidents of this nation prove by evidences that the inheritance of tribal people are not only confined in a particular region but also their sporadical dispersions are emblemed from remote hilly tracts and forest regions of sub-Himalaya to North-Eastern regions, the Mountain belt between Narmada and Godavari rivers of Central India and in Western Ghats pervading from Wynad to Kaniyakumari of South part of India (Sinha, 1990). Still now, the tribal people are inhabiting in isolation and they have the limited contact with the people of other communities. As a result of this, their customs, norms, traditional beliefs, etc. are preserved to a large extent. Various social scientists, specially anthropologists are highly acquainted for their ideal contribution in conducting the extensive studies on social, cultural and economic life and also demographic dimensions of different Indian tribal groups. Their stated findings in this regard are highlighted in a squinted manner:

Economic Character/Occupation

Regional influences are so much concerned to vary the economic character/ occupation of the tribal groups of India. It is substantial that every tribal group is involved to practise a particular work as primary occupation whereas their other activities are expressed under the category of secondary occupation. Keeping in view the overall activities, Majumdar & Madan (1996) classified the tribal occupation into food gathering, agriculture, shifting cultivation, crafts, pastoralism, labouring, etc. By initiating another indepth studies, Vidyarthy & Rai (1977) further made a very relevant classification indicating forest hunting type, hill cultivation, plain agriculture, simple artisan, pastoral type, folk artisan, service and trade, etc. Various studies of Bhowmick (1963) comprise that avoiding criminal activities, Lodha tribal groups of West Bengal are going to be motivated themselves to practise agriculture whereas daily labour, hunting, fishing, crafting, fuel selling, business, etc. are practised by them as the sources of supplementary income. According to the study of Enthoven (1975), it has been acquainted that as hereditary servants, Dubla tribal groups of Gujarat are devoted to the lord groups. In very rarely cases, they earn through cultivation, dairy farming, fishing, fuel selling, crafts, collection of roots, tubers, Mahua flowers, etc. The retrospective report of Atkinson (1981) reveals the primary as well as secondary occupation of Raji tribe of Kumaun Himalaya. This study highlights that most of the tribal households practise agriculture, animal husbandry, tailoring, etc. as their primary occupation. Traditional hunting, gathering and crafting occupations are implicated with their life as secondary sources of income.

A prolong study, conducted by Bose (1981) among Garo

tribe of Meghalaya reports that both male and female of them are involved in shifting cultivation whereas a large number of them practises daily wage labour but service under government are far less common. The available information, collected by Bhanu & Saheb (1983) comprise that the traditional occupations of Irula tribe of Tamil Nadu are hunting and trappering of porcupines, rats and snakes. But slowly they are motivating themselves to practise settled cultivation, agricultural labour, plantation labour, etc. By another study of Som (1993), it is known that the occupations various communities of different villages in Orissa are depended on the sets of environment. This study also specifies that most of the villagers are engaged to practise agriculture, labour, soil conservation, selling indigenous products, etc. Due to lack of land, Hill Korwa tribe of Madhya Pradesh, studied by Pandey & Tiwari (1996) are mainly assorted to earn through daily labour whereas their secondary occupations are associated with various forest products. Study of Sharma (1988) focuses that the main occupation of Bharia tribe of Madhya Pradesh are agriculture, farm labour, pastoral, basketry, leave plate making, etc. Minor forest products also play the important role in their livelihood. In this regard, an important study, conducted by Patra (2001) communicates that Raji tribe of Uttaranchal are not confined in hunting and food gathering stages. Occupations of the present generation are dispersed in cultivation, fuel selling, crafting, fishing, etc. In spite of these, more or less the Raji economy is influenced by the existence of shifting cultivation.

Household Income

Income is regarded as the key factor for the development of socio-economic status. But in population dynamics, determination of sources of income is assumed as very difficult. It is substantial that fertility is incorporately related with socio-economic status whereas socio-economic status is depended on sources of income. However the total household income is generated by the earning of all members of a particular family. The fluctuation in quantity of household income is also depended on the number of earning members, their type of activity, etc. In this regard, Bhasin's studies (1990) among Bhutia of Sikkim and Gaddi of Himachal Pradesh are concered to point out the annual income. His collected information define that yearly income of most of the families are varied from rupees 10,001 to 15,000/- An intensive investigation of Mahanta (1993) among a multicaste Assamese village reports about three category of income groups. Per month earning capacity of lower and middle income groups are varied from rupees 50 to 200/- and rupees 201 to 1200/- respectively whereas upper income group illustrate their monthly income from rupees 1201 to 2001/-

For an average estimation of monthly income, study of Sabat & Dash (1996) reveals a clear picture among Khand tribe of Orissa. Their assessment specifies that most of the households earn rupees 2001 to 2500/- per month. In very rarely cases, some of the households elaborate their monthly earning amount above rupees 3000/- Another comparative study, conducted by Basu (1998) emblems the approximate income of Santal tribe and Lodha tribe of West Bengal. Large number of Santal and Lodha earn monthly rupees 500 to 900/- whereas possibility of monthly rupees 1000 to 1999/- are earned by only a few families. For getting a clear information about the economic position of Bharia tribe of Madhya Pradesh, Sharma's study (1998) is very useful. This study specifies that the average monthly income of Bharia tribe is rupees 543/- which is comparatively lower than the average monthly income of Gond tribe (rupees 658/-). In the context of income variation, his study clarifies that due to very remote inhabitation, Bharia tribal groups are no more facilitated by continuous work opportunity which curtails their monthly income.

Ownership of Land

It is a consent that most of the tribal people in India are landless. For their livelihood, they are to be depended on wage labour and collection of forest products. Very less number of tribal groups are come under identification to have their little quantity of land portion. But these land holder groups are mostly deprived by unavailability of written document of their land. By simple plotting, they generally demarcate the boundary of their land. For the purpose of shifting cultivation, understandingly they acquire the plots of forest land according to their requirement of food grains. Now a days, the policy of State Government is implemented to give them the deed of their cultivated land. However, in the context of land ownership, various studies have been conducted among different tribal groups. Studies of Mishra (1976) focus a very typical situation about land ownership of tribal population of Tripura. It is a legend that inspite of ownership of entire kingdom, the king of Tripura did not desire to ascribe the title of 'Landlord' from tribes who were practising "Jhum" cultivation. Even census book of the state (1968) does not make any report of inclusion the 'Jhum' cultivated land in land tenure system. By a descriptive report of Tiwari (1984), it is known that land alienation is considered as the most acute problem among Hill Korwa tribal groups of Madhya Pradesh. His study comprises that mainly the Ahir groups are charged for forcibly encroach the fellow land of Hill Korwa. They alienate the land of the tribe through transfer the name, mutation and purchase the land falsely presenting the name of other tribal groups.

Various studies, conducted by Nair (1987) point out that Khasi, Jaintia and Garo tribes of Meghalaya are the shifting cultivators. Their forest based cultivating land is mutually distributed to the whole tribal groups of specific area. According to the study of Fernandes (1993), it is followed an acquaintation with pattern of communal ownership of shifting cultivated land among Khond Tribe of Orissa and Gond tribe of Andhra Pradesh. Such communal ownership is sometimes considered as the sign of harmony for making a link between them and nature. His commitments also imply that among them, the land alienated persons are regarded as trustees. In the context of land ownership system, the study of Sastry (1993) is also very significant. His study makes a clear statement that most of the Chenchus of Andhra Pradesh are landless. Some of Chenchus cultivates their land without having any written document. As a reason, they were assorted to come on conflict with the forest department. For avoiding such situation, forest department launched an act to make boundary of the forest land. So the remaining land is plotted to the Chenchus without conferring any deed of Government.

Housing Condition and Facility Available

Incorporating the traditional rules and regulation, housing

construction is varied from one tribal community to another. But it is real that more or less, tribal housing condition is found very poor. Most of the tribal houses are made of muddy walls with bamboo thatched roofs. They are not aware to provide any ventilation facility in their housing construction. Even due to shortage of space, their domestic animals are also accommodated in their living room. In regarding the matter, study of Tiwari (1984) informs that Hill Korwa tribal groups of Madhya Pradesh build up their cluster types of house within a few hours and as desired, they also dismantle within no time. They generally bound their housing ground by almost one meter height of muddy wall. For making new houses, they make thatched or tiled roof and set on the prepared muddy walls. They use one room for living and another room for kitchening and storing purposes. All the raw materials required for housing construction are collected from their nearest forest. According to the various studies of Khan (1987), poor housing condition is come to notice among different communities of Uttar Pradesh. Due to unavailability of ventilation facility in constructed houses, most of the family members are exposed to come under respiratory and other infectious diseases.

Bhasin's studies (1990), conducted among different communities in Sikkim and Himachal Pradesh express that most of their houses are made of muddy wall whereas its roofs are prepared by combinely wood and bamboo with thatches. Stone houses are rarely built by them. They are habituated to decorate their houses with various wooden flowers and colours. Cow-sheds are usually constructed very closely with their living room. Courtyards are found to every house. In another study, Kar & Gogoi (1993) report that Nocte tribe of Arunachal Pradesh prepare rectangular shaped houses using the wooden pillars. Roof is made of leafs (Toko). Under the platform of their huts, they store the productive materials and accommodate their cattle. Their housing place is not demarcated by wall or fence. Different types of hut and its constructed materials of Bhil tribe of Madhya Pradesh are focused by the study of Thakur & Thakur (1994). Generally they settle down their huts on the high hill. They make stone wall and use grasses, leafs or tiles for covering the upper surface of the roof. For providing long durability, they use beams of 'Khajur' tree (Phoenix Sysvestria) under the roof of house. A similar type of study, conducted by Kumar (1998) reports that Kacharis tribe of Nagaland are acquainted to have 'Nablai' means cluster houses. Their houses are constructed with timber superstructure, bamboo walls with mud plastered and also thatched roof. For saving their houses from constantly blowing strong wind and cyclone, they prepare the bamboo wall- boundary. A very relevant assessment in the context of house making among Kawar tribe of Madhya Pradesh is comprised by the study of Tiwari (1998). They construct rectangular shaped hut and use for multi-purposes. Except bed room, 'Kothi' is used as biggest for storing the agricultural products. They build up another room for worshipping the 'God' and for kitchening purposes. 'Dhenki' is considered as the another space which is always fixed with any part of Verandah.

Place of Residence

Almost all tribal groups of India are traditionally inhabiting in rural belts. They generally select their place of residence where the sources of livelihood are easily available in a close distance. Even many tribal groups are settled down in forests or hilly forest tracts to collect the forest products for their daily life. So place of residence is considered as a great component to make an impact mainly on the economic status. In this regard, study of Tiwari (1984) reports that the houses of Kamar tribe of Madhya Pradesh are settled on the middle or top portion of hills in a forest area. For constructing their cluster types of house, firstly they select location considering both natural and supper natural aspects. Selection of their residential place is also depended on close distance of water supply, availability of forest resources, etc. In this regard, very supportive studies of Bhasin (1990) focus that the residences of different communities of Sikkim are settled down on the slope of various hills bearing a neat and clean acquaintation. Most of the village communities of Himachal Pradesh build up their residences in muddy and filthy on slope of hills. The muddy and filthy basements are very weak and there is a chance to be washed by extreme current of rain water. So, their most of the houses may be depreciated during rainy season.

The report, produced by Kar & Gogoi (1993) reflects that in the context of place of residence, any dearth of space is not followed in Nocte tribal villages of Arunachal Pradesh. Their houses are constructed generally in huddle condition. Through divination, the village site is selected by their priest. If there is a presumption of any kinds of ominous, then priest exhibits his right to avoid the place and suggests them to shift in other area for residential purpose. According to the study of Soni (1998), it is acquainted that Bhil tribe of Madhya Pradesh generally construct their residences on high hills. The purposes of such high location are to watch their cultivated land, feel privacy to profane intake the local wine, save their unifying cultural atmosphere, etc. Beside this, their such constructions on hills are considered as the abode of God and Goddesses. In the context of settlement places of Kawar tribe of Madhya Pradesh, a changing phenomenon is noted by the study of Tiwari (1988). In spite of rural dwelling, some of them construct complex types of residence achieving the modern thoughts. Settlement pattern of the most of villages are found as linear and situated on plain land. As multi-ethnic villagers, the location of their clusters is separated from other caste groups. Generally Kawar do not allow to reside with the neighbours who belong to low caste groups as compared with them.

Family Structure

Family structure indicates the number of total family members who inhabit in a common residence and share the common food from the single kitchen. However, structure of family is varied from one community to another. Large family size is generally existed among most of the tribal communities of India. According to the study of Banerjee & Bhatia (1988), three types of families are run among Gond tribe of Madhya Pradesh. Their small family is consisted of less than four members. From 5 to 8 members are registered in medium family whereas nine members and above are represented in large family. Their study reveals that son-preference is highly prevalent in most of the Gond families. Expecting birth of male offspring, they desire to perform frequent child births and as a result, medium to large families are constituted among them. In a very sophisticated manner, study of Vithal (1992) comprises that among Chenchu tribe of Andhra Pradesh, 2 to 7 members are generally constituted in the family whereas average family size is estimated as less than 4 members. After marriage, the new couples are usually separated from parents' family. In that situation, nuclear families are organised by short listed members.

Study of Sabat & Dash (1996) reveals that there is an existence of four types of family among Kondh tribe of Orissa. Small family is formed by below 3 members whereas medium family is shaped by 4 to 6 members. Beside, this, 7 to 9 members and above 10 members are categorized for constituting large and very large family sizes respectively. But large family as well as joint size family is rarely found among them. Moreover, 4.5 members are measured as their average family size. Their study also indicates an important correlation between fertility and family size. In the context of family structure, the available information about Bharia tribal groups of Madhya Pradesh are unveiled by the study of Sharma (1998). Among them, both nuclear and joint families are existed. In nuclear family, average family size is constituted by 5 members whereas joint family consists of 8 to 9 members. This study also makes an another type of correlation between family structure and work force. Through mutual understanding, adequate family members in joint family share the total activities and complete within a short period of time. But due to very small family size, specially in nuclear family, the members generally feel uneasy by workload.

Religion

Religion is thought as the response of human beings to the apprehension of power which may be supernatural or supersensory. For adjustment, the human beings are effected by the power which is perceived as supernatural. So, in this context, religion is presumed as the expression of manner of effected people. More or less religion belief is commonly found in every primitive as well as modern society. But the style of presentation of this religious belief is varied from one to another society. According to the study of Jay (1974), it is informed that Maria Gond tribe of Maharashtra is devoted to follow their traditional religion. They worship 'Persa Pen' cult and 'Kalikankali' river. 'Lingo' is respected as their main deity. Both the 'Perma'and

'Pujari' not only continue their duties as priests and medicine men but also they perform magical practice. In accordance with the study of Breeks (1983), it is also known that Kurumba primitive tribal groups of Nilgiri Hill of Tamil Nadu are professed as Hinduism. They are heartily devoted to their primordial God 'Siva'. Except their family and clan deities, they propitiate their regional deities like - Kuribettaray, Vanadevatari, Marithai, Kalimma and others. Study of Dutta (1983) also makes a tremendous expression on religion belief among Miji tribe of Arunachal Pradesh. They believe their traditional religious system and worship both spirits and regional deities. They celebrate their famous 'Khan Puja' one time in every year. In the context of religion identity, Miji groups are found to be trifurcated into Hindu, Buddhist and Christian. A monographic study of Tiwari (1984) reflects that Hill Korwa tribe of Madhya Pradesh are so much addicted to believe to their traditional religious system. They confer the great faith on supernatural power and worship 'Sigir Dev, Gauri, Mahadeo and Parvati' God and Goddesses. 'Khudia Rani' is highly respected as their important deity. In the month of July and August, they celebrate 'Haryali' festival for the purpose of greenness. By offering the new crop of 'Kutki', to the ancestors, they also celebrate 'Kora' festival in the month of September.

The another intensive research work of Chakaraborty (1990) expresses that Great Andamaneses of Andaman Island are eager to have traditional religious belief. His report is enabled to introduce 'Billikhu' a respected deity among the tribe. They worship this deity during the ceremonies of birth, marriage and adolescence periods. Now a days, they keep the picture of Hindu God and Goddesses and visit temple. Most of the Andamaneses resort to Hindu religion whereas the supporters of Christian and Buddhist religious are far less common. In this regard, Saika's study (1994) among Angani Naga of Nagaland points out their over all religious belief and rituals which are concerned with supernatural forces, powers and deities. They are confirmed that nature is alive and not visible and for avoiding natural calamity, social, familial and also personal problems, they try to appease the God by sacrificing cows, dogs, cocks with liquor (wine), etc. Most of the Agami Naga are very much influenced to embrace themselves in Christian religion. Various studies of Thakur & Thakur (1994) also report that religion or 'animistic' beliefs are eagerly existed among Munda, Oraon and Santal communities. Even in any place of their nearest forest, a few pipal trees are identified as a sacred or abode of God 'Basudeo' and these trees are never cut by them. Their perception is that due to the disturbance of their relationship with spirits, they have a chance to be affected by various diseases. Another study of Saha & Saha (1998) comprises that Santal tribe of Orissa are the worshipper of Hindu God and Goddesses. Their religion is not concerned with one's sin and atonement. Sometimes, they perform the various magics and witchcrafts for entertainment. The available information consisting of the socio-cultural life of Bharia tribe of Madhya Pradesh is presented by the study of Sharma (1998). In the context of religion, they celebrate 'Dushera, Deepawali, Holi' and other festivals. They worship their indigenous God 'Baba Dev' .and participate in 'Hardeo and Bhim Deo' ceremonial programmes. Study of Patra (2001) also makes a clear statement about the religious organization of Raji tribe of Uttranchal. Raji are the worshippers of Hindi deities. Beside this, the various local deities like – 'Nanda Devi, Kali, Mallikarjun, Khaudia, Gano Devata and others' are also worshipped by them. They appease both benevolent and malevolent spirits by conducting propitiation.

Education

In over all socio-economic development, impact of education is assorted to play a great role. Basically, the trend of educational attainment measures the improvement of the society. The level of education is also considered as an important indicator for assessing the entire process of progress. The other significant variables of education affect demographic behaviour which is concerned with marriage, fertility, mortality and migration. In the context of educational study, Hutton (1922) is appreciated as the pioneer researcher of Naga Phom tribe of Nagaland. His study confers that due to rarely available school in the area, girls have less scope to be educated as compared to boys. Study of Tiwari (1984) specifies that among Hill Korwa tribe of Madhya Pradesh, scholarship as well as incentive-attraction is regarded as the important factor for increasing the number of enrolment of the children in the school. His investigation also defines that for receiving the amount of scholarship, initial admission of children is taken place but after that, they intentionally abandon the school environment. So naturally their attendance is far less common in the school register. Study of Patnaik (1989) also presents that Saora tribe of Orissa prefer to formal education. But due to extreme poverty, their continuous educational progress is in hindrance. Sex discrimination among them is a real factor which gives high freedom to the boys in coming school as compared to girls.

By the studies of Sinha (1990), poor economic condition among various tribal groups of North-East and Island regions is highlighted as the reason of low educational attainment. His studies emphasize that most of the tribal children are pressurized to contribute a substantial part of their household economic activities. So instead of school education, their maximum motivational approaches are concentrated to support their families from financial deprivation. Educational status of Taro tribe of Manipur is also acquainted by a very analytical study of Singh (1995). His report focuses that age at marriage and both fertility and mortality rates are fluctuated by their educational attainment. Higher educated persons have a tendency to bear low fertility rate. Their male literacy rate is comparatively higher than female. Same trend of low female literacy rate as compared to male among Bhotia tribal groups of Uttar Pradesh is presented by the study of Chachra & Bhasin (1998). Their study also informs that as key factor, specially female education influences the demographic behaviour.

Age at Marriage

Marriage is considered as the socially recognized biological tie between husband and wife. Through marital alliance, the couples are socially permitted to enjoy sexual intercourse and share all socio-economic activities residing in a same house. There is an important factor that tribal communities of India prefer to come in marital alliance at early age. Even, the system of child marriage is also prevalent among those aboriginals who are closely contacted with the customs of Hindu religion. It is a çonsent that early age at marriage is connected with their various social as well as economic factors. Usually economic activities of tribes are totally depended upon the cooperative joint cadre work of husband and wife. After getting married, the new couples try to sustain the stable economic situation. Beside this, due to non-payment or very less payment of bride price, the marriage is generally held as early as possible. So, by conducting early marriage, they not only assure the sexual satisfaction but also try to acquire the better economic advantage. But early age at marriage is assorted to have a negative role for influencing high fertility. Nair & Kateswer (1987) are acquainted as the well-known researchers in this field. Their studies express that socio-cultural, psychological and economic factors are incorporately related to give preference the early age at marriage of various communities of North Karnataka. By indepth inquiry, it is revealed that after menarche, the girls are considered as adequate enough for qualifying marriage. Even for the delay of marriage, parents generally afraid of plausible sexual exploitation of their girls. Beside this, delay marriage is not only a social stigma for the parents but also it is risky, financially expensive, etc. In this regard, studies of Bhasin (1990) also make an indication about moderate age at marriage of Bhotia tribal groups in Uttar Pradesh. Before marriage, the marriageable boys and girls are socially allowed to come on pre-marital sexual relationship on trial basis. During this period, if understanding between boys and girls is not satisfactory, then marriage is normally cancelled. But the begetting progeny is usually accepted by their society approved rules and regulations.

A descriptive study, conducted by Sharma (1990), comprises that child marriage is highly prevalent among Bharia tribal groups of Madhya Pradesh. Most of their parents are designated as the trustworthy to the traditional rules and norms and morally pressurized to continue the marriage of their offsprings as early as possible. A comparative study of Mutharyappa (1993) assesses that in Karnataka, age at marriage of Jenu Kuraba tribal groups is lower than Kadu Kuraba. But marriage of girls of both the groups is performed before puberty. The relevant report of Roy (1995) also reflects the significant information about the age at marriage of Kokna tribe of Maharashtra. In accordance with their social norms, they start to practise marriage of their girls from the age of 10 years. But due to their socio-cultural upliftment and loyalty of Government policy, the present generation of both sexes is achieving significant progress in practicing marriage at adult age. A relevant study of Singh (1995) highlights a variation on age at marriage of girls and boys among Taro tribe of Manipur. Almost five years age difference is recorded between the marriageable girls and boys. Due to conduct of early age at marriage, their females have a higher chance to conceive frequently but high reproductive wastage is caused as the hindrance of their over population growth. In another study of Singh (1995) reports that Khond tribe of Orissa prefer to early age at marriage. But sometimes due to non-payment of bride price, the marriage of girls is delayed or cancelled. An investigation, conducted by Samal, et al. (1996) implies that among Jaunsaria tribe of Central Himalaya, the average age at marriage of girls is measured as 13.18 years. Their study also clarifies that the reasons of early age at marriage are associated with their traditional socio-cultural. barriers rather than economic problems.

Socio-cultural impact on age at marriage to Kumuni caste groups and Bhatia tribal groups are discussed by the studies of Chachra & Bhasin (1998). These communities are totally implicated with their traditional orthodox and as a result, their motivational approaches are concentrated to practise early age at marriage. Another study, conducted by Maheo & Kella (2000) defines that due to the positive impact of education, most of the Naga of Manipur come in marital alliance at moderate age (22.7 years). In their study, it is also revealed that very few illiterate Naga are married at early age. In this regard, study of Patra (2001) attempts to investigate the marriage of Raji women in Uttranchal. His collected information imply that after puberty, the parents are eager to take responsibility for the marriage of their daughters as easily as possible. So naturally their marriage is performed at early age. In the context of socio-demographic study of Yadav, et al. (2001), the age at marriage is considered as a relevant associated component among Lohar Gadiya of Madhya Pradesh. Their study mentions that there is no any remarkable variation of age at marriage between males and females. But due to semi-nomadic nature, illiteracy, poor economic condition, etc., they prefer to early age at marriage.

Age at Menarche

Menarche is phenomenon as an important physiological episode in the life of every woman. The term menarche is expressed by secreting the first regular flow of blood from the womb of girl and it's periodical continuation is maintained upto the particular upper age. However, the age at menarche means the age at first menstruation which is started from a specific age of girls. From menstruation, the girls are promoted to the stage of maturity and capable to conceive. In the context of the matter, studies of Bhasin (1990) confer the general information about the upper age at menarche (15.58 years) of girls of Lepcha and Bhutia communities of Sikkim. These studies support that in hot climate, temperate zone and cold region, the average age at menarche is varied from low to medium and then high respectively. The heavy body weight indicates the acceptance of better nutritional food items and bearing of continuous good health which have a great impact to ȧttain menarche at early age. By the studies of Singh & Shukla (1992), it is known that the average menarchieal age of Rana Tharu, Jogia Tharu, Donguria Tharu, Khatara Tharu and Pachhmaha Tharu tribal females of Uttar Pradesh is 13.52 years. Their studies further define that the age at menarche is depended on the climate, geographical, socio-cultural conditions and genetic and non-genetic factors.

Various studies of Balgir (1994), Choudhury, et al. (1994) & Singhal, et al. (1994), conducted among eight exogamous tribal groups of Assam, Mirdha tribe of Orissa and different communities of Punjab express that 13.01 years, 13.0 years and 13.47 years respectively are measured as their average age at menarche. Studies of Balgir further clarifies that the age at menarche is not only associated with occupation, educational level, family size, food habit, living condition, birth rank and climate but also it is concerned with genetic factor. Comments of Choudhury, et al. (1994) extend that due to close affinity with higher caste groups, the mean menarcheal age of Mirdha women is found to be accounted higher as compared to other tribal women. For the variation of menarcheal age, food items are the important responsible factor which is concerned by the study of Singhal, et al. (1994). According to the study of Sharma & Chowdhary (1995), it is acquainted with 13.69 years as the average

age at menarche of Gond women of Maharashtra. Their study reveals that fertility is higher of those women who attained menarche below the age of 13 years. Various studies of Barua (1996) indicate that among the tribal groups of North-East India, menarche is not only confined in biological phenomenon, but also it is related with rites, rituals, prohibitions, superstitions, etc. In accordance with the study of Sengupta & Rajkhowa (1996), 12.51 years age as the mean menarcheal age of Ahom tribal women of Assam. They additionally remarks that except all reasons, rural-urban residence is focused as the important factor for the variation of menarcheal age. By the studies of Elizabeth, et al. (2000) and Maheo & Kalla (2000), it is found to be measured 13.06 years and 14.59 years as the mean menarcheal age of Thoti tribal women of Andhra Pradesh and Mao Naga tribal women of Manipur respectively. Their studies comprise that normally girls are to be married before the age at menarche which is concerned as the reason of high fertility. In this regard, Patra's study (2001), conducted among Raji tribal women of Uttaranchal reports 13.40 years as their mean age at menarche. This study also specifies that for influencing menarcheal age, socio-economic conditions, nutritional status, geo-physical environment, etc. are responsible.

Age at Menopause

Menopause is a biological term having meaning as the symbolic end of womanhood in the life of all women. From this stage, ovulation and menstruation are consequently stopped and ceased the reproductive function of women. However, the age at menopause is varied from one to other women. The variation of menopausal age is depended on food habit, socio-economic status, environmental and genetic factors. Various studies, conducted by Bhasin (1990) report that the mean menopausal age of women among different communities of Sikkim is measured as 44.59 years whereas Gaddi tribal women are attained on menopause at the age of 44.99 years. His studies further focus that except hot climate, body weight of women is also implicated to determine the menopausal age. Study of Sengupta & Rajkhowa (1997) specifies that 46.32 years as the mean age of menopause of Ahom tribal women of Assam. This study also defines that the age at menopause is fluctuated in accordance with nutrition, socio-economic status, environment, altitude, climate, heredity, rural-urban residence, family size, etc. Sometimes various physical symptoms like - hot flushes, headache, insomnia, itching, etc. are created after stopping the menstruation cycle.

Sonowal tribal groups inhabit throughout the Assam region. Study among them, conducted by Kalita & Sengupta (1997) repots 47.22 years as the mean age at menopause of the women. Their study emphasizes that food habit is importantly associated with the age at menopause. In this regard, study of Maheo & Kalla (2000) depicts that the mean age at menopause of the Mao Naga women of Manipur is estimated as 45.23 years. Their study expresses that higher menopausal age of women always extends the reproductive span of life which usually influences high birth rate. By the study of Majumdar (2001), 42.40 years is acquainted as the mean age at menopause of Mahato women of West Bengal. Due to odd environmental factor and malnutrition, Mahato women attain menopause at very low age. Further, the study of Patro (2001) makes an estimation of mean menopausal age as 45.23 years of Raji tribal women of Uttaranchal. His study also indicates that menopausal age may be varied by the influence of socio-cultural and environmental factors. As they are indigenous tribe, genetic factor may not be responsible to differentiate the menopausal age of women.

Fertility

Fertility means the actual reproductive performance of women or couples. Basically it indicates the number of produced both living and death children of women. The actual fertility performance of women is totally dependent on physiological function and socio-cultural practices. Potential form of fertility is influenced by physiological factors from biological angles whereas the conditioning social environment is embraced by socio-cultural factors. In this regard, the studies of Bhasin (1990) express that fertility of various communities of Sikkim and Himachal Pradesh is influenced by both biological and socio-economic factors. Among them, traditional Hindu culturists are pronatalist and their socio-economical well status is established by producing large number of children. After bearing specially son, their women not only make themselves socially eligible to acquire the family properties for inheritator but also assume the support and cordial affection from their husbands. In this context, study of Barua (1992) highlights that fertility of Turung tribe of Assam is associated with biological factors consisting of age at menarche, age at marriage and age at menopause and also socio-cultural factors concerning to religious, educational and economic status. Report of Kshatriya, et al. (1993) depicts that total fertility rate per woman of Bison Horn Madia is varied from 5.46 to 5.60. Their study also attributes that low socio-economic status, odd environment, insanitation, unawareness to health and poor health care practices, etc. are transgressed as the reasons of their high fertility.

A study report, made by Choudhury, et al. (1994) exhibits that high fertility is presented by those Mirdha women of Orissa whose age is varied from 15 to 50 years. Their study also clarifies that worst environment, poverty, illiteracy, unawareness to family planning practices, etc. are the contaminated factors of their high fertility. Further, a comparative study of Pandey (1994) specifies that due to conduct early age at marriage, the tribal women of Jabalpur in Madhya Pradesh have an achievement of higher fertility than non-tribal women. According to the study of Khongsdier & Ghosh (1995), it is followed that more or less fertile aged women among Khasi tribe of Meghalaya are unmarried. As a reason, their fertility is assorted low as compared to the national fertility rate. By the study of Sengupta & Chakravarty (1995), it is acquainted that among tribal groups of Assam, fertility is correlated with various factors. Their study confers that low fertility is registered in joint family as compared to nuclear family. Similarly, the women of rural belt give higher fertility than urban setting. In connection with this, study of Pandey & Tiwari (1996) reports that due to poverty, deplorable low literacy, early age at marriage, etc., Hill Korwa tribe of Madhya Pradesh sustain high fertility. But after birth, due to continuous struggle, very less number of children are survived and as a result, their population growth is almost constant. Study, conducted by Chaudhary & Devi (1997) also makes an exploratory analysis on differential fertility among Meitie community of Manipur. Their study imparts that the illiterate couples achieve the higher fertility rate (6.20) than the fertility rate (2.67) of the educated couples. Wives of rickshaw pullers confer the low fertility rate as compared to those who practise agriculture.

A very significant study of Guha (1997) reveals that higher female death in reproductive age group, late marriage, nomadic in nature, indigenous birth control practice, etc. are focused as the transgressed reasons of low fertility among the Bhotiya tribal communities of Uttar Pradesh. Studies of Chaturvedi, et. al. (1998) indicate that among various rural communities of Assam, fertility is increased by improving the educational level and occupational status of mothers. Knowledge, attitude and practice of birth control devices are directly associated with the education. So educated mothers generally desire low fertility as compared to others. Among Abujhmaria tribe of Madhya Pradesh, very high fertility (39.9) is reported by the study of Pandey & Goel (1999). Their study clarifies that most of the women are found in the fertile age group. Beside this, they are in tension of high infant mortality and due to illiteracy, they are almost unaware to practice family planning devices. So, all these are the attributed reasons of their high fertility. Study of Elizabeth, et. al. (2000) points out the significant information about various measures of fertility rate among Thoti tribe of Andhra Pradesh. Generally Thoti women present the increasing trend of fertility rate upto their age of 29 years. Their crude birth rate, general fertility rate, etc. are found to be high due to incorporate better ante natal and child care facility. Similar study, conducted by Patra (2001) reports that among Raji of Uttaranchal, high rates of infant and child mortality influence the couples to take part in reproduction which elaborate high fertility. Further, study of Yadav, et al. (2001) explains that low acceptance of family planning devices, lack of proper medical facility, high child mortality, etc. are the considered as the reasons of high fertility among Lohar Gadiyas of Madhya Pradesh.

Mortality

Mortality means the permanent extinction of all signs of life from living body. It is substantial that after birth, mortality may be occurred at any time. But every incident relating to mortality is associated with many causes. The indebted causes are not only related with biological factors but also its adequate extensions are incorporated with many social factors. In this regard, studies of Bhasin (1990), conducted among Gaddi tribal groups of Himachal Pradesh are very important for measuring the high death rates and assessing its related reasons. Her studies indicate that low level of education, insanitation, inadequate medical services, etc. are the transgressed reasons of their high crude death rate. Beside this, high pre-natal as well as infant death rate is sensitively linked with biological as well as socio-cultural factors. Report of Kshatriya, et al. (1993) depicts that Bison Horn Madia tribe of Baster district in Madhya Pradesh are positioned below the poverty line. In this situation, they intake poor quality of food items which lead diseases specially for children and pregnant women. They usually use their household compound for family as well as cattle domestication purpose. Moreover, immunization of both ante-natal and infants are almost ignored. So all these are contaminated as the reasons of various diseases prostrating to death. Study of Adak (1994) implies that greater percentage of infant and children are measured to pass away of those Khasi mothers of Meghalaya who are illiterate, got married at early age, involved in miscellaneous works, attended delivery by neighbours, non-immunized, etc. Further, a comparative study of Khongsdier (1995) also exhibits that Christian Khasi are somewhat advanced in education and financial condition and as a result, they may afford better medical facility which protects their high offsprings loss as compared to the non-Christian Khasi.

Study of Sabat, et. al. (1996) expresses the different demographic parameters of Kandh tribe of Orissa. Their report mentions that due to acute scarcity of potable water, insanitation, unfavourable environment, very poor access of modern health care facility, etc., the various communicable diseases are aggravated and their infants are deteriorated day to day. According to the study of Choudhary, et. al. (1997), it is reported that foetus loss of Santal and Phariya tribal groups of Rajmahal Hills in Bihar are associated with genetic profile and nutritional status. Their high infant mortality is attributed as the reasons of weaning, improper supplementary foods, contact with sick and unhealthy persons, new environment, etc. Study of Pandey & Goel (1999) remarks that usually the illiterate Abujhmaria tribe of Madhya Pradesh ignore to use the family planning devices and as a result, frequent child births are performed among them. Their less medical facility connected to financial problem is not enough to protect all infants. So high mortality is prevalent among them. Such study, conducted by Sharma & Sharma (1999) reports that high infant mortality rate (242) among Gond tribe of Madhya Pradesh are transgressed as the reasons of preference of male sex, very less hospitalized delivery, etc. In this context, study of Elizabeth, et. al. (2000) defines the genetical deformation of high death among Thoti tribe of Andhra Pradesh. Their explanations focus that as a result of high degree of inbreeding, usually the harmful recessive genes form the homozygous condition which leads the genetic disorders and the persons are attacked by sickle cell anemia and thalassaemia and influence death. Study of Pandey, et. al. (2001) highlights that high child mortality among Kamar tribe of Chattisgarh is not only linked with biological factors but also it is related with household occupation, income, maternal and child health care, etc. An over all study of Patra (2001) consists of various factors which are responsible for high mortality among Raji tribe of Uttaranchal. His study generally emphasis that low socio-economic condition, malnutrition, poor health care facility, traditional way of delivery, etc. are the attributed reasons for influencing high death rate.

Selection Intensity

In population group, the maximum potential rate is generally measured by selection intensity. It is real that fitness of population is totally depended on heredity but for measuring its potential rate, index of opportunity for natural selection is used. Under natural selection, differential fertility and differential mortality are considered as the two important components which are responsible to transmit the gene frequencies in population. Combining in a particular manner, the one going pattern of differential fertility and mortality measure the expression of fitness of population. In this context, no any change is indicated by 'zero' symbol whereas the maximum change of potential rate is estimated by the index of opportunity for natural selection (Livingston & Spuhler, 1965). In human population group, the different theoretical controversies are existed on natural selection. But on the basis of the maximum amount of differential fertility and mortality in population group, the indirect method for computing the index of total selection was first formulated by Crow (1958).After almost one decade, this method was renamed and acquainted as the index of opportunity for natural selection (1966). Later on, including embryonic mortality component, Johnston & Kensinger (1971) modified this formula. According to them, the index 'I' is referred to the total amount of selection having two components which are known as fertility (If) and mortality (Im). It computes the proportion of all selection and completed heritability of fitness which have the chances to be increased with specific birth and death rate. It is defined that the influence of genetic component in differential fertility and differential mortality is so much small as compared to the effect of host environment comprising physical, cultural, socio-economic and behavioural factors (Cruze-Coke, et. al., 1966). So, instead of total intensity, it presents only its upper limit (maximum) for the purpose of potential action of natural selection which is introduced as 'Total Index of Opportunity for Natural Selection'. By incorporating the embryonic mortality, Johnston & Kensinger (1971) modified the index of Crow (1958) and then subsequently many studies were conducted in different parts of the world.

According to the study of Spuhler (1962), it is specified that due to high differential fertility, total selection intensity is converted into high among industrial population whereas their mortality is estimated as very low. A very vast study of Salazano (1963) indicates that index of selection is also influenced by culture, behaviour and other factors which are indebted for fitness of population. Study of Barrai & Fraccaro (1964) also points out that opportunity of natural selection among nomads are generally found high as compared to settled laps. A comparative study (between two industrial sub-groups) of Gupta (1980) also mentions the various socio-economic components which are related to determine the natural selection. In this regard, study of Basu, et. al. (1988) measures the embryonic death (0.016) and pre-reproductive death (0.209) and also selection due to fertility (0.148) among Halba tribe of Madhya Pradesh and clarifies that their biological as well as socio-cultural factors are very much associated with differential fertility and mortality. Further, study of Khongsdier (1994) expresses that in connection with religion, selection intensity is varied between Christian Khasi and Non-

Christian Khasi of Meghalaya. Further, study of Sudhakar, et. al. (1998) reports that except genetic factor, selection intensity among Lappala Velama caste of Andhra Pradesh is varied in the context of well developed rural and semi urban inhabitants who are facilitated by better health care. A very intensive study of Langstieh (2001) comprises that as a reason of genetic drift among Muslim Khasi of Meghalaya, a strong chance is suggested by the co-efficient of breeding isolation. Their mortality component is very low as compared to fertility which is come from total selection potentiality. Such study of Patra (2001) also reports that among Raji tribe of Uttaranchal, differential mortality is very high due to the causes of low degree of socio-economic development, unspecified fever, dirrhoea, tetanus, dysentery, low amount of maternal and child health care, unsafe delivery, malnutrition, occupational exploitation of mothers, absence of immunization, etc.

Migration

Migration is considered as an important factor in demographic change. It is defined that migration means the change of residential place from one to another area. Usually, population concentration and sources of natural products are always well balanced by the process of migration. As a transitional way, people migrate from one to another village, one to another district and even from one to another country. But among tribal people, migration is usually conducted from one to another area and even hardly from one to another district. Due to extreme poverty, tribal people generally come from one to another area for seeking work opportunity. Various studies of Bhasin (1990) elaborate that due to the cause of major epidemiological importancy, Lepcha, Bhutia, Nepalese and other ethnic groups were migrated in Sikkim and formed a plural society. Now a days, they are involved in trading, road side labouring, constructional working, etc. According to the study of Pal (1995), it is unveiled that Oraon tribal groups of Chotanagpur Plateau in Bihar were migrated many times from one to another area. History implies that migrating deliberately from Konkan Coast (Western Coast) and Narmada river of Western Coast, they arrived in Rhotasgarh and its adjoining hill areas of Sahabad district in Bihar. There, being defeated by Aryan, they dislodged

Rhotasgarh and resettled in Rajmal hill areas. Further, they were economically, socially and culturally deprived by the British government and other dominant groups and in that situation, they were fruther migrated in North Bengal, Assam and other places.

The explanations about the causes of migratory process are given by the studies of Prasad & Rao (1996). Their studies report that due to heavy draught, the various rural communities of Andhra Pradesh were migrated from own place, district and even state to outside for getting job opportunity. Such way, their economic requirement helped to generate a new tradition with the outsiders and progress their socio-cultural life over a period of time. Study of Adak & Chaudhury (1996) confines that the higher population growth of Tripura is not only depended on births over deaths but also associated with immigration over emigration. Even their studies specify that one-fourth population of the state are increased by the reason of immigration. In this regard, the study of Sharma & Sharma (1999) focuses that the Gond tribe of Maharashtra are generally not ready to migrate. They are patriarchal tribe and only through legal marriage, their female migration is performed. Gonds are clan exogamous tribal groups. In case, the marriage is conducted between the bride and groom who belong to same clan, they are pressured to emigrate from their native land. Their study also reveals that these tribal groups also migrate due to the reasons of flood, drought, earth-quake, famine, etc.

Maternal and Child Health Care

Maternal care indicates the care by providing nutritional food, health care facility, safe delivery, proper rest, etc. to the women during their ante natal, natal and post natal periods. In other side, child care means the care which is implicated at the time of delivery and post delivery periods by applying safe delivery, proper breast feeding, nutritional food items, immunization and medical facility. In First and Second Five-Year Plans (1951-56-61), maternal and child care were seriously accepted by Ministry of Health, Government of India. During Fifth Five-Year Plan, family planning with maternal and child health care services were launched as a part of minimum needs.

The main purpose of these activities was to provide minimum health services and nutrition to the vulnerable pregnant women, lactating mothers and pre-school children (Kanitkar, 1979). Now adays, health service activities are implemented as child survival and safe motherhood programmes. In this regard, the studies of Bhasin (1990) are very important for focusing the special food items which are consumed by the pregnant women among various communities of Sikkim and Himachal Pradesh. Due to fear of abnormally increase the size and stomach trouble of would to be born baby, most of the pregnant women avoid to intake the nutritional and fatty substances and some particular vegetables respectively. For respecting to their social taboos, they also eat certain fruits and meat of animals. It is a very peculiar that only after delivery, the new born mother is initiated with locally prepared strong alcoholic drink. Normally, the new born mothers practise breast feeding upto minimum three months and then slowly introduce the supplementary food items instead of feeding.

Studies of Rajyalakshmi & Geervani (1992) express that during pregnancy period, the Jatapu, Savara, Godaba and Kondadora tribal women in South India consume yellow pumpkin, legume vegetables, gourds and beans. As nutritional foods, they are also very much addicted to eat tender bamboo shoots and mushrooms which are collected form their locality. By introducing the substitute foods, most of the Jatapu women practise weaning at the age of above 1 year of children whereas Savara, Godaba and Kondadora women elaborate breast feeding upto the age of 2 years of their children. Another studies of Mishra (1993) report that the maximum mothers of various communities of Orissa initiate breast feeding to their babies above 60 hours after their birth. But they continue breast feeding upto 24 months. Study of Basu, et. al. (1994) comprises that 84 percent of Kheria women in Orissa do not change their scheduled diet whereas only 10 percent women reduce their quality of food intake during their pregnancy period. Almost 50 percent pregnant women are immunized but delivery of most of the women is performed at home. Upto the age of 3 years, 69 percent, 75 percent and 71 percent offsprings of Kheria are immunized against BCG, DPT and Polio drop respectively. By the study of Karmakar (1995), it is acquainted that due to early age at marriage and malnutrition during pregnancy period of tribal women of Singhuhum district in Bihar, generally they face the pregnancy related complications and bear the low birth-weight of child.

In the context of maternal and child health care of Khairwar tribal groups of Madhya Pradesh, study of Pandey, et. al. (1996) reports a very inefficiency attitude. Normally the routine-wise activities are not changed by the women during their pregnancy period. They use unsterilized knife and blade for cutting the umbilical cord of new born. In case of complicated delivery, their pregnant women are kept in dedication for the mercy of God. Similar study of Rajaratnam, et al. (1997) expresses that maternal and child health care of Malto tribe of Bihar are varied from one socio-cultural and ecological setting to another. During pregnancy period, most of their women (87 percent) are not aware to take tetanus. By the help of local 'Dais', almost all women are delivered at home. They practise colostrum feeding but immunization against the various diseases of new born babies is almost ignored. Studies of Bhuyan (1999) yield a very clear picture about the maternal and child health care related to food, rest, safe delivery, post natal health, etc. among Bodo, Mishing, Dimasa and Karbi tribal groups of Assam. Normally, the pregnant women are implicated to obey their food taboos. Only 25 percent pregnant women accept special food items whereas most of the women consume alcoholic beverages during pregnancy period. Almost all women continue their routine works. Being influenced by their socio-cultural orthodox, they are restricted not to move to certain places. His studies specify that 90 percent deliveries of women are performed at home. Special care to neo-nates is almost neglected among them. It is stated that 47 percent mothers start breast feeding immediately after birth of child. Only 36 percent mothers continue breast feeding to their child till next conception. By initiating supplementary foods to their child, 89 percent mothers practise weaning.

Various studies, conducted by Nanda & Niranjan (1999) exhibit that among different scheduled tribes of India, maternal care is depended on the place or residence, occupation, educational status, etc. Rural illiterate inhabitants always present their negligence view whereas better occupational and educational status achieves a motivational approach to practise ante-natal care. Studies of Nayak & Babu (2001) reveal that most of the scheduled castes and scheduled tribes of Orissa prefer to conduct delivery at their home. Almost 50 percent of their deliveries are assisted by the entire supervision of their traditional birth attendants and relatives. Tetanus toxim and iron and folic acid tablets are started to accept by more or less pregnant women. By the study of Patra (2001), it is known that maternal and child health care are almost unexposed among Raji tribe of Uttaranchal. Their most of the deliveries are taken place at home by the help of non-medical professionals. Only 29 percent of their children are fully immunized. The other relevant studies of Prasad & Nagaraj (2001) make a comparative account that deliveries, conducted at home in various communities of Andhra Pradesh are merely lower than institutional deliveries. They are just slowly motivating themselves to prefer to the medical professionals in connection with their maternal and child health care.

Health Seeking Behaviour

Health is a state of complete physical, mental and social well being whereas disease indicates the illed health or disturbance and requires immediate remedy. It is real that in particular environment, health and disease are depended on resources of both biological and cultural factors. In simple as well in tribal societies, phenomena of health and disease are totally related with socio-cultural factors. Through the over all analysis of socio-cultural milieu, it is clear that medical aspect is fully associated with health problem. In connection with the acceptance of modern medical services, tribal people are slowly emerging from their socio-cultural boundary. Keeping in view, the studies of Pandey & Saxena (1988) are very much concerned to focus the demographic and health seeking behaviours, connected with socio-cultural diversity among various tribal and non-tribal groups of Madhya Pradesh. Their studies confer that population density, female literacy rate, growth rate, achievement of maternal and child health care, rate of family planning adoption, etc. of tribal population, are indisposed as compared to non-tribal population. In this regard, the detail information about food, nutrition and morbidity of Jatapu, Savara, Gadaba and Kondadora tribal groups of South India are conveyed by the studies of Rajyalakshmi &

Greevani (1992). Their studies impart that health problems of these tribal groups are caused by mainly scabies and dermatis. They are also suffering from malnutrition, infection, gastic disorders, bronchitis, B-complex deficiency, anemia and other diseases. In the prepared report, their suggestions imply that as mitigation, health education, idea about personal hygiene, mobile health care facility, etc. are essentially required for them. Study of Kar & Gogoi (1993) defines that due to extreme poverty, Nocte tribal groups of Arunachal Pradesh always involve in continuous work without having any rest. By frequent attack of mosquito, malaria disease related mortality is specified as very high. Beside this, worm, stomach disorder, scabies, pox, pain, cough, headache, vomiting, diabetes, hypertension, hypotension, tuberculosis, tetanus, polio, etc. diseases are more or less prevalent among them. As prevention, they worship their various specific deities sacrificing the coconut, hen and others. For treatment, they also use to prefer the herbal medicines. But when all rituals, sacrifices, herbal medicines, etc. are failed to achieve the positive result, then they generally come to treat their diseases under modern medical personnel. Study of Chattopadhyay & Prasad (1995) remarks that Nicobarese of Nicobar Island are very innocent in the context of the quality and quantity of food intakes which are required for their children in accordance with various stages of physical growth. Most of them are prostrated to bear poor health by the affect of gastro intestinal disorders, bronchial disorders, malaria, scabies and other diseases. Modern way of treatment is almost unexposed to them.

A very important study, conducted by Ghoshmaulik and Karmotapatra (1995) discloses that Juang tribe of Orissa are affected by various diseases but their modern aleological aspects are almost nil. Most of them are treated their diseases under 'Shaman' (village medicine man). Due to unavailability of well equipped PHC or Hospital in their locality, the disease affected persons obviously feel uneasy to go far distant medical centre from Juang villages. So usually they are to be avoided the modern medical facilities and motivated to take treatment from their indigenous medicine man. Study of Bhagwat & Chirmulay (1997) reveals the traditional healing practices among rural people of Karnataka. Traditional systems of treatment are usually practised through variety of techniques which are associated with herbal, animal and kitchen materials. In accordance with the types of disease, they also practise magico-religious, acupuncture, acupressure and messages and other particular techniques. Report of the study of Bajpai & Mitra (1998) confers that Hill Korwa tribe of Madhya Pradesh do not feel worry suffering from their diseases during 2 to 3 days. In connection with the treatment of their diseases, they rarely prefer to the modern clinical facility. Due to apathy to the medical practitioners and lack of useful medicine in PHC or Hospital, they prefer to their beneficial ethno-medicines for the treatment of their illed persons. For focusing the health care practices among the various tribal groups of Visakhapatnam, a report is prepared by the study of Rajpramukh (1998). His study emphasizes that except the diseases of digestive disorder, more or less they are suffering from arthritis, skin disease, infection by mite burrows, anemia, malaria, etc. For the treatment of such diseases, they are socio-culturally. motivated to their traditional medicine man. According to the study of Datta (1999), it is highlighted that by the influence of Buddhism, treatment of diseases of most of the Singpho in Arunachal Pradesh are depended on nature and natural resources connected with plants and other available materials. They extremely believe that evil spirits and witchcrafts are directly or indirectly related with the effect of all diseases. So, they usually prefer to the magico-religious practices for treatment. Study of Pandey & Tiwari (2001) reports that Pando tribal groups of Madhya Pradesh are identified not to have a common sense about the healthy persons. For the treatment of illed persons, they prefer to 'Gunia' or traditional healer who serves herbal medicine without asking any cash payment. In accordance with the severity of disease, 'Gunia' is requested to take the fowel, coconut, locally prepared wine, etc. In this regard, study of Sharma (2001) depicts the socio-cultural relation with health hygiene among Gond tribe of Madhya Pradesh. Inhabiting in unhygienic surroundings, they are bounded to accept the contaminated foods and impured water and as a result, they are frequently suffering from malaria, asthma, conjunctivitis, ear-nose and throat infection, itches, digestive disorders, malnutrition and other diseases. Their socio-cultural norms influence them to practise traditional healing for the treatment of almost all diseases.

Family Planning

Family planning is considered as the systematic planning for bestowing the welfare activities of family members. Specially, it indicates some suitable methods which are committed to adopt for controlling the undesired child birth. However, the importance of family planning in India was first officially recognized in 1952. But the family planning programme was implemented to use from Fourth Five-Year Plan. The main objectives of the family planning are concentrated to decrease birth rate of less than 39, to influence the couples for conducting small family size in their society, to develop their personal knowledge about various family planning methods and to supply the various necessary family planning devices and equipments.

India is the second largest populated country in the world and its most of the people are positioned under financially backward condition. In this regard, the special reference is imparted to the tribal people who not only bear the financial deprivation but also submit themselves to lead a low socio-cultural life style. They firmly believe their customs and traditions. They usually prefer to the low age at marriage. Their both birth rate and death rate are unexpectedly high. Generally, high death rate is directly associated with high birth rate. Taking into consideration the situation, it is stated that health services and birth control devices are much required for these tribal people.

In the context of different components of birth control device among tribal communities of India, various studies have been conducted and assessed the valuable findings. In this regard, studies of Bhasin (1990) define that many communities of Sikkim and Himachal Pradesh rarely practise birth control devices. In practicing birth control devices, a biasness is highly incorporated to pressurize specially females as compared to males. Educational impact is importantly associated with birth control devices. Beside this, their higher population growth is also saved by observing prolonged abstinency and odd ecological settings. A comparative study of Piplai (1993) furnishes that only 7 percent and 19 percent couples of Oraon and Tamang tribal communities respectively of Jalpaiguri district in West Bengal practise family planning devices while they are getting the equal opportunity. Their significant number of couples prefers to adopt vasectomy and tubectomy whereas loop, pill and condom are rarely accepted by them. An important report of Sharma & Sharma (1993) presents that almost 46 percent of tribal women of Udaipur district in Rajasthan are trained by short term orientation of 'Family Planning Programme' of Government of India. These trained women powerfully motivate others to adopt various contraceptives. Inspite of this, 61 percent and 21 percent of these tribal groups are not ready to use any birth control devices till give birth to their desired at least 2 male children and more than 2 male children respectively. By the study of Basu, et. al. (1994), it is known that Dudh Kharia tribe of Orissa are the extreme followers of their traditional orthodox. Influencing with their traditional socio-cultural norms, related to child birth as the gift of God, 62 percent of them deny to receive family planning devices. Very specifically their comments elaborate that after giving births of 3 to 4 desired children, they generally prefer to use contraceptives. Study of Mutharayappa (1995) highlights the actual reasons of family planning adoption among Marati Nayak, Male Kudiya and Korago tribes of Karnataka. Getting compensation of Rs.100/- to 150/- and other incentives, they are motivated to adopt family planning methods. Further another study of Mutharayappa (1998) points out that Jenu Kuruba and Kadu Kuruba of Karnataka usually use their indigenous family planning methods while their number of population is no more enough.

Studies of Chchra & Bhasin (1998) express that most of the Kumauni and Bhoita communities of Uttar Pradesh are experienced about various contraceptive methods but users are rarely identified among them. Due to prefer to male offsprings, more offsprings, health problems, unawareness about methods, will not be doing and others, they are sometimes demotivated to use contraceptives. By the users' claim concerning to dizziness, bleeding, back-pain, bodyache, weakness, swollen and other physical problems, the non-users are also irritated for avoiding family planning practices. In the context of knowledge, attitude and practice of birth control devices, study of Mahapatro, et. al. (1999) is considered as significant one. Their study assesses that among Bhattra tribe of Madhya Pradesh, modern family planning methods are classified into five types. The physical type consists of practices of condom, intra uterine device, pill, etc. whereas rhythm is embodied in physiological method. Coitus interrupts is regarded under psychological method. Gelly, cream, oral pill, etc. are come under bio-chemical substances whereas abstinence and ritual taboos are considered as the family planning method under social practice. Among them, it is found to be estimated that 95 percent, 16 percent and also 8 percent are experienced in regarding to knowledge, attitude and practice of various family planning methods respectively. Further such study of Maheo & Kalla (2001) reports that in the context of Knowledge, attitude and practice of birth control devices, 66 percent, 30 percent and 13 percent Mao Naga respectively are found to be measured. Most of the birth control practitioners prefer to use condom (34 percent), natural substance (30 percent) and intra uterine device (24 percent) whereas sterilization (10 percent) and. pill (2 percent) are adopted very rarely. Their study also emblems that practices of birth control devices are corroborately associated with education, socio-economic status, average fertility rate, etc. Another study, conducted by Pandey & Tiwary (2001) presents various components concerning to socio-cultural aspects and health practices among Pando Tribal groups of Madhya Pradesh. In connection with family planning devices, their study expresses that most of the Pando (87 percent) have an experience about knowledge but all are not assembled in practicing. Even among family planning practitioners, almost all members prefer to use natural substance, nirodh, pill, etc.

AIMS AND OBJECTIVES OF THE STUDY

Every research study is purposeful. It always accomplishes the acquaintation with the answers of questions through the perseverance of scientific procedures. It is a common parlance that by the performation of research study, all types of information are accumulated and then analysed for investigating the hidden truth which is unveiled to all. By initiating the maximum efforts, a systematic assessment is made on the over all matter and then reasonable proposal is imparted for possible remedy. In this regard, the present research is concentrated to study the demographic parameters which are possessed on various factors. In this regard, socio-economic as well as biological factors are predominantly responsible. For determining the reasons of indebted factors, the main aims and objectives for the present study are stated as follows:

1. To study the ethnographic account of Saharia,
2. To study the measures of population composition – age-sex composition i.e. age-sex distribution, dependency ratio, index of ageing, sex ratio, masculinity proportion, economic and educational characteristics, marital status, etc.,
3. To study the measures of fertility – crude birth rate, general fertility rate, age specific fertility rate, total fertility rate, mean age at child bearing, general marital fertility rate, age-specific marital fertility rate, child women ratio, etc. and the measures of mortality-crude death rate, age-specific death rate, infant mortality rate, neo-natal and post-neonatal mortality rates, etc.,
4. To study the biological determinants like-age at menarche, menopause and the indices of the total natural selection (following Crow, 1958 and Johnston & Kensinger, 1971),
5. To study the maternal & child health care, health seeking behaviour, family planning practices and utilization pattern, etc.,
6. To compare the present population with tribal and non-tribal population groups of India.

CHAPTER - II

RESEARCH DESIGN AND METHODOLOGY

In this chapter, the research design, research methods, sampling, etc. are described in regarding the subject matter of the research. Pilot study and preliminary investigation are also included in the context of its purposes. For collecting the different types of data, the various methods, data collection schedules, process of data analysis, measuring, etc. are incorporated in a systematic manner. Moreover, this chapter consists of the reasons of Saharia selection, area selection and the problems faced during field work.

However, for the present research study, six Saharia villages under Barai block, Gird subdivision of Gwalior district in Madhya Pradesh have been selected purposively. Various relevant methods have also been decided in accordance with the various stages of this research work. These are stated in the following ways:

Research Design

Research design was considered as an arrangement of condition for data collection and also data analysis in a systematic manner. At the initial stage, research design was thought as a conceptual structure and within this, the various relevant methods were experiencely arranged for accumulating the various information. In different contexts, it was presumed as the blue print about the selected field area and the community for the present study. Beside this, by the help of this blue print, all types of probably suitable method like-data collection, measurement and analysis procedures were systematically decided for minimizing the research related vital problems. For the present study, this research design was defined as an advanced research plan which was required for data collection and analysis of research materials. It was also imperative that an efficient and suitable research design should be made ready before going to the research operation. Through this research design, different research related ideas were organised in a form for checking up the defects and inadequacies. Even such a prepared design was given to the supervisor or experts for adding their own comments and for further possible critical evaluation. Taking into consideration the objectives, time, budget and other aspects, research design was aware to decide the advanced methods for collecting relevant data and the techniques for processing and analysing of those collected data. By the entry of errors in the design, there was a chance to upset the entire research work. In regarding this, research design was prepared with great care to avoid the possible errors. So, research design, an event was a large amount of dependable reliability for expectant result of the research and by which, the firm foundation was constituted for full and perfect edifice of the research work.

Research Methods

For the present research operation, research methods included the particular methods which were to be applied for collecting the research related information. By logical consideration, research methods were accustomed to pursuit for collecting the real data. Sometimes, research methods encouraged to collect the rigorous information also. However, among various data collecting methods, literature survey, interview, observation, case study, genealogy and rarely questionnaire were decided as objectives and logical and even free from personal bias or prejudice. Regarding the decided objectives and methods, all possible questions of various components were systematically arranged in the schedule for collecting the relevant information from different respondents. These research methods were dealt to collect the demonstrable good quality of information. Generally, a guidance was provided by the rules of logical proof of various research methods and these forwarded the systematic investigation procedure. It is postulated that the satisfaction and internal stability were achieved by applying the various decided research methods in the study field.

Sampling

In research design, sampling was understood as a smallest unit of a larger whole and it was an important role relating with the present research. Before going to the field of this present research, it was very required to achieve the humble knowledge about the given population, their concentration and their socio-cultural as well as biological aspects. All such preliminary information were acquired through literature survey. Available literatures were enabled to indicate that the major concentrations of Saharia tribe were estimated in Barai block of Gird subdivisional area. It was also informed that as primitive tribe, they were passing socio-economically backward and isolated life. It was further informed that the dispersals of Saharia were recorded in 21 districts but their large number of population was accounted in Gwalior and Morena districts of Madhya Pradesh. Beside this, among all subdivisions of Gwalior district, the maximum Saharia were centrally distributed in the Gird subdivision. Comparing with the increasing rate of national population, it was speculated that the estimated population were the chances to be increased in number. In this regard, 300 to 400 households in various villages under Barai block of Gird subdivision were decided as sample size for the present study. There was also a presumption that this sample size would be able to supply the relevant information regarding the objectives. Taking into consideration, the distribution of Saharia tribe in various subdivisions of Gwalior district, the Barai block of Gird subdivision was selected purposively. In the second stage, the adjoining both close distance and far distance villages of Barai block were selected by random sampling technique.

Pilot Study

For the present study, the Barai block of Gird subdivision and its adjoining villages were selected for collecting the information. Interview with the subject canvassing an interview schedule was formed to arrange the basic tools for data collection. Well planned interview schedule consisting of both open ended and close ended questions were prepared for this research purpose.

Before finalising the schedules, a pilot study was performed (from 3rd to 11th January, 1999) for checking up the initially prepared schedules and for determining the field situation. Through pretesting the schedules, the necessary correction and modification were made keeping in view of the objectives of the study. The purpose of pretesting the schedule was to rectify the errors and to incorporate the modification so as to make it more useful one. Beside this, the field area was confirmed and lodging, fooding, etc. were decided in the field area as convenient as possible. The data to be collected from the officials, villagers and including all concerned were informed accordingly.

Preliminary Investigation

For the purpose of this research work, a preliminary investigation in over all research methods has been considered as the fundamental step. Through this investigation, attempts have been formulated to come in important and relevant insight of various involved components in the whole scope of research work. In fact, the involved components have been focused in regarding their population structure, concentration, settlement pattern, development strategy and its impact, educational attainment, disease and therapeutics, family planning, etc., for the present study. At the household level, observation and informal interview or discussion methods have been applied for collecting the information about their attitudes towards the structure of family size and formation, living standard, concept of modern education, notion of modern doctor and medicine, awareness to family planning methods, development aspects, migration, etc. from almost five families of every selected village. Beside this, state, district, subdivision, block and village level various relevant data like - Saharia settlement pattern, household, demographic structure, concentration, history of origination, soil, flora, fauna, communication system, electricity, medical facility, living standard, material and soci-cultural aspects, family planning methods, development schemes, etc., have been additionally accumulated from different libraries, offices, village political leaders, religious heads and experienced elders. For the present study, preliminary investigation has been required to gain an over all guidance on location and distance of villages, distribution of population, household list, attitude of respondents and speed of answering of questions, responds' errors, social barriers, acceptability, suitability of research method, duration of time, probable cost, etc.

Data Collection

Through preliminary investigation, an over all practical experience has been achieved about significant insight into various involved aspects of Saharia. Before entering the relevant information into schedule, most of the respondents have been interviewed thoroughly. By asking various questions, their attitude, manner, co-operativeness, answering performance, etc., have been determinated in a systematic manner. Generally, the oldest person in every family of selected Saharia villages has been regarded as head. Sometimes, head of the family has been found to be very old and facing ageing problem. In such situation, his eldest son or daughter has been considered as the head who has openly supplied most of the information. Following the attitude of respondents, confidential information relating to women have been collected from wives corroborating with the presence of husbands. Duration between menarche and marriage and between marriage and pregnancy have been carefully estimated by cross examining the statements of wife with her own age, present age of the child, important social events of the year, etc. Similarly, the age at death of child has been estimated taking into account the mentioned factors. The large number of arranged questions of various components in schedule has been asked and collected answers from every household of six selected villages. All the parameters of interview (and observation) have been systematically arranged in various schedules which are stated in the following manner:

General Schedule: Information pertaining to name of district, subdivision, block, bank, post office, village, community hall, guest house, educational institution, Hospital or dispensary, electric facility, irrigation facility, principal crops, rain fall, seasonal disease, multipurpose training centre, loan, development programmes, etc. were systematically arranged in this schedule.

Village Schedule: Information regarding sources of water, fauna, flora, soil, settlement pattern, village path/road, drainage, bank, post office, electricity, medical facility, village market, school, communication system, sanitation, community place, worship place, industries, number of Saharia population, household, number of non-Saharia population, household, name of elected gram Pradhan, traditional gram Pradhan, development programmes and others were included this schedule.

Household Schedule: This scheduled was comprised by the information of the name of respondent, relationship with others, age, sex, marital status, language, house type, food and drink, dress and ornaments, implement and utensils, family structure, clan, change of clan (after marriage), property inheritance, social hierarchy, status of women, birth, marriage, divorce and remarriage, death, religious organisation, political organisation, education, development programmes, etc.

Occupational Schedule: This schedule consisted of the information about occupation of grand father, father and present generation, landed property, animal husbandry, hunting, gathering, tribal craft, business, labour, service, dependency, total income, total expenditure, indebtness, source of indebtness and others related information.

Living Standard: This schedule was charged to confer the information about the types of residence, storeyed, made by, number of room and purposes, arrangement of water, source of fuel, light supply, awareness for sanitation and so on.

Mass Media and Education: Information about enjoyable instrument (Radio, Tape Recorder, T.V.), communication by, connection, types of enjoyable movie, educational facility, stipend facility, desireness, satisfaction, preference for male/female education, reading of newspaper, news of T.V. or Radio, etc., were covered by this schedule.

Development Aspects: This schedule was helped to collect the information about provided development schemes, purpose, number of benefited families, interest, process of repaying installments, etc.

Fertility Schedule: Data relating to the age at menarche, age at menopause, age at marriage, consanguineal/affinal marriage, duration, age at child birth, age at marriage of son/daughter, result of pregnancy (one generation), etc. were collected by this schedule.

Maternal and Child Care Schedule: Cultural practices-fatalism, selection of doctor place of delivery, delivery attendant, material used to cut naval cord, breast feeding, lactation, weaning practices, immunization, etc., were the important information, collected by this schedule.

Health Seeking Behaviour : In this schedule, it was prepared the various questions relating to health condition, duration of sickness, reasons of sickness, visit any Hospital/PHC, doctor preference, comment about Hospital/PHC, accepted medicine or not, last five years records of sickness, etc.

Mortality Schedule: Information associated with dead record of last one year, causes of death, consulted for deceased person, etc. were systematically arranged in this schedule.

Migration Schedule: This schedule was concerned to the information about family particulars at migration, adopted cultural norms, sexual intercourse, whether pregnant women migrated, child born occurred, abortion, any body died, etc., during migration, reasons of migration and others.

Family Planning Schedule: Information relating to the awareness of family planning, view on offsprings, awareness of conception, adopted methods, adopted by husband/wife, problem felt, method of abortion, preference on male/female, ideal number of male/female, etc., was emboded in this schedule.

Total Duration of Field Work

For the purpose of this research work, all primary data were collected from six Saharia villages of Barai block, Gird subdivision in Gwalior district. In this context, duration was estimated from preliminary investigation to the completion of main data collection of every household. Preliminary investigation was started from 4th February, 1999 and continued upto 16th February, 1999 and then systematically household data collection was started and completed on 6th December, 1999. In the mean time, due to physical problem, data collection was discontinued for a few days. However, almost ten months were expensed for collecting all types of primary data from every Saharia household.

Data Analysis

Data analysis has been considered as an important task for preparing an ideal report. It has been taken as computation of all possible measures and seeking various relationships, existed in collected data. Data analysis has always been done following the objectives of the study and without having any bias. For analysis the various types of data of particular component, it has been assembled the different formulae which are stated in the following manner:

Demographic Analysis

For the present study, the various demographic variables have been utilized and these are as follows:

A. Measure of Population Composition –

1. Distribution of population by age and sex and its percentage.

B. Measure of Economic Activity-

1. Crude Activite Rate (CAR) $= \dfrac{\text{Economically Active Population}}{\text{Total Population}} \times 100$

2. General Activity Rate (GAR) $= \dfrac{\text{Economically Active Population}}{\text{Population Aged (15-59)}} \times 100$

C. Dependency Ratio –

1. Young Age Dependency Ratio (YADR) $= \dfrac{\text{Population Aged (0-14) Years}}{\text{Population Aged (15-59)}} \times 100$

2. Old Age Dependency Ratio (OADR) $= \dfrac{\text{Population Aged 60 + Years}}{\text{Population Aged (15-59)}} \times 100$

3. Total Dependency Ratio (TDR) $= \dfrac{\text{Population Aged (0-14) Years} \;\; \text{60 Years}}{\text{Population Aged (15-59)}} \times 100$

4. Index of Ageing (IA) $= \dfrac{\text{Population Aged 60 + Years}}{\text{Population Aged (0-14) Years}} \times 100$

D. Measure of Educational Aspects -

1. Literacy Rate (LR) $= \frac{\text{Number of Literate population}}{\text{Total Population}} \times 100$

2. Age/Sex Specific Literacy Rate (A/SSLR) $= \frac{\text{Literate Population in an Age Group}}{\text{Total Population of that Age Group}} \times 100$

3. Various Levels of Educational Attainment - By Age and Sex.

E. Marital Status and Distribution -

Distribution of Population by Marital Status, Sex and Age Group.

F. Measure of Fertility -

1. Sex Ratio (SR) $= \frac{\text{No. of Female in Population}}{\text{No. of Male in Population}} \times 1000$

2. Masculinity Proportion (MP) $= \frac{\text{No. of Male in Population}}{\text{No. of Total Poulation}} \times 100$

3. Measure of Child-Women Ratio -

(i) Child-Women Ratio (CWR) $= \frac{\text{Children Aged (0-4) Years in a Population}}{\text{Women of Reproductive Age Group (15-49)}} \times 1000$

(ii) Child-Women Ratio (CWR) $= \frac{\text{Children Aged (5-9) Years in a Population}}{\text{Women of Reproductive Age Group (15-49)}} \times 1000$

(iii) Child-Women Ratio (CWR) $= \frac{\text{Children Aged (0-9) Years in a Population}}{\text{Women of Reproductive Age Group (15-49)}} \times 1000$

4. Crude Birth Rate (CBR) $= \dfrac{\text{No. of Live Births Durings the Year}}{\text{Mid-year Population}} \times 1000$

5. General Fertility Rate (GFR) $= \dfrac{\text{No. of Live Births in a Year}}{\text{Mid-year Female Population in Reproductive Age Group (15-49)}} \times 1000$

6. Age Specific Fertility Rate (ASFR) $= \dfrac{\text{No. of Live Births in a Particular Age Group of Women}}{\text{Mid-year Female Population of the same Age Group}} \times 1000$

7. Total Fertility Rate (TFR) $= \dfrac{5\times \sum_{15-19}^{45-49} \text{ASFR}}{1000}$

8. Gross Reproduction Rate (GRR) $= \dfrac{5\times \sum_{15-19}^{45-49} \text{ASFR}}{1000}$ For Female Live Births

9. Mean Age of Child Bearing (MACB) $= \sum_{MidPoint=15}^{49} \dfrac{\text{Mid-Point of the Age Group} \times \text{ASFR}}{\text{ASFR}}$

10. Age Specific Marital Fertility Rate (ASMFR) $= \dfrac{\text{No. of live Births in a particular Age Group}}{\text{Mid-year Female Population (Wed-lock) of the same Age Group}} \times 1000$

11. General Marital Fertility Rate (GMFR) $= \dfrac{\text{Number of Live Births in a Year}}{\text{Mid-Year Female Population (Wed-lock) of the same Age Group (15-49) Years}} \times 1000$

12. Total Marital Fertility Rate (TMFR) $= \dfrac{5 \times \sum_{15-19}^{45-49} \text{ASMFR}}{1000}$

G. Measure of Mortality –

1. Crude Death Rate (CDR) $= \dfrac{\text{Number of Deaths During the Year}}{\text{Mid-Year Population}} \times 1000$

2. Age-Specific Mortality Rate (ASMR) $= \dfrac{\text{Number of Deaths in a Particular Age-Group}}{\text{Mid-Year Population of the Same Age Group}} \times 1000$

3. Still Births Rate (SBR) $= \dfrac{\text{Number of Still Births During the Year}}{\text{Number of Live Births and Still Births During the Year}} \times 1000$

4. Peri-natal Mortality Rate (PMR) $= \dfrac{\text{Number of Still Births and Infant Deaths of Less than 7 Days During the Year}}{\text{Number of Live Births and Still Births During the Year}} \times 1000$

5. Neo-natal Mortality Rate (NMR) $= \dfrac{\text{Number of Infant Deaths Aged upto 28 Days During the Year}}{\text{Number of Live Births During the Year}} \times 1000$

6. Post Neo-natal Mortality Rate (PNMR) $= \dfrac{\text{Number of Deaths abov 28 Days to less than one Year During the Year}}{\text{Number of Live Births During the Year}} \times 1000$

7. Infant Mortality Rate (IMR) $= \dfrac{\text{Number of Infant Deaths During the Year}}{\text{Number of Live Births During Year}} \times 1000$

8. Under-Five Mortality Rate (U5MR) = $\dfrac{\text{No. of Deaths Under-Five Years Children During specified Year in a Population}}{\text{Total no. of Live Births During that Specified Year in that Population}} \times 1000$

9. Child Mortality Rate (CMR) = $\dfrac{\text{No. of Deaths of 1 to 15 Years Children During Specified Year in a Population}}{\text{Total no. of Live Births During that Specified Year in that Population}} \times 1000$

10. Cause Specific Death Rate (CSDR) = $\dfrac{\text{Number of Deaths by particular cause}}{\text{Total Population}} \times 100{,}000$

H. Selection Intensity –

For the present study, Crow's (1958) and Johnson & Kensinger's (1971) methods have been additionally applied to compute the index of opportunity for natural selection. For this purpose, the reproductive histories have been considered of those respondents (females aged 45 years and above) who completed their reproductive span of life.

The index of opportunity for selection (I_1) following Crow (1958) has been calculated as:

I_1 = $I_m + I_f / P_s$; where $I_m = P_d / P_s$; and $I_f = V_f / (x)^2$

[I_m = Index of opportunity for selection due to mortality (mortality from birth to reproductive age – below 15 years).

I_f = Index of opportunity for selection due to fertility;

X = Average number live birth per women aged 45 years and above who have completed their reproductive life span;

V_f = Variance of number of live births;

P_d = Proportion of pre-reproductive death;

P_s = Proportion of survivors from birth to reproductive age].

The index of opportunity for selection (I) following Johnson & Kensinger (1971) has been calculated as: $I_2 = I_{me} + I_{mc} / P + I_f / P_b P_s$;

Where $I_{me} = 1 - P_b / P_d$, $I_{mc} = P_d / P_s$; $I_f = V_f / (x)^2$; $P_b = 1 - P_{ed}$

[I_{me} = Index of opportunity for selection due to embryonic mortality;

I_{mc} = Index of opportunity for selection due to pre-reproductive morality (morality from birth to reproductive age);

P_{ed} = Proportion of embryonic deaths;

P_b = Proportion of survivors to birth;

$\dot{P}_d$ = Proportion of pre-reproductive deaths]

For conducting the present research, field area was selected at different Saharia villages under Barai block, Gird subdivision of South-West part of Gwalior district. Barai block is regarded as the heart of all Saharia villages. At initial stage of this present research, this area was investigated and decided there for availability of maximum Saharia families. The reasons for selecting the tribe, area and villages are as follows:

Selection of Saharia

The local dialect of Saharia is 'Khariboli' which is incorporately related with Hindi language. So, at the time of data collection, it was faced severely the language problem. They are one among seven primitive tribes of Madhya Pradesh and reside in the remote hilly-forest regions where no anthropological with reference to demographic work has been done by the former anthropologists. So, it was required to investigate them systematically with precision view. Beside this, most of the beneficiary schemes of Government are emerging for primitive tribes. But still now, they are undeveloped and isolated from the main stream of national life. Whether they are accepting these schemes or not, if accepted then how much they are benefited by these schemes and other parameters have also been covered by the present study.

Selection of Area

The maximum Saharia are inhabiting in Barai block, Gird subdivision of Gwalior district. As a reason, this block area was selected expecting possible better communication and accommodation facilities. To reach in any Saharia village, it would not be expended more amount and time. Beside this, very few anthropologists surveyed this area long before and their data collection was mainly limited only in ethnographic components. Even they could not enable to present the satisfactory conclusion.

Selection of Village

Only the Saharia are inhabiting in every selected village. A few villages are settled down in a close distance of Barai block and other villages are situated far distance from this block area. So, it could be enabled to observe the differentiation between the life style of close distance villagers and far distance villagers of this block. Beside this, the expected sizable samples were easily covered in every village.

The Research Work and Problems Faced

Research work comprising the extended study of a community and the way of life of this community people, is the co-experience of anthropologist. This is considered as the source of information and after collecting, researchers generalize these at home. In simple word, the research work has been meant by a vision quest. On this ground, Young (1960) has defined this research work in the following words, "We may define social research in the systematic method of discovering new facts or verifying old fact, their sequences, interrelationships, casual explanations and natural which govern them."

Research problems always refer to those problems which are come either theoretically or practically to the researchers and taking into consideration, the researchers want to obtain the suitable solution of problems. In ordinary way, it may be said that various problems existed in various conditions but then and there, every problem should be solved or faced by ideal researchers. During the field work among Saharia under Barai block, many problems were faced and also solved. These problems are described in the following manner:

The local dialect of Saharia is called "Khariboli." This dialect is incorporately related with Hindi language. But the pronunciation is somewhat different from Hindi language. So at initial stage, language problem was faced sometimes. But with the help of hostel students and other people, this problem was solved satisfidely.

When I was introduced to them, they looked me as a Government official - census worker. According to their speculation, they were investigated for the personal interest of field worker. However, by explaining the bonafide and academic purposes, it was possible to convince them. When they enquired my identification, I introduced myself as a university research scholar. They were satisfied and felt pride and then provided permission to select the families and respondents for the present study.

In second time, when I contacted with respondents for collecting more information and cross checked the collected information, then they showed their reluctance simply by saying that they had already supplied all information and they had no time for supplying again other information. After convincing them any way, I further collected data which contained more necessary information and then cross checked the previous collected information.

Generally, the male and female and also their adult children used to stay in the field or forest for their various purposes. The children, who stayed at home, were unable to supply information and even they also felt shame. By consulting with them, the suitable time was decided (mainly morning, evening and night) and then all necessary information were collected.

Most of the Saharia are illiterate and careless. For their illiteracy and carelessness, they were unable to supply all kinds of accurate information relating to date of child birth, age of the child, etc. So, depending on associated incidents and my personal field experience, it was possible to gather information from such respondents.

They are more addicted to drink the local wine (Handia/Daru). Specially at evening, they were habituated to drink wine and after drinking, they practised abnormal behaviour. In that condition, they were unable to supply any information.

A few selected villages are settled down some distance from the camp (Panihar). Due to hilly and broken road, any transport system was not available to reach in such villages. Inspite of such odd situation, those villages were also covered on foot.

Many times, the Government administrators or agencies visited in the Saharia inhabitat villages for various purposes and they always showed that they were more advanced or civilized than Saharia. Even, they sometimes provoked them by practising the various misbehaviours. In that condition, they had no any firm confidence to the new comers. But, by using various satisfactory words, the rapport was established with them and then the adequate information were started to collect.

At initial stage, it was presumed that within the decided period of time, all types of data collection would be completed. But sometimes for my physical disturbance, it was not possible to collect all kinds of information and as a result of this, field study was sometimes delayed.

Limitation of the Study

Limitations of the study are stated in the following manner:

1. Due to some reasons, higher statistical tools like – linear equation, multiple regression, coefficient of correlation, etc. could not be used in the study.
2. Detailed interview of medical doctors and other functionaries could not be done because of their busy schedule.

CHAPTER - III

ETHNOGRAPHIC PROFILE OF TRIBES AND SAHARIA AS A WHOLE

This chapter consists of the analytical descriptions of tribes, primitive tribes, their distributions, zonal variations, history of Gwalior and geographical situation. In a very formative manner, this chapter also initiates an intervention to embody the origination – history of Saharia, their geo-physical environment, settlement pattern, infrastructural condition, ethnic composition, economy, socio-cultural perspectives, education, development aspect, etc.

ETHNOGRAPHIC PROFILE OF TRIBES

The word 'Tribe' is evolved to have different meanings but Latin Root is confined in the collective aspersion of its origination. Instead of tribe, the Middle English term states 'Tribuz' which is meant to introduce three dimensions with having variation from one country to another. Roman asserts as political division whereas Greek is studded to explain as equal with fraternity. In this regard, Irish also accepts this as synonymous word with family or community bearing the same surname. The Colonial masters, concerned to the communities usually elude the word tribe and liberally use the term – primitive, savage, barbarious, uncivilized, preliterate, little community, aborigin, native, etc. In an exponent discussion, Dictionary of Anthropology (Winick, 1957) defines, "Tribe is a social group, usually with a definite area of living, dialect, cultural homogeneity and unifying social organization. It may include several subgroups as sibs or villages; a tribe ordinarily has a leader and may have a common ancestor and patron deity. The families or small communities making up the tribe, are linked together through social, religious, family or blood relation". By conferring different evidences, the sacred Puranas and other Epics postulate that for inhabiting in forest and practicing aboriginal folk, many groups of people were secluded as 'Tribe'. Later on, those groups were introduced as 'Asuras, Dasys, Nishades, Rakhasas' and others (Bhowmick, 1990).

More or less, concentrations of the tribal people have been enumerated in most of the countries of the world. A lot of evidences supports that from ancient time to the present state, tribal people are depressed and unable to avoid their miserable situation. Without having any experience about the socio-cultural orthodox of tribes, the Colonial emperors implemented their cruel administrative rules and regulations. As a result, tribal people were effected very much and then they organized the fragmentary rally in various parts for making insurrections against the ruler groups. During this susceptible period, many anthropologists like – Saligman, Evan Pritchard, D.R. Nadel, et.al. were deputed to conduct socio-cultural research studies among tribal people specially in Colonial kingdoms. In America, tribal as well as non-tribal people were also facing some acute social problems related to mal-adjustment in highly, industrialized exploitation, colour difference between Red Indians and Racial groups and others. Arrounding these sentimental issues, people came into violence which was suddenly erupted throughout the continent. For making neutralization and integration of such emotional problems, anthropological studies were also required further.

In Indian sub-continent, tribal people are inhabited in farthest corner of various provinces. Under British rules, tribal people were never studied to improve their socio-cultural status or preserve their unifying culture. The main purpose of these rulers was pursued to secure peace without establishing any economic development (Sahu, 1982). After eighteenth century, British Government just prepared an 'Act' for demarcating all backward classes into wholly excluded area and partially excluded area (Saxena, 1962). But after getting independence, free India has been inspired to furnish an elaborated democratic

'Constitution'. This evolves the constitutional rules and regulations sustaining different provisions for all citizens of India. But special provisions have been given to the Scheduled Castes and Scheduled Tribes who were detached from the main stream of national life. For bestowing the socio-cultural upliftment process through various projects, all tribes have been enlisted under the Article '342' of the Constitution of India and then they are acquainted as 'Scheduled Tribes'. Among Scheduled Tribes, 74 groups all over the country have been further categorized as more backwarded as well as primitive tribes for the reasons of their small size of community, pre-agricultural stage of economy, high extent of isolation, low level of literacy, etc. (in fifth five year plan). Etymology makes an wimp that 'primitive' means 'aboriginal or very old'. Actually primitive tribes are designated to those who have been originated earlier than other tribes. But there is no any existence of such identification in Anthropological literatures. However, the purpose of this identification is to turn them from their stagnated life and redirect to avail the modern facilities by providing the various development schemes. At a glance, state-wise distributions of identified primitive tribal population are depicted in the following Table 3.1.

TABLE: 3.1
State-wise Distribution of Identified Primitive Tribal Population of India for the Year of 1971, 1981 and 1991

Name of Identified Primitive Tribe	*State/Union Territory*	*Number of Population*		
		1971	*1981*	*1991*
1	2	3	4	5
Abujhamaria	Madhya Pradesh	1300	15500	17016
Baiga	Madhya Pradesh	–	120387	134357
Bharia	Madhya Pradesh	1589	1614	2012
Hill Korwa	Madhya Pradesh	–	19041	27109
Kamar	Madhya Pradesh	13600	13500	13110
Saharia	**Madhya Pradesh**	**207174**	**260816**	**417171**
Birhor	Madhya Pradesh	738	561	925
Kathodi	Gujarat	2939	3665	3234

1	2	3	4	5
Kotwalia	Gujarat	12902	16130	18835
Padhar	Gujarat	–	12731	13446
Siddi	Gujarat	4482	5600	6896
Kolgha	Gujarat	29464	25030	33096
Saharia	Rajasthan	26796	39808	–
Buxas	Utter Pradesh	–	34195	42027
Raji	Utter Pradesh	–	371	494
Asur	Bihar	7026	7783	8345
Birhor	Bihar	3464	4377	7671
Birjia	Bihar	3628	4057	4106
Hill Kharia	Bihar	127002	141771	83591
Korwa	Bihar	18717	21940	20221
Malpaharia	Bihar	48636	79322	14078
Pahariya	Bihar	14651	24102	–
Sauria Paharia	Bihar	59047	39269	–
Savar	Bihar	3548	3014	–
Marram Naga	Manipur	5123	6544	–
Reangs	Tripura	64722	84004	–
Birhor	Orissa	248	142	–
Bonodo	Orissa	3870	4431	–
Didayi	Orissa	3055	3654	5990
Dongria Khond	Orissa	2676	6067	7666
Juang	Orissa	3181	2834	5774
Kharia	Orissa	1259	1259	1438
Kutia Khnad	Orissa	3016	4735	6479
Lanjia Soura	Orissa	4223	8421	10644
Lodha	Orissa	1598	1598	2052
Mankidia	Orissa	133	133	130
Paudi Bhuyan	Orissa	4424	8872	10926
Soura	Orissa	2845	2917	3420
Birhor	West Bengal	–	658	–

1	2	3	4	5
Lodha	West Bengal	45906	53718	–
Toto	West Bengal	–	675	–
Boda & Gutab Gadaba	Andhra Pradesh	25108	27732	35182
Bondo, Khond & Parengi Porojay	Andhra Pradesh	12347	16479	20721
Chenchu	Andhra Pradesh	24178	28434	30680
Dongria & Kutia Khond	Andhra Pradesh	34382	39408	63154
Kolam	Andhra Pradesh	26498	21842	39457
Konda Reddy	Andhra Pradesh	42777	54685	64841
Konda Savara	Andhra Pradesh	28189	–	35309
Thoti	Andhra Pradesh	1785	1416	1696
Katkaria	Maharastra	146785	174602	–
Kolam	Maharastra	56061	118073	–
Maria Gond	Maharastra	53400	66750	–
Jenu Kuruba	Karnataka	–	29092	26608
Koraga	Karnataka	–	12041	16422
Kadar	Kerala	1120	1503	1521
Kattunayakan	Kerala	5565	8803	11001
Kurumbas	Kerala	1319	1283	1267
Cholanaikayan	Kerala	306	234	360
Koraga	Kerala	1200	1098	1300
Irulas	Tamil Nadu	–	36383	30000
Kattu Naickan	Tamil Nadu	–	36383	–
Kota	Tamil Nadu	1188	604	–
Kurumba	Tamil Nadu	–	105757	–
Paniyan	Tamil Nadu	6093	6393	–
Toda	Tamil Nadu	930	875	–
Jarwa	Andaman & Nicobar Islands	–	200	200
Onge	Andaman & Nicobar Islands	–	102	98
Sentinelese	Andaman & Nicobar Islands	–	80	100
Shompen	Andaman & Nicobar Islands	212	214	135
Great Andamanese	Andaman & Nicobar Islands	–	28	28

In the context of global view point, Indian sub-continent is appertained to occupy the position of second largest tribal population (after Africa). Concentrations of tribal people are dispersed crossing one to another political boundary of the states and union territories of India. Their scatterdly inhabitations are highly noticed in different remote areas. However, for almost same racial live stock, similar characteristics, better understanding of demographic situation and others, Indian sub-continent is permutated in to seven tribal zones (Sinha, 1990; Sharma & Sharma, 1999). In these zones, the important tribal groups and their socio-cultural aspects are briefly discussed in the following manner:

North-Eastern Zone: Location of north-eastern tribal zone is pervaded throughout Arunachal Pradesh, Assam, Manipur, Meghalaya and Mizoram. This zone is noticed as the inhabitation of plentiful tribal groups like the Adi, Khowa, Singpho, Chakma, Garo, Khasi, Kuki, Aimol, Chiru, Moyan, Sema, Hajong, Nega, Mikir, Bhil, Bhutia, Lepcha, Oraon, Santal, Riang and other tribes. Their physical appearances impart an aspersion that they belong to the Mongoloid racial live stock. They generally select their ideal inhabiting location which is surrounded by natural resources. Shifting cultivation is resorted as their primary occupation whereas hunting, gathering, fishing, labouring, basket making, etc. are practised as secondary purposes. These tribal groups are non-vegetarian and addicted to drink rice beer (O-deng). They are endogamous and prefer to polygamy system of marriage. For ensuring the normal delivery of expectant mother, they arrange worship and sacrifice animals or birds. They usually bury the dead body. There, traditional political organization is existed for justifying all social disputes. These tribal people are devoted to propitiate both benevolent and malevolent God and Goddess to secure peace and appease respectively.

Eastern Zone: Eastern tribal zone consists of Bihar, Jharkhand, Orissa, Sikkim and West Bengal. The originations of 132 tribes and their sub-groups are identified all over the states of this zone. The Asur, Baiga, Birhor, Gond, Oraon, Munda, Santal, Bhutiya, Chenchu, Ho, Lodha, Rajur, Saora, Bhutia, Lepcha, Garo, Kora, Nagessia, Rabha, Toto and others are considered as highly noticeable tribes whose physical appearances are committed to report as the descendants of the Mangoloid racial live stock. These tribes traditionally practise hunting and gathering occupations. Shifting cultivation and rarely settled cultivation are also practised by them. Lodha tribal grpups of this zone are highly appreciated for making the decorated bridal palanquin. They are tribal endogamous but clan exogamous and negotiation marriage is preferred to them. There is the existence of active traditional village Council consisting of headman, assistant headman, priest and messengers. They investigate the socio-cultural problems and take the necessary action. Their hearty respect is concentrated to the religious belief. By making prayer to their primordial God, they solicit for prevailing peace and better harvesting.

Northern Zone: Northern tribal zone embodies Himachal Pradesh, Uttar Pradesh and Uttaranchal. Concentrations of the Bhot, Gaddi, Gujjur, Kanaura, Swangla, Bhutia, Buksa, Raji, Tharu and other important tribes are come to notice throughout this zone. Their physical characters report that they are originated from Mongoloid racial live stock. These tribal groups are habituated to tolerate the extreme cold weather. Inspite of their socio-cultural similarity, they are permutated in accordance with their occupational differences. The typical example of Bhutia tribal groups reports that they are traditionally involved in business of borax, tails of yaks, herbs, musk, etc. Traditionally Rajis practise nomadic hunting and gathering occupations whereas other tribal groups earn through agricultural labour. They are endogamous and patrilineal tribal groups. According to special requirement, they also sometimes devote themselves in practicing levirate, surrorate and cross cousin marriage. They observe name giving ceremony as auspicious day. After death, they generally cremate the dead body. Their traditional political head is empowered to justify all socio-cultural despites. They worship all Hindi deities for various purposes.

Central Zone: Central tribal zone is extended in Madhya Pradesh and Chhatisgarh where largest tribal people are settled down. Due to occupy the central place and produce highest tribal population, this zone is acquainted as tribal heart of India. However, this zone is adorned by birth of the Baiga, Bharia, Bhil, Birhor, Gond, Halba, Kamar, Karku, Kharia, Kol, Hill Korwa,

Munda, Parja, Saharia and other tribes whose physical structures indicate that they belong to Proto-Australoid racial live stock. Specially during summer season, these tribal groups face problem of inadequacy of water. Wage-earning, fuel selling, rickshaw pulling, crafting, etc. occupations are practised to pass their daily life. They use to eat 'Rabbi' made by millet and chuti combinely (coarsely ground). They prefer to negotiation marriage which is extremely prohibited to conduct in same clan. Both remarriage and widow marriage are rarely practised among them. They observe child birth as very auspicious day. Their dead body is buried projecting face upwards and directing head towards south. As patrilineal tribe, father's properties are equally transmitted to his sons. Their active traditional political organization is functionised to maintain socio-cultural norms and justify the conflicts. They are inspired to worship the Hindu God and Goddesses.

Western Zone: Western tribal zone consists of Dadra & Nagar Haveli, Gujarat, Goa, Daman & Diu, Maharastra and Rajasthan. There is followed the sporadical dispersions of the Dhosia, Kokna, Verli, Barda, Bhil, Dubla, Gond, Koli, Pomla, Siddi, Andh, Baiga, Birhul, Halba, Kamar, Oraon, Parja and other tribal groups. The physical appearances of these tribal groups are concerned as the descendants of Prota-Australoid racial live stock. Hunting and gathering are resorted as their traditional occupations. But at the present state, they are practising wage labour. Except negotiation, elopement process of marriage is also conducted among them. After birth of the child, the new born mother has to observe impureness during six days. They are socially permitted to cremate or bury the dead body. As patrilineal tribes, father's properties are transmitted through male line. In every tribal group of this zone, there is existence of a recognized traditional political organization to give the prorogation only to the male for justifying the socio-cultural disputes by the direct supervision of 'Gameti or Mukhia' or headman. They use to celebrate the various deities like – 'Miri Mata, Hindole Devi' and others without having any acceptance of even water.

Southern Zone: The extension of southern tribal zone is followed throughout Andhra Pradesh, Karnataka, Tamil Nadu and Kerala. Almost all regions of this zone are habituated by153 tribal groups and their sub-groups. The Andh, Bhil, Chenchu, Gond, Jatapu, Khond, Koya, Kulia, Yanadis, Barda, Irular, Kota, Toda, Yerava, Aradan, Kadar, Uraly, Malasar, Koraga, Solasa and others are come to notice as important tribal groups whose physical structures report that they belong to the Caucasoid and Proto-Australoid racial live stocks. Collecting honey, roots, tubers, leaves, tamarind, etc. and practicing slash and burn (Kumri) cultivation, they exist their daily life. In an exceptional case, Toda tribal groups of this zone adopt pastoral life and milking and churning are practised as their main sources of economic subsistence. Due to female infanticide among them, there always runs the inadequacy of marriageable girls which motivate them to practise polyandry marriage. Clan exogamy is performed whereas remarriage and divorce are rarely permitted among them. After birth of child, they observe birth pollution during seven days. By worshipping ancestors, they bury the dead body. After death of father, inheritance is passed through male line. The famous traditional 'Kula Panchayat' system of Chenchu tribe is going to be destroyed and side by side, the modern political body is empowered even in every village panchayat level. They are inspired for propitiating to the God of mountain (Towoit), God of sacred place (Townor) and others.

Island Zone: Island tribal zone is constituted by Andamanese, Jarawas, Nicobarese, Onges, Sentinelses, Shom Pens, and other tribes who inhabit in Andaman, Nicobar and Lakshadweep. In accordance with their physical appearances, they are assessed that they belong to Negrito and Mongoloid racial live stocks. Hunting and gathering are reported as their traditional occupations. But now a days, they are also motivating to practise fishing, basket making, etc. Their partial economic need is also fulfilled by horticultural labouring. For consuming and commercial purposes, they sometimes domesticate pig and goat. In this tribal zone, both male and female are almost naked. Sometimes, they use leaves and bark of tree just for covering their sex part only. But recently, the present generation start to wear the small clothes. They are clan exogamous but in special cases, they are socially permitted to marry with the girls who are not related consanguinely for minimum two ascending generations. The monogamy system of marriage is preferred to these tribal groups. They have no any awareness to observe the birth pollution. They generally bury the dead body and for respecting religious faith, they celebrate the burial ceremony. After death, father's properties are equally distributed to sons. Specially Nicobareses are so much addicted to obey their traditional political organization which regulate their social rules and norms. They purposively worship 'Soni Mata, Devi Mata' and other deities.

Indian subcontinent is embellished to evolve 623 tribes and their sub-groups comprising 8.08 percent of the total population. Their deliberated sporadical dispersion are demarcated on hilly and plain forest regions (Sachchidananda & Prasad, 1996). It is rationalistic that Madhya Pradesh is appreciated to embrace the highest tribal population (22.73 percent) whereas Andaman & Nicobar and Lakshawdeep are acquainted to restrain the lowest tribal population (below 1 percent). It is substantive an additional charge that there is no existence any tribal population in Haryana, Punjab, Chandigarh, Delhi and Pondicherry. As compared with the total population of the states in the nation, Mizoram (94.75 percent) and Andaman & Nicobar (5-10 percent) are estimated to possess the highest and lowest percentage of population respectively (Census, 1991). However, as the tribal heart of India, Madhya Pradesh presents 22.27 percent tribal people, out of total populations who are concentrated in various regions (Map 3.1). Approximately, they are measured as the one-fourth of the total tribal population of this country. Population size of these tribal groups is also varied considerably. In this regard, it is contrived here the typical examples of Gond and Bhil tribal groups whose populations have been exceding 35 lakhs and 15 lakhs respectively. Andh Bharia and others are concerned to have almost a significant number of population in this state. Beside this, less than one thousand populations have also been measured to divulge in Birhor and Kolam tribal groups.

AREA AND SAHARIA PEOPLE

Among total of 46 identified Scheduled tribes (according to Schedule Tribe order), 7 groups have been declared as primitive tribes in Madhya Pradesh. Among these primitive tribal groups, Saharia is an important tribe and its total population is enumerated

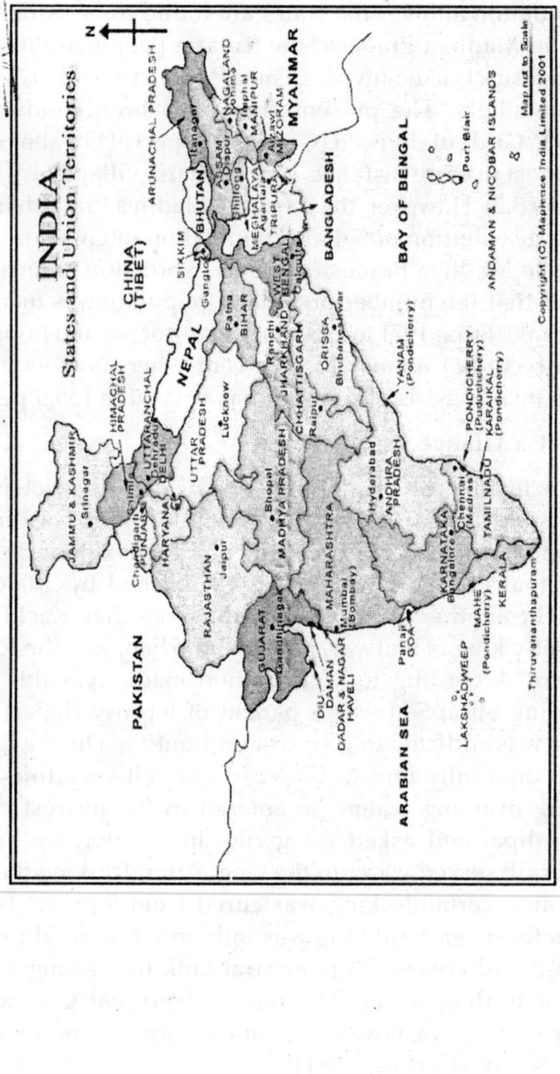

Map 3.1: Location of Madhya Pradesh in India

as 417171 implying 2.70 percent, out of total tribal population (Census, 1991) in this state. The sporadical concentrations of Saharia are not only limited by political boundary in Madhya Pradesh but also their dispersals are located in Rajasthan, Andhra Pradesh, Orissa, Bihar and very rarely in West Bengal. Their total population all over the states are found to be estimated as 7,95,134. In Madhya Pradesh, the Saharia people are inhabited in various districts like-Shivpuri, Guna, Morena, Gwalior, Vidisha, Datia and others. The present study has been conducted in Barai block, Gird subdivision (Gwalior proper) of Gwalior district where almost in close distance, some Saharia villages are settled down (Map 3.2). However, the census of Madhya Pradesh informs about the distribution of Saharia population in Gwalior district as well as in Madhya Pradesh. It is an expression of measuring parameter that the number of Saharia population is increasing at a faster rate. From 1971 to 1981, increasing of Saharia population has been recorded almost 25.9 percent whereas from 1981 to 1991, this increasing is also noticed as very high (55.9 percent).

District at a Glance

The history of origination of Gwalior district is very controversial. The earlier evidences support that Gwalior was originated from the spell of 'Gwalher'. The maxim of 'Ferishta' indicates that present Gwalior was established by 'Malch and Malwa'. The another controversy emphasises that 'Kachhwaha' chief- a petty king of Kutwar, named Suraj Sen, was the founder of Gwalior. According to a circulation made available in the legend, King Suraj Sen was a patient of leprosy (leper). More or less, he was addicted to go forest for hunting. During hunting operation on a hilly forest, 'Gopagiri', he felt very thirsty and for getting drinking water, he entered in the nearest cave of 'Sidh Gwalipa' and asked for giving him water. By his own vessel, hermit served water to the king. After drinking the given sacred water, certainly king was cured from leprosy. For this miracle activity, grateful king was influenced to build up a fort on this hill and enlarged the natural tank for storing a heavy amount of healing water. The name of present Gwalior was kept after the name of 'Gwaliawar' and enlarged tank was named as 'Suraj Kund' (Census, 1981).

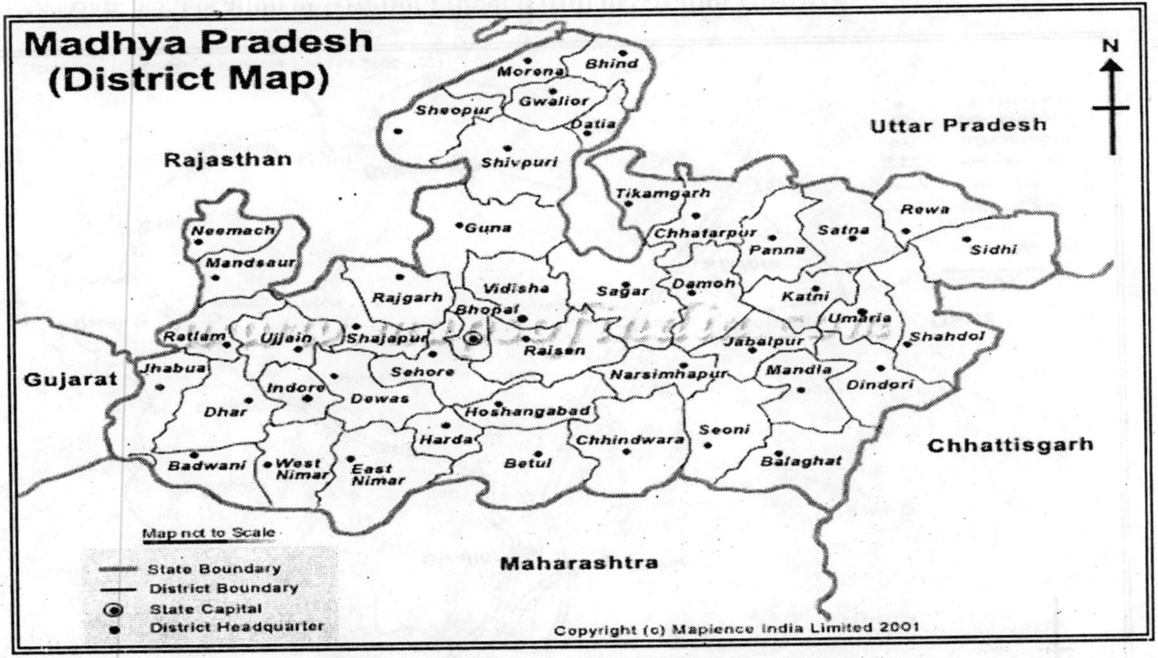

Map: 3.2: Location of Gwalior District in Madhya Pradesh

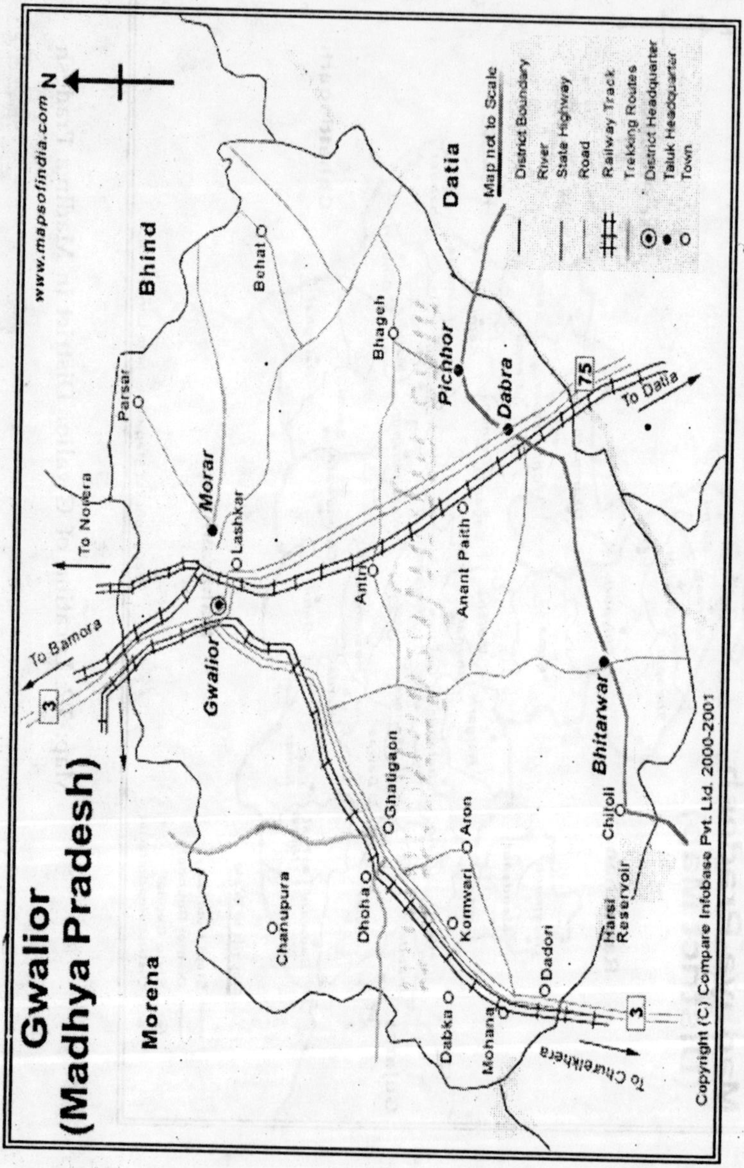

Map: 3.3: Location of Gwalior Proper (Grid) in Gwalior District

In November, 1956, Madhya Pradesh was recognised as a new state and from there, the present studied area was included as an integrated district of the state. Taking into consideration for better administrative facility, district Gwalior district was divided into three tahsils (subdivisions) viz.; Gwalior (Grid), Pichore (Dabara) and Bhander. The name - Gird has been become uncommon in accordance with the change of time and it is presently known as Gwalior proper.

In Gwalior district, the location of Gwalior proper, Pichore and Bhander tahsils are followed on South-West, North-East and South-East corner respectively (Map3.3). The district Gwalior is bounded by various other districts. Morena and Bhind districts are situated on the North and North–East corner and East side respectively. Shivpuri and Datia districts of Madhya Pradesh and Jhansi district of Uttar Pradesh are located on the South side of Gwalior. The approximate longitude and latitude have been estimated as 26.14 N and 78.10 E respectively. A major part of this district is covered by undulating hills and forests. Almost uncomfortable weather is run throughout the year. In winter season, temperature is varied from 8^0c to 13^0c whereas in summer season, its variation is noted from 30^0c to 38^0c. Rainfall is medium and it is fluctuated from 66 cms. to 84 cms. Naturally, all kinds of fauna and flora are found throughout the area.

The present research study has been performed among six Saharia villages namely - Banera, Bijli Ghor, Prem Nagar, Bhatpura, Gandhipura-North and Gandhipura-South under Barai block (under Gwalior proper) of Gwalior district in Madhya Pradesh. All studied villages are almost centrally located to Barai block. Banera village is settled down at a distance of 3 km. to the South-East corner of Barai block. Bijli Ghor is situated at a distance of 1 km. to the South-East corner whereas Prem Nagar village is located at a distance of half km. to the South side of Barai block. In North side, Bhatpura village is established and it is 3 km. away from Barai block. Gandhipura-North and Gandhipura-South villages are seated at a distance of 10 km. to the South – East corner of Barai block (Map 3.4).

History

Saharia have been constituted as one of the primitive

tribal group in Madhya Pradesh as well as in India. The available information support that they are the member of a very widespread 'Kolarian' tribe (Thakur & Thakur,1994). Their sporadical dispersals are located from North Madhya Bharat in the Centre to Andhra Pradesh and Orissa on the Eastern coast of India. In various parts of this country, they are acquainted with various names like-Saharia, Sabara, Sora, Sawara, Savar, Saora, Sahariya, etc. Still now, the early history of origination and migration of Saharia tribal group are not exactly clear. Some controversial issues about Saharia are yet to be explored. Due to some sudden natural calamities, the present Saharia perhaps have migrated from the Western part of India.

The etymological point of view defines that the literal meaning of 'Saharia' is acquainted as companion of tiger. This opinion further emblems that the word 'Saharia' is divided into two independent words like - 'SA' and 'HARIA' and these are assorted to have a separate meaning. 'SA' means companion and 'HARIA' means tiger which have been described in the riddle-verse of saint Surdas. From the Persian word 'Sher', the name Saharia has been originated and indicated the meaning as jungle or forest. Legend describes that once upon a time, 'Lord Shiva' blessed them to have access to the jungle as like as 'Sher' meaning tiger or lion and from there, they were named as 'Saharia'. In the Vadic literature, the remark of 'Aitrava Brahman' wimps that Sahara are the well-defined tribe. Puranas also confer a great evidence of specification that Sahara are the 'Vindyamauliks' which ascribe them as the original inhabitants of the Vindhyas.

It was defined that at Aranyakanda in Ramayana, there was a description of Rama who visited the Sabara region and met with a pious Sabara lady. A vague mention is also expressed about Sabara at Santiparva in Mahabharat. Mazumdar's (1994) argument incurred on the collected record from military expedition describes that as late as 8th century, the area of Pallava Malla of South India was the land of Sabara (Sabhor). Banbhatta & Dandin (7th century A.D.) argued that the Vindhyas were considered as the stronghold of them. Even poet Vikapati (also 7th century A.D.) narrated about Vindhyachal which was regarded as the shrine of the Sabara – goddess and there, human sacrifice was practised by leaf-wearing Sabaras. The valuable collective

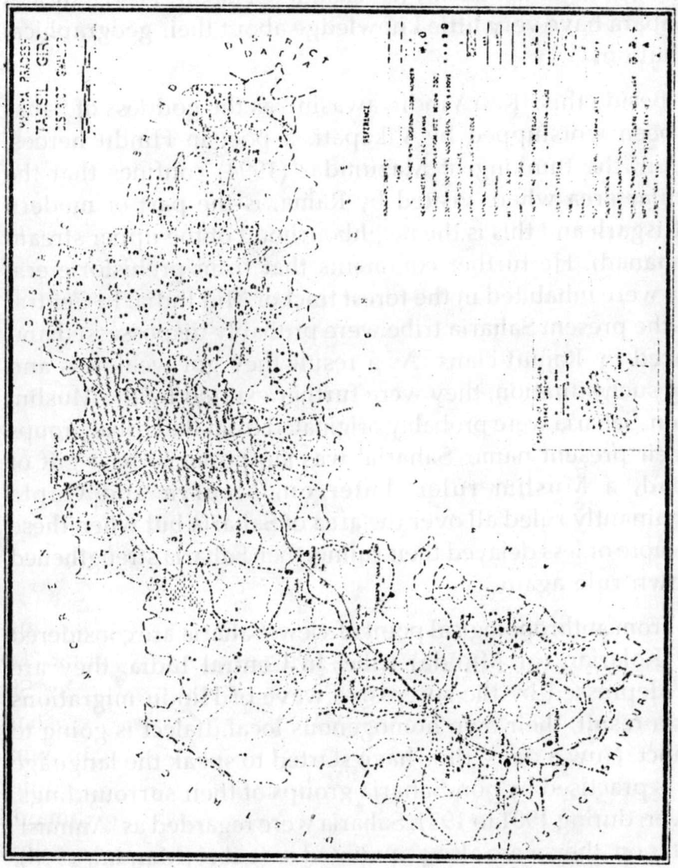

Map: 3.4: Location of Study Area in Gwalior Proper (Subdivision)

remarks of Pliny and Ptolemy (cf. Thakur & Thakur, 1994) indicates that Sabara have very little knowledge about their geographical distribution.

Beside this, 'Kali Vindhyawasini' as the goddess of Sabar have been worshipped by Vikapati, a poet in Hindu heroes. Later on, the thinking of Mazumdar (1994) confines that the particular area where visited by Rama, is the part of modern Chhattisgarh and this is the neighbourhood of the upper stream of Mahanadi. He further comments that from prehistorie era, Sabara were inhabited in the forest tract of Mid India. In Central India, the present Saharia tribe were probably dispossessed and displaced by Rajput clans. As a result they got weakness and during such situation, they were further exerted by the Muslim invasion. Saharia were probably originated from Bhil tribal groups and their present name 'Saharia' was supposed to be a gift of Sahabad, a Muslim ruler. Later on, Maurya and Gupta predominantly ruled all over the area of Saharia but when these rulers more or less delayed their ruling, then Saharia strengthened their own rule again.

From anthropological point of view, Saharia are considered as the Kolarian (or Munda) tribe. In Central India, they are totally depressed by the successive wave of Hindu migrations and as a result, their own homogenous local dialect is going to be extinct. Now a days, they have started to speak the language which is practised by non-Saharia groups of their surroundings. However, during 1901 to 1921, Saharia were regarded as 'Animist' and later on, they were also acquainted as 'tribe' (Mandal, 1998). In the census report of 1981, Saharia tribal groups were identified as 'Aboriginal' and then categorized as 'Primitive' tribe.

Climate

In this region, the uncomfortable climate is generally recorded throughout the year. From the end of February to June, the days are counted as hotter. May is phenomenon as the hottest month in the year. In the peak of the summer season, temperature rarely comes down below 35^{0}c but during these months, temperature varies from 37^{0}c to 42^{0}c. From the month of November to January, the coldest days are estimated in the year and during these days, temperature varies from 7^{0}c to 12^{0}c.

Rainfall

The maximum rainfall is measured during the monsoon month (June and July). Rain fall is normally started from the middle of June and continued upto September month. The annual rainfall of this region is recorded as medium and it is varied from 70 cms. to 90 cms. Due to such type of rainfall, water is logged anywhere during long time and soil is used as extent favourable for agricultural products. During this time, the maximum humidity is present in air and atmosphere is normally misty.

Water Sources

In the six studied Saharia villages, the sources of purified drinking water are totally unavailable. In this area, there is no stream, canal, lake, dam, etc. as water sources. So, they are depended on the water of well and tube-well for both their drinking and other purposes. In rainy season, the logged water on the lower land is sometimes collected for various purposes. But in hottest summer season, when well and tube-well do not get the water layer, then they are pressurized to collect very little quantity of water from far distant villages.

Soil

Various types of soil are found all over the region. Regarding the quality, colour, retentive of moisture, etc., the people of this area have classified their cultivable soil into four categories which are stated as Kala Jamin, Bhokta Jamin, Retili Jamin and Kakrala Jamin (Soni,1985). Kala Jamin is regarded as black soil which is very suitable for maize, wheat, jawer and vegetables cultivation. Bhokta Jamin is acquainted as yellow soil and it produces varieties of paddy, peas, flax, gram, etc. Retili Jamin is considered as sandy soil. Dadar jawar (another variety), peas, gram, and others are also grown in this soil. Lastly, Kakrala Jamin is known as soil of forest area and this soil is used for millet, urad, math, etc., production. Due to rough and hilly tracts, some parts of the soil of this region are consisted as very poor and not suitable for cultivation (Verma, 1978).

Flora

Almost 30 percent land of this area is under forest. The

entire forest area is more or less covered with various types of grass. Among all, the Phool Bahari grasses are specially referred to make the famous broom. Bamboo is at randomly grown throughout the region. Beside this, the teak plantation is continued by the forest department. Among fruit bearing trees, tendu, char, Mahua, etc. are found all over the region. Generally, they are addicted to drink local wine (Daru) which is prepared by Mahua-flowers. Dhawra (Anogeissus latibolia), Sal (Shorea robusta), Kauha (Teminalia arjuna). Bija (Pterocarpus marsupium), etc. are grown as the big trees in various forests of this area.

Fauna

Both the herbivorous and carnivorous animals are found in different forests of this region. The ancient history again informs that once upon a time, plentiful tigers and panthers were available in their forests. At present, these animals are not totally extinct but they are. much reduced in number. Various herbivorous animals are also existed and among them, sambhar cheetal, barking deer, neelgai or blue-bull, cow, bear, wild boar, deer, mouse deer and others are important. These animals are also going to be reduced in their number. Due to deforestation, hiddenly hunting, lack of available drinking water and food, limited production, etc., these animals are come down in number and even some animals are going to be extinct. In continuation of such unfavourale environment, these forest animals will have no chances to be existed in coming days.

Settlement Pattern

Most of the tribal villages are dispersed. The first ecological unit is regarded as hamlet (Phalaya) of a tribal village. On this ground, Aurora (1972) wrote, "Hamlet is an important recognizable ecological unit of the residential pattern of village society." According to the study of six Saharia villages, it is evidenced that one tribal group (Saharia) lives in one separate hamlet. They generally construct their houses on middle higher ground of the hill. The main purposes of such type construction on middle ground of the hill are as follows: to save themselves from extreme current of water specially in rainy season, to keep watch on their agricultural field, to follow their grazing livestocks, to isolate their own family members from common people just for preserving the homogeneity of their culture, to maintain the direct connection with their propitiable God and Goddesses through their constructed abode, etc.

They generally avoid to build up their houses on top of the hill. As reasons, they express their difficulty to ride on the top of the hill or come down to the lower ground of the hill by them and also specially by their livestocks. Beside this, they are unable to carry their agricultural products and water from foot to the top hill. Saharia scatterdly live in a hamlet. Their small types of house are constructed on a very limited ground and these are shown as like as cluster. More than 25 families are togetherly followed in every hamlet. Before construction of their houses, they generally consult with their main Pujari (priest) and propitiate the ground offering hen. Normally, Saharia are not habituated to shift their settlement site. One particular place is selected for their permanent habitation. They have no any written document or deed of their residential land but for their agricultural land, Government has already started to confer them the deed. Due to their poverty, they use to sell their landed property to the non-tribal money lenders and landlords with very chief rate. As a result, they are going to be landless. In that condition, Government has ruled out that the non-tribal people are restricted not to purchase the landed property from the tribes. Beside this, the deed of tribal property purchased by non-tribal groups is liable to be invalid under the operation of Government rule.

Village Path or Road

In Saharia inhabitat villages, the concrete road is totally absent. Only the village Bijli Ghor and Prem Nagar are settled down near to the concrete road of Barai block. The other studied villages are located far distant and those villagers are not benefited by the facility of better road. Even there, rarely Kachha road is found available. Only through the undulating hilly foot path, these villages are connected with another villages.

Drainage

There is no existence of any proper drainage system in Saharia inhabitat villages. In natural way, the rain water passes from high to low land. Due to the effect of heavy rainfall in monsoon month, the strong flow of rain water is at randomly directed anywhere from high to low land. As a result of at random directions of heavy rain water, sometimes their clusters are damaged partially or fully. Beside this, after bathing and washing, the used dirty water is generally logged anywhere in their surroundings and created the insanitation concerning with unhealthy situation.

Bank and Post Office

As per the present study among Saharia villages, it is a clear observation that they have neither any bank nor any post office facilities. Beside this, most of the Saharia do not require to go any bank or any post office. The available information make an aspersion that in very rare cases, a few Saharia take banking and postal facilities from Barai block and sometimes also from Panihar. If it is required to provide them the banking loan or postal facilities, then they are informed by the Government officials to produce themselves in bank or post office which are available in Bari or Panihar.

Electricity

Government officials inform that according to Government sanctioned scheme, every Saharia family in any village is facilitated by free of cost electric power. It is substantial that Government authorities have restricted their service by supplying the electric power upto the main poster of entrance of all studied villages. From this main poster, they have taken very loose electric connection upto their residences depending on their own expense and responsibility. They are consuming this electric power for lighting and sometimes television purposes.

Medical Facility

In Saharia villages, Government Hospital or dispensary is not available. Only a Government Hospital is existed in Barai block. Beside this, some private doctors are practising in Barai block and also in Panihar. Most of Saharia have complained that in Hospital/PHC, there is neither any experienced staff nor availability of any useful medicine. So, generally they have abandoned to take treatment facility from the Hospital. They are turning to prefer to the medical facility from private doctors by expensing own amount. Beside this, the mobile doctors occasionally visit their villages and supply them the necessary medicines with free of cost. Sometimes the immunization programmes are also performed subsequently in every Saharia village.

Village Market

Village market is also not depicted in any Saharia village. They generally purchase their necessary commodities from the shops of Barai block and Panihar. Beside this, a market is rendered in Barai block once in a week and there, all participants are not only belonged to Saharia tribal group but also the multi-ethnic populations are concerned to share their high extent of consultation. Apart from selling and purchasing, the significance of this weekly market is to exchange their information among relatives who are living in distant villages. The suitable boys and girls are also selected to conduct the negotiation marriage. The various socio-cultural, political, criminal and other important news are also widely communicated through this market. The postman also distributes letters to the villagers in market. Now a days, a few general stores are inaugurated in some Saharia villages and they are also getting benefit from these shops.

School

In every Sahara village, a free primary school is established but school building is not available in a few villages. Due to lack of school building particularly in some villages, teachers organize the classes under the shade of a big trees. Available information and own observation support that only one teacher is appointed for one school. The middle school and high school are totally absent in their villages. After crossing the primary level of education, they have to come either to the school of Barai block or Panihar for upper education or abandon the school education. It is a consent that generally children do not go to school because of their poverty and carelessness attitudes of elders. Moreover by the efforts of elders, children are not influenced or enforced to attend school regularly.

Communication

Due to the undulating hilly rocks and uneven terrain, any conveyance is generally not allowed throughout all villages. So, in this regard, most of the Saharia villages are almost isolated from one to another. In spite of this, sometimes villagers maintain their link only by using footpath. But footpath is also submerged during rainy season (Sharma, 1994). The actual condition of Bhatpura is stated that except for a few kilometers of connecting Kaccha road, this village is completely lack of communication. Some families in Bijli Ghor and Prem Nagar villages have constructed their residences on almost foothill. They (only two families) hardly maintain their transportation specially scooters. Cycle, bullock cart, jeep, etc. are more or less used to connect upto the foot hills of Banera, Gandhipura-North and Gandhipura-South villages during dry season. But inside the hamlet, any conveyance even cycle is not suited. After using bullock cart, the villagers keep it in a particular safety place on the lower belt of their residential hill.

Sanitation

It is a remarkable observation that the cluster types of house are generally constructed in insanitary condition. A deep notice in this regard confirms that most of the families use same houses for living themselves as well as for accommodating their livestocks. There is found no bathroom or latrine facility in their hamlets. After bathing or washing, the dirty water is more or less overlapped on their surroundings. Due to the lack of drainage system, generally human and animal dung, urine, dirty water, etc. are accrued to make environmental pollution of their hamlet area. In that aggravated insanitory condition, different types of insect like- houseflies, mosquitoes, cockroaches, leeches, etc., are grown in a large extent. These germful insects usually attack and as a result Saharia peoples are frequently affected by various diseases.

Community Hall

According to the present research work, it is confirmed that in every Saharia inhabitat village, a little or big community hall is found available. For the purpose of its construction, all Saharia collectively contribute some materials and then build up a cluster type of hut on a particular place in every hamlet. By the financial help of Government, a big and decorated community hall has been constructed in the village - Bijli Ghor. Very reliable information, collected from various sources specify that Saharia use their community hall for several purposes. After completing the daily routine works, they generally gather in the community hall and enjoy song and sometimes dance. There, all villagers exchange various information which are originated from different incidents throughout the day. In this hall, generally it is vague to pass on all types of riddle from old to young generation. Propitiation of village deities and communal festivals are also performed here. Due to shortage of enough space in their huts, sometimes their guests are accommodated here for passing only night. Keeping in view on multi-purpose activities, their community hall may be regarded as a figure of informal school.

Ethnic Group of the Village

Saharia are generally considered as uni-ethnic tribal group. According to the study among six Saharia villages, it is a noticeable point that they have the tendency to stay in a hamlet where all belong to their own Saharia community. Their attitudes indicate that they are not agree to mingle with other tribe or caste groups. It can really be said that they are very much shy. Due to their such character, they always feel isolated themselves and do not want to come on main focus for mixing with another caste groups. Beside this, they think that by mixing with non-Saharia groups, their unique traditional socio-cultural identity have a chance to be hampered. So, they are isolately inhabiting in a hamlet on hill which is located far distant from the modern civilization. Such type of remote inhabitation is not only saved their own traditional culture but also they are free from the abuse of untouchability.

Physical Appearance

Physical appearance of Saharia tribal groups is followed as very ugly and they are not habituated to bath regularly. Physical figure of Saharia indicates that they are generally of medium stature. But, short to medium stature of Saharia are also identified in a few exceptional cases. Their skin colour is generally dark but some times it is varied from dark to brown. Coarse, straight and dark hairs are seen on their head. Their face and nose are found as broad but on their nasal root, sometimes a depression is located. Head of Saharia tribe is rectangular and obliquity of the eyes is viewed. Owing to the above stated physical appearances, they come under Dravidian racial groups.

Language

In broad sense, Saharia-speaking language is comprehend as like as Hindi but in precision context, it is clear that they are habituated to speak their regional language which is colloquially known as 'Khariboli' (Mandal, 1998). It is reported that this language is pronounced as the admixture of Hindi, Rajasthani and Malwi accents. By the effect of Bundelikhandi dialect, Saharia are also influenced to speak a recognised local language which is identified as 'Sohariya'. To continue the communication among both inter and intra groups, they use the Indo-Aryan language and this is also acquainted as 'Hadoti' or 'Harauti' (Singh, 1994). The Devnagari is evident as the only script which is used for their writing purpose.

House Type

Traditionally, Saharia dwell in a very simple type of hut or house which is not well built. In a few stipulated days, their hut may be built up but within a few hours, it may be dismounted (Tiwari, 1984). Following their own traditional pattern, they construct their cluster types of residence either on a plateau or on the slope of a mountain (Mandal, 1998). Rectangular shaped houses are generally constructed and arranged in rows facing a common side of their hamlet. Beside this, small tie huts are also built up by them. Usually their huts consist of one room, verandah and small open space to use for cooking purpose and sometimes for sleeping purpose specially in summer season (Sahu, 1998). After consulting with '*Janter*' (Magician), they generally select one side in the room for sleeping purpose. To build up a hut, sometimes their suitable place is decided by '*Pujari*' (Priest). The Saharia huts are made of mud, grass, leaf, bamboo, wood, stone (rarely), etc. Now a days, some Saharia people are constructing the cemented residences by the Government beneficiary loan scheme.

Economy

It is obviously known that most of the tribal communities in India are positioned under extremely backward condition and poverty stricken (Thakur & Thakur, 1994). Their dispersed location is generally followed the remote hilly and plain forest regions where modern technological advances are very rarely touched still now. So, these tribal groups are mostly depended on ecology which plays an important role in forming their economic structure (Mandal, 1998). Among all tribes in Madhya Pradesh as like as in India, Saharia are recognized as a primitive tribe who prefer to inhabit at a close distant of forest for collecting considerably the various forest products. Their indispensable economy is significantly influenced by environment which is regarded as the impact of ecology. The post economic history of Saharia tribal groups implies that they traditionally adopted the nomadic life and practised shifting cultivation, hunting, gathering, pastoralism, etc. (Prabhu, 1983). But now a days, they are going to change their previous economy and come on food production stage by settled cultivation.

The settled cultivation is conducted as their primary subsistence of occupation whereas animal husbandry, hunting, gathering, fuel selling, etc., are supplemented as their secondary occupations. But due to lack of cultivated land, most of the Saharia have become daily wage earners, instead of settled cultivation (Singh, 1994). The bonded labour abolition rules of Government (1975) are not profoundly acquiesced among them. Due to their poor financial condition, some of them are appointed as bonded labour under landlord or contractor specially in interior area comprising modified formation. Whereas significant number of Saharia also adopt handicraft, business and service as their main occupational pursuitence.

However, very low number of landed Saharia cultivate wheat, jawar, bajra, maize, paddy, mustard seeds and also sometimes varieties of vegetables. Pig, cow, dog, goat, sheep, etc., are mainly found as their domestic animals. They are generally engaged to do agricultural labour but now a days, they are labouring as stone cutter under the contractor. For their economic benefit, the co-operative farming was also organised among them under the development scheme of Madhya Pradesh

Government but this was also not succeed. From their nearest forests, they collect fruits, edible roots, tubers, mahua flowers, honey, tendu leaves, gum, fuel, etc. and sometimes sell these in their local markets. Their hunting and gathering practices are totally banned by Government. But in rarely cases, they confidentially hunt birds, fowls, monkey, rabbit, wild boar, peacock, cock, etc., from their nearest forests. Besides, they are very skilled to make baskets, mats, various leaf plates, ropes, etc. Collecting grass from jungle, they prepare specially the 'Phool Bahari' broom which is highly popular throughout the region.

Food and Drink

Due to poor economic condition, most of the Saharia can not afford to take meals two times in a day. Generally bread is considered as their staple food. They prepare bread or roti from wheat, maize, millet, etc. They consume roots, tubers, leaves, etc. which are collected from their nearest forests. Non-vegetable food items are much preferred to them. Occasionally they eat rice with non-vegetable food items concerned to egg, fish, chicken, birds, meat of goat, pork, etc., whatever is hunted from the forests. Sometimes they purchase their choiceable vegetables from their local markets. They celebrate various festivals by preparing 'Dal-bati' as special food item in their locality. For cooking the food items, they use mustard oil and sometimes various milk products. Mahua flowers are used to prepare their local wine (Daru) and men (and sometime women) usually take this alcoholic drink, specially at evening. On a festive occasion, they purchase such drink and take it with variety items of cooked food.

Dress and Ornaments

As interior inhabitation, Saharia are almost unexposed from modern civilization. According to the present study conducted in various Saharia villages, it is found that they are using very simple types of traditional dress. Saharia men put on a 'dhoti' and 'kurta' (half shirt) and sometimes aged persons use 'languta' (small cloth) to cover their sex part only. On festival time, they also tie 'feta' (turban) around their forehead. Women wear saree (ladies dhoti), ghaghara (peticoat) , ordi (bodice) , saluka (blouse), orhni with ghaghra, etc. Children are usually found in naked condition. At the time of marriage ceremony, generally the bride wears various colorful dresses and these are not so different from non-Saharia people. Now a days, the young males start to wear pants and shirt whereas shalwar suit and shirt are used to wear by young females. Red and deep blue are accepted as their preferable colours. Comparatively, women are more attracted to wear the varieties of ornaments than men. Due to their poverty, they are unable to purchase the costly ornaments which are made of gold. Instead of gold, they use the ornaments of silver, zinc, brass, iron, glass, plastic, etc. Both men and women put on necklace but bangles, ear rings, finger rings, etc. are worn particularly by women. From their local market, they generally purchase their all dresses and ornaments. Saharia women are enthusiastic to decorate their face, hands and foots with tattooing marks.

Implements and Utensils

Through slow and gradual mental development, the superior position is occupied by men in the animal kingdom. From ancient era, men had to make various implements for the purpose of hunting and protecting themselves from wild animals. Beside this, they had to prepare various utensils for collecting the hunts and gathering food materials from the forest. During the era, they prepared so many implements and utensils only for their own purposes. But with the changing period of time, implements and utensils preparation techniques were modified and sometimes changed. Saharia, a descendant group of this ancient people, are considered as a unique example for making the various implements and utensils. Now a days, they prepare implements and utensils not only for their own purposes but also by selling these materials, they earn little amount. However, for hunting purpose, they make bow and arrow, spear thrower, etc. and for cultivation and other purposes, plough, axe, spade, yoke, scythe, ladder, iron bar, etc. are made by them. Various implements and traps are also prepared and used to catch the various fishes specially in rainy season. By making various implements like-hearth, karai, dish, vessel, basket, mat, broom, etc., they are much praised among non-Saharia people.

Family

Family is regarded as the first structural and functional unit among Saharia. Their perception indicates that family is the smallest social group consisting of parents and their biological and adopted offsprings residing in a same house and sharing the common hearth. But sometimes, unmarried sister, married brother and son (with wife) also inhabit in family. Nuclear type of family is commonly found but in a few cases, evidence of some joint families is also existed among them. After marriage, they generally live in partrilocal as well as neolocal residence. Normally, father is respected as the supreme powerful man in family. He not only directs the family members for involving in various activities but also regulates the family budget (finance). Both joking and avoidance relations are also followed among them. In this context, their socio-cultural rules and regulations define that a Saharia woman has to avoid her husband's father and elder brother. By keeping the veil, she is directly restricted not to talk with them and not to see them. Jocking relation is permitted to conduct with wife's younger brother and sister and husband's younger brother and sister.

Clan

The available information emblem that Saharia are committed to endogamous group and they are divided into thirteen patrilineal exogamous clans or 'gots or gati' (Crooke, 1896). But fourteen clans are recorded by Singh (1994) and about fifty clans are also recorded by Sahu (1998). So many exogamous lineages of Saharia are originated by the division of every clan. Totemistic in nature is generally perpetuated among most of the clans and specific deities like-plant, animal, etc. are worshipped by specific clan members. Some clan members also worship common deities because they believe that common deities have been begotten from common origin. Traditionally, they believe that the members of same clan are the descendent of a common ancestor. According to the study among Saharia, it is confirmed that the members of a largest populated clan are always dominated and all privileges are enjoyed by them in every hamlet. But direct or indirect relation and co-operation are always continued among different clan members. The members who belong to particular one clan are not restricted to take food from other clan members. Feeling certain inauspicious, they always respect the totemic objects and keep distance from killing and also eating all these. Clan endogamy is strictly prohibited among Saharia.

Kinship

Among Saharia, kinship is a very relevant term which is implicated with their socio-cultural orthodox. The present study informs that all Saharia are bounded together in groups by kinship relation. Both affinal and consanguineous kinship relations are conferred among them. Marital alliance is allowed among the socially or legally recognized affinal kins. But due to present same blood, biological relation as well as marital alliance is totally prohibited among consanguineous kins. In Saharia society, it is evident that both jocking and avoidance relations are existed. Jocking relationship is conducted between a man and his wife's younger sister or brother and also a woman and her husband's younger sister or brother. Avoidance relations are extremely acted between a man and his wife's' parents, younger brother's wife, maternal nephew's wife and others.

Property Inheritance

Patriarchal society approved rules and regulations are imparted among Saharia. According to the information from various respondents, it is confirmly perpetrated that only sons are allowed to inherit their father's properties. After marriage of sons, they usually leave their father's house and separately construct the new residence for them (new couples). In that situation, father does not give any properties to those separated sons. Sons have to maintain their family budget depending on their own income. But after death of father, all properties both moveable and immovable of deceased father are equally divided among all sons by the direct interference of village panchayat. A few cases inform that if any son provides any special care in old age condition of father, then he gets some extra movable properties as compared to other brothers. Daughters of deceased person have no right to inherit any properties, they are socially permitted to accept only the husband's properties. As inheritator, if there is no any son of deceased father, then his properties may be divided among sister's or brother's sons as per the decision of society members. The widow of deceased person can choice any son for staying with him as a family member.

Social Hierarchy

Saharia are usually inhabiting the interior hilly and plain forest regions. They have no any direct contact with advanced community people and in this context, they feel themselves as isolated and untouchable. In regarding the position of their social hierarchy, it is expressed that they have no objection to eat food which is prepared by superior or equal community people. But they are not agree to eat food which is cooked by other inferior community people. Clan exogamy and tribal endogamy are generally followed among them. In any condition, they are not socially allowed to come in marital alliance with any non-Saharia community people. Violating this rule, if any body of them selects the life partner who belongs to other community, then their traditional village Panchyet justify the case and as punishment, the wrongdoer is charged to pay the decided amount within the stipulated period of time and feed them or otherwise leave his native hamlet.

Status of Women

Saharia are acquainted as the members of patriarchal society. Males are always behaved as the dominant groups on females. Their society approved rules and regulations indicate that the women are not considered as property inheritators. At early age, their marriages are generally organised by the decision of father. Family management and domestic works are considered as their lion part of daily activities. Beside this, cultivation, daily labour, craft, child caring and child rearing, etc., are also practised by the women in Saharia society. In most of their families, the earned amount is expended by the permission of husbands. Men govern all vital decisions and women just support these. But a reverse character comprises that all ritual activities are performed by the direct involvement of women. In spite of all these socially discriminated rules, friendship behavior is usually continued between husband and wife and both of them are satisfied.

Birth

As an important phenomenon, child birth is celebrated among Saharia. Before child birth, the expectant mother is usually shifted in a new hut which is temporally built up for her delivery purpose. Otherwise, if new hut is not built up within stipulated period, then the expectant mother is replaced in a particular room of their own inhabitat hut where delivery is conducted by the help of elderly knowledgeable mid-wife of their own community. This is also evident that sometimes, the child birth is taken place in the forest where the would to be mother has gone for collecting various forest products. In that condition, other accompanied women are studded to take care the delivery and shift the new born child and mother from the forest to house. Praying to the God for longevity of new born child, Saharia mid-wife cuts the umbilical cord. Sometimes first delivery is practised in the parents' house of expectant mother. Their traditional rules make wink that the news of male child birth is heralded by the firing of gun and then they enjoy throughout the day as auspicious. Rounding the new born child and mother, the village-women present their folk songs and dances. During six days, the members of that family observe pollution and then they thoroughly clean the house with the mixture of cow dung and water. After completing purificatory bath ceremony, they arrange 'Chati Puja' which is worshipped by the village priest. Final purificatory bath ceremony is again celebrated on 30th day after child birth and then mother is generally allowed to come on her old routine. They enjoy collective song and dance whereas 'Tona-totka' is also practised to save the new born child from the evil spirits. In every ceremony, molasses is distributed to the invitees.

Marriage

Among Saharia, marriage is considered as the socially recognized relationship between man and woman and by which they are permitted to stay in a common residence, co-operate in all activities, attain sexual cohabitation and procreate offsprings. Tribal endogamy and clan exogamy rules for marital alliance are strictly governed among them. Their society approved rules inform that they are allowed to practise monogamy but in some special cases, they are permitted to practise polygamy. By the influence of Hindu society, they are exposed to practise early marriage. Usually, negotiation marriage is organised but marriage by service, marriage by exchange, marriage by elopement, etc. are also rarely performed among them. In their society, parallel cousin, cross cousin and junior levirate marriages are prohibited but junior sorrorate marriage is allowed to practise. Dowry and bride price (vardan) are not considered as important thinkable matter for the marriage. As dowry, the bride's father generally endows a few forests to the groom and from there, he is restricted to collect any product from those gifted forests. Generally, they use palanquin (palki) and bullock cart to carry the bride-groom and party respectively. If road is not suitable, then they move depending on foot. In bride's place, groom and party stay for one day and night and next day, after completing the remaining activities of marriage ceremony, they return home. According to their traditional customs, band is restricted to employ in marriage ceremony. But instead of band, copper plate is beaten for making a loud noise. Generally, their priest (Pujari) is requested to perform the marriage. Their Hinduized marriage rules indicate that both the bride and groom revolve seven times around the nuptial fire for making a witness of their marriage. Vermilion on forehead, hair parting and wearing of finger-ring are followed as the symbol of married women. Lastly, an exclusive assessment defines that their marriages are not so much expensive. The bride's father serves bread of jawar, jwar kharhi, dal, vegetables, etc. for feeding the bride- groom party. They are patriarchal tribe and after marriage, the new groom with bride usually dwells in patrilocal residence.

Divorce and Remarriage

Divorce and remarriage are rarely practised among Saharia. Divorce is generally allowed on the ground of adultery, insanity, maladjustment, cruelty and others. Getting complaint from any one of the couple, the tribal council (mainly by the presence of punch) enquire the case and on the basis of reality of stated allegation, they come to declare for divorce. After divorce, if the woman marries with another person, then the paramour is asked for fine (Ghagra) by the council. Some amount of this asked money is given to her previous husband and remaining amount is expensed for communal feast. The previous husband is also permitted to marry if he gives the amount as fine to his pervious wife and serves such type of communal feast. According to the study, no any evidence is recovered for prohibition against widow remarriage. Generally widow is restricted to marry her deceased husband's younger brother (levirate) but widower is permitted to marry his deceased wife's younger (if unmarried) sister (sorrorate). On the ground of widow remarriage, both the bride price and dowry are usually avoided among them.

Death

In life cycle, death is considered as the last closing chapter of human beings. Most of the Saharia speculate that after death, God takes away the soul of dead person. They generally cremate the dead body. But in some cases, the gathered information support that after death, the dead body of very old person is cremated or. buried (Tiwari, 1984). With employing music, they carry the male dead body towards cremation place. In case of female, they cremate the dead body with her ornaments, except those ornaments which are made of gold and silver. Their traditional rules and regulations define that in the house of deceased family, food is not cooked during three days. Neighbours, villagers and friends prepare food in their own houses and supply to the bereaved persons. Bathing and washing activities on fourth day is performed by the help of village priest. If the bereaved family members do not have any financial problem, then they celebrate the occasion by providing single feast.

Religious Organization

The manifold concepts of Saharia imply that without religious activities, life is unstable. As supreme God 'Bhagwan' is respected among them. They believe that world is created by the desire of this supreme God. This great soul is not confined in a temple or abode or in particular area, He is loitering all over the universal. However, they traditionally worship the various deities like- Behran, Thakur, Bhumij, Naharsingh, Ghatoiya and others for various purposes. Mata is a female deity and She is acquainted with several names like - Sitla Devi, Sardamai, etc. Whenever, the villagers are suffered from the disease of chicken pox, then they offer different fruits, sweets, cooked food, etc. to appease Her. In this regard, sometimes She is worshipped by the help of village priest. Beside this, the God Molishugh, Tejajee and Nahardeo are also propitiated for the safe from typhoid disease, snake bite and tiger attack respectively. Various taboos are also importantly obeyed by this community people. For performing the various puja-festivals, they are not limited to call only their traditional priest (Pujari), even in the present state, they are allowed to request the Hindu Brahmin (Pandit). By the influence of Hindu community, Saharia are motivated to enjoy Diwali, Holi, Raksha Bandhan, Dussehara and other festivals.

Political Organisation

Now a days, the existence of both traditional and modern political oraganisations are followed in every Saharia village. In their traditional political organisation, the post is hereditary occupied by the head and he is designated as 'Sahrama or 'Makadom' (Sahu, 1998)..Beside this, Patel, Barhai, Prodhan and Jankar are regarded as the subordinates of Sahrama. The members of this political body not only regulate their socio-cultural homogeneity but also justify the various disputes and punish the offenders. But slowly, this traditional political organisation is disappeared and they are motivated to convert in modern political organisation. The leaders of such modern political organisation are selected by election through public secret vote. They generally prefer to the leaders who are educated, talkative, free from hesitation, capable to attend any meeting with Government officials, experienced about outer world affairs, co-operative, commendable beneficiary nature and so on. Their main duties are to govern for justifying the internal conflicts and involve themselves for over all communal development.

Motive of Education

The available information for the present study elaborate that most of the Saharia are illiterate, very poor and scatterdly live in the interior area. For their illiteracy, they can not understand the importance of modern school education. They always struggle for economic subsistence and as a result, they usually motivate their children to support them by collecting the livelihood from their local forests. So, instead of school education, their children are to be pressurized for collecting the food materials from their early age. In that condition, school education is almost unexposed to their offsprings. For providing the financial benefit and increasing their literacy rate, Government have already adopted multi-dimensional tribal development schemes. Under such schemes, every enrolled children in the school is possessed to get thirty five rupees (Rs. 35/-) per month (excluding wheat, books and uniform). In this regard, their children are just enrolled in the school register for accepting the monthly sanctioned amount and other commodities. In connection with this, very significant statements reveal that at the end of every month, the attendance of enrolled children is estimated as maximum but after availing all benefits, their attendance is decreased unexpectedly. So, it is clear that as an inducement of education, they do not send their children in school. Most of the Saharia comment that the proposed education system in their local school is not satisfactory. In a very simple manner, a large number of Saharia expresses that they prefer to male education, instead of female. On educational perspective, the personal exclusive interviews indicate that gender variations are totally ignored among them and both male and female are allowed to go to school for achieving educational benefit. Just to focus on the outside incidents, newspapers are also occasionally read by a few educated Saharia. Further, it is informed that some of them frequently listen the news of Radio whereas a significant number of them are identified as the viewers of T.V. news and other programmes.

Mass Media

Radio and television are considered as the electronic magic which carpet and transport the various activities throughout the day and night to the millions of people of far away places. As technological revolution, these are the invention of twentieth century which are transforming much of the world and its impacts are profoundly providing on our social, political and cultural life. (Emercy, Ault & Ager,1965). Radio, television and newspaper are used as most powerful medium of communication and these have immense capabilities for spreading any news within certain period of time. By the effect of these mass-media like - radio, television and news paper, people may change their attitude, generate awareness about sanitation, nutrition, hygiene, disease, family planing methods, etc. In the present study, it is elaborated that the radio and television are found in every hamlet but the availability of news paper readers are identified as insufficient number. Newspaper is not purchased by any Saharia people but after coming to Barai block or Paniahr, some of them read news paper occasionally.

Movie

Movie is considered as an important invention among various enjoyable resources. It is very substantial that the enjoyment of movie is not only limited for urban people but also its great pleasure is perceived by the rural people. In spite of their inhabitation in remote area, isolation from modern civilization, poverty, etc., they are assuring more or less this facility. The exclusive interviews confer that most of the Saharia are enthusiastic but due to financial problem, they can not afford to purchase the television. Some of them are enjoying the various types of movie in cinema hall of Gwalior district, video hall at Barai block and through television in their hamlet. After completing the daily activities, they generally gather in a residence of their hamlet where television is available and enjoy the various telecasting programmes or cinema.

Education

In over all development process, education is regarded as the most essential issue. Education is used as an important powerful instrument for socio-economic upliftment (Sinha,1996). Through educational attainment, people may achieve activeness, confidence, skill, comprehensiveness, belief, attitude of argument, commitment, etc. and these are much required to inhabit him in an ideal society. Educational improvement of particular society in a particular place are ensured if their matched educational policies are carefully adopted during long time (Tiwari,1984). The effect of ecology on education is not neglected, it plays an important role in learning attitude. The favourable environment endeavours an interesting learning opportunity and by which, the complicated exercise is also comprehend as simple one (Gregory, 1998). Due to illiteracy and poverty, most of the people are suffering from socio-cultural deprivation and in that anxious condition, they are losing their activeness and motivation. As a result, they feel themselves as weak, powerless, dependent, vulnerable, isolated, etc. In such hopeless circumstances, co-operative education is preferred and by which they not only influence themselves but also borrow the exact direction for progressive social and economic change (Shah, 1999). Generally, women are acquainted as conservative element and habituated to stay behind the screen. Inspite of equal opportunities received by both men and women, a comprehensible measurement ensures that the changeable performance of women is slower than men. Because women are tied by various traditional socio -cultural rules and regulations. For providing a new shape in the context of socio-cultural dimension, women education is considered as an important phenomenon (Jena, 1994).

The present study indicates that most of the Saharia are not enthusiastic to accept the formal education for their offsprings. As an effect of this attitude, the literacy rate among them is deplorable low. According to the census report (1981), their literacy rate is found to be estimated as 2.74 percent whereas male literacy rate (4.99 percent) is higher than female literacy rate (0.39 percent). The available information yield that as incentive, educational scholarship under Government beneficiary schemes have been recommended for primary school going children of Saharia as well as other primitive tribes of Madhya Pradesh. To accept the monthly amount of such Scholarship, the enrolment of the children in school register is increased but the attendance of the children in school is investigated as very low. The present study confirms that various socio-cultural parameters are responsible for the low attendance of children in the school. For their poverty, they enforce their children to collect the edible food materials and fuel from their nearest forests. Beside this, elders have to go out for earning purpose and due to their absence at home, their older children are to be responsible to protect their youngers. Most of the Saharia are illiterate and as a result, they are unable to provide any educational guidance to their children. Their presumption is that both the non-Saharia and outsider teachers are not co-operative and their careless attitudes always demotivate their children to gain the educational benefit. Even their thinkings concentrate that as belonged to Saharia community, their children are always hated and also sometimes punished by those teachers. For these reasons, their children are hesited to come in close contact with teaching groups. In other side, the common text books pertaining very hard lessons are recommended for the students of every class without special concerning the level of Saharia children. Even in these books, their children do not find the Saharia dialectically descriptions of own socio-cultural activities and the stories of their own forefathers. So, usually their children are not interested to follow such types of text book. Further, another information ensure that all educational policies of Government are implemented during a short period of time and in this time bound, Saharia are initially inspired to send their children in school but due to over the duration of such educational policies, their children are demotivated to roll back from school attending. As the reasons of above stated consequences, their ultimate literacy is increasing very slowly as compared to the literacy rate of other Indian population.

Development of Saharia

The tribal communities of India are very poor, pre-agriculturist, illiterate, isolated, exploited by dominant groups and so on. For the over all improvements of tribal population, the founding fathers of this nation were aware from early stage of beginning. Regarding to the basic needs of these tribal groups, the various Government development schemes were launched occasionally. Through these development schemes, a few tribes are going to be elevated towards the mainstream of national life. Such development schemes were introduced by various names like-IRDP (Integrated Rural Development Programme), TRYSEM, (Training of Rural Youth for Self-Employment), DWCRA, (Development of Women and Children in Rural Areas), ITDP, (Integrated Tribal Development Project), NREP (National Rural Employment Programme), JRY (Jawahar Rojgar Yojana), etc., under different five year plans. The major objectives of most of the schemes are to alleviate the poverty from tribal areas. Beside this, the other objectives are incorporated to improve their socio-cultural and educational status.

Various development programmes are started and even some launched development programmes are also continued in Saharia area. The Madhya Pradesh Government has already inaugurated to provide land to the landless Saharia, under the section 170B (Land Revenue Code of Madhya Pradesh Government). Beside this, the provided land plots are to be cleaned, levelled, bounded, etc., for suitability of cultivation. Under the development schemes, the better seeds, fertilizer, insecticides, pump sets for irrigation, etc., are to be supplied by Government with very cheap rate. Also they are to be trained by new technique of agricultural science to produce better crops for two or three times in a year from one plot of land. As a result, it is an expectation that they will slowly convert themselves from shifting to settled cultivation. There is also an another scheme implemented for plantation of bamboo, tendu, mahua, kachuwa, achar, etc., in their local forests and by collecting the raw materials from these trees, they are to be improved their economic status. The different loan schemes relating to bamboo works, broom making, leaf cup manufacturing, mat-making, poultry, goatery farm, fisheries, purchasing bullocks, housing, etc., are sanctioning many times and establishing the Gramin Bank in the locality, Government tries to give them the sanctioned amount within short period of time and by which they not only save themselves from the exploitation of middlemen but also certainly they can invest the received amount for their desired purpose. Free Hospital facility, free family planning, free drinking water facility, free nutritional food facility specially for pregnant women and others have already been launched for Saharia. Their school going children are also attracted by scholarship, mid-day meal, books and uniforms.

CHAPTER - IV

SOCIO-ECONOMIC IMPACT ON DEMOGRAPHIC AND HEALTH CHARACTERISTICS OF SAHARIA

In this chapter, an attempt has been made to explain the demographic profile of Saharia. Various parameters of fertility, mortality, migration, maternal and child health care, health seeking behaviour and family planning have been analysed in the context of various socio- cultural, economic and biological factors. In this chapter, the various parameters of fertility, mortality, migration, maternal and child health care, health seeking behaviour and family planning have also been discussed in a comparative framework of tribal and non-tribal population groups of Madhya Pradesh as well as other parts of India.

BACKGROUND CHARACTERISTICS

Madhya Pradesh is a hill-locked state and situated in the central region of India. In the country, almost one-eight part of the forest area is covered by this state. In terms of land area, Madhya Pradesh is the largest state and its total population has been found to be achieved sixth position in the country. For providing the better administrative facility, this state has been divided into 12 administrative divisions, 45 districts, 317 sub-divisions and 459 development blocks.

Saharia are one of the primitive tribe who inhabit in various hilly and forest regions of this state. The present study indicates that their settlement patterns are isolated in nature and they have a limited contact with other tribal as well as non-tribal societies. As a result, their indigenous social rules, regulations, customs, norms, beliefs, folk activities, etc. are preserved till now to a great extant. Keeping in view of their social, cultural and economic life, a large number of social scientists conducted their studies in various times. (Tiwari, 1984; Singh, 1994; Thakur & Thakur, 1994; Mandal, 1998). But most of their studies pertained a very little attention on various parameters of demographic dimension.

In a tribal and non-tribal society, one's own unique rules, regulations, customs, norms and others are always respectively maintained for directly or indirectly controlling their socio-cultural systems. It is a reality that early age at marriage and non-utilisation of family planning methods are considered as the important socio-cultural systems which influence fertility and lack of nutritional food, insanitation, paucity of clinical facility, etc. aggravate diseases and hence frequent deaths are taken place among population groups. Generally, health or absence of disease is considered as biological fitness of human body. But in social as well as in psychological perception, biological fitness is totally depended on socio-cultural aspects of health. This biological fitness is also related with nutrition, age at menarche, menopause, marriage, child birth, lactation, breast feeding, etc. So, biological condition with socio-cultural aspects determinate the various fertility and mortality rates of demographic parameters (Behura, 1991; Sahu, 1998; Kshatriya, 2000).

Background characteristics in this regard are very much required to understand the various aspects of studied population. It indicates the studied villages, total population including males and females, land holding pattern, types of residence, types of transportation, arrangement of water, etc. It not only conveys the message of socio-economic status of population but also makes association with various demographic parameters.

In terms of land area, Madhya Pradesh is the largest hill-locked state and it's almost one-third part is identified as forest area. According to the Census 1991, Madhya Pradesh occupies sixth position in all populated states in India. However, among multi-ethnic population, 46 tribal groups and their sub-groups are inhabiting throughout the area. Further among these (46) tribal groups, seven have been declared as the primitive tribes wherein Saharia is important one. Madhya Pradesh is predominated as an agricultural state and economy of most of the people is based on agricultural products and labour force (77 percent). During 1990-91, per capita income of this state is very low (Rs.4,021/-) as compared with India (Rs.4,974/-). Crude birth rate, crude death rate and infant mortality rate of the people of Madhya Pradesh have been estimated as 34.4, 12.7 and 104.0 respectively. Health status of the population of this state is very poor. Literacy rate has been found to be deplorable low (44.2 percent). Maternal and child health care, immunization, water supply and sanitation, etc. have not been launched in a large extent. For reducing socio-cultural barriers and population growth, mass media and interpersonal communication are utilized and through these, all are explainly acquainted with the various methods of contraceptives and the positive aspects of contraceptive use (NFHS, 1992-93).

Distribution of Households and Population

In the present study, the available data on distribution of village-wise Saharia house-holds and population are depicted in the Table 4.1. The study reveals that the maximum population are recorded in Bhatpura village (25.8 percent), followed by Bijli Ghor (23.5 percent), Gandhipura - South (22.5 percent), Gandhipura - North (11.6 percent), Prem Nagar (9.5 percent) whereas Banera village shows the lowest percentage of population (7.1 percent). Bhatpura is an old fashionable village and due to lack of work opportunity, its population are decreasing by the process of out migration. In other side, Banera is a new settled village and due to availability of work, its population are increasing as a reason of in migration. However, this study exhibits an estimation of total 1668 population who belong to 333 households of six villages whereas 895 and 773 are males and females respectively.

TABLE: 4.1

Village-wise Distribution of Households and Population of Saharia

Sl. No.	Name of Various Villages	Number of Households	Population			
			Male	Female	Total	Percent
1.	Benera	26	63	55	118	7.1
2.	Bijli Ghar	84	207	185	392	23.5
3.	Prem Nagar	33	90	68	158	9.5
4.	Bhatputa	71	226	204	430	25.8
5.	Gandhipura-North	39	107	87	194	11.6
6.	Gandhipura-South	80	202	174	376	22.5
	Total	**333**	**895**	**773**	**1668**	**100.0**

Land Holding Pattern

Saharia are very poor and their most of the families are landless (88.0 percent) whereas only 12.0 percent families have acquired very little size of land (Table 4.2). Their history of origination indicates that they were hunters and food gathers and their economy was based on forest products. So they were

TABLE: 4.2

Distribution of Land Holding Pattern Among Saharia

Land Holding (in Acres)	No. of Households	Percentage
Landless	293	88.0
< 1	17	5.1
1- 2	8	2.4
2-3	10	3.0
3-4	3	0.9
4 >	2	0.6
Total	**333**	**100.0**

ignorant to acquire the land. But due to illegal operation, now the forests are gradually vanishing and their forest based economy is going to be disappeared. So, instead of hunting and food gathering, they are motivated to practise labour, craft, animal husbandry, etc. Even, it has also been informed that due to extreme poverty, some landholder Saharia sold their land to the landlords (Zamindars).

Types of Residence

Types of residence are the important denominator for assessing the socio-economic status. Most of the Saharia are very poor and due to their poverty, they are unable to build up pacca residences. As a result, it is found to be measured 38.1 percent, 34.8 percent and 21.4 percent families who inhabit in bamboo, thatched and wood-made residences respectively. Only 5.7 percent families are found to have cemented residences, built up by the help of Government beneficiary loan (Table 4.3). Actually for constructing their houses, they use those materials which are available in their locality. They construct their cluster types of rectangular hut on the middle top slope of the mountain. They have also a supported explanation that such type of location is very safe for themselves from various aspects. In rainy season, their huts are not dismantled by the extreme flow of water. Beside this, from their residences, they can easily watch their grazing live-stocks and their agricultural land. They presume that due to construct their abode on such location, they may

TABLE: 4.3

Types of Residence Among Saharia

SL. No	*Types of Residence*	*Number of Households*	*Percentage*
1	Thatched (Very Poor)	116	34.8
2	Bamboo Made (Poor)	127	38.1
3	Wooden (Medium)	71	21.4
4	Cemented (Good)	19	5.7
	Total	**333**	**100.0**

enable to gain benediction from their primordial God. So, they not only save themselves from natural calamity but also isolate themselves from another communities for existing their own unique tribal culture. Through a detail explanation, it is also clearly understood that if they build up their huts on the top of the hill, then it is always difficult to go on the top with their live-stocks and even they are also unable to carry their agricultural products on the top of the hill.

Types of Transportation

It is apparent from the Table 4.4, the inconvenience communication and transportation systems among Saharia are highlighted with various reasons. Due to uneven ridges and undulating hilly foot path, generally, the conveyance is not allowed inside the four villages. Only in the village - Bijli Ghor and Prem Nagar, 0.6 percent families use two wheelers and 3.9 percent families use bullock-carts whereas bicycle is used by 33.9 percent families in all villages. But there is found 61.6 percent families who maintain communication depending on foot. The village - Bhatpura, Gandhipura-North and Gandhipura-South are delinked specially in rainy season. Then these villagers are to be faced food problems and even they observe hungry two or three days continuously.

TABLE: 4.4
Types of Transportation Among Saharia

SL. No	*Types of Transportation*	*Number of House holds*	*Percentage*
1	Bicycle	113	33.9
2	Two Wheeler	2	0.6
3	Bullock cart	13	3.9
4	On Foot	205	61.6
	Total	**333**	**100.0**

Arrangement of Water

Water is very important one among all essential commodities. But availability of water sources are rarely found among Saharia inhabitat area. According to the present study, 40.3 percent Saharia families are come to the notice who depend on water of well. Among them, 38.7 percent families collect water from both well as tube-well whereas 17.4 percent families are committed to take water of tube well (Table 4.5). Government has provided only a few tube-wells in Saharia inhabitat area but most of the tube-wells are not in function. Beside this, due to extreme hot in summer season - specially in May-June months, tube-wells do not get water layer and then 3.6 percent families collect water from pond of another villages. It is also reported that they are always facing the deficiency of purified water.

TABLE: 4.5

Arrangement of Water from Difference Sources Among Saharia

Sl. No.	*Sources of Water*	*Number of Households*	*Percentage*
1	Well	134	40.3
2	Tube-well	58	17.4
3	Well & Tube-well	129	38.7
4	Pond	12	3.6
	Total	**333**	**100.0**

Sources of Light and Fuel

It is an observation that under Government scheme, all the families in every Saharia village are facilitated by free of cost electric power. But, they are regulated to consume electric power only for lighting purpose. Saharia generally collect dry-wood from their nearest forests and use it for fuel purpose. In very rarely cases, it is found that a few Saharia (who are in service) use kerosene for cooking purpose.

In every Saharia village, the free of cost electric power is served by Government. But due to their financial problem, they are unable to purchase the wire for the permanent electric fitting in their residences. In some households of service holders, kerosene is used for cooking purposes. From nearest forests, Saharia generally collect the dry-wood which is used for fuel purpose.

Types of Family

The collected information for the present study reveal that both nuclear and joint families are existed among Saharia. Most of them belong to nuclear families (91.3 percent) whereas joint families (Table 4.6) are far less common (8.7 percent). There are various evidences that Saharia are the followers of their socio-cultural orthodox. After marriage, sons are to be separated immediately from their parents' house and as a reason, the nuclear families are increased, instead of joint families. Saharia are very poor and as a result of poverty, they are unable to arrange the required food materials for all members (of joint family) which play an effective role for the formation of nuclear family.

TABLE: 4.6
Types of Family Among Saharia

Sl.No.	*Types of Family*	*No. of Families*	*Percentage*
1	Nuclear	304	91.3
2	Joint	29	8.7
	Total	**333**	**100.0**

Food Habit

Due to extreme poverty, Saharia are not able to arrange two square meals in a day. As staple food, they eat bread of wheat, maize, millet, etc. They sometimes consume roots, tubers, leaves, etc. whatever are available in their nearest forests. They are non-vegetarian. Occasionally they eat rice with egg, fish, birds, chicken, pork, etc. "Dal-bati' (mixture of dal, rice and a few vegetables) is consumed as a very special food on a festive occasion in their locality. Most of them are very much addicted to drink their local wine "Daru". After completing their routine work, they usually desire to be refresh by taking such alcoholic drink.

Village Path/Road

According to the present study, the collected data highlight to draw the unavailability of concrete road in all Saharia villages. Among six inhabitat villages, only the village – Bijli Ghar and the village - Prem Nagar are situated near to the concrete road of Barai block. The other all distant villages are connected with Barai block by Kachcha road. Inside every village, there are undulating hilly footpaths which connect all their clusters.

Types of Various Mass Media

The electronic mass media is the gift of modern technology. But in rural area, it's use is far less common. The available data reveal that among Saharia, only 36.3 percent households are interested to follow television (11.7 percent) and radio (22.5 percent) programmes because television and radio are available in their households (or in the households of their neighbours). After going in their market named Barai or Panihar, they feel very difficulties to read the newspaper and as a reason, newspaper readers (2.1 percent) are rarely found among them (Table 4.7). Beside this, due to financial problem, 66.7 percent Saharia households are unable to follow any sort of mass media related activity.

TABLE: 4.7

Types of Various Mass Media Used by Saharia

Sl. No	*Types of Mass Media*	*Number of Head Households*	*Percentage*
1	Television Available(B/W)	39	11.7
2	Radio Available	75	22.5
3	News Paper Reading	7	2.1
	Total	**121**	**36.3**
4	Not Used any Mass Media	212	66.7
	Grand Total	**333**	**100.0**

Types of Enjoyable Movie

Enjoyment of various movies is mostly concerned with financial status and standard of education. Due to financial problem, most of the Saharia are not enabled to see the movies at Cinema Hall. But through own television and video hall, established in their locality, they use to enjoy various movies. The present study depicts that among Saharia, 54.3 percent heads of the families are interested to enjoy the various movies whereas 45.7 percent heads of the families do not watch any movie. However among viewers, romantic movies are interestingly followed by large percentage of heads of families (29.1 percent) whereas sex (6.3 percent), social (9.3 percent), war (6.0 percent) and violence (3.6 percent) movies are rarely preferred to Saharia (Table 4.8).

TABLE: 4.8

Types of Enjoyable Movie Among Saharia

Sl. No	*Types of Enjoyable Movie*	*Head of Families*	*Percentage*
1	Romantic	97	29.1
2	Sex	21	6.3
3	Social	31	9.3
4	War	20	6.0
5	Violence	12	3.6
	Total	**181**	**54.3**
6	Not Watched any Movie	152	45.7
	Grand Total	**333**	**100.0**

POPULATION COMPOSITION

A demographic profile and related socio-economic characteristics of the household population are presented in a systematic manner. It also includes the study concerned to the various components of population composition, such as, the measures of age-sex composition, marital status, social, economic and educational characteristics, etc. In addition, several back-ground characteristics of individual female respondents, such as, economic, socio-cultural, physical environmental background as well as their menarcheal age, age at menopause (if applicable) and attitude/preference in relation to the family size and sex composition of children (which constituted the independent determinants) etc. are discussed. In population dynamics, the study of population composition is considered as a most fundamental aspect. Population composition is taken as the internal structure of a population group with regard to one or more demographic traits, such as age, sex, marital status and economic activities, educational characteristics, etc. at a stipulated period of time.

Population by Age and Sex Composition

Every population group has unique structure which can be described in terms of its age and sex composition. The structure of a population is closely associated with the number of births, deaths and migrations. In general, these events do not occur in the same pattern acrossing all the age groups and both the sexes of all the populations. It is because that population differs from one to another with respect to their structure. The age and sex composition depict the basic demographic situation of a population in a region. It substantially influences the capacity or potentiality for future population change. Simultaneously, it itself gets influenced by past population changes, i.e. by vectors of fertility, mortality, migration, nupituality operating in a population or area. In other words, it provides comprehensive insight into several characteristics of a population or area. An understanding of the same is therefore the first and foremost thing in any population dynamic study and must proceed any further population analysis. However, the present data on age component are collected in terms of completed whole or full years. Then all these (age data) are categorized into five years age groups (cohorts) instead of single year numbers. Using these standard five years age cohorts, the age and sex composition of the studied Saharia tribal group are presented in the following Table 4.9.

Age Composition

The age composition of a population is a good indicator of the type of population under study. If a population is a developed one, the proportion of people in higher age groups are to be more, otherwise, the reverse is happened, i.e. if the proportion of people in the younger age group is more, then the population is a developing one which is generally the case in India. In this country, the percentage of population in 0-14 age group is estimated high as 36.1 percent (SRS, 1992). In the present study, it is followed that age specific distribution of Saharia indicates a young age structure and developing or growing population by comprising 47.2 percent of the population who are assembled in the 0-14 age group (Table 4.9). As opposed to the population in 0-14 age group, 48.8 percent and 4.0 percent of the population are found in 15-49 and 50+ age groups respectively which indicate a high mortality or low survival to old age. High fertility, lack of old age care, improper nutrition and low level of socio-economic conditions of Saharia may be attributed for this state of age composition.

Sex Composition

The sex composition of a population is accepted as significant one in demographic analysis, since it is a potential source to study the dynamics of population growth. It also indicates the relative level of development of an area. The balance between the sexes is an important aspect of population. Many economic and social relationships are closely linked to the balance or disparity between the number of males and females. Sex composition may be studied with reference to the sex ratio. The sex ratio of a region may also be affected by the development activities of the region. However, for the present study, two basic measures are used to determine the sex composition of the Saharia population, i.e. (i) sex ratio and (ii) masculinity proportion (Table 4.9).

Sex Ratio

In most of the population groups, the number of males and females tend to be nearly equal, with males out numbering females at the younger ages and females out numbering males at the older ages. From the demographic point of view, situation of near equality measures that each sex has an adequate supply of mates so that the population can replenish its losses due to mortality from the successive age cohorts. It appears to be true that social, economic and community life are affected in many ways by large imbalances in the sex composition (Bogue, 1964). It is widely known that sex ratio in most of the developing countries are tilted in favour of males, unlike the trend observed in developed one. Even in the country, the variation of sex ratio acrosses different regions that India is quite great. According to the Census 1991, the highest and lowest sex-ratio is found in Kerala (1036) and Arunachal Pradesh (859) respectively. Sex ratio of Saharia is found to be measured as 863.68 (Table 4.9) which indicates higher proportion of males than females - a characteristic of developing region and lower than Madhya Pradesh (985) and India (972).

Sex ratio of Saharia is found comparatively higher (863.68) than Raji (858.0), Scheduled Caste of Himachal Pradesh (850), Lepcha (849), Sherpas (744) and others and lower than Gond (986.8), Kamar (906.0), Hill Korwa (954.4), Jaunsarias (889), Johar Bhotia (1132), Rang Bhatia (1209), Marchha Bhotia (1168), Kumauni Caste (998), Bhotia (981), Brahmin (890), Rajput (870), Gaddis (870), Bhutia (996), Mao (1012), Bodhs (956), Baltis (961), Arguns (928), Brokpas (947), Dalu (1060), Santal (913), Lodha (902), Dudh Kheria (1098), Malia (1888.8), and others. Early age at marriage, frequent child births, low status of women, inadequacy of infrastructural facilities, strong male sex preference, low level of literacy, untrained delivery attendance, improper medical care, low socio-economic status, etc. may be the concomitant factors for their low sex ratio. Thus, the increased female work force participation rate tends to reduce discrimination against females. A woman's work has a stronger significance than man's work and the increased participation of mother in work force improves the status of girl children. Female work force participation rate may be one of the important factors leading to higher sex ratio (Rosenzweig & Schultz, 1982; Bardhan, 1984; Chaudhuri, 1996). Female health care specially in rural area is not concerned by any body. Birth of female child in the family is not accepted with pleasure and even female death is bothered without extreme mourn as compared to male. Due to unscientific delivery, the expectant mothers are to be expired in large number which influences low fertility.

TABLE: 4.9
Distribution of Family Members by Age and Sex, Sex Ratio and Masculinity Proportion Among Saharia

Age Groups (in Year)	*Males*	*(%)*	*Females*	*(%)*	*Total Number*	*(%)*	*Sex Ratio*	*Masculinity Proportion*
0-4	137	15.3	118	15.3	255	15.3	861.31	**53.7**
5-9	150	16.8	132	17.1	282	16.9	880.00	
10-14	136	15.2	114	14.7	250	15.0	838.23	
0-14	**423**	**47.3**	**364**	**47.1**	**787**	**47.2**	**860.52**	
15-19	110	12.3	87	11.2	197	11.8	790.90	
20-24	79	8.8	82	10.6	161	9.7	1037.97	
25-29	82	9.2	67	8.7	149	8.9	817.07	
30-34	59	6.6	74	9.6	133	8.0	1254.23	
35-39	61	6.8	33	4.3	94	5.6	540.98	
40-44	32	3.6	19	2.4	51	3.1	593.75	
45-49	18	2.0	12	1.6	30	1.8	666.66	
15-49	**441**	**49.3**	**374**	**48.4**	**815**	**48.8**	**848.07**	
50-54	9	1.0	11	1.4	20	1.2	1222.22	
55-59	5	0.5	10	1.3	15	0.9	2000.00	
60-64	8	0.9	7	0.9	15	0.9	875.00	
65-69	6	0.7	5	0.6	11	0.7	833.33	
70+	3	0.3	2	0.3	5	0.3	666.66	
50+	**31**	**3.4**	**35**	**4.5**	**66**	**4.0**	**1129.03**	
Total	**895 (53.7%)**	**100.0**	**773 (46.3%)**	**100.0**	**1668**	**100.0**	**863.68**	

Masculinity

Masculinity proportion is the other measure of sex composition depicting the balance of the sexes in a population, in terms of proportions or percentages at a specified time. Generally, it may be defined that in a population, sex composition is measured by masculinity proportion. It is just the percentage of males in a population. Since the sex ratio is found to be low among Saharia whereas the masculinity proportion of them is estimated 53.7 as high (Table 4.9). Masculinity proportion of Saharia is found high (53.7) as compared to Brahmin (52.91), Rajpaut (53.48), Gaddis (53.48), Bodhs (51.10), Baltis (51.00), Brokpas (51.40), Arguns (51.90), Bhutias (51.10), Madhya Pradesh (51.40) and India (51.73) but low as compared to Scheduled Caste (54.05), Lepchas (54.09), Serpas (57.35) and others. Their high masculinity proportion may be attributed as the reasons of strong male sex preference, early age at marriage of women and frequent child births, low socio-economic status, etc. Inadequate educational and medical facilities available to female, poor infrastructural condition, lack of nutritional food, etc. are also the possible reasons of their high masculinity (Bhasin, 1990; Kapoor, 1996; Patra, 2001).

Marital Status

The status of individual with regard to marriage is a fundamental aspect of a population composition. The key-index to population growth is not the number of fecund females, but the number of cohabiting fecund females in most of the population of the world; marriage is the first step in the formation of a biological family. The marital status distribution is an important factor for affecting fertility. Marital status has demographic, social, religious and legal significance. Therefore marital status composition is yet another essential part of population dynamics. It is not simply the number of fertile females who influence the level of fertility in a population, but the number of married fertile females. This is because, in most societies, all but a small fraction of child bearing occurs within marriage which is the socially and legally recognized child bearing institution. In the present study, the marital status distributions in general, have indicated that in Saharia population group;. (i) the percentage of unmarried males is higher (30.2 percent) than females (26.0 percent) and the unmarried population are declined above the age of 9 years; (ii) the percentage of unmarried males (23.4

percent) is high as compared to females (19.6 percent); (iii) the majority of children under 14 years are not married; (iv) the majority of population above 15 years are married; (v) the married females (in wed lock) population in reproductive age group are higher which have the chances of high fertility; (vi) widowers or divorces are very low which have also the chances to high fertility (Table 4.10).

TABLE: 4.10

Age and Sex-wise Distribution of Marital Status Among Saharia

Age Group (in Year)	Unmarried			Married			Widow(er)/Divorced			Grand Total		
	M	F	Total	M	F	Total	M	F	Total	M	F	Total
0-4	137	118	255	0	0	0	0	0	0	137	118	255
5-9	150	132	·282	0	0	0	0	0	0	150	132	282
10-14	136	112	248	0	2	2	0	0	0	136	114	250
15-19	74	71	145	36	16	52	0	0	0	110	87	197
20-24	5	2	7	74	80	154	0	0	0	79	82	161
25-29	0	0	0	82	67	149	0	0	0	82	67	149
30-34	1	0	1	58	74	132	0	0	0	59	74	133
35-39	0	0	0	60	32	92	1	1	2	61	33	94
40-44	0	0	0	32	19	51	0	0	0	32	19	51
45-49	0	0	0	17	9	26	1	3	4	18	12	30
50-54	0	0	0	9	8	17	0	3	3	9	11	20
55-59	0	0	0	5	10	15	0	0	0	5	10	15
60-64	0	0	0	8	4	12	0	3	3	8	7	15
65-69	0	0	0	6	4	10	0	1	1	6	5	11
70+	0	0	0	3	2	5	0	0	0	3	2	5
Total	503	435	938	390	327	717	2	11	13	895	773	1668
Percent	30.2	26.0	56.2	23.4	19.6	43.0	0.1	0.7	0.8	53.7	46.3	100.0

(M=Male, F=Female)

Dependency Ratio

Dependency ratio of a population indicates the proportion of consumer group and producer group (Thomson & Lewis, 1965). Dependency ratio measures the impact of age composition on the livelihood activity of a population. It is estimated in reference to the proportion of young (0-14 years) and old (60+ years) in the total population who are presumably economically inactive and proportion of population at productive ages (15-59 years). In other words, it attempts to describe the burden of dependency or dependency load that is supported by potentially economically active population. The dependency ratio can be estimated in parts, thereby separately measuring the dependency load of youth and aged. The sum of young age dependency ratio and old age dependency ratio are equal in the context of total dependency ratio. The three parameters, viz., young age dependency ratio (YADR), old age dependency ratio (OADR) and total dependency ratio (TDR) are measured in the present study. The dependency (derived from the age distribution of a population) is based on the fact that most of the members of a society are consumers and only some members are producers (Thomson & Lewis, 1965). The dependency also reflects the level of development of a region (i.e. the higher the dependency load lower the level of development).

Young Age Dependency Ratio (YADR)

The young age dependency ratio (YADR) among Saharia is found to be measured as 92.58 (Table 4.11). In the study population too, the young age dependency ratio is come to notice relatively higher (92.58) than Abujhmaria (86.9), Lohar Gadiyas (92.30), Bodhs (63.09), Baltis (80.09), Brokpas (73.04), Arguns (50.09), Brahmin (70.82), Rajputs (69.65), Scheduled Caste of Himachal Pradesh (86.00), Gaddis (75.18), Raji (73.10), Dharchula (80.00), Juhar Bhutia (56.53), Marcha Bhutia (49.01), Lepchas (77.84), Bhutias (81.94), Hindus (61.43), Buddhists (78.42), Mao (64.52), Kand (53.31), Madhya Pradesh (65.50) and India (73.30). It may be attributed that due to high population growth under 15 years age group that means high fertility as a by product of transition from food gathering to food producing stage, low socio-cultural status, etc., the young age dependency ratio of Saharia is come to high.

Old Age Dependency Ratio (OADR)

The percentage of population above 60 years among Saharia is found to be low (1.9 percent). As a reason, their old age dependency is reduced. Among them, survival to old age group is also not high. So, the problem of ageing is far less common. However, the old age dependency ratio (OADR) is found to be estimated as 3.64 (Table 4.11) which is comparatively lower than Abujhmaria (7.1), Lohar Gadiyas (5.7), Bodhs (9.69), Baltis (5.54), Brokpas (7.35), Arghuns (5.81), Brahmins (7.12), Rajputs (5.79), Scheduled Castes (5.16), Gaddis (5.98), Dharchula (3.88), Johar Bhutia (4.02), Marcha Bhutia (4.74), Lepcha (3.79), Bhutias (6.27), Hindus (4.16), Buddhists (4.80), Mao (8.82), Kand (8.01), Madhya Pradesh (6.5) and India (12.0). It may be attributed that due to lack of old age care, after marriage immediate separation from parents, low socio-economic condition, high mortality in senior groups, etc., their old age dependency ratio is prostrated to low.

Total Dependency Ratio (TDR)

The total dependency ratio (TDR) indicates the sum of the young age dependency ratio and the old age dependency ratio. For the present study, total dependency ratio among Saharia is found to be measured as 96.22 (Table 4.11). Comparing to different population groups of Madhya Pradesh and India, Saharia total dependency ratio (96.22) is exhibited higher than Abujhmaria (93.00), Lohar Gadiyas (92.87), Bodhs (72.78), Baltis (85.63), Brokpas (80.39), Arghuna (55.9), Brahmins (77.94), Rajputs (75.44), Scheduled Caste (91.16), Gaddis (81.16), Buksa (95.52), Jhunsari (79.09), Raji (80.00), Dharchula (83.88), Johar Bhutias (60.55), Marcha Bhutia (58.75), Lepchas (81.63), Bhutias (88.21),Hindus (65.59), Buddhists (83.22), Mao (73.34), Kand (61.62), Madhya Pradesh (72.10) and India (85.30) but it is lower than Tharu (103.09). Comparatively higher population growth below the age of 14 years age group is mentioned as the main contaminated reason of their high total dependency ratio.

Index of Ageing

The index of ageing measures the relative number of old persons in a population. The ageing of population (i.e. whether the population is 'Young' or 'Old') can be described by the ratio of old persons aged 60 years and above to the young population aged 0-14 years. It also indirectly measures the young and old population groups. This index, in general, is found low when the proportion of population under 15 years is high and vice-versa. Hence, in developing countries with high fertility, this is usually come to low (16.0); while the state of Kerala, it is found rather high (22.0) denoting a somewhat 'old' population with low fertility, as noticed in developed region (Chachra & Bhasin, 1998). The index of ageing among Saharia is found to be measured as 3.94 (Table 4.11) which is very low as compared to Lohar Gadiyas (6.1), Bodhs (15.96), Baltis (6.91), Brokpas (10.07), Arghuns (11.60), Brahmins (10.05), Rajputs (8.31), Scheduled Castes (6.00), Gaddis (7.95), Raji (8.53), Dharchula (4.86), Johar Bhutia (7.11), Marcha Bhutia (9.67), Lepchas (4.88), Bhutias (7.65), Hindus (6.77), Buddhists (6.12), Madhya Pradesh (10.0) and India (16.0) but high as compared to Rajput (3.63) and Scheduled Castes (3.38) of Uttar Pradesh. It may be attributed that due to high proportion of population (growth) under 15 years and high mortality in aged (old), ageing index of Saharia is prostrated comparatively to low.

TABLE: 4.11
Dependency Ratios and Index of Ageing Among Saharia

Sex	*Below 15 Years*		*15-59 Years*		*60 Yrs. & also*		*Dependency Ratio*			*Index of*
	No.	*%*	*No.*	*%*	*No.*	*%*	*Young*	*Old*	*Total*	*Ageing*
Male	423	25.4	455	27.3	17	1.0	92.96	3.74	96.70	4.01
Female	364	21.3	395	23.7	14	0.8	92.15	3.54	96.04	3.85
Total	**787**	**47.2**	**850**	**51.0**	**31**	**1.9**	**92.58**	**3.65**	**96.22**	**3.94**

Number of Members in the Family

Family is a social unit consisting of parents and their

biological and adopted offsprings residing in a same house and sharing a common hearth. In a family, the number of member is varied in accordance with type of family. Both nuclear and joint families are existed among Saharia. But the number of nuclear families is very high as compared to joint families. After marriage of son, the immediate separation from parents is the attributed reason of nuclear family formation. In the present study, the number of members in a family is varied from 2 to 11 whereas mean number of members in a family is found to be measured as 5 (Table 4.12). The number of joint families is very low. So, the mean number of members (in a family) is depended on the number of offsprings in nuclear families. Due to high fertility, the number of children is increased but decreasing as the cause of high mortality.

TABLE: 4.12

Number of Members in a Family Among Saharia

Number of Members in Family	*Number of Families*	*Percentage*
2	10	3.0
3	60	18.0
4	66	19.8
5	67	20.2
6	66	19.8
7	42	12.6
8	15	4.5
9	6	1.8
10	0	0.0
11	1	0.3
Total	**333**	**100.0**
Mean Number of Member	5	

Clan-wise Distribution of Population and Sex Ratio

In the present study, the available data highlight the

existence of twenty one partilineal exogamous clans among Saharia. This study also further confers that Kheria is recorded as the highest populated clan (26.4 percent) and its members are dominated in the society. In other side, ue to inadequate number of population, the members of Digoria clan (0.2 percent), Shonoria clan (0.3 percent) and others are always depressed by dominant groups (Table 4.13). Sex ratios in different clans are varied from 500.00 (each in Dongia and Negtelia Clans) to 1500.00 (Shonoria clan). Socio-cultural rules and regulations are also varied from one clan to another. In regarding fertility performance, some specific clan members prefer to both male and female sex equally whereas some others like better only the birth of male offsprings. Even this type of clanwise variation is followed in using the family planning methods. Some clan members do not agree to use any family planning method whereas some others prefer to modern contraceptive devices. But a few clan members till now believe their traditional methods of birth control. Clan-wise mating pattern is also another socio-cultural aspect which depicts that marriage in same clan is extremely prohibited among Saharia. Marriage is usually performed in different clans, so they are clan exogamous.

TABLE: 4.13
Clans-wise Distribution of Population and Sex-Ratio Among Saharia

Sl. No	*Name of Clans*	*No. of Males (Percentage)*	*No. of of Females (Percentage)*	*Total Population (Percentage)*	*No. of Families (Percentage)*	*Sex Ratio*
1	2	3	4	5	6	7
1	Shoria	25 (2.8)	16 (2.1)	41 (2.5)	10 (3.0)	640.00
2	Gobaria	47 (5.3)	30 (3.9)	77 (4.6)	18 (5.4)	638.29
3	Kheria	229 (25.6)	212 (27.4)	441 (26.4)	91 (27.4)	925.76
4	Monia	40 (4.5)	31 (4.0)	71 (4.2)	15 (4.5)	775.00
5	Belhoria	29 (3.2)	20 (2.6)	49 (2.9)	9 (2.7)	689.65

1	*2*	*3*	*4*	*5*	*6*	*7*
6	Digoria	2 (0.2)	1 (0.1)	3 (0.2)	1 (0.3)	500.00
7	Shelia	39 (4.4)	49 (6.4)	88 (5.3)	14 (4.2)	1256.41
8	Deboria	10 (1.1)	8 (1.0)	18 (1.1)	5 (1.5)	800.00
9	Ataria	23 (2.6)	18 (2.3)	41 (2.5)	9 (2.7)	782.60
10	Dhoria	115 (12.8)	84 (10.9)	199 (11.9)	35 (10.5)	730.43
11	Dongia	4 (0.4)	2 (0.3)	6 (0.3)	1 (0.3)	500.00
12	Negtelia	4 (0.4)	2 (0.3)	6 (0.3)	2 (0.6)	500.00
13	Norboia	28 (3.1)	25 (3.2)	53 (3.2)	10 (3.0)	892.85
14	Barodia	93 (10.4)	83 (10.7)	176 (10.6)	34 (10.2)	892.17
15	Badratia	100 (11.2)	88 (11.4)	188 (11.3)	39 (11.7)	880.00
16	Jabrolia	52 (5.8)	43 (5.6)	95 (5.7)	18 (5.4)	826.92
17	Sholanki	12 (1.4)	8 (1.0)	20 (1.2)	4 (1.2)	666.66
18	Paria	7 (0.8)	8 (1.0)	15 (0.9)	3 (0.9)	1142.85
19	Ghoria	7 (0.8)	8 (1.0)	15 (0.9)	3 (0.9)	1142.85
20	Shonora	2 (0.2)	3 (0.4)	5 (0.3)	1 (0.3)	1500.00
21	Chandia	27 (3.0)	34 (4.4)	61 (3.7)	11 (3.3)	1259.25
	Total	**895 (53.7%)** 100.0	**773 (46.3%)** 100.0	**1668** (100.0)	**333** (100.0)	**863.68**

ECONOMIC CHARACTERISTICS

The capability of the work force, engaged actively in any productive and gainful economic activity is a basic economic characteristic of a population. It is therefore an importance in a study on population dynamics, since all demographic processes and economic characteristics are believed to influence each other directly or indirectly; and it is closely linked with development and well being of a population.

Types of Occupation: Generation-wise

Practice of various occupations is changed in accordance with the situation faced by next generation. In the past, hunting was not only regarded as the source of livelihood but also it was an indication of higher social status. Due to shortage of forest animals and restriction on hunt, this way of occupation is going to be extinct. Instead of hunting, labour, agriculture, craft, etc. are practised by most of them. In the present study, an attempt is made to exhibit the changing pattern of occupations from grand father generation to parent and then present generation. In grand father generation, most of the Saharia practised hunting (56.4 percent) because hunts were available in the forests. Except this, they tried to improve their status by practicing hunting operation. But in father generation, daily labour occupation was highly preferred to large percentage of households (58.5 percent). Beside this, very less percentage of households (12.3 percent) was involved in agricultural works for their livelihood. But the households of daily labour occupation (70.2 percent or 69.1 percent, out of 333 - Table 4.15) are highly increased in present generation (Table 4.14). Hunting, food gathering, animal husbandry, agriculture, bonded labour, tribal craft, business and service are practised by very less percentage of households. So, according to these changing occupational trends, hunting practice is going to be extinct due to unavailability of forest and also Government restriction on game. In stead of hunting, they are motivated to practise daily labour. Most of the Saharia are landless. So now a days, daily labour is practised as their only dependable source of income.

TABLE: 4.14

Types of Occupation: Generation-wise Among Saharia

SL. No.	Types of Occupations	Grand Father (Percentage)	Father (Percentae)	Present Generation (Percentage)
1	Hunting	184 (56.4)	12 (3.7)	1 (0.3)
2	Food Gathering	22 (6.8)	9 (2.8)	5 (1.5)
3	Animal Husbandry	20 (6.1)	27 (8.3)	11 (3.4)
4	Agriculture	22 (6.8)	40 (12.3)	38 (11.7)
5	Daily Labour	40 (12.3)	191 (58.5)	229 (70.2)
6	Bonded Labour	21 (6.4)	22 (6.7)	15 (4.6)
7	Tribal Craft	17 (5.2)	25 (7.7)	16 (4.9)
8	Business	0 (0.0)	0 (0.0)	2 (0.6)
9	Service	0 (0.0)	0 (0.0)	9 (2.8)
	Total	**326** (100.0)	**326** (100.0)	**326** (100.0)

Distribution of Families According to Present Occupation

All Saharia families are distributed in accordance with the primary and secondary occupations. In every family, some of the members are involved full time in primary occupation whereas others expense part time by practicing secondary

TABLE: 4.15
Distribution of Families by Primary and Secondary Occupations Among Saharia

SL. No.	*Primary Occupations*	*Total Families (Percentage)*	***Secondary Occupations***	***Total Families (Percentage)***
1	Hunting	1 (0.3)	Hunting	13 (3.9)
2	Food Gathering	7 (2.1)	Food Gathering	34 (10.2)
3	Animal Husbandry	12 (3.6)	Animal Husbandry	47 (14.1)
4	Agriculture	40 (12.0)	Agriculture	26 (7.8)
5	Daily Labour	230 (69.1)	Daily Labour	59 (17.8)
6	Bonded Labour	17 (5.1)	Fuel selling	56 (16.8)
7	Tribal Craft	14 (4.2)	Craft	44 (13.2)
8	Business	2 (0.6)	Business	9 (2.7)
9	Service	9 (2.7)	Transporter	4 (1.2)
10	Begging	1 (0.3)	Fishing	41 (12.3)
	Total	**333 (100.0)**	**Total**	**333 (100.0)**

occupation. The available data exhibit that among ten multiple choices, the maximum percentage of families are engaged in primary occupations concerning daily labour (69.1 percent), followed by agriculture (12.0 percent) and bonded labour (5.1 percent) whereas rest of the families have an involvement in practicing tribal craft (4.2 percent), animal husbandry (3.6 percent) and others (Table 4.15). In secondary occupations, the maximum percentage of families carries on as a profession of daily labour (17.8 percent), followed by fuel selling (16.8 percent) and animal husbandry (14.1 percent) whereas transportation is practised by minimum percentage of families (1.2 percent). Due to inhabit in remote and undulating hilly area, they have less opportunity to attach with the occupation of business and transportation.

Sexwise Distribution of Population for Primary and Secondary Occupations

In human life, occupation is considered as the base to make performance of all activities. For surviving on earth, any living organism requires foremost importancy on food which is resourceful from occupation. However, involvement in various occupations is varied from one region to another and from one community to another.. In Saharia tribal area, the opportunity of work is not available throughout the year. Whenever they get any type of work, they generally involve themselves to do it without having any delay. The available data for the present study depict that the involvement of males in primary (57.0 percent) as well as in secondary occupation (57.3 percent) is found to be high as compared to females (Table 4.16). Malnutrition and inadequate medical facility are caused for their physical problem and due to non-adoption of family planning devices, they can not avoid frequent conceptions and child births which make an inequal sharing in economic activity. As primary occupation, hunting (0.1 percent), business (0.2 percent) and begging (0.2 percent) are practised by the minimum percentage of Saharia whereas daily labour is carried on as an important occupation by the maximum percentage of people (68.2 percent). With respect to secondary occupation, it is an observance that business and daily labour are practised by the minimum (0.1 percent) and the maximum (34.8 percent) percentage of Saharia people respectively.

TABLE: 4.16
Sex-wise Distribution of Population for Primary and Secondary Occupations Among Saharia

SL. No	Primary Occupations	Total Population Male (%)	Female (%)	Total (%)	Secondary Occupations	Total Population Male (%)	Female (%)	Total (%)
1	Hunting	1	0	1	Hunting	6	0	6
		(0.2)	(0.0)	(0.1)		(1.6)	(0.0)	(0.9)
2	Food Gathering	19	9	28	Food Gathering	12	11	23
		(3.6)	(2.3)	(3.1)		(3.1)	(3.8)	(3.4)
3	Animal Husbandry	26	13	39	Animal Husbandry	19	16	35
		(5.0)	(3.3)	(4.3)		(4.9)	(5.6)	(5.2)
4	Agriculture	86	48	134	Agriculture	89	67	156
		(16.6)	(12.2)	(14.7)		(23.1)	(23.3)	(23.2)
5	Daily Labour	324	297	621	Daily Labour	131	103	234
		(62.4)	(75.7)	(68.2)		(34.0)	(35.9)	(34.8)
6	Bonded Labour	17	0	17	Fuel Selling	58	47	105
		(3.3)	(0.0)	(1.9)		(15.1)	(16.4)	(15.6)
7	Tribal Craft	34	24	58	Tribal Craft	27	31	58
		(6.6)	(6.1)	(6.3)		(7.0)	(10.8)	(8.7)
8	Business	2	0	2	Business	1	0	1
		(0.4)	(0.0)	(0.2)		(0.3)	(0.0)	(0.1)
9	Service	9	0	9	Transporter	12	3	15
		(1.7)	(0.0)	(1.0)		(3.1)	(1.1)	(2.3)
10	Begging	1	1	2	Fishing	30	9	39
		(0.2)	(0.2)	(0.2)		(7.8)	(3.1)	(5.8)
	Total	519 (57.0%)	392 (43.0%)	911	Total	385 (57.3%)	287 (42.7%)	672
		100.0	100.0	(100.0)		100.0	100.0	(100.0)

Crude Activity Rate

In the present study, the various crude activity rates are computed for persons, as well as either sex, since the sex differentials are usually found substantial throughout the world, more so, in developing countries, like India. Crude activity rate of Saharia in primary occupation is found to be measured as 54.61 percent whereas 57.98 percent and 50.71 percent rates are for males and females respectively (Table 4.17). Crude activity rate of Madhya Pradesh has been estimated as 52.67 percent whereas males project a comparatively higher rate (52.67 percent) than females (56.95 percent). As compared to Madhya Pradesh, crude activity rate of India has also been found to be low (49.30 percent) and there, 54.74 percent and 43.71 percent are for males and females respectively (Census, 1991). Therefore, it is noticed that Saharia crude activity rate is comparatively higher than the crude activity rate of Madhya Pradesh and India. Crude activity rate always depends on the financial position of a particular population. Better financial position always decreases the crude activity rate whereas poverty and other barriers have a tendency to increase it. Most of the primitive tribal groups are poverty stricken and as a result, they are to be involved themselves in practicing various works from their childhood stage which usually help to increase their crude activity rate. So, financial problem is assessed as the reason of high crude activity rate of Saharia primitive tribe.

General Activity Rate

Economic characteristics of a population are greatly affected by its age composition and hence the general activity rate is also computed to study the ratio of persons engaged in any gainful and productive economic activity to the population at the working age, i.e. 15-59 years. The general activity rate in primary occupation of Saharia is found to be measured as 107.17 percent whereas 114.00 percent and 99.24 percent are for males and females respectively (Table 4.17). Due to poverty, they have to seek work opportunity. Whenever they are introduced by any type of working activity, then they generally involve themselves. So, the percentage of working population is remarkably increased and as a result, their general activity rate is also found to be measured high.

TABLE: 4.17
Crude and General Activity Rate Among Saharia

	Primary Occupation		*Secondary Occupation*	
	Crude Activity Rate	*General Activity Rate*	*Crude Activity Rate*	*General Activity Rate*
Male	57.98%	114.00%	43.01%	84.61%
Female	50.71%	99.24%	37.12%	72.65%
Total	**54.61%**	**107.17%**	**40.28%**	**79.05%**

Family Income and Expenditure

Yearly income of Saharia households varies in accordance with the types of work. Usually, income of a few service holders (4.5 percent) are measured high (above Rs.10000/-) as compared to the persons of other occupations. However, the maximum families (19.5 percent) yearly earn Rs.6500/- to 7000/-, followed by 13.5 percent (Rs.5500/- to 6000/-), 12.0 percent (Rs.6000/- to 6500/-), 10.9 percent (Rs.7000/- to 7500/-) whereas the minimum families (0.3 percent) earn below Rs.3000/-, followed by 1.2 percent (Rs.3500/- to 4000/-), 1.5 percent Rs.3000/- to 3500/-), 2.1 percent (Rs.9000/- to 9500/-). The average household income is found to be estimated as Rs.6035/- (Table 4.18). After all, it may be assessed that in regarding the expenditure, income of Saharia households are not sufficient. In Saharia inhabitat area, work opportunities are not always available. Beside this, the collected information illustrate that landlords (Jamindars), contractors and others always exploit them (labour groups). Due to poverty, they usually demand works during long time. But instead of their paid works, they are pressurized to receive very little amount by the exploiter groups. So, their contributed works and the value of works are inconsistent and these are come to notice as the reason of the low average income.

In the present study, the available data also depict that almost all Saharia expense their earnings for the purpose of fooding and dress and ornaments. Besides fooding and dress-ornaments, most of the Saharia expense their amount for housing, drinking and puja-festival purposes. Some families are unable to maintain all family budgets whereas some families' income and expenditure are equal. Only a few families are identified who deposit very little amount after maintaining all family budgets. The other families are unable to bear their family budget and they generally borrow the amount from money lenders or contractors (with high interest) for the purpose of fooding, clothing, housing, treatment, marriage and drinking.

TABLE: 4.18
Family Income and Expenditure of Last one Year Among Saharia

Income (in Rupees)	*No. of Families*	*%*	*Expenditure on Items*					
			Food No. of Family	*House No. of Family*	*Drinking No. of Family*	*Dress-ornaments Family*	*Utensils No. of Family*	*Puja-Festival No. of Family*
<3000	1	0.3	1	1	0	1	0	0
3000-3500	5	1.5	5	5	5	5	2	2
3500-4000	4	1.2	4	4	4	4	1	3
4000-4500	9	2.7	9	9	9	9	7	6
4500-5000	16	4.8	16	16	15	16	13	13
5000-5500	31	9.3	31	30	29	31	28	28
5500-6000	45	13.5	45	44	42	45	44	43
6000-6500	40	12.0	40	38	39	40	39	39
6500-7000	65	19.5	65	62	62	65	65	65
7000-7500	36	10.9	36	35	36	36	36	35
7500-8000	21	6.3	21	21	19	21	21	21
8000-8500	12	3.6	12	11	11	12	12	12
8500-9000	15	4.5	15	13	15	15	15	15
9000-9500	7	2.1	7	7	7	7	7	7
9500-10000	11	3.3	11	10	11	11	11	11
10000>	15	4.5	15	13	14	15	15	15
Total	**333**	**100.0**	**333**	**316**	**318**	**333**	**316**	**315**

TABLE: 4.19
Indebted Families and Its Purposes Among Saharia

Indebted Amount (in Rupees)	*No. of Families*	*%*	*Expenditure*					
			Food No. of Family	*Cloth No. of Family*	*House No. of Family*	*Treat-ment No. of Family*	*Drinking No. of Family*	*Marri- No. of Family*
<200	6	10.3	2	0	2	0	0	2
200-300	8	13.8	4	2	0	2	0	0
300-400	11	19.0	6	3	0	1	0	1
400-500	9	15.5	2	6	1	0	0	0
500-600	5	8.6	3	2	0	0	0	0
600-700	5	8.6	3	1	0	0	1	0
700-800	6	10.3	1	4	0	0	1	0
800-900	2	3.5	1	1	0	0	0	0
900-1000	0	0.0	0	0	0	0	0	0
1000-1100	1	1.7	1	0	0	0	0	0
1100-1200	0	0.0	0	0	0	0	0	0
1200-1300	0	0.0	0	0	0	0	0	0
1300-1400	2	3.5	1	0	0	0	1	0
1400-1500	1	1.7	0	0	0	0	1	0
1500 >	2	3.5	1	0	0	1	0	0
Total	**58**	**100.0**	**25**	**19**	**3**	**4**	**4**	**3**
%	**17.4**	**100.0**	**43.1**	**32.7**	**5.2**	**6.9**	**6.9**	**5.2**

Indebted Amount and its Purposes

Most of the Saharia families earn very little amount from all sources. It is substantial that all their earned amount is not enough to maintain their family budget. So for maintaining their family budget, either they have to sell any property otherwise borrow the amount from money lenders or contractors with high interest. Last one year record indicates that 17.4 percent families (out of 333) were indebted various amounts for different purposes. The maximum households (19.0 percent) were indebted

Rs.300/- to.400/-, followed by 15.5 percent (Rs.400/- to 500/), 13.8 percent (Rs.200/- to 300/-), 10.3 percent (below Rs.200/). Whereas 3.5 percent households were indebted the highest amount (Rs.1500/-). Most of the families (43.1 percent) expended their indebted amount for fooding whereas very less number of families (5.2 percent) expended for the purpose of housing and marriage (Table 4.19).

EDUCATIONAL CHARACTERISTICS

In all socio-economic aspects, education is thought as the most influential factor in differentiating people's social and demographic behaviour. Education is also regarded as an integral component for development and well-being. Hence the study of educational characteristics of a population in a region is deemed essential for the study on population dynamics. In fact, such characteristics are believed to affect the reproductive behaviour, use of contraceptives, health of children, proper hygienic practices and status of women. Beside this, educational characteristics of a population also focus insight into the 'output' of the educational system in an area. Very often social scientists use education as a socio-economic indicator.

Literacy Rate

Education usually makes an aspersion to literacy which means that a person is able to read and write. The literacy rate is also known as crude literacy rate indicating the number of literate persons in a population group at a specified time. However, the various measures of literacy are usually estimated for both sexes to assess the gender difference which is substantial in many developing countries including India. Literacy rate of Saharia is found to be measured as 23.2 percent whereas 28.2 percent and 17.7 percent are for male and female literacy rates respectively. But literacy rate of Saharia with age of 5 years and above is also found to be estimated as 26.6 percent whereas 32.6 percent and 20.2 percent are for male and female literacy rates respectively (Table 4.20). So, in the study, Saharia male literacy rate is found comparatively higher than female literacy rate. In the context of comparative assessment, Saharia literacy rate is found lower (23.2 percent) than Gond (26.4 percent), Abujhmaria (26.9 percent), Jogia Tharu (29.4 percent), Kaharia Tharu (40.0 percent), Pachnimahan Tharu (27.2 percent), Raji (33.6 percent), Lepcha (43.3 percent), Bhutia (35.4 percent), Tarao (48.9 percent), Gaddis (23.3 percent), Brokpas (42.1 percent), India (29.6 percent) and others. Literacy rate of Saharia is also found to be high (23.2 percent) when it is compared to Danguria Tharu (19.2 percent), Sherpas (9.5 percent), Yanadis (8.3 percent), Madhya Pradesh (21.5 percent) and others. It may be attributed that due to their extreme poverty, they have to involve in works from very early age and in that condition, they have no excess time to takepart in school education. Due to high extent of illiteracy in parental generation, Saharia children can not achieve any influential approach to the modern education. Beside this, Saharia literacy rate is low due to largely rural settings of the region and relatively inadequate educational facilities, lack of motivation and negative attitude towards female education, etc.

TABLE: 4.20

Literacy Rate Among Saharia

Category	*Literacy Rate (As percent of Total Population)*	*Literacy Rate (As percent of Total Population 5 Years and Above)*
Male	28.2	32.6
Female	17.7	20.2
Total	23.2	26.6

Age Specific Literacy Rate

Various measures of age specific literacy rate is further computed by classifying 5 years age group of the population. In this context, male and female literacy rate is also shown separately in the following Table 4.21. The comparison of literacy rate in different age groups of Saharia with micro-level estimates is revealed that the rate of 5-9 age group is higher (47.7 percent) than the rate of 10-14 age group (29.0 percent). In the age group of 0-4 and 5-9 years, generally children are not capable to provide any working support to their parents. So, they are just enrolled in the school register for getting Government scholarship and free of cost food materials, books, uniforms, etc. which probably show as the reasons of their comparatively higher literacy rate.

TABLE: 4.21

Age Specific Literacy Rate (Literate Percent by Age and Sex) Among Saharia

Age Group in Years	Illiterate						Literate					
	Male		Female		Total		Male		Female		Total	
	No.	%	No.	%	No.	%	No.	%	No.	%	No.	%
0-4	131	10.2	115	9.0	246	19.2	6	1.6	3	0.8	9	2.3
5-9	49	3.8	48	3.7	97	7.5	101	26.0	84	21.7	185	47.7
10-14	66	5.1	72	5.6	138	10.7	70	18.1	42	10.9	112	29.0
15-19	78	6.1	83	6.5	161	12.6	32	8.3	4	1.0	36	9.3
20-24	72	5.6	81	6.3	153	11.9	7	1.8	1	0.3	8	2.1
25-29	70	5.5	67	5.2	137	10.7	12	3.1	0	0.0	12	3.1
30-34	50	3.9	74	5.8	124	9.7	9	2.3	0	0.0	9	2.3
35-39	55	4.3	33	2.6	88	6.9	6	1.6	0	0.0	6	1.6
40-44	28	2.2	18	1.4	46	3.6	4	1.0	1	0.3	5	1.3
45-49	13	1.0	12	0.9	25	1.9	5	1.3	0	0.0	5	1.3
50-54	9	0.7	11	0.9	20	1.7	0	0.0	0	0.0	0	0.0
55-59	5	0.4	10	0.8	15	1.2	0.	0.0	0	0.0	0	0.0
60-64	8	0.6	7	0.5	15	1.2	0	0.0	0	0.0	0	0.0
65-69	6	0.4	5	0.4	11	0.8	0	0.0	0	0.0	0	0.0
70+	3	0.2	2	0.2	5	0.4	0	0.0	0	0.0	0	0.0
Total	**643**	**50.2**	**638**	**49.8**	**1281**	**100.0**	**252**	**65.1**	**135**	**34.9**	**387**	**100.0**

But slowly the literacy rate is reducing towards upper age groups of Saharia. They contribute working support to their parents or independently pass the family life. Some persons of various upper age groups have been literated by the help of non-Government voluntary organizations, National Literacy Mission and others.

Motive for Educational Attainment

Education is a most fundamental aspect of entire progress. But the motive of educational attainment varies from one person to another and even from one community to another. In the present study, 63.7 percent Saharia families are recorded to have the desire for providing better education to their children. Due to unavailability of own story (tribal related) in the book and absence of teachers who belong to their own community, 56.1 percent heads of the households are not satisfied to the local educational system. Similarly, 63.7 percent heads of the households prefer to male education, instead of female (Table 4.22). Because educated males can involve themselves to achieve better agricultural knowledge, face in competition for getting

TABLE: 4.22
Motive for Educational Attainment Among Saharia

Sl. No.	*Motive for Education*	*Yes (Percentage)*	*No (Percentage)*	*Total (Percentage)*
1	Desire of Education	212	121	333
		(63.7)	(36.3)	(100.0)
a	Satisfaction on Local Education	93	119	212
		(43.9)	(56.1)	(100.0)
b	Preference of Male Education	135	77	212
		(63.7)	(36.3)	(100.0)
c	Preference of Female Education	77	135	212
		(36.3)	(63.7)	(100.0)
2	Read News Paper	23	310	333
		(6.9)	(93.1)	(100.0)

Government job, etc. Beside this, by appointing as a teacher in their school, they will be enthusiastic to incorporate the special attention for teaching to the Saharia children. Among them, 36.3 percent heads of the households prefer to female education because enrolled females not only get the monthly stipend but also by achieving this type of formal education, they will teach their offsprings and maintain their family budget properly. According to the study of Unisa (2000), son preference in educational attainment is reported by 79.3 percent in Haryana, 82.5 percent in Rajasthan, 82.6 percent in Madhya Pradesh, 92.8 percent in Assam, 75.0 percent in Kerala and 74.4 percent in Andhra Pradesh.

TABLE: 4.23

Reasons of Preference for Male Education Among Saharia

Sl. No	*Reasons of Male Preference*	*No of Families*	*Percentage*
1.	For Better Agriculture	17	12.6
2	For Better Job	18	13.3
3	For High Status	7	5.2
4	For Teaching to Saharia	16	11.9
5	For Free From Bonded Labour	.12	8.9
6	For Free From Social Exploitation	10	7.4
7	For Government Scholarship	20	14.8
8	For Increasing Literacy Rate	6	4.4
9	For Maintaining Family Income	7	5.2
10	For Increasing Monthly Income	7	5.2
11	For Understanding Govt. Dev. Schemes	9	6.7
12	For Overall Positive Guidance	8	5.9
	Total	**135 (63.7%)**	**100.0**

Reasons of Preference for Male Education

In all traditional dimensions of Indian society, it is importantly visualized that son has the prime right to occupy the central place for taking decision of family formation. Their perception is that existence of son preference in educational attainment is irrespective in accordance with their socio-economic tradition. The present study expresses that education for male is given preference over female for various reasons. The maximum percentage of Saharia prefer to the education of son for better job (13.3 percentage), followed by better agriculture (12.6 percent), teaching to Saharia, etc. (Table 4.23). For male educational attainment, the minimum percentage of Saharia are committed to give preference due to the reason of increasing literacy rate (4.4 percent), high status (5.3 percent), maintaining family income (5.2 percent), understanding Government development scheme (5.2 percent), etc.

TABLE: 4.24

Reasons of Preference for Female Education Among Saharia

Sl. No	*Reasons of Female Preference*	*No. of Families*	*Percentage*
1	For Teaching Their Offsprings	11	14.3
2	For Better Job	5	6.5
3	For Maintaining Family Budget	4	5.2
4	For Better Food Preparation	3	3.9
5	For Marriage in High Status	3	3.9
6	For Proper Child Care	15	19.5
7	For Developing Women Status	4	5.2
8	For Entertaining Equal Life (As Male)	4	5.2
9	For Getting Government Scholarship	13	16.9
10	For Increasing Literacy Rate	4	5.2
11	For Changing Life Style	6	7.8
12	For Maintaining Better Health	5	6.5
	Total	**77 (36.3%)**	**100.0**

Reasons of Preference for Female Education

Female education plays an important role for entire development of the society. It is practical that the educated female can achieve an art to maintain their health status and procreate healthy child. In urban areas, female education is accepted equally as like as male whereas rural settings have an illustration of male dominancy in educational attainment. Female education is almost ignored among tribal society. In spite of this, some Saharia prefer to female education for various reasons. The present study finds out that in this group, the maximum percentage of Saharia prefer to female education for the purpose of proper child care (19.5 percent), getting Government scholarship (16.9 percent), teaching their offsprings (14.3 percent), etc. (Table 4.24). In other side, female education is preferred to the minimum percentage of Saharia due to the reason of better food preparation (3.9 percent), maintaining family budget (5.2 percent), maintaining better health status (6.5 percent), etc.

BENEFICIARY LOAN

It is a provision that every year, many development programmes are being launched specially for primitive tribes. Under such development programmes, loan facility is considered as important one. Due to extreme poverty, all Saharia family members are very eager to get the Government beneficiary loan. The available

TABLE: 4.25

Beneficiary Loan Accepted Families in Last One Year Among Saharia

Sl. No	*Purpose for Various Loans*	*Number of Families*	*Percentage*
1	Bullock Purchasing Loan	17	14.8
2	Goatery Loan	21	18.3
3	Poultry Loan	19	16.5
4	Fishery Loan	9	7.8
5	Mat-Making Loan	23	20.0
6	Bamboo Work Loan	20	17.4
7	Stone Hosing Loan	1	0.9
8	Cemented Building Loan	5	4.3
	Total	**115 (34.5%)**	**100.0**

data depict that 34.5 percent families have already been benefited by various loans (Table 4.25). Stone housing loan has been accepted by only 0.9 percent family, followed by 4.3 percent (cemented building loan) and 7.8 percent (fishery loan). Mat-making loan has been provided to the maximum families (20.0 percent), followed by 18.3 percent (goatery loan), 16.5 percent (poultry loan) and

14.8 percent (bullock purchasing loan). Some loan benefited families have claimed that due to negligence of some Government officials, the sanction amount as loan has been delayed to receive. After all, loan benefited families are very pleased because their financial position is comparatively better than other families. Due to better financial position, their literacy rate is going to be comparatively high which plays a great role in better demographic situation.

FERTILITY REGULATING FACTORS

In demographic study, fertility regulating factors are considered as significant because its direct or indirect influence is incorporated to the various components of demographic structure. Age at menarche, age at menopause, age at marriage, duration between marriage and conjugal life, duration between marriage and first child birth, duration between menarche and first child birth, etc., are the major fertility factors which have the important role in demographic situation.

Age at Menarche of Women

Kisch (1910) is honoured as the pioneer researcher for first introducing the term menarche. As a biological phenomenon, it gets expression in women's body to point out an important stage of life. Menarche indicates the specific stage of first periodical regular flow of blood from womb in all the healthy normal females. At a particular level of biological development, the girls begin to menstruate for the first time and that is continued for a period of four to five days. The menstrual cycle is usually one of twenty eight days and the estimated blood loss is varied from 50ml. to 200 ml. (Barua, 1996). Menarche – the first menstruation, is a well defined milestone which denotes the functional development of the female reproductive system, although a few initial cycles are anovulatroy. It is a clear hint of puberty and much of the adolescent growth spurt has already passed by the time of its onset (Prakash & Pathmanathan, 1992). However, menarche is not a final phenomenon of sexual maturation but probably because of endocrine regulation is connected with other phenomena of puberty and growth processes including influence on adult body size (Wolanski, et.al., 1998). Usually it is considered as an important physiological episode in life of women. The term menarche, the sign of puberty among girls experiencing physiological changes from childhood, refers to the first appearance of menstruation. After all the age of first menstruation start is taken as the age of puberty or the age of maturity and from this stage, females are biologically capable to conceive.

For making a comparative study of menarche, all Saharia women and their daughters are distributed in different age groups. The present study depicts that the maximum percentage of women attained menarche at the age of 14 years (48.1 percent) and 13 years (38.7 percent) whereas 15 years and 12 years are measured as the menarcheal age of only 5.7 percent and 7.5 percent women respectively. In other side, the maximum percentages of daughters got menarche at the age of 13 years (53.6 percent) and 14 years (33.9 percent). Only 1.8 percent and 10.7 percent daughters started menstruation cycle at the age of 15 years and 12 years respectively. The mean age at menarche of women (respondents) and their daughters are found to be estimated as 13.5 ± 0.84 years and 13.3 ± 0.66 years respectively (Table 4.26). So, it is found that menarcheal age of mothers is lightly high as compared to daughters. Comparatively low menarcheal age of daughters is attributed as the reasons of somewhat socio-cultural improvement, occupational change, achievement of low literacy rate, nutritional food, etc.

However, age at menarche of Saharia women (13.5 years) is high when compared to Gond (12.8 years), Kamar (13.49 years), Rana Tharu (13.26 years), Katharia Tharu (13.1 yeaars), Pachhimaha Tharu (13.44 years), Brahamin of Jammu & Kashmir (13.25 years), Rajput of Jammu & Kashmir (13.07 years), Tai Turung (12.43 years), Ahom (12.51 years), Sinypho (12.59 years), Sonowal (12.45 years), Garo (12.55 years), Mirdha (13.40 years), Kondh (13.40 years), Thoti (13.06 years) and others but it is low when compared to Hill Korwa (13.67 years), Munda (14.65 years), Abujhmaria (15.0 years), Dongia Tharu (14.0 years), Juhar Bhotia (15.1 years), Rang Bhotia (16.0 years), Marcha (16.18 years), Mahajan (13.55 years), Bodhs (15.43 years), Baltis (14.79 years), Arghuns (14.65 years), Gaddis (14.01 years), Brokpas (14.85 years),

Schedule Caste of Himachal Pradesh (14.04 years), Lepcha (15.55 years), Mao (14.59 years), Gond 13.69 years), Gonda (14.32 years) and others. Variation of menarcheal age is depended on occupation, educational status, food materials, environmental factors and others.

TABLE: 4.26

Age at Menarche of Mothers and Daughters Among Saharia

Age at Menarche (in Years)	*No. of Mothers*	*%*	*No of Daughters*	*%*
12	25	7.5	12	10.7
13	129	38.7	60	53.6
14	160	48.1	38	33.9
15	19	5.7	2	1.8
Total	**333**	**100.0**	**112**	**100.0**

Mean ± S.D. = 13.5 ± 0.84 Mean ± S.D. = 13.3 ± 0.66

Age at Menopause of Women

With increasing age, various morphological and physiological changes are accompanied in the life of women. The reproductive life of women is come to end with varying degree of suddenness with the menopause – a largely human phenomenon (Potts & Selman, 1979). In other words, menopause is considered as the most critical biological event in the body and from this stage, the reproductive function of women is completely ceased by consequently arresting the menstruation flow of blood and ovulation (Sengupta & Rajkhowa, 1996; Kalita & Sengupta, 1997). Sometimes, the term 'menopause' is acquainted as the symbolic end of womenhood because the women who attained menopause are not capable to conceive. However menopause is a very complex process of changes which occur in the biological structure of women, accompanied by a variety of events, sometimes resulting in extremely unpleasant symptoms which comprise hot flushes, headaches, insomnia, itching, etc. (Mastana, 1996).

According to the Table 4.27, it is found that the maximum percentage of Saharia women came to menopause stage at the age of 44 years (34.4 percent) and 45 years (28.1 percent) whereas 18.7 percent, 9.4 percent and 9.4 percent women attained menopause at the age of 43 years, 46 years and 47 years respectively. However for the present study, the mean age at menopause of women is found to be measured as 44.6 ± 1.17 years. The mean reproductive span for the women is also estimated as 31.1 years. The mean age at menopause of Saharia women is found comparatively higher (44.6 ± 1.17 years) than the mean age at menopause of Kamar (43.0 years), Bodhs (44.49 years), Baltis (44.39 years), Brokpas (44.12 years), Scheduled Caste of Himachal Pradesh (44.32 years), Gaddis (44.41 years), Brahmin of Himachal Pradesh (44.1 years), Bhutia (42.46 years), Buddhists (44.33 years) and others but lower than Arghuns (45.68 years), Rajput of Himachal Pradesh (44.81 years), Lepchas (47.00 years), Ahom (48.0 years), Sonowal (47.22 years), Khamiyang (46.25 years), Garo (45.85 years), Meities (44.95 years), Muslim (45.08 years), Mao (48.69 years), Vedic Brahmin (45.53 years), Kondh (44.96 years), Thoti (47.35 years) and others. The differences in age at menopause in different population or in different sub-groups of the same population may be influenced by genetical and environmental factors. Since the Saharia, like most of the

TABLE: 4.27

Age at Menopause of Women Among Saharia

Age at Menopause (in Years)	*Number of Women*	*Percentage*
43	6	18.7
44	11	34.4
45	9	28.1
46	3	9.4
47	3	9.4
Total	**32**	**100.0**

Mean ± S.D. = 44.6 ± 1.17

Indian populations are strictly endogamous group, the contribution of genetical factors for any difference in menopausal age can not be ruled out. Malnutrition, low socio-economic factors, environmental and genetic factors, rural urban residence, family size, etc. may be attributed to the possible reasons for determining the menopausal age of women (Friseh, 1974; Bongaarts, 1980; Beall, 1983; Sengupta & Rajkhowa, 1996; Kalita & Sengupta, 1997; Majumdar, 2001).

Age at Marriage

In the field of sociological and anthropological researches, marriage is considered as an important bio-cultural phenomenon in social institutions. Marriage is a biological tie but recognition is provided by society approved rules and regulations. It directly contributes to form family whereas, the over all cultural aspects of a society are widely concerned by marriage. As a reason, it is defined that human being is the primary component of a family and begotten of human being as well as family formation is the absolute outcome of marriage alliance. In a broad sense, marriage is thought as the socially approved sexual relationship between man and woman. It is a relation of one or more men to one or more women having a sexual gratification with a social sanction of cohabitation and offspring born out of the union is a socially legitimate issue, having an existing equal social status. It is primarily an organized institution for regulating sex behaviour in absence of which, there prevails promiscuity that is sexual anarchy (Bhattacharya, 1972). There is no doubt that through sex gratification forms, the dominant motive of marriage in any society, its "need for a dependable social mechanism for the care of children and also transmission of culture from one generation to the other" can not be ignored (Morab, 1988).

In various stages of development, marriage is regarded as a social institution which is endured through some changes among all groups of people in different parts of the world. Till update, marriage institution is guided by a number of rules, norms, customs, rituals, etc. in all societies including preliterate, literate, educated, developing, underdeveloped or developed.

Social disharmony is conducted by the violation of such social rules and regulations. The guiding forces and unique features of respective marriage regularities in every ethnic group ensure to form the well distinctiveness of a society. It is generally found that among traditional societies, both boys and girls are encouraged by ancient laws. As an effect, they are motivated to conduct marriage at early age. The early age at marriage specially of females helps to determine the high reproductive span of women. Fertility is declined due to late marriage (Busfield, 1972). Whereas higher age at marriage usually performs lesser reproductive span which reduces high child birth.

Through this socially recognized institution, a couple gets the liberties to cohabit and share the economic, reproductive and child rearing functions of a family. In this regard, the mean age at marriage indicates average time of family formation. Generally, though not universally, it is only within the confines of a marriage that a woman is initiated into child birth in most of the societies. Therefore, age at marriage is a very important demographic and health characteristic. Age at marriage, though in itself a factor for influencing population growth, is also an effect of socio-economic status, education, urbanization, status of women, etc. (Caldwell, et. al. 1983; Bhasin, 1990; Kapoor, 1996). Taking into consideration the over all perspectives, Government personnel have been influenced to implement the policy which is concerned to the fixation of marriageable age for both male and female. According to the Indian Marriage Restrain Act, 1976, it has been ruled out that age at marriage of male is 21 years whereas of female is 18 years.

Age at Marriage of Husbands and Wives

The available data for the present study reflect that marriages of Saharia male groups are started from 14 years and continued up to 23 years. From the Table 4.28, it is visualized that the maximum percentage of husbands got married at the age of 17 years (27.9 percent), 18 years (22.3 years), 19 years (18.0 percent), etc. Whereas the minimum percentage of husbands came in marital alliance at the age of 23 years (0.3 percent), 22 years (0.6 percent) 21 years(1.5 percent), etc So, through the study, it may be assessed that with the increasing of age up to 17 years, number of marriage is increased. But after the age of 17 years, the number of marriage is gradually decreased and makes a reverse relation between the age at marriage and number of marriage. Lastly the mean age of marriage of men is found to be measured as 17.6 ± 1.23 which is comparatively lower than the age (21 years) decided by Marriage Restrain Act, 1976.

TABLE: 4.28
Age at Marriage of Husbands and Wives (Respondents) Among Saharia

Age at Marriage Marriage	*No. of Males*	*%*	*No. of Females*	*%*
12	0	0.0	4	1.2
13	0	0.0	71	21.3
14	7	2.1	165	49.6
15	14	4.2	82	24.6
16	55	16.5	10	3.0
17	93	27.9	1	0.3
18	74	22.3	0	0.0
19	60	18.0	0	0.0
20	22	6.6	0	0.0
21	5	1.5	0	0.0
22	2	0.6	0	0.0
23	1	0.3	0	0.0
Total	**333**	**100.0**	**333**	**100.0**

Mean ± S.D. = 17.6 ± 1.23 Mean ± S.D. = 14.0 ± 0.80

The present study also confers that the maximum percentage of women were married at the age of 14 years (49.6 percent), followed by 15 years (24.6 percent) and 13 years (21.3 percent). Very rarely cases, marriages of women were performed at the age of 17 years (0.3 percent), 12 years (1.2 percent) and 16 years (3.0 percent). Here it specifies a very observable point that the number of marriage is correlated with the increasing age up to 15 years and then produces a reverse relation. The mean age at marriage of Saharia women is calculated as 14.0 ± 0.80 years which is also found low as compared to the age decided (18 years) by the Act. Their low age at marriage is transgressed as the reasons of poverty, deplorable low literacy rate, low socio-cultural status, high extent of isolation, limited contact with other community people, etc.

Age at Marriage of Respondent's Sons and Daughters

By the impact of modern education and socializing with the people of other communities, a very little change is pertained in the context of age at marriage of the respondent's sons and daughters anong Saharia. In the present study, it is noticed a comparative account of age at marriage between sons and daughters, sons and respondents and daughters and mothers among Saharia. Among them, the maximum percentage of marriages of sons were organized at the age of 18 years (36.8 percent), 19 years (19.4 percent) and 16 years (16.3 percent) whereas minimum percentage of marriages of sons were also organized at their age of 22 years (2.0 percent), 21 years (3.1 percent), 14 years & 15 years (4.1 percent each) and 16 years & 20 years (7.1 percent each). The mean age at marriage of sons is found to be estimated as 17.9 ± 1.41 years (Table 4.29). The mean age at marriage of fathers (respondents) is also found as 17.6 years (Table 4.28). So, it is an observation that due to somewhat socio-cultural improvement, the mean age at marriage of sons is found comparatively higher than those of respondents. In other side, the available data depict that the maximum percentage of daughters were married at the age of 14 years (39.7 percent), 15 years (23.1 percent) and 13 years (15.4 percent) whereas minimum percentage of marriages of daughters were also held at their age of 18 years (2.6 percent), 17 years (6.4 percent) and 16 years (12.8 percent). Therefore, the mean age of marriage of daughters is found to be estimated as 14.6 ± 1.22 years. Whereas the mean age at marriage of mothers (respondents) is also found as 14.0 years (Table 4.28). So, it is come to notice that the mean age at marriage of daughters is comparatively higher than that of mothers. This investigation also informs that due to the impact of modern education, media (T.V., Radio & Newspaper), social workers, various voluntary organizations and so on, they are slowly being demotivated from their traditional socio-cultural orthodox and try to come with the main stream of national life. Their early age at marriage is converted into adult marriage and then naturally, their total span of fertile age is going to be reduced for imparting a significant role in fertility controlling behaviour.

TABLE: 4.29
Age at Marriage of Sons and Daughters Among Saharia

Age at Marriage (Years)	*No. of Sons*	*%*	*No. of Daughters*	*%*
13	0	0.0	12	15.4
14	4	4.1	31	39.7
15	4	4.1	18	23.1
16	7	7.1	10	12.8
17	16	16.3	5	6.4
18	36	36.8	2	2.6
19	19	19.4	0	0.0
20	7	7.1	0	0.0
21	3	3.1	0	0.0
22	2	2.0	0	0.0
Total	98	100.0	78	100.0

Mean ± S.D. = 17.9 Years ± 1.41 Mean ± S.D. = 14.6 Years ± 1.22

For child bearing and rearing, age at marriage of women is considered as an important indicator. In the present study, the mean age at marriage of Saharia women is found to be 14.0 years which is low as compared to Abujhumaria (15.3 years), Hill Korwa (14.9 years), Gond (15.5 years), Kamar (14.23 years), Gonds (16.0 years), Juhar Bhotia (19.05 years), Rang Bhotia (19.01 years), Marchha Bhotia (18.71 years), Kumauni Caste (15.87

years), Bhutia Tribe (16.01 years), Brahmin (19.81 years), Rajput (18.32 years), Scheduled Caste (18.42 years), Gaddis (18.22 years), Baltis (17.5 years), Brokpas (16.8 years), Arghuns (17.7 years), Lepchas (18.08 years), Bhutias (19.20 years), Buddhists (18.46 years), Tai Turung (21.47 years), Garo (19.63 years), Dalu (15.53 years), Pnar (19.64 years), Meities (19.09 years), Muslim (16.40 years), Mao (22.7 years), High Caste Bengali (23.20 years), Mahatos (15.95 years), Mirdha (17.13 years), Malia (15.5 years) and others but high as compared to Thoti (12.88 years). As compared with reported communities (except Thoti), it is an observation that the mean age at marriage of women among Saharia is very low. The mean age at marriage of Saharia men is also very low (17.6 years) as compared to reported population groups. Due to their illiteracy, low socio-economic condition and absence of close contact with others, till now they are innocent about the negative impact of early age at marriage. Beside this, as early as possible, Saharia fathers are ready to perform the marriage of their daughters. Because, after marriage of daughters, they feel relaxation from all social as well as moral responsibilities. Fertility is declined due to late marriage (Busfield, 1972). Different studies also provide evidences that early age at marriage of girls among various communities is usually conducted and their fertility rate is comparatively higher than others. Even, the use of contraceptives has no any significant role for fertility control where early age at marriage is normally preferred (Nag, 1974; Conde, 1978; Dyson & Moore, 1983; Chaudhuri, 1984).

Duration Between Marriage and Conjugal Life

The performance of conjugal life is totally depended on socio-cultural atmosphere. After marriage, suddenly the couples are not permitted to entertain sexual intercourse among Saharia. The present study depicts that 5.7 percent, 77.2 percent and 17.1 percent respondents (couples) performed sexual restriction below 1 year, 1 year and 2 years after marriage respectively (Table 4.30). It is reported that after their marriage, some another social activities are continuously held during a stipulated period of time. Within this period, sexual intercourse is totally restricted among them. Beside this, the duration between marriage and conjugality is also depended on the age of bride. If the marriage is conducted at very early age of bride, then this duration is normally extended up to maximum according to their society approved rules and regulations. Their perception is that without completing their social activities after marriage, if they come on sexual enjoyment, then there is a maximum possibility of misfortune at any time. So, to avoid such suspense or to please the dreadful evil eyes, they generally observe abstinence during below 1 year, 1 year and sometimes 2 years. Marriage and certainly conjugality have a direct impact on the high fertility.

TABLE: 4.30
Duration Between Marriage and Conjugal Life Among Saharia

Duration in Year(s)	*Number of Couples*	*Percentage*
Below 1	19	5.7
1	257	77.2
2	57	17.1
Total	**333**	**100.0**

Interval Between Marriage and First Child Birth

Due to observe the remaining socio-cultural activities after marriage, performation of sexual intercourse is usually delayed among Saharia. The present study exhibits that child births were occurred by 5.1 percent, 61.3 percent, 26.7 percent, 6.3 percent and 0.6 percent couples after 1 year, 2 years, 3 years, 4 years and 5 years of their marriage respectively. So, the mean age of interval between marriage and first child birth is found to be estimated as 2.4 ± 1.44 years (Table 4.31). Interval between marriage and first child birth is mainly depended on age at marriage of women, age at menarche, duration of the act of sexual intercourse, etc. If sexual intercourse is performed within short period of time after marriage, then child birth is also occurred within short interval. Government officials, voluntary organizers, health workers and others occasionally visit this area and by various explanations, they try to motivate them not to bear offsprings at early age and within shorter interval after marriage. For extending the duration between marriage and first child birth, various agencies concerned to health serve pills, condoms, etc. to Saharia with free of cost. Sometimes their physical disturbance is also responsible to restrict the child birth within close interval. Shorter interval between marriage and first child birth always influences high fertility (Sahu, 2001).

TABLE: 4.31
Interval Between Marriage and First Child Birth Among Saharia

Interval in Year(s)	*Number of Couples*	*Percentage*
1	17	5.1
2	204	61.3
3	89	26.7
4	21	6.3
5	2	0.6
Total	**333**	**100.0**

Mean ± S.D. = 2.4 ± 1.44

Duration Between Menarche and First Child Birth

Menarche is a biological symbol which indicates the adultness of females to conceive. After menarche, certainly females are to be married in Saharia community. Sometimes the marriage of females is arranged before menarche and in that condition their child birth is also delayed. Duration between menarche and first child birth among Saharia is depended on the duration between menarche and marriage and also marriage and conjugality through sexual intercourse. The available data for the present study express that among them, 3.0 percent, 31.2 percent, 42.4 percent, 18.3 percent, 3.9 percent, 0.9 percent and 0.3 percent women gave birth their first child after 1 year, 2 years, 3 years, 4 years, 5 years, 6 years and 7 years duration respectively from menarche. The mean duration between menarche and first child birth is found to be measured as 2.9 ± 1.01 years among Saharia women (Table 4.32). Usually, the aged Saharia think that after attaining menarche, their daughters are matured to bear child and in that condition, they should perform their (daughters) marriage. This study also reports that some women were married before attaining menarcheal age. So, naturally their child birth was held after longer duration of marriage. If after menarche, marriage is not held within short period of time, then the occurrence of first child birth is normally delayed. Beside this, after marriage, if sexual restriction is observed during long time, then first child is also given birth after long interval. After marriage, first child birth is sometimes delayed due to adopt various family planning methods which help to extend the duration between marriage as well as menarche and first child birth. In such study of

TABLE: 4.32

Duration Between Menarche and First Child Birth of Women Among Saharia

Duration (in Years)	*Number of Women*	*Percentage*
1	10	3.0
2	104	31.2
3	141	42.4
4	61	18.3
5	13	3.9
6	3	0.9
7	1	0.3
Total	333	100.0

Mean ± S.D. = 2.9 ± 1.01

Mutharyappa (1993), a report is made that most of the children of Jenukurumba and Kadukurumba tribes of Karnataka were given birth children after two years duration of menarche of women. Shorter interval between menarche and first child birth influences high fertility.

Age Difference Between Husbands and Wives

Age difference between husband and wife is considered

as a significant contribution to the performance of fertility. The present study, conducted among Saharia confers that age difference between couples varies from 1 year to 8 years. In the study, 3 years age difference is found to be entertained by the maximum percentage of couples (28.9 percent), followed by 4 years (27.0 percent), 2 years (17.1 percent) and 5 years (13.5 years). Whereas age difference between the minimum couples is calculated as 7 years (0.6 percent), followed by 8 years (0.9 percent), 1 year (5.7 percent) and 6 years (6.3 percent). The mean age difference between all couples of Saharia is found to be estimated as 3.5 ± 1.35 years (Table 4.33). Obviously it is known that when their sons are physically fit to earn, then their fathers try to perform their marriage as early as possible. But suitable adult girls/brides are normally not selected within certain period of time. In that circumstance, marriageable males are to have patience for sometimes or even during a few years for their marriage.

TABLE: 4.33
Age Difference Between Husbands and Wives Among Saharia

Age Difference in Year (s)	*Number of Couples*	*Percentage*
1	19	5.7
2	57	17.1
3	96	28.9
4	90	27.0
5	45	13.5
6	21	6.3
7	2	0.6
8	3	0.9
Total	**333**	**100.0**

Mean ± S.D. = 3.5 Years ± 1.35

When choiceable girls are searched, then they do not care on the age factor of those girls. So longer age difference is naturally identified between the couples of such cases. Study of Sahu

(2001) reports that among Malia community of Orissa, 6.8 years is imparted as the mean age difference between spouses. Age difference among tribes is also depended on various socio-cultural beliefs, customs, norms, etc. Usually low socio-cultural status is seen to have a great impact on longer duration of age difference between couples. Marginal age difference between spouses does not have any deficiency whereas longer age difference between them sometimes yields a negative effect on their reproductive performance or capacity. Longer age difference between spouses also leads to large number of pregnancy wastage. As a result, there is a possibility to have low number of conception which always negatively effects fertility.

FERTILITY

Fertility is considered as the actual reproductive performance of women. But generally, it indicates the number of children which were produced by the women. It is defined that fertility of women is totally depended on physiological function and socio-cultural practices. Fertility potential form is influenced by physiological factors from biological angles whereas the conditioning social environment is embraced by socio-cultural factors. In simple words, fertility means the actual reproductive performance of woman or couples. Some demographers prefer to use the word natality, instead of fertility. However, attempts have been made to study the association of culture with fertility behaviour among certain tribes through social and demographic variables. These studies have taken culture as an independent variable determining the fertility behaviour. Because among different tribes, every aspect of life from birth to death is being influenced by the prevalence of customs, beliefs and notions which are practised in their day-to-day life. Though fertility is a biological phenomenon, there is a number of other factors influencing the levels and differentials of fertility among tribal groups. Various demographers usually measure the fertility differentials by taking into account women's income, occupation, education, family type, age at menarche, age at marriage, etc. (Dandekar & Dandekar, 1953; Dandekar, 1959; Roy Burman, 1961; Nag, 1962; Das, 1973; Thomson & Lewis, 1965; Vidyarthi & Rai, 1977; Sahu, 1983; Basu & Kshatriya, 1989).

MEASURES OF FERTILITY

Although there is a wide gap between the potential level of fertility (fecundity) and actual performance of the potentiality (fertility), in reality it has to rely upon the latter method for measuring the actual fertility performance. The measures of fertility ratios and rates help in understanding the relation between the general conditions of the people and level of fertility. Various fertility measures are calculated for the population understudy in order to study the trends in fertility level. An attempt is also made to study the relationship between fertility and socio-cultural factors particularly occupation, income, education, age at marriage, as these influence differential fertility.

The ability of a population to adapt to its environment depends on its fertility and population growth. Fertility is a genetic concept that encompasses a complex time – dependent process covering events ranging from exposure to intercourse and child bearing to the formation and dissolution of unions. It is basically a complex multivariate system representing a set of different reproduction strategies. Though reproduction is a biological phenomenon, levels in fertility can be influenced by socially controlled norms and practices.

Child-Women Ratio (CWR)

The child-women ratio (also called general fertility ratio) is a commonly used measure of fertility which is calculated from the age-sex distribution. Very simply, it is defined as a ratio between number of children and number of women in reproductive age group. Child-women ratio (CWR) is used as an indicator of fertility when more detailed measures are unavailable. Sometimes it is treated as the measure of effective fertility, as it does not consider the births of children dying early in life. In other words, it reflects only the number of surviving children of less than 5 years (or 9 years) of age. But this ratio is affected by distribution of women respecting to the age in the reproductive period, dramatic changes in mortality (infant and early childhood mortality) and migration, which in turn are influenced by several independent determinants of the population components. In the present study, child-women ratios for

$Co\text{-}_4/W_{15\text{-}44}$, $C_{5\text{-}9}/W_{20\text{-}49}$ and $Co\text{-}_9/W_{15\text{-}49}$ among Saharia are found to be measured as 667.78, 570.46 and 1238.25 respectively (Table 4.34). It is revealed that child-women ratio among Saharia is high (1238.25) as compared to Kamar (1141.31), Brahamin (994.38), Marcha Bhotia (770.64), Juhar Bhotia (734.46), Bhotia (1040.00), Jaunsaria (1150.00), Mao (545.45), Dalu (860.80), Pnar (869.60), Kandh (695.00), Madhya Pradesh (812.53), India (659.00) and others. In other side, child-women ratio is depicted comparatively lower than Rajput (1244.13), Scheduled Caste (1281.55), Darchula Bhotia (1285.71), Raji (1264.71), Buksha (1411.00), Tharu (1538.00) and others. Preference of male child and very less percentage of family planning adoption, low socio-cultural status, poverty, illiteracy, lack of awareness, high mortality, etc. are attributed as the reasons of their high child-women ratio.

Crude Birth Rate (CBR)

Crude birth rate (CBR) plays an important role in fertility rate. It is defined that crude birth rate is a ratio of total registered live birth to the total population, also in some specific year, also multiplied by 1000. In the present study, crude birth rate among Saharia is found to be measured as 43.76 (Table 4.34). Saharia crude birth rate is noticed comparatively higher than Bhil (43.5) Gonds (43.0), Abujhmaria (39.9), Jaunsaria (32.0), Kumauni Caste (26.23), Marchas (35.98), Johari (15.64), Dharchula (24.16), Bhotia (23.54), Marcha Bhotia (35.98), Bodhs (24.46), Baltis (23.57), Brokpas (27.17), Arghuns (14.25), Muslim Gujjar (42.2), Brahmin (25.8), Rajput (21.7), Gaddis (28.4), Santal (37.2), Lodha (31.2), Kora (41.81), Dudh Kharia (38.5), Madhya Pradesh (35.1), India (32.7) and others but lower than Kamar (53.04), Lohar Gadiyas (44.3), Raji (46.03), Buksha (61.14), Juhar Bhotia (48.21), Rang Bhotia (53.61), Scheduled Caste (48.8) and others. The male sex preference, paucity of family planning methods adoption, illiteracy, etc. are contaminated as the reasons of very high crude birth rate among Saharia. It may be attributed that low socio-economic status, early age at marriage, transitional life from food gathering to food producing stages, high infant and child mortality, etc. are the reasons of high crude birth rate (Barua, 1992; Kshatriya et.al., 1993; Kapoor, 1996; Yadav, et.al, 2001). Crude birth rate is also influenced by education, medical facility, communication system, environmental condition, financial status, family size, etc. (Davis & Blake, 1956). Crude birth rate is implicated with marriage, conception, induced abortion, postpartum infacundability, etc. Even high fertility is entertained for preferring to particular sex specially in developing countries (Bongaarts & Potter, 1983; Arnold, 1992).

General Fertility Rate (GFR)

The simplest over all age limited measure is defined as general fertility rate (GFR), accounted as the number of births of per 1000 women who are in child bearing age. General fertility rate does not indicate a definite pattern except that though the crude birth rate is moderate, general fertility rate is high. This makes a hint that the number of women in 15-49 age group is less as compared to the total population. In the present study, general fertility rate among Saharia is found to be measured as 244.96 (Table 4.34) which is comparatively higher than Gonds (229.88), Kamar (177.02), Lohar Gadiyas (76.17) Jaunsarias (125.0), Kumauni Castes (108.87), Marchhas (128.44), Johari (56.49), Dharchulas (95.23), Bhotia Tribe (86.48), Raji (213.2), Juhari Bhotia (175.2), Marcha Bhotia (162.41), Rang Bhotia (186.4), Bodhs (95.70), Baltis (98.59), Brokpas (119.05), Arghuns (49.81), Muslim Gujjar (18.70), Brahmin (93.3), Rajput (83.9), Scheduled Caste (201.5), Gaddis (110.5), Santal (168.0), Lodha (133.3), Dudh Kharia (164.0), Thoti (132.62), Soliga (188.0), Madhya Pradesh (140.01), India (166.6) and others. Early age at marriage, illiteracy, less family planning adoption, socio-cultural disadvantage, etc. are the attributed reasons of high general fertility rate among Saharia.

Age Specific Fertility Rate (ASFR)

Age specific fertility rates (ASFR) reveal the distribution of frequencies of birth among women according to age. It is more accurate than the estimation of crude birth rate. This is due to the fact that only the women in child bearing age are considered here and not the whole population, the emphasis being made to a specific period of time in relation to live births and women. In a population, a detailed picture of fertility at a specified time/period can be obtained by examining the schedules of age specific fertility rates, since the age of mother is an important factor affecting the fertility level and the rate of child bearing is not uniform throughout all ages. In fact, fertility is usually heavily concentrated between ages 20 to 29 years. In the present study among Saharia, age specific fertility rate is found to be measured as highest (328.35) in those women who are in 20-24 years age group, followed by 269.84 (25-29 years), 264.73 (15-19 years), 222.22 (30-34 years), 130.43 (35-39 years), and 125.00 (40-44 years) whereas the women of 45-49 age group do not have any age specific fertility rate (Table 4.34). The highest age specific fertility rate of India is reported as 314.5 in those reproductive mothers who are in the age group of 20-24 years. It is also reported that in population groups, the highest age specific fertility rates vary from 20-29 age group (SRS, 1993). Since the relatively high fertile reproductive periods are observed in the age group of 20-29 years and women in that age group may be encouraged to adopt family planning devices. But due to paucity of family planning adoption, higher fertility in the stated age group is entertained among Saharia.

Total Fertility Rate (TFR)

The total fertility rate (TFR) presents a single index of total fertility. It is the sum of age specific birth rates of women, at each age group from 15 to 49 years. The total fertility rate represents the same population of women as a general fertility rate, but takes account of the distribution of the year's births among women of different ages. Hence, it is a far more effective measure of summarizing the frequency of births of a particular year. This method is concerned itself only to women who are in fertile age group. Among Saharia, total fertility rate and total fertility rate per woman are found to be measured as 6702.70 and 6.70 respectively (Table 4.34). Further, total fertility rate per woman among Saharia is revealed higher when compared to Halba (5.89), Madia (6.00), Muria Gond (5.10), Lohar Gadiyas (4.60), Muria (5.64), Bnaria (5.95), Kamar (4.6), Jaunsarias (3.84), Kumauni Caste (3.08), Marchas (4.20), Johari (1.93), Dharchulas (2.68), Bhotia Tribe (2.75), Buksha (5.70), Juhar Bhotia (6.20), Marcha Bhotia (6.30), Rang Bhotia (5.80), Bodhs (2.79), Baltis (3.12), Brokpas (3.09), Arghuns (1.66), Brahmin (3.29), Rajput (3.27), Scheduled Caste (5.91), Gaddis (3.51), War Khasi (6.11),

Santal (5.5), Lodha (3.3), Kondh (3.60), Dudh Kheria (5.39), Mirdha (3.41), Manue Kolam (5.51), Chenchu (5.7), Yanadi (4.10), Thoti (3.40), Kota (3.73), Irula (5.03), Madhya Pradesh (4.90), India (3.60) and others but lower when compared to Raji (7.40) and others. Low socio-economic status, high extent of illiteracy, male sex preference, high infant and child hood mortality, family planning less adoption, early age at marriage, etc. may be mentioned as the important reasons of their high total fertility rate per women.

Gross Reproduction Rate (GRR)

Gross reproduction rate (GRR) indicates the average number of female children expected to be born per women during her entire reproductive span, if there is no mortality and the fertility schedules represented by the age specific fertility rate continue to remain the same. In other words, this rate suggests how effectively mothers are replacing themselves with daughters (ignoring mortality), who would bear the next generation. Hence, this is also considered as the replacement index. In the present study, gross reproduction rate and gross reproduction rate per woman among Saharia are observed to be estimated as 2742.25 and 2.74 respectively (Table 4.34). Gross reproduction rate per woman among Saharia is found to be comparatively higher than Kamar (2.36), Kumauni Caste (1.50), Marchas (2.04), Johari (0.94), Dharchulas (1.31), Bhotia Tribe (1.34), Bodhs (1.70), Baltis (1.53), Brokpas (1.55), Arghuns (0.38), Kandh (1.44), Thoti (1.84), Madhya Pradesh (2.00), India (1.70) and others but lower than Raji (3.54) and others. Early age at marriage of female, very low spread of literacy, high infant and childhood deaths, low socio-economic status, etc. may be attributed as the reasons of their high gross reproduction rate.

Mean Age of Child Bearing (MACB)

The mean age of child bearing (MACB) indicates the average age of child bearing of women. Differences in the pattern of child bearing can be measured in terms of mean age of child bearing or fertility. It describes the age pattern of fertility of a synthetic cohort of hypothetical group of women, viewed as having in their life times similar fertility experience recorded in the calendar year. In general, it is understood that high mean age of child bearing usually influences high fertility of population and a substantial fraction of total fertility relates to the latter years of child bearing. On the other hand, in low fertility populations, the mean age is lower and a small fraction of total fertility occurs in latter years of child bearing. In the present study, the mean age of child bearing of women among Saharia is found to be estimated as 29.30 years (Table 4.34) which is comparatively higher than Kamar (29.23), Brahmin (27.16), Rajput (24.60), Scheduled Caste (26.59), Kumauni (25.84), Johari (27.28), Dharchulas (24.93), Bhotias (27.93), Brahmin of Himachal Pradesh (29.30), Rajput of Himachal Pradesh (28.81), Bodhs (26.6), Brokpas (25.20), Arghuns (25.20), Chhetris (23.01), Limboos (26.37), Scheduled Caste of Sikkim (27.84), Madhya Pradesh (26.9), India (27.4) and others but lower than Marchas (30.46), Scheduled Caste of Himachal Pradesh (32.62), Gaddis (29.61), Baltis (30.50), Lepchas (31.64), Bhutias (30.20), Buddhists (30.93) and others. Early age at marriage, low socio-cultural status, high infant and child mortality, etc. may be attributed as the reasons of their high mean age of child bearing.

MARITAL FERTILITY RATE (MFR)

All the women in the fertile age do not participate in the reproduction, particularly in countries where tradition and customs do not permit the unmarried women to become mothers. Hence, the actual populations at risk of potential child bearing are currently married women of the fertile age groups. Marital status of women is indicated by martial fertility rate (MFR). It defines the fertility rate of those married women who are in wed-lock status.

General Marital Fertility Rate (GMFR)

The general marital fertility rate (GMFR) is a more refined measure which takes into account the number of married women (in wed-lock) in the child bearing age. It is a better fertility measure than general fertility rate (GFR). General marital fertility rate is important in the Indian societies as only marital fertility is socially and legally recognized. The general marital fertility rate among Sahara is found to be measured as 248.29 (Table 4.34). The general marital fertility rate among Saharia is depicted comparatively higher than Kamar (231.41), Brahmins (144.75), Rajputs (162.33), Kumauni (165.6), Marchas (194.44), Johari (90.9), Dharchulas (135.59), Raji (227.64), Brahmin of Himachal Pradesh (122.2), Rajput of Himachal Pradesh (115.0), Scheduled Caste of Himachal Pradesh (236.8), Gaddis (145.1), Bodhs (144.4), Baltis (137.3), Brokpas (153.9), Arghuns (75.60), Lepchas (141.3), Bhutia (154.93), Buddhist (148.51), Chhetris (211.53), Limbroos (117.65), Kandh (213.11), Madhya Pradesh (185.00), India (173.60) and others but lower than Scheduled Caste of Sikkim (297.30) and others. Saharia general marital fertility rate is noticed high. Paucity of family planning adoption, early age at marriage, illiteracy, etc. may be contaminated as the reasons of their high general marital fertility rate.

Age Specific Marital Fertility Rate (ASMFR)

Another measure of fertility computed for ('currently') married women (in wed-lock) for different age groups is the age specific martial fertility rates (ASMFR). The age patterns of marital fertility rates for Saharia are observed to be measured as 264.70, 328.35, 269.84, 222.22, 136.36 and 62.50 in those married women who are in the age groups of 15-19 years, 20-24 years, 25-29 years, 30-34 years, 35-39 years and 40-44 years respectively (Table 4.34). Whereas the women of 45-49 years age group do not present any age specific fertility rate. The age pattern of marital fertility rate for India is also nearly similar to the pattern of age specific fertility rate found among Saharia. It is also found to be recorded that age specific marital fertility rate is very high in those women who are in the age group of 15-29 years (SRS, 1993). Early age at marriage, illiteracy, very less use of family planning methods, etc. may be perhaps as the reasons of their high age specific marital fertility rate.

Total Marital Fertility Rate (TMFR)

Like total fertility rate, the total marital fertility rate (TMFR) is the cumulative value of age specific marital fertilities at the end of the reproductive period. It indicates the average number of children expected to be born per married woman during the entire span of reproductive period, if the age specific marital fertility rates (on which the rate is based) continue to be the same and there is no mortality. The total marital fertility rate and total marital fertility rate per woman among Saharia is found to be measured as 6419.85 and 6.41 respectively (Table4.34). This study also presents that Saharia total marital fertility rate per woman (6.41) is found comparatively higher than Kamar (6.34), Brahmins (3.01), Rajputs (4.80), Scheduled Caste (5.31), Kumauni Caste (4.75), Marchas (5.61), Juhar Bhotia (4.14), Dharchulas (2.8), Bhotia (4.29), Bodhs (5.20), Baltis (3.50), Brokpas (6.0), Arghuns (2.90), Madhya Pradehs (5.30), India (4.90) and others but lower than Raji (7.38), Kandh (6.70) and others. High extent of illiteracy, early age at marriage, paucity of family planning adoption, male sex preference, etc. are the attributed reasons of their high total marital fertility rate per woman.

Gross Reproduction Rate (GRR) in Wed-Lock

In relation to martial status, the gross reproduction rate (GRR) indicates the live birth female children of per thousand women who are in wed-lock condition. The gross reproduction rate is the average number of daughter that would be born to a woman (in wed-lock) during her life time if she passed through the child bearing ages experiencing the average age specific fertility pattern of a given period (often a year). The gross reproduction rate was widely used in the 1930s and 1940s as an indicator of fertility trends whereas the total fertility rate is more often quoted in current work (Wilson, 1985). Simply, this rate suggests how effectively mothers are replacing themselves with daughters (ignoring mortality) who would bear the next generation. Hence this is also considered as replacement index. The gross reproduction rate and gross reproduction rate per woman among Saharia are found to be estimated as 2752.15 and 2.75 respectively (Table 4.34). Low level of socio-cultural status, high extent of illiteracy, early age at marriage, high infant and child mortality, etc. are the attributed reasons of their high gross reproduction rate.

TABLE: 4.34
Measures of Fertility Among Saharia

Sl. No.	*Fertility Indicators*	*Calculation*
1	Child-Women Ratio (CWR) of (0-4) years	667.78
	Child-Women Ratio (CWR) of (5-9) years	570.46
	Child-Women Ratio (CWR) of (0-9) years	1238.25
2	Crude Birth Rate (CBR)	43.76
3	General Fertility Rate (GFR)	244.96
4	Max. Age Specific Fertility Rate (ASFR) of (20-24) years	328.35
	Min. Age Specific Fertility Rate (ASFR) of (40-44) years	125.00
	No. Age Specific Fertility Rate (ASFR) of (45-49) years	0.00
5	Total Fertility Rate (TFR) per Women	6.70
6	Gross Reproduction Rate (GRR) per Women	2.74
7	Mean Age of Child Bearing (MACB)	29.30
8	General Marital Fertility Rate (GMFR)	248.29
9	Max. Age Specific Marital Fertility Rate (ASMFR) of (20-24 years)	328.35
	Min. Age Specific Marital Fertility Rate (ASMFR) of (40-44) years	62.50
	No. Age Specific Marital Fertility Rate (ASMFR) of 45-59) years	0.00
10	Total Marital Fertility Rate (TMFR) per women	6.41
11	Gross Reproduction Rate (GRR) per Women in Wed-lock	2.75

Lastly, the present study points out that Saharia are the members who belong to traditional society. Most of them are illiterates and positioned under socio-economically backward condition. Still now, occupational status of a major group is found in transitional life from food gathering to food producing stages. They lag behind in the field of education and have achieved very little literacy rate. As per their marital status is concerned, they are to be married at very young age. In respecting to the traditional socio-cultural orthodox, large number of Saharia prefer to conduct frequently births of male child. They are not aware to the sanitation and their living standard is very low. Due to paucity of proper medical facility, their still birth, infant and child mortality rates are noticed as very high. In the context of family planning, modern birth control devices are rarely adopted by them. So, illiteracy, low socio-cultural life, poor economic status indicating transitional life from food gathering to food producing stages, early age at marriage, insanitation, paucity of medical facility, family planning non-adoption, etc. are the transgressed reasons of their high child-women ratio, crude birth rate, general fertility rate, age specific fertility rate, total fertility rate, gross reproduction rate, general marital fertility rate, age specific marital fertility rate, total marital fertility rate and gross reproduction rate of women in wed-lock. Under these circumstances, it is highly suggested to implement urgently the long time multi-stages development schemes which will not only improve their educational as well as socio-economic status but also smoothly motivate them to come on better status of fertility.

DIFFERENTIAL FERTILITY

In any society, the performance of differential fertility behaviour of women is affected by both socio-cultural and biological factors. For identifying these fertility differential factors, the intensive micro-level field studies have been conducted among Saharia. In the study, an attempt is made to examine the various factors which are responsible for their differential fertility. The mean number of children ever born (per ever married woman) is estimated under the study. The children ever born is installed the same as the parity of a woman. Apart from the number of children ever born, the number of children surviving (currently living children per ever married woman) is additionally studied. It may be mentioned here that this variable is also utilized to estimate the child loss per woman (discussed latter in this chapter). It is an observation that the differentials in mean number of children surviving (still living) are smaller than the differentials in mean number of children ever born. The occurrences of high fertility and relatively high levels of infant and child mortality among Saharia may be caused in this trend. In this regard, it is a statement that several independent determinants may influence the fertility level in the study populations. The collected information between all these are discussed in the following manner:

Fertility Differentials by Land Holding Pattern

Among rural populations, the land ownership or size of land owned by the households is considered as the important indicator of economic resources, as well as the possible role of the same population processes. For the present study among Saharia, the mean number of children ever born increases as the size of land holding (household) increases. Among them, it is noticed that relatively large ownership of land (4 acres >) may be contributing to the increasing in mean number of children ever born (4.00) and reversely, no land or relatively small size of land owned tends to comparatively the lower mean number of children ever born (3.70 or 3.05). Both land less and land ownership groups (4 acres >) require more children for labouring and excess agriculture respectively (Table 4.35). So, ultimately their mean number of children ever born is found comparatively higher than others.

In other side, relatively larger size of land ownership (4 acres >) tends to the high mean number of children surviving (3.50) whereas no ownership of land (Table 4.35) or comparatively low size of land ownership (1 acre <) tends to low mean number of children surviving (2.83 or 2.82). The variation may be attributed that due to large size of land, more children may have certain economic benefits. The land less small farmers may be limiting the family size since the small amount of land owned may get further fragmented. Additionally, some of the observations are conducted in the area and implicated that some people have not owning land or little land, they have no relatively high economic standing. But others are benefited by owing to the emergence of other allied activities or services as promising economic pursuits and in this regard, an assessment is made that certain socio-cultural attributes are not responsible for fertility conducive.

So, the differentials in mean number of children surviving per woman by size of household land among landless is low and the estimation seems to increase with increase in size of land holding. It is observed that there is an increase in the number of children surviving with the increase in size of landholding, similar to the pattern of differentials in number of children ever born with reference to land ownership.

TABLE: 4.35
Fertility Differential by Land Holding Pattern Among Saharia

Land Holding (in Acre)	*Mean No. of Children Ever Born*	*Mean No. of Children Surviving*
Land Less	3.70	2.83
<1	3.05	2.82
1-2	3.12	2.87
2-3	3.40	2.90
3-4	3.66	3.00
4 >	4.00	3.50

Fertility Differential by Types of Residence

The type and quality of residences are an aggregate of determinants which characterize the immediate physical environment of human beings. These also indicate the level of living standard or the socio-economic status of households or some other extents. In dynamics of population components, the impact of housing condition have a significant role. In the present study among Saharia, the available data depict that relatively better housing condition (good) contributes the decreasing mean number of children ever born (3.56) whereas very poor quality of residences (Table 4.36) confer comparatively the increasing mean number of children ever born (4.10). The number of families is very high but the family status is very low in very poor and poor quality of residences. Whenever, the couples go out for work, then either they have to carry on their infants or drop out at home without any supported persons or care takers. For avoiding this unhealthy situation, they beget more offsprings for providing a supporting responsibility to elders for younger groups. In this regard, the mean number of children ever born is increased in very poor and poor quality of residences (Singh, 1986; Mahadevan, 1989)

In other side, the mean number of children surviving increases as the quality of residence increases. Good or medium quality of residences tend to increase Table 4.36) the high mean number of children surviving (3.10 or 3.21) whereas very poor quality of residences have a tendency to influence low mean number of children surviving (2.66). So, it is noticed that the mean number of children ever born and mean number of children surviving are influenced by the quality of residences. Due to insanitation, mosquitoes attack, etc., the very poor quality of residences are not saved for living and as a result, its mean number of children surviving is comparatively lower than others (Bhasin, 1990; Nag, 1998).

TABLE: 4.36
Fertility Differential by Types of Residence Among Saharia

Sl. No.	*Types of Residences*	*Mean No. of Children Ever Born*	*Mean No. of Children Surviving*
1.	Thatched(Very Poor)	4.10	2.66
2.	Bamboo Made(Poor)	3.59	2.76
3.	Wooden (Medium)	3.98	3.21
4.	Cemented (Good)	3.56	3.10

Fertility Differential by Types of Transportation

Most of the Saharia inhabitat villages are settled on undulating hilly-forest region and there, transport system is very poor (except the village Bijli Ghor and Prem Nagar). Transportation by bus or jeep is totally absent there. Due to comparatively better financial condition, a few service holders are able to transport by two wheeler and also bicycle. But due to financial problem, the maximum Saharia transport by foot and bullock cart. Comparatively better socio-cultural status, literacy in different educational levels, high adoption of birth control devices, etc., are the attributed reasons which influence the low mean number of children ever born (Table 4.37) of two wheeler (3.54) and bicycle (3.59) users and vice-versa for foot (4.13) and bullock cart (3.97) users.

In other side, due to provide adequate medical facilities, nutritional foods, better living standard, etc., the mean number of children surviving are found to be comparatively higher (Table 4.37) in those who use two wheeler (3.19) and bicycle (3.12) and vice-versa for foot (2.69) and bullock cart (2.73) users. It is substantial that the communication facilities in terms of improved transports not only increase mobility but also these are responsible for new ideas about family formation. Inadequate transportation plays a significant role for arresting development activities (Miro & Potter, 1980; Bhasin, 1990).

TABLE: 4.37
Fertility Differential by Types of Transportation Among Saharia

S.No.	*Types of Transportation*	*Mean No. of Children Ever Born*	*Mean No. of Children Surviving*
1.	Bicycle	3.59	3.12
2	Two Wheeler	3.54	3.19
3	Bullock Cart	3.97	2.73
4	On Foot	4.13	2.69

Fertility Differential by Sources of Water

Sources of water collection indicate the quality of water which have an impact in fertility differential. For the present study among Saharia, comparatively the higher mean number of children ever born (3.83) is found to be estimated in those households who collect water from pond (Table 4.38), whereas the water of tube-well tends to increase lower mean number of children ever born (3.46). Generally the literate persons in various educational levels are more or less acquainted with the quality of water in regarding the sources. Influencing with the formal education, most of them try to form small family size by adopting various family planning methods. So, usually their mean number of children ever born is low as compared to others.

But in case of the mean number of children surviving, the water of tub-well tends to increase comparatively higher (2.96), followed by 3.85 (well and tube-well), 2.79 (well). The mean number of children surviving have a tendency to be increased lower (2.75) in those households who arrange water from pond (Table 4.38). In Saharia inhabitat areas, more or less good quality of water is available only in tube-well as compared with well and pond. The mean number of children surviving is high (2.96) in those households who use the water of tube-well. It may be attributed that the water of tube-well is purified and by the use of this water, their children are saved from water borne and infectious diseases. So, it forms a real ground that the quality of water and the mean number of children surviving are positively correlated among Saharia.

TABLE: 4.38

Fertility Differential by Sources of Water Among Saharia

Sl. No.	*Sources of Water*	*Mean No. of Ever Children Born*	*Mean No. of Children Surviving*
1	Well	3.67	2.79
2	Tube-well	3.46	2.96
3	Well & Tube-well	3.65	2.85
4	Pond	3.83	2.75

Fertility Differential by Types of Mass Media

The available data for the present study express that when television or radio or newspaper is used in Saharia houses or in their immediate neighbourhood (Table 4.39), then the mean number of children ever born is found low (3.40 at aggregate level) as compared to non-users (3.81). Hence, it appears that the expose of mass-media is often considered important in influencing the population components, may also have certain bearing in the study areas. It is further noticed that those who experience more media exposure have lower number of child births, desire fewer children and tend not to emphasize traditional reasons, such as, by preference for wanting another child and intend to use family planning methods sooner (Kagicipasi, 1979).

In other side, the present study defines that when television or radio or newspaper is used, the mean number of children surviving (Table 4.39) is found relatively high (2.87 at aggregate level) as compared to non-users (2.80). Mass-media users are so much benefited by following the proper child caring and rearing, nutritional food for child, the way of prevention of some diseases, etc. Getting an ideal achievement, they are enabled to practise remedial components which enhance their mean number of children surviving. Beside this, an exclusive observation retains that television viewers have a comparatively higher mean number of children survival (2.96) than .radio (2.82) and newspaper (2.85) users. Clarification incurred of this aspect presents that in tribal area, the various programmes of television are viewed with more interest and the viewers can easily remind the maximum outcomes as compared to the activities covered by radio programmes and newspaper. So, it may be assessed that the television programme is found as tremendous one which effectively maximizes the higher mean number of children surviving.

TABLE: 4.39
Fertility Differential by Types of Mass Media Used Among Saharia

SL. No.	Types of Mass Media Used	Mean No. of Born Children Ever	Mean No. of Children Surviving
1.	Television	3.48	2.96
2.	Radio	3.32	2.82
3.	News Paper	3.42	2.85
4.	Not Used any	3.81	2.80

Fertility Differential by Types of Movie Viewed

Cinema hall is not existed all over the Saharia inhabitat area They generally watch the various movies from video hall and television which are more or less available in their locality. In very rarely cases, a few Saharia watch movies from cinema halls of Gwalior district city. In this context, the present study depicts that the mean number of children ever born tends to increase high among the heads of households of move viewers (3.77 at aggregate level). It may be attributed that after enjoying various movies (specially sex and romantic), they get excitement which effects in the act of fertility performance. Beside this, comparatively the higher (Table 4.40) mean number of children ever born (3.95) is recorded among sex related movie viewers as compared to violence & war (3.75 each), romantic (3.61) and social (3.58). As a reason, it is explained that sex related movie viewers are more excited than others. They are influenced to conduct frequently sexual intercourse which increases high fertility.

TABLE: 4.40
Fertility Differential by Types of Movie Viewed Among Saharia

Sl. No.	*Types of Watched Movie*	*Mean No. of Children Ever Born*	*Mean No. of Children Surviving*
1	Romantic	3.61	2.93
2	Sex	3.95	2.95
3	Social	3.58	2.80
4	War	3.75	2.45
5	Violence	3.75	2.75
6	Not Watched any	3.63	2.83

In this study, the available data are also enabled to show that the mean number of children surviving among the heads of households of non-movie viewer (Table 4.40) tends to increase high (2.83) as compared to different types of move viewers (2.77 at aggregate level). Paucity of child caring and rearing awareness, financial problem, insanitation, etc. may be mentioned as the possible reasons of their comparatively low mean number of children surviving. Even the mean number of children surviving varies in accordance with the types of movie viewers. Due to the different reasons as explained, the mean number of children surviving tends to increase from 2.45 (war), 2.75 (violence), 2.80 (social), 2.93 (romantic) to 2.95 (sex) among Saharia.

Fertility Differential by Family Types

Family formation is a very significant approach for conferring the ideal size of the family. The mean number of children ever born and mean number of children surviving are varied in accordance with the types of family. In the present study among Saharia, it is observed that the mean number of children ever born is comparatively higher (Table 4.41) in nuclear families (3.68) than joint families (3.37). As a reason, it may be stated that in joint families, young couples are frequently separated, so that coital frequencies are minimized and the chances of conception is correspondingly reduced (Nag, 1965).

TABLE: 4.41

Fertility Differential by Family Types Among Saharia

Sl. No.	*Type of Families*	*Mean No. of Children Ever Born*	*Mean No. of Children Surviving*
1.	Nuclear Families	3.68	2.86
2.	Joint Families	3.37	2.68

Further the mean number of children surviving is found comparatively lower (Table 4.41) in joint families (2.68) than nuclear families (2.86). Among Saharia, the traditional socio-cultural orthodox is highly appreciated by the members of joint families. Even inspiring with their socio-cultural rules and regulations, they usually prefer to get the medical facility for ailment from their traditional healer. Unscientific treatment for their children is no more enough and even sometimes it tends to decrease their child surviving. Various studies conducted in various parts of India support that the mean number of children ever born is high in nuclear families as compared with joint families. Lack of privacy of the couples, financial problem, traditional belief to the socio-cultural norms, etc. are the attributed reasons of low mean number of children surviving (Bhasin, 1990; Sengupta & Chakravarty, 1995; Choudhary & Devi, 1997).

Fertility Differential by Occupations of Wives (Respondents)

Considering the occupational status and fertility, it is revealed that among Saharia, the women, engaged in food gathering occupation have the highest mean number of children ever born (3.85), followed by 3.78 (tribal craft), 3.67 (agriculture), etc. (Table 4.42). In other side, the lowest mean number of children ever born is recorded in beggar family (3.00). Food gathering is a traditional occupation which often requires minimum or nil educational qualification and do not perceive the upward occupational mobility and also this is conducive to large family size. Beside this, women with tribal craft and agriculture need more working hands which tend to have a high mean number of children ever born (Bhasin, 1990; Choudhury & Devi, 1997; Chachra & Bhasin, 1998; Nag, 1998; Majumder-Paul, 2001). The lowest mean number of children ever born of the women, engaged in begging occupation may not be determined due to very little sample size.

TABLE: 4.42
Fertility Differential by Occupations of Wives Among Saharia

Sl. No.	*Types of Occupation*	*Mean No. of Children Ever Born*	*Mean No. of Children Surviving*
1	Food Gathering	3.85	2.71
2	Animal Husbandry	3.50	2.83
3	Agriculture	3.67	2.90
4	Daily Labour	3.65	2.73
5	Tribal Craft	3.78	2.84
6	Household Work	3.63	3.14
7	Begging	3.00	2.00

In this study, the highest mean number of children surviving (3.14) is comprised in those women who involve in household work, followed by 2.90 (agriculture), 2.84 (tribal craft), etc. (Table 4.42). The women with household work occupation are comparatively better in financial position and always concentrated to continue the domestic activities including proper child caring and rearing, fresh and nutritional food feeding to their children, etc. which have a great impact to increase their high mean number of children surviving. Due to financial problem, the women, practised begging occupation are unable to provide the nutritional foods, medical facility, etc. to the children and as a result, they are failed to achieve the high mean number of children surviving.

Fertility Differential by Occupations of Husbands (Respondents)

The mean number of children ever born and children surviving are always varied in accordance with the types of occupation among Saharia. The highest mean number of children ever born is found to be recorded in those husbands (Table 4.43) who practise hunting occupation (4.00), followed by 3.73 (bonded labour), 3.71 (agriculture), etc. Among Saharia, hunting is a traditional occupation and most of the husbands, involved in this occupation are illiterate. Due to their illiteracy, they have no any intention to reduce family size. Even, they are not exposed to adopt any family planning methods, so their mean number of children ever born is come to notice high as compared with other occupation practitioners (Choudhury & Devi, 1997; Nag, 1996; Majumder, 2001). Due to admixture with the other caste groups, literate in various educational levels, large extent of family planning adoption, etc., the husbands of service (3.33) and other occupations tend to achieve lower mean number of children ever born.

The mean number of children surviving is implied to be higher (Table 4.43) when husbands are service holders (3.11), followed by 3.00 each (business and hunting). The service holders are not only educated but also they are in comparatively better financial position. So, due to better financial position, they are aware to the proper child caring and rearing by providing the safe delivery, nutritional foods, medical facility, etc. which have a positive impact on their high mean number of children surviving. The husbands of food gathering occupation are illiterate and they are always facing financial problem. In other side, by influencing with their old thinking, they take the medical facility from their indigenous traditional healer and for their financial problem, they are not able to purchase the nutritional foods and other required commodities which tend to reduce their mean number of children surviving (2.60). So, the present study makes a clear statement that the types of occupation and the mean number of children ever born and mean number of children surviving are positively correlated with each other.

TABLE: 4.43

Fertility Differential by Occupations of Husbands Among Saharia

SL. No.	*Types of Occupation*	*Mean No. of Children Ever Born*	*Mean No. of Children Surviving*
1.	**Hunting**	4.00	3.00
2.	Food Gathering	3.40	2.60
3.	Animal Husbandry	3.60	2.81
4.	Agriculture	3.71	2.92
5.	Daily Labour	3.65	2.80
6.	Bonded Labour	3.73	2.73
7.	Craft	3.68	2.85
8.	Business	3.50	3.00
9.	Service	3.33	3.11

Fertility Differential by Household Income

The present study exhibits that among Saharia, the mean number of children ever born decreases with an increase of annual income. The mean number of children ever born is specifically found to be highest (3.89) when annual income is almost lowest (Rs.3000/- to 3500/-), followed by 3.81 (Rs.3500/- to Rs.4000/- and 3.79 (Rs4000/- to 4500/-) whereas lowest mean number of children ever born (3.00) is achieved in that household whose annual income is estimated below Rs.3000/- (Table 4.44). It may be attributed that the largely rural set-up and relatively low level of development of the study areas, in general, are the reasons of encouragement to those households who are with relatively low income and desire more children. Beside this, the low income groups are mostly illiterate and living in socio-cultural backward position and also they are not aware to use the birth control devices which enhance their high mean number of children ever born (Nag, 1998).

TABLE: 4.44

Fertility Differential by Household Income Among Saharia

Imcome (in Rupees)	*Mean No. of Children Ever Born*	*Mean No. of Children Surviving*
<3000	3.00	2.00
3000-3500	3.89	2.67
3500-4000	3.81	2.74
4000-4500	3.79	2.89
4500-5000	3.71	2.73
5000-5500	3.66	2.94
5500-6000	3.64	2.81
6000-6500	3.63	2.85
6500-7000	3.66	2.82
7000-7500	3.61	2.80
7500-8000	3.70	2.90
8000-8500	5.53	2.79
8500-9000	3.57	2.88
9000-9500	3.48	3.07
9500-10000	3.46	3.12
10000>	3.44	3.13

Further this study prepares that the mean number of children surviving increases with the increase of income. Above Rs.10000/- annual household income groups are enabled to show the highest mean number of children surviving (3.13), followed by

3.12 (Rs.9500/- to 10000/-), 3.07 (Rs.9000/- to 9500/-), etc. (Table 4.44) whereas below Rs.3000/- annual household income group tends to have the lowest mean number of children surviving (2.00). The higher mean number of children ever born and lower mean number of children surviving are found in comparatively low income group than in high income group (Agarwala, 1966). Specially for rural families, the initial effect of increased income is likely to be an improvement in health and nutritional levels which can significantly increase the mean number of children surviving (Ridkar, 1969; Chachra & Bhasin, 1998; Nag, 1998; Maheo & Kalla, 2000).

Fertility Differential by Clanwise Distribution of Families

The available data for the present study make an existence of total 21 clans among Saharia. The highest mean number of children ever born is found to be gained in Shonoria clan (5.00), followed by 4.05 (Jaborolia), 4.00 each (Digoria & Ghoria), 3.97 (Badratia), 3.83 (Kheria), etc. (Table 4.45) whereas Dongia, Negtelia and Sholonki clans reveal the achievement of lowest mean number of children ever born (3.00 each). It is informed that socio-cultural rules and regulations are varied from one to another clan. Some clan members are totally illiterate and in respecting to their socio-cultural orthodox, they do not use the modern family planning methods and as an effect, their mean number of children ever born is recorded comparatively higher than those who use family planning methods.

In other side, the maximum mean number of children surviving is found to be measured in Shonoria clan (4.00), Ghoria clan (3.33), Badratia clan (3.15), etc. whereas Dongia clan (2.00), Deboria clan (2.20), Sholonki clan (2.25), etc. (Table 4.45) produce the minimum mean number of children surviving. It is mentioned that some clan members are literate in different educational levels and they are financially advanced as compared to others. They are capable to expense a part of amount for their child care which enhances child survival. Clan by determining access to health, nutritional level, education, etc. facilities influence their high mean number of children surviving and vice-versa (Sharma & Sharma, 1999).

TABLE: 4.45
Fertility Differential by Clan-wise Distribution of Families Among Saharia

SL. No.	Name of Clans	Mean No. of Children Ever Born	Mean No. of Children Surviving
1.	Shoria	3.50	2.70
2.	Gobaria	3.77	2.94
3.	Kheria	3.83	2.97
4.	Monia	3.60	2.80
5.	Belhoria	3.22	2.44
6.	Digoria	4.00	3.00
7.	Shelia	3.42	2.57
8.	Deboria	3.00	2.20
9.	Ataria	3.66	2.88
10.	Dhoria	3.48	2.65
11.	Dongia	3.00	2.00
12.	Negtelia	3.00	2.50
13.	Norboia	3.20	2.40
14.	Barodia	3.55	2.70
15.	Badratia	3.97	3.15
16.	Jaborolia	4.05	2.94
17.	Sholonki	3.00	2.25
18.	Paria	3.33	2.66
19.	Ghoria	4.00	3.33
20.	Shonoria	5.00	4.00
21.	Chandia	3.81	2.90

Fertility Differential by Education of Wives (Respondents)

Most of the Saharia women are illiterate. Only a few wives are literate but their different educational levels are failed to reach in high school standard. Education of wives has a significant role in fertility performance. In the present study among Saharia, the collected information show that literate in different higher educational levels is far less common. Except a few women, all are illiterate and their mean number of children ever born is found to be higher (3.67) than the literate women (Table 4.46) in various education levels (2.66 at aggregate level). Even among literate women, the lower mean number of children ever born (2.00) is begotten by the women of middle school educational level than lower primary and upper primary (3.00 each). Education may be said to be affecting fertility directly or indirectly but through various indirect channels, such as higher age at marriage, age at first child birth, greater knowledge pertaining to fertility regulation, etc. control the mean number of children ever born. Even duration of schooling i.e. levels of education tends to influence the mean number of children ever born (Choudhury & Devi, 1997; Das & Saikia, 1999; Maheo & Kalla, 2000).

TABLE: 4.46

Fertility Differential by Education of Wives Among Saharia

SL. No.	*Wife's Educational Level*	*Mean No. of Children Ever Born*	*Mean No. of Children Surviving*
1.	Illiterate	3.67	2.85
2.	Lower Primary	3.00	2.50
3.	Upper Primary	3.00	2.50
4.	Middle School	2.00	2.00
5.	High School	0.00	0.00

The mean number of children surviving is also affectively influenced by various levels of education of wives. In this study, the mean number of children surviving (Table 4.46) is found to be higher (2.85) among illiterate women as compared to the women of various educational levels (2.33 at aggregate level). Even, with the increase of various educational levels, the mean number of children surviving tends to reduce. So, it is an assessment that women's education and the mean number of children surviving are in inconsistent relation. But in regarding their mean number of children ever born, the mean number of children surviving is positively correlated among them. Due to very humble number of educational attainment of the women, their educational achievement can not vary the total mean number of children surviving.

Fertility Differential by Education of Husbands (Respondents)

The present study comprises that among Saharia, the educational characteristic of husbands too, appears to influence fertility as the mean number of children ever born is less (2.96 at aggregate level) when they are literate and more when they are illiterate (3.76). Also, the mean number of children ever born is lower when husbands are more educated, that means a decline in number of children ever born (Table 4.47), noticed from lower primary (3.27) to high school level (2.57). Most of the educated husbands use various contraceptive methods and as a result, their mean number of children ever born is found comparatively lower than illiterate (Majumder, 2001).

TABLE: 4.47

Fertility Differential by Education of Husbands Among Saharia

Sl. No.	*Husband's Educational Level*	*Mean No. of Children Ever Born*	*Mean No. of Children Surviving*
1.	Illiterate	3.76	2.88
2.	Lower Primary	3.27	2.61
3.	Upper Primary	3.20	2.60
4.	Middle School	2.81	2.63
5.	High School	2.57	2.42

The mean number of children surviving is found in inconsistent relation among the husbands of various education levels. This depicts that illiterate husbands contribute the higher (Table 4.47) mean number of children surviving (2.88) than literate in various educational levels (2.57) (at aggregate level). But, with the increase of educational levels, the mean number of children surviving tends to increase (2.61 to 2.63), except the education of high school level (2.42). In comparison with the mean number of children ever born, the present study assesses a positive correlation which indicates that with the increase of educational levels, the mean number of children surviving tends to increase. Due to low attainment in various educational levels of husbands, the mean number of children surviving (2.57) is very low as compared to illiterate (2.88). However, due to awareness, comparatively better financial position, socio-cultural advancement, etc. the educated husbands are much careful to their children's health and nutritional level which influence their high mean number of children surviving.

Fertility Differential by Mating Pattern Regarding with Educational Levels

Mating pattern between husband and wife in regarding their educational levels and average fertility are incorporately related with each other. The mean number of children ever born and mean number of children surviving among Saharia differ in accordance with the mating pattern between couples with regarding their educational levels (Table 4.48). The mean number of children ever born is found to be higher (3.74) when mating was performed between illiterate couples as compared to the couples of various educational levels (3.11 at aggregate level). It is further specified that the mean number of children ever born tends to decrease when mating was performed between the couples of illiterate and lower primary (3.50), illiterate and high school (3.20), upper primary and middle school (3.00) and middle school and high school (2.00) respectively. Due to use the various family planning methods by the couples of literate in various educational levels, their trend of mean number of children ever born is recorded to be low.

In other side, the mean number of children surviving among illiterate couples is high as compared to literate (2.49 at aggregate level). But in regarding the various educational levels of couples, sometimes the mean number of children surviving is found in inconsistent relation due to very low educational attainment of the couples (Table 4.48). In this study, the mean number of children surviving is positively correlated when it is compared to the mean number of children ever born. For providing proper child caring and rearing, medical facilities, nutritional foods, etc., the couples of various educational levels are found to be achieved a comparatively high mean number of children surviving.

TABLE: 4.48

Fertility Differential by Matting Pattern Regarding with Educational Level Among Saharia

Sl. No.	*Wife's Educational Level*	*Mating*	*Husband's Educational Level*	*Mean No. of Children Ever Born*	*Mean No. of Children Surviving*
1	Illiterate	X	Illiterate	3.74	2.88
2	Illiterate	X	Lower Primary	3.50	2.50
3	Illiterate	X	Upper Primary	3.00	2.00
4	Illiterate	X	Lower Primary	3.23	2.81
5	Illiterate	X	Upper Primary	3.50	2.85
6	Illiterate	X	Middle School	3.22	2.66
7	Illiterate	X	High School	3.20	2.60
8	Lower Primary	X	Middle School	3.50	2.50
9	Upper Primary	X	Middle School	3.00	3.00
10	Upper Primary	X	High School	3.00	2.00
11	Middle School	X	High School	2.00	2.00

(7 Husbands Expired / Divorced)

Fertility Differential by Beneficiary Loan Accepted Families

As primitive tribe, Saharia have the opportunity to receive the beneficiary loan schemes for their financial as well as socio-cultural upliftment. Among them, the loan accepted families enjoy the better financial status than others. In this regard, the present study is going to determinate the impact of their financial status which is associated with ever born and surviving of their children. The mean number of children ever born is recorded as high (Table 4.49) in those households who did not get any loan (3.62) as compared to loan benefited families (3.57, at aggregate level). The available information postulate that due to frequent child deaths in the households, they usually take a decision to initiate frequent child births which enhance their mean number of children ever born. Further, a comparative account presents that the mean number of children ever born is found high in mat-making loan and bamboo work loan benefited families (3.95 each), followed by 3.64 (bullock purchasing loan), 3.63 (poultry loan), etc. whereas stone housing loan benefited families present the lowest mean number of children ever born (3.00). In this context, a clarification is made that the mean number of children ever born among loan benefited families is varied in accordance with the acceptance of contraceptive devices.

TABLE: 4.49

Fertility Differential by Beneficiary Loan Accepted Families Among Saharia

SL. No.	*Name of Various Loans*	*Mean No. of Children Ever Born*	*Mean No. of Children Surviving*
1.	Bullock Purchasing Loan	3.64	2.88
2.	Goatery Loan	3.57	2.76
3.	Poultry Loan	3.63	2.78
4.	Fishery Loan	3.44	2.55
5.	Mat-Making Loan	3.95	3.21
6.	Bamboo Work Loan	3.95	3.15
7.	Stone Housing Loan	3.00	3.00
8.	Cemented Building Loan	3.40	2.60
9.	No Loans	3.62	2.79

The mean number of children surviving is recorded comparatively higher (2.86, at aggregate level) in various loan benefited families than those who did not get any loan (2.79). Among various loan accepted families, the highest mean number of children surviving is shown by those who were benefited by mat-making loan (3.21), followed by 3.15 (bamboo work loan), 3.00 (stone housing loan), etc. (Table 4.49) whereas fishery loan benefited families present the lowest mean number of children surviving (2.55). Due to comparatively better financial position, the loan benefited families are enabled to expense their amount for the purpose of nutritional food items and modern clinical facility, etc. which tend to increase their mean number of children surviving.

Fertility Differential by Age at Menarche

Menarche is a biological event which has a significant effect in fertility performance. In the present study, it is found that among Saharia, the mean number of children ever born tends to decrease at the age at menarche increases from 12 to 15 years. The highest mean number of children ever born is measured in those women whose menstruation was started at the age of 12 years (3.92), followed by 3.89 (13 years), 3.49 (14 years) whereas the lowest mean number of children ever born (3.10) is presented by those women who attained first menstruation cycle at the age of 15 years (Table 4.50). The age at menarche is usually influenced by many socio-cultural as well biological factors. Their early age at menarche determines the early age at marriage which also exposes early child birth and due to get long duration of reproductive span of life by early menstruation, their mean number of children ever born is come to be high. The increase in menarcheal age is also accompanied by some physiological change which subsequently has substantial effect on fertility (Talwar, 1967). Women with the early onset are more fecund than ones with late age at menarche leading to earlier pregnancy and earlier child births for a given exposure to the risk of conception (Freedman, et.al., 1981; Udry & Cliquet, 1982). The women having menarcheal age between 13-14 years have higher fertility than those on either side of menarcheal scale and thus are at selective advantage (Sharma & Chowdhury, 1995). According to the study of Nag (1998), the women of relatively late onset of menarche seem to lower fertility but the impact of relatively early onset on fertility seems not exactly clear among all.

In other side, the present study depicts that the mean number of children surviving tends to decrease with the increase of menarcheal age of women (except 13 years age at menarche). The highest mean number of children surviving is estimated in those women whose menarche was started at the age of 13 years (3.06), followed by 3.04 (12 years), 2.70 (14 years) whereas age at 15 years menstruated women present lowest mean number of children surviving (2.26). The late age at menarche (around 15 years) is the indication of maternal physical problems which minimize their frequent conceptions (Table 4.50). So, their mean number of children surviving is come to low. Beside this, the maternal diseases usually transfer into the natal body which also affect on the surviving power of the children. Therefore, it may be attributed that the low mean number of children surviving is usually achieved by late menstruated women.

TABLE: 4.50
Fertility Differential by Menarcheal Age of Women Among Saharia

Age at Menarche (in Year)	*Mean No. of Children Ever Born*	*Mean No. of Children Surviving*
12	3.92	3.04
13	3.89	3.06
14	3.49	2.70
15	3.10	2.26
< 13.5 Mean	3.90	3.05
13.5 Mean >	3.29	2.48

Fertility Differential by Reproductive Span of Life of Women

The average fertility is also depended on reproductive span of life of women among Saharia. In the present study, the mean number of children ever born tends to increase with the increase of reproductive span of life of women. The highest mean number of children ever born is exhibited by those women whose reproductive span of life runs above 30 years (5.70), followed by 4.64 (25-30 years), 4.56 (20-25 years) whereas lowest mean number of children ever born (Table 4.51) is shown by those women whose reproductive span of life is estimated below

5 years (2.80). Longer reproductive span of life generally exposes to the oldness of women. For frequent child births within this longer reproductive span of life, they are enabled to present comparatively the higher mean number of children ever born than others. Beside this, they are normally traditional minded and exposing with such type of attitude, they are not enthusiastic to prefer to the modern contraceptive family planning devices which may also be attributed as the reason to have their high mean number of children ever born.

In other side, the mean number of children surviving increases with the increase of reproductive span of life of women among Saharia. The highest mean number of children surviving is come to notice (Table 4.51) in those women whose reproductive span of life is continued above 30 years(4.85), followed by 3.75 (20-25 years), 3.71 (25-30 years) whereas lowest mean number of children surviving is presented by those women whose reproductive span of life is run below 5 years (2.04). Long reproductive span of life generally exposes the oldness of women. Usually the aged women gain comparatively better experience through a few child deaths. After that, they are capable to protect their children from frequent deaths and as a result, their mean number of children surviving is got high as compared with other women.

TABLE: 4.51

Fertility Differential by Reproductive Span of Life of Women Among Saharia

Reproductive Span of Life of Women	*Mean No. of Children Ever Born*	*Mean No. of Children Surviving*
<5	2.80	2.04
5-10	3.13	2.33
10-15	3.32	2.49
15-20	3.71	2.89
20-25	4.56	3.75
25-30	4.64	3.71
30>	5.70	4.85

Fertility Differential by Age at Marriage of Women

Usually, the tribal people practise early age at marriage. High fertility performance by early age at marriage has a significant role in population growth and dynamics. The initiation of cohabitation and child bearing as a biological factor are generally sanctioned by society-approved rules and regulations. Late marriage generally reduces the child bearing and reproductive span of life. In the present study among Saharia, the available data comprise that the mean number of children ever born tends to decrease with the increase of age at marriage of women (except 17 years age at marriage). The highest mean number of children ever born is found to be measured in those women who were married at the age of 12 years (4.50), followed by 4.23 (13 years), 4.00 (17 years) whereas the lowest mean number of children ever born is presented by those women (Table 4.52) whose marriage was held at the age of 16 years (2.90). Early age at marriage indicates the longer duration of reproductive span of life of women. So, within this period of time, women normally have a chance of frequent child bearing which influences the high mean number of children ever born. Beside this, frequent child deaths are usually prevalent in tribal society. Feeling fear of frequent child deaths, the women of long reproductive span of life (i.e. married at early age) experiencely come to the frequent child births and these are attributed as the causes of their comparatively early age at marriage and high mean number of children ever born. Many studies have demonstrated the lower fertility for those women who marry late compared to those who marry at younger age (Agarwala, 1962, 1966; Driver, 1963; Wyon & Gordon, 1971). Age at marriage of women affect their fertility performance, since marriage marks the beginning of reproductive life of a couples. Over all, early age at marriage has a great importancy to influence high fertility (Chachra & Bhasin, 1998; Nag, 1998; Maheo & Kalla, 2001).

The mean number of children surviving tends to decline with the incline of age at marriage of women (except 17 years age at marriage of women). The highest mean number of children surviving is recorded in those women (Table 4.52) whose marriage was held at the age of 12 years (3.50), followed by 3.39 (13 years), 2.75 (14 years) whereas lowest mean number of children surviving is achieved by the women who were married at the age of 16years (2.20). Early age at marriage as well as early age at menarche of women increases long duration of reproductive span of life. Within this reproductive span of life, they experiencely tolerate their frequent child deaths which influence their high mean number of children surviving.

Further, this study confers that the mean number of children ever born (4.09) and mean number of children surviving (3.19) are found to be high in those women (Table 4.52) whose marriage was held below their mean age at marriage (14.0 years) as compared to the mean number of children ever born (3.80) and mean number of children surviving (2.93) respectively in those women whose marriage was held above the mean age at marriage (14.0 years >). This is also attributed that early age at marriage ensures long reproductive span of life and within this period, the frequent child deaths experiencely support their high mean number of children surviving.

TABLE: 4.52

Fertility Differential by Age at Marriage of Women Among Saharia

Age at Marriage of Woman (in Years)	*Mean No. of Children Ever Born*	*Mean No. of Children Surviving*
12	4.50	3.50
13	4.23	3.39
14	3.56	2.75
15	3.50	2.58
16	2.90	2.20
17	4.00	3.00
<14.0 Mean	4.09	3.19
14.0 Mean >	3.80	2.93

Fertility Differential by Settlement Pattern

In the present study, it is found that the mean number of

children ever born (3.66) and mean number of children surviving (2.87) of settled Saharia are comparatively higher than the mean number of children ever born (3.62) and mean number of children surviving (2.78) of migrants (Table 4.53). The settled households require comparatively many hand works by giving birth to a number of offsprings. Even the another information, collected by exclusive interview express that they rarely use the family planning methods whatever are more or less highly used by migrants Saharia. Because migrant's villages are settled down near to block area surrounding Government Hospital. In this regard, their mean number of children ever born is enhanced as compared to migrants. It is also an attribution that due to comparatively better financial position, the settled families can afford the nutritional level and medical facility for their children and as a result, their mean number of children surviving is high as compared to migrants.

TABLE: 4.53

Fertility Differential by Settlement Pattern Among Saharia

Sl. No.	*Settlement*	*Mean No. of Children Ever Born*	*Mean No. of Children Surviving*
1.	Migratory	3.62	2.78
2.	Settled	3.66	2.87

Fertility Differential by Infant Mortality

Information relating to fertility differential impart that the mean number of children surviving is recorded to be highest in those Saharia women who gained experience of 3 infant deaths (7.75), followed by 6.51 (2 infant deaths), 4.33 (1 infant death) whereas the lowest mean number of children surviving (2.37) is presented by those women who did not loss any infant (Table 4.54). In this context, it is a very effective clarification that the mean number of children surviving tends to increase high with the increase of past infant death experiences. Various nations, pertained to high fertility have high rates of infant and child mortality which reinforce high fertility attitude of couples (Bogue, 1969; Chandrasekhar, 1972). In this study, an assessment is made that preferably tribal people consciously or sub-consciously are seeking many births to achieve a certain desired number of surviving children and to recompensate (for) the child loss in view of either the past experience and relatively high mortality condition. Even, comparatively high infant mortality of the present study is also attributed as the reason of high mean number of children surviving by the past experience, concerned to a number of infant deaths.

TABLE: 4.54
Fertility Differential by Infant Mortality Among Saharia

Age Groups of Cohort	*No Infant Death Mean No. of Children Surviving*	*One Infant Death Mean No. of Children Surviving*	*Two Infant Deaths Mean No. of Children Surviving*	*Three Infant Death Mean No. of Children Surviving*
15-19	0.75	2.52	0.00	0.00
20-24	1.44	4.19	4.62	0.00
25-29	2.27	5.00	5.90	7.25
30-34	2.17	6.10	6.83	8.00
35-39	3.73	7.50	7.00	0.00
40-44	4.00	7.25	7.00	8.00
45-49	5.66	5.00	7.50	0.00
50-54	5.28	5.50	8.00	8.00
55-59	6.66	0.00	7.66	8.00
60-64	0.00	6.00	8.88	0.00
65-69	7.00	6.00	9.00	0.00
70>	0.00	7.00	8.00	0.00
Aggregate	**2.37**	**4.33**	**6.51**	**7.75**

MORTALITY

Only three components are responsible to change the population structure. Among these components, mortality is considered as one whereas the others are being fertility and migration. It is postulated that human beings are mortal. They have to die once upon a time after birth. In other words, after birth, permanent extinction of all signs of life from body is taken place and it is meant as death. The United Nation and World Health Organization combinely defined (1970), "Death is the permanent disappearance of all evidences of life at any time after birth has taken place (post natal) cessation of vital functions without capacity of resuscitation". According to this definition, it is clearly understood that only after live birth, death is occurred. So, a close link is always performed between mortality and live birth. Hauser & Duncan (1959) defined death by saying, "Death prior to complete expulsion or extraction from its mother of a product of conception, irrespecting of the duration of pregnancy, the death is indicated by the fact that after such separation the foetus does not breathe or show any other evidence of life, such as breathing of heat, pulsation of umbilical cord or definite movement of voluntary muscles". Normally a child stays in the womb of mother during 28 weeks. Keeping in view on this matter, the World Health Organization indicates that this remain 28 weeks should be registered as deaths (cf. Raj, 1982).

Very clearly, mortality indicates the permanent extinction of all signs of life from living body and it is occurred at any time after birth. It is not performed without any cause. Biological as well as social factors are indebted for every death. In other words, mortality is considered as a continuous force of attrition, tending to reduce populations - a major negative force in the balance of vital processes. It is noticed that the tribal mortality is quite distressing, specially when seen in the context of Indian national population. The differences can be attributed to the prevailing socio-economic, cultural and health care practices. The poor food habits contribute the malnutrition specially among children and pregnant mothers which lead to increase susceptibility to morbid conditions. Maternal care is largely neglected and the expectant mothers to a great extent are not inoculated against tetanus. From the inception of pregnancy to its termination, no specific nutritious diet is consumed by the women. The consumption of iron, calcium and vitamins during pregnancy is poor. Most of the deliveries are conducted at home attended by elderly ladies of the household. Vaccination and immunization of infant and children are inadequate. In addition, extremes of magico-religious beliefs and taboos tend to aggravate the problems which influence high mortality (Dandekar & Dandekar, 1953; Dandekar, 1959; Ghosh, 1970; Sharma, 1978; Sirajuddin & Basu, 1984; Murthy, 1987).

MEASURES OF MORTALITY

Population analysis necessitates study of mortality which trends to understand the demographic structure of a population. Mortality along with fertility and migration is responsible for a population's demographic profile. It is a biological phenomenon and an inexorable force inducing population and social changes. The levels of mortality define fitness, survival and growth of a population. Mortality is also an excellent indicator of economic, social status and well being of people of a region or to precise, a pointer of development. It is the process whereby deaths occur in a population. Differences in mortality are generally found among various sub-populations either at a particular time or between different cohorts. The various factors affecting differential mortality are far from being clearly understood; climate, diet and life style more generally are all subjects of current research. Moreover, there may be strong underlying interaction factors since the choice of residence, occupation and others may be related to health in the first place, leading to selectivity among the sub-populations studied (Wilson, 1985). However, various measures of mortality and its related components of Saharia are stated in the following manner:

Crude Death Rate (CDR)

Crude death rate (CDR) is the most common and widely used measure of mortality, describing the frequency with which death occurs in a population at a specified time/period. Heer & Smith (1968) said "Crude death rate may be defined as the ratio of the number of deaths which occur within a given population during a specified year, to the size of death population at mid year". Obviously, it is simplest method of finding out death rate because what is required to be known is only the total population and number of deaths, occurred in particular period. Crude death rate reflects a population's age structure as well as the prevailing patterns of mortality. In the present study, crude death rate among Saharia is found to be measured as 25.77 (Table 4.55). Keeping in view the comparison, Saharia crude death rate is noticed to be higher than Gond (23.19), Ahujhmaria (14.90), Bhils (15.53), Jaunsarias (11.85), Juhar Bhotia (12.79), Rang Bhotia (16.11), Marcha Botia (13.12), Brahmin (7.61), Rajput (8.08), Scheduled Caste (12.54), Marchas (8.22), Johari (18.12), Dharchulas (10.01), Brahmin of Himachal Pradesh (12.9), Rajput of Himachal Pradesh (11.8), Bodhs(19.84), Baltis (18.87), Brokpas (21.16), Arghuns (16.91), Buddhists (19.8), Hindus (17.8), Mao (3.1), Santal (10.9), Lodha (11.8), Dudh Kharia (11.8), Santal of Orissa (13.0), Thoti (5.32), Madhya Pradesh (12.60), India (9.3) and others but lower than Oraon (25.88), Gonds (40.08), Lohar Gadiyas (47.19), Kamar (46.57), Raji (47.6), Mina (40.7) and others. It is assessed that among Saharia, the reported high crude death rate may be attributed as the reasons of paucity of modern clinical facility, high extent of illiteracy, financial problem, negligency to the immunization, unfavourable environmental factor, lack of nutritional foods, insanitation, low socio-cultural status, careless to maternal and child health care, early age at marriage, insecure life of aged persons, etc.

Age Specific Mortality Rate (ASMR)

Age specific mortality rate (ASMR) is another method of finding out death rate. The mortality risks, faced by human beings vary sharply with age. Hence to understand the over all death rates, age specific death rates are also studied, as these can separate the component of mortality from the effect of age composition of a population. However, the age specific death rates among Saharia are recorded as the capital letter 'U' pattern with the mortality high among the young and old age groups. Mortality is high for the 0 - 4 age group (82.35), after that it reduces for the following age groups with few exceptions (Table 4.55) and again picks up at around age fifty onwards (133.33). Mortality rate among children is usually high. Thereafter pressure of death decreases. But when old age comes, then the pressure of death again increases. In comparison to the various population groups, the pattern of age specific mortality rates among Saharia is found almost similar (SRS, 1993; Chachra & Bhasin, 1998; Nag, 1998; Sharma & Sharma, 1999; Patra, 2001). High age specific mortality rate is mostly due to low level of socio-cultural factors, non-availability of medical facility, illiteracy, early age at marriage of girls, early and frequent child bearing of women by unskilled mid-wife, careless attitude on child, new born mothers and aged groups, etc. (Dandekar, 1975; Ware, 1981; Rosenweig & Schutlz, 1982; Dasgupta, 1990; Preston, 1990).

Still Birth Rate (SBR)

Still birth is a term which makes a wimp to determinate an accountation of reproductive wastage. Pearl (1939) defined that still birth "in strict logic and definition means an infant born dead at or near term". It is usually regarded as the foetal death. Further, foetal death indicates the death which is occurred before the complete expulsion or extraction from the womb of mother. From 28 weeks of conception to the exact child bearing period, the embryonic loss is accounted as still birth or foetal death. Due to separation from gestation, the foetus is unable to practise breathing or show any other evidences of life such as beating of heart, pulsation of the umbilical cord or definite movement of voluntary muscles. In the present study among Saharia, still birth rate (SBR) is found to be measured as 26.66 (Table 4.55). Taking into consideration in a comparative account, it is noticed that still birth rate among Saharia is comparatively higher (26.66) than Kamar (25.91), Brahmin (10.2), Rajput (11.6), Scheduled Caste (17.8), Buddhists (22.2), Madhya Pradesh (12.3), India (11.6) and others but lower than Hindu Khasi (31.6), Christian Khasi (34.6) and others. Low socio-economic status, high extent of illiteracy, negligence to maternal care specially during pregnancy period, malnutrition, unscientific delivery, etc. are the attributed reasons of their high still birth rate (Banerjee, et.al. 1976; Sharma & Sharma, 1999).

Peri-natal Mortality Rate (PMR)

Early neo-natal death (death of infant within first week of life), late foetal death (after 28 weeks of gestation) and still birth together constitute peri-natal mortality. In simple words, it includes late foetal mortality and a position of infant mortality which indicate early neo-natal death. Peri-natal mortality rate (PMR) is also a sensitive index reflecting standards of mother and child health care prior to and during pregnancy and child birth and also during the first week after birth: as well as the availability and effectiveness of other social development measures (Devi, 1979). Peri-natal mortality rate among Saharia is found to be measured as 54.79 (Table 4.55) which presents comparatively higher than Brahmin (29.6), Rajput (34.8),Scheduled Caste (25.7), Madhya Pradesh (52.9), India (44.3) and others but lower than Kamar (59.26), Marchas (75.0), Johari (60.0), Dharchulas (81.0), Brahmin of Himachal Pradesh (63.9), Rajput of Himachal Pradesh (56.2), Scheduled Caste of Himachal Pradesh (92.3), Bodhs (69.77), Baltis (96.15), Brokpas (90.91), Arghuns (71.43), Buddhists (88.9) and others. Unsatisfactory maternal and child health care services, personal unhygiene, traditional and unscientific delivery attendance in most of the births, delivery at home, careless on ante-natal and post natal checkup, early age at marriage and frequently child births, illiteracy, poverty, etc., are the attributed reasons which influence their high peri-natal mortality rate.

Neo-natal Mortality Rate (NMR)

Neo-natal mortality refers to deaths which are occurred under four weeks after birth of child. It is generally observed that deaths occurred during the neo-natal period are primarily caused by biological factors which indicate neo-natal mortality, attributed to endogenous or ante-natal causes. In the present study, 54.79 is found to be estimated as the neo-natal mortality rate (NMR) among Saharia (Table 4.55). In comparison with other studies, it is noticed that neo-natal mortality rate among Saharia is comparatively higher than Rajput (16.0), Scheduled Caste (30.76), Marchas (14.28), Johari (40.0), Dharchulas (50.0), Bodhs (24.39), Hindus (35.1), Khasi (17.2), Garo (33.9), Mizo (3.5), India (47.2) and others but lower than Kamar (68.23), Raji (137.9), Brahmin (75.8), Rajput of Himachal Pradesh (69.0), Scheduled Caste of Himachal Pradesh (94.4), Baltis (81.63), Brokpas (100.0), Buddhists (66.7), Thoti (108.1), Madhya Pradesh (64.5) and others. Although the impact of ante-natal and delivery care on survival during first month of the life is less than the effect on mortality risks at later stages, it is nonetheless very large.

Children of mothers who receive no such care, have a higher neo-natal mortality rate than the rate for children of mothers who receive both ante-natal and delivery care. Such differentials are more impressive because women who have pregnancy-related complications, their babies have a relatively high risk of death. High neo-natal mortality rate may also be attributed as the reasons of unhygienic weaning practice, paucity of medical facility, unscientific delivery, negligence on maternal and child health care, illiteracy, low socio-economic status, etc.

Post Neo-natal Mortality Rate (PNMR)

Post neo-natal mortality refers to the deaths which are occurred between four weeks and one year of children's age. The post neo-natal deaths are most sensitive to socio-economic factors as compared to biological factors. Post neo-natal mortality is also attributed to exogenous or environmental causes. Normally, most of the infant deaths are accounted in post neo-natal mortality. In the present study, post neo-natal mortality rate (PNMR) among Saharia is found to be measured as 68.49 (Table 4.55) which presents high as compared to Kamar (53.51), Brahmin (28.57), Rajput (32.0), Scheduled Caste (7.69), Brahmin of Himachal Pradesh (40.2), Rajput of Himachal Pradesh (36.6), Hindus (35.1), Khasi (24.8), Garo (18.1), Mizo (19.5), Madhya Pradesh (41.2), India (25.5) and others but low as compared to Johari (80.0), Dharchulas (100.0), Raji (206.9), Scheduled Caste of Himachal Pradesh (122.2), Bodha (73.17), Baltis (81.63), Brokpas (100.0), Arghuns (76.92), Buddhists (111.1) and others. Paucity of medical facility, early age at marriage and frequent child births, delivery at home by untrained 'Dai' (mid-wife), malnutrition, negative attitude on immunization, low socio-economic status, high extent of illiteracy, etc., are the attributed reasons of their high post neo-natal mortality rate.

Infant Mortality Rate (IMR)

Infant mortality rate (IMR) is one of the most important measure of mortality, as it estimates the mortality in that segment of the population, where it is usually extremely high. It is regarded as the good indicator of health status of a population and is one of the most vital demographic parameter which indicates the level of socio-economic development of a community or society. It is the mortality of live-born infants who have not reached their first birth day. Infant mortality is a major contributor to deaths in populations with high mortality but it is reduced almost to insignificant in many developed countries, making one of most striking aspects of mortality improvement (Wilson, 1985). The infant mortality rate is also considered as an excellent indicator of the situation of medical and public health facilities in an area and altogether with literacy rate and life expectancy, it hints the quality of development and human well being in a region. It also accounts for a large chunk of all deaths and affects the attitude, behviour of parents towards family size and structure. In the present study, infant mortality rate among Saharia is found to be measured as (123.28) which is noticed comparatively higher (Table 4.55) than Jaunsarias (82.0), Brahmin (28.27), Rajput (48.0), Scheduled Caste (38.46), Johari (120.0), Rajput of Himachal Pradesh (113.3), Bodhs (97.56), Arghuns (76.92), Hindus (70.18), Mao (43.5), Khasi (42.0), Garo (52.0), Mizo (23.0), Dalu (103.6), Pnar (119.2), Zemi (86.1), Kora (72.1), Santal (94.8), Lodha (99.2), Mirdha (116.0), Hill Kolam (70.59), Manue Kolam (68.0), Madhya Pradesh (85.2), India (78.5) and others but lower than Abujhmaria (130.0), Gonds (242.0), Muria (123.50), Kamar (196.60), Lohar Gadiyas (144.30), Juhar Bhotia (152.0), Rang Bhotia (212.0), Marcha Bhotia (158.7), Marchas (142.8), Dharchulas (150.0), Raji (344.8), Brahmin of Himachal Pradesh (125.4), Scheduled Caste of Himachal Pradesh (263.2), Baltis (163.26), Brokpas (200.0), Buddhists (177.77), Kutia Konda (197.7), Dudh Kheria (202.4), Dongaria Kondh (153.11), Kandh (153.8), Santal (127.0), Thoti (162.16), Soliga (188.0) and others.

High infant mortality is influenced by various factors. There are no maternal and child welfare centres in the vicinity of the area. People are not aware to the immunization for the children from early stage and ante-natal and post natal periods of the mother. Due to nuclear family formation and non-availability of supporting persons at home, the infants and young children are carried to the working places by their mother's back or just left behind alone at home. They are exposed to all types of infection and health hazards in the field and at other working places. Due to busy in economic requirement, mothers usually initiate less attention to look after their children and their own health. Beside this, congenital mal-transformation, immature birth, illiteracy, low socio-economic status, discrimination in the context of less care to female children, mal-nutrition, insanitation, poor infrastructure, non-availability of purified drinking water, etc., are the attributed reasons of high infant mortality rate.

Under-five Mortality Rate (U-5MR)

Under five mortality considers all deaths from 0 to under five years of age. In other words, it is the addition of infant mortality and child mortality. This mortality can also be defined as the probability of dying before the fifth birth day. However, under five mortality rate (U-5MR) is also an another important measure of mortality which is recently being promoted as the main pointer of the state of children, as well as human and economic progress in the region (UNICEF, 1991). More so, because in low-mortality populations, mortality risks between age 1 year and 5 years are also low and the infant mortality rate can be used as a reasonable single index of child mortality but in populations with higher mortality, relatively high proportions of deaths occurred between age 1 year and 5 years as well as and so the under five mortality rate is a more important index of over all child mortality, although the infant mortality rate remains a crucial measure (UN, 1992). It is found that under five mortality rate among Saharia is measured as high (82.35 in Table 4.55) when compared to Marchas (42.85), Rajput (56.0), Brahmin (42.85), Khasi (57.96), Garo (79.01), Mizo (31.91), India and others but low as compared to Kamar (132.3), Scheduled Caste (84.60), Johari (240.0), Dharchulas (350.0), Raji (724.10), Bodhs (195.12), Baltis (244.90), Brokpas (300.0), Arghuns (153.85), Madhya Pradesh (130.30) and others. It may be mentioned that due to malnutrition, negligence to child health care, paucity of medical facility, low socio-economic status, etc., their under five mortality rate is high.

Child Mortality Rate (CMR)

Child mortality takes into consideration the children deaths from one year to less than five years. It can be also defined as the probability of dying between the first and fifth birth day. Child mortality is not only limited to measure the dead children in a population but also it assesses the socio-economic disbalancies which are indebted for deaths. The United Nations first celebrated as the International Year of Child in 1979. Since then the scientists all over the world, particularly the demographers and social scientists have taken interest to find out the causes and patterns of child mortality. However, it is well known that infant and child mortality rates are the good index to understand the general health status of a population. In comparison to different population groups, it is found that child mortality rate (CMR) among Saharia is found to be measured as 62.82 (Table 4.55) which is higher than Marchas (28.57), Brahmin (14.28), Rajput (8.0), Scheduled

TABLE: 4.55
Various Measures of Mortality Among Saharia

Sl. No.	*Mortality Measures*	*Calclulation*
1.	Crude Death Rate (CDR)	25.77
2.	Max. Age Specific Death Rate > 4 & 55< Age Groups	329.19
	Min. Age Specific Death Rate in 10-34 Age Groups	7.59
	No Age Specific Mortality Rate in 25-29 & 45-49 Age Groups	0.00
3.	Still Birth Rate (SBR)	26.66
4.	Peri-natal Mortality Rate (PMR)	54.79
5.	Neo-natal Mortality Rate (NMR)	54.79
6.	Post Neo-natal Mortality Rate (PNMR)	68.49
7.	Infant Mortality Rate (IMR)	123.28
8.	Under Five Mortality Rate (UFMR)	82.35
9.	Child Mortality Rate (CMR)	62.82

Caste (46.15), Khasi (15.9), Garo (27.1), Mizo (8.9), Madhya Pradesh (49.3), India (33.4) and others but lower than Kamar

(123.3), Johari (120.0), Dharchulas (200.0), Raji (379.3) and others. Low level of socio-economic status, high extent of illiteracy, malnutrition, negligence attitude to child care, weaning practice without proper balanced substitute diets, inadequacy of modern clinical facility, old communication system, lack of purified drinking water, etc. are the attributed causes of their high child mortality rate.

Reasons of Death of Last one Year

Reasons of death are one of the important aspects of mortality study. A clear and broad picture, drawn in favour of mortality on the basis of data on reasons of death help in understanding various aspects of death among various ethnic groups provide an indication of their awareness as regards their health practices as well as the activities of the concerned public health authorities which when properly analyzed, may be useful for planning medical measures (Bhende & Kanitkar, 1991). In all the countries of the world, most of the deaths take place due to diseases and all the diseases are depended on biological as well as socio-economic factors.

In the present study among Saharia, it is found that the maximum deaths were occurred due to pneumonia (20.9 percent), malaria (13.8 percent), tuberculosis (11.6 percent), gastric (9.3 percent), diarrhoea (9.3 percent), etc. (Table 4.56). Low standard of living, poor quality of food habit, hard work, malnutrition, insanitation, lack of purified drinking water, low level of socio-cultural status, unfavourable environment, etc. are the attributed reasons of such diseases (Bhasin, 1990; Adak, 1994; Sharma & Sharma, 1999; Kshatriya, 2000). Due to poverty, illiteracy, socio-cultural rules and regulations, inadequacy of Government health centre, etc., their traditional healers are initially given preference for the treatment of their diseases. But when the treatment of traditional healers is considered no more enough to control the diseases, then they generally come under the treatment of modern doctors. During long time continuous suffering, modern doctors are sometimes unable to control their diseases by providing the proper treatment and then as a result, the illed persons loss their survival power.

TABLE: 4.56

Reasons of Death of Last one Year's Record Among Saharia

Sl. No.	*Reasons of Deaths*	*Percentage*
1	Pneumonia Disease	20.9
2	Malaria Disease	13.8
3	Typhoid Disease	7.0
4	Gastric Disease	9.3
5	Anemia Disease	4.7
6	Diarrhoea Disease	9.3
7	Tuberculosis Disease	11.6
8	Jaundice Disease	6.7
9	Diabetes Disease	4.7
10	Indigestive Disease	4.7
11	Accident Case	2.3
12	Disease not Identified	7.0
	Total	**100.0**

From the foregoing discussion, it may be pointed out that Saharia are one of the primitive tribes and have a strong low socio-economic impact on their life style. Most of the Saharia are landless and they are to be engaged in primary sector as wage earners. Due to paucity of water resources, they usually drink uncleaned and impured water. As interior inhabitation, they lag behind in the field of education and have achieved very little literacy rate. In respecting to their traditional society approved rules and norms, they are to be come on marital alliance at very early age. The awareness of family planning contraceptive methods is almost nil. Therefore, early age at marriage and family planning non-acceptance are the two important reasons which expose them to conduct frequent child births. In such circumstances, the early aged mothers are generally prostrated containing very low health status. Immunization and medical check-up for ante-natal, natal and post-natal stages are mostly neglected among them. Even a major group of people are to be affected by various seasonal as well as malnutritional diseases. So, poor socio-economic status, malnutrition, impured drinking water, high extent of illiteracy, early age at marriage and frequent child births, non-acceptance of family planning methods, unawareness on immunization, paucity of modern medical facility, worst environment, etc. are contaminated as the reasons of affecting various diseases which influence their frequent deaths. As a result, Saharia crude birth rate, age specific death rate, still birth rate, peri-natal, neo-natal and post neo-natal mortality rates, infant mortality rate, under five mortality rate and child mortality rate are quite distressing, specifically when compared to most of the tribal and non-tribal population of India. Finally, it is suggested that urgently a long-time multi-stages development scheme should be implemented among this tribal inhabitat area. Under this scheme, first priority should be given to improve their financial condition, educational status, availability and quality of drinking water and medical facility. Implementing such development scheme, occasionally demographic, biological as well as medical and socio-economic studies should also be conducted to review the improvement of launched projects and then an expectation may be furnished about them as socio-economically as well as demographically advanced Saharia.

DIFFERENTIAL MORTALITY

In demographic study, many important factors relating to parental socio-economic condition, biological aspects, maternal status, etc. are determined for its association with loss and surviving of the children. Any other study does not further specify that maternal factors, environmental contamination, nutrient deficiency, injury and personal illness control are the five factors which are identified as the determinants of child survival (Moseley & Chen, 1984). Child mortality rate exhibits a pronounced inverse association with a wide variety of socio-economic variables. Of all the variables examined, the one factor emerged as the strongest and most consistent determinant of census tract variations in infant or child mortality is the proportion of low income families (Stockwell & Wicks, 1984). But according to Kost & Amin (1992), infant and child mortality may be said to be affected by two sets of factors - factors related to reproductive or maternal characteristics and socio-economic factors. However, in the context of various socio-economic as well as biological factors, mortality differentials are discussed in the following manner:

Mortality Differential by Land Holding Pattern

Information, collected for the present study depict that among Saharia, the child loss ratio is found comparatively high among landless (0.236) than (Table 4.57) land holding groups (0.115 at aggregate level). But specially among land holder groups, the size of land ownership in influencing the proportion of child loss does not seem to be very clear. However, land holder groups are comparatively better in financial position than landless groups. So, due to better financial position, their family budget is prepared consisting of medical services, nutritional foods, standard of living, etc. which reduce their frequent child loss.

TABLE: 4.57

Mortality Differential by Land Holding Pattern Among Saharia

Land Holding (in Acres)	*Child Loss Ratio*	*Child Survival Ratio*
Landless	0.236	0.764
<1	0.076	0.787
1-2	0.148	0.851
2-3	0.147	0.852
3-4	0.100	0.819
4>	0.125	0.875

In other side, this study further reveals that the child survival ratio is found to be measured comparatively lower among landless (0.764) than land holder groups (0.818 at aggregate level) and even with the increasing of land-size, child survival ratio is also increased (Table 4.57). Due to comparatively better financial position, the land holder groups are able to fulfill all requirements and as a result their child survival ratio is found high. Study of Flinn (1986) also supports that individuals with more land tend to have more reproductive successes.

Mortality Differential by Types of Residence

The maximum child loss ratio among Saharia is come to the notice in those households who inhabit in thatched made residences (0.253), followed by bamboo made residences (0.230) and wooden residences (0.194) whereas lowest child loss ratio (Table 4.58) is presented by those who inhabit in cemented building (0.064). The housing condition is attributed as the actual aggregate of determinant which constitutes the immediate physical environment of human beings and effects mortality mainly through the elements of exposure. It may be noted that housing characteristics are also roughly indicative of the level of living (thereby reflecting the socio-economic status of the residents) which is in turn, influenced by a number of factors. Mainly very poor (thatched) and poor (bamboo made) quality of residences are available in Saharia inhabitat area. Inhabiting in such residences, they are not able to face heavy rain fall, extreme cold and hot weather and as a result, most of their children are affected by various diseases which enhance frequent deaths. So, in this regard, their child loss ratio is recorded high.

Again, this study focuses that the maximum child survival ratio is implied in cemented residences (0.936), wooden residences (0.806) and bamboo made residences (0.768) whereas the minimum child survival (Table 4.58) ratio is recorded in thatched residences (0.747). Generally, standard of living (good) protects children from various diseases which increases comparatively higher child survival ratio. A great contribution of Benjamin (1965) makes an attention to the difficulty separating the effects of housing characteristics from other determinants of child mortality while this is highly correlated with social class, social status, income, unemployment and place of residence. Preston, 1975,

1980; Potts & Selman, 1979 and Tabah, 1980 have remarkable statements that changes in environmental factors such as quantity and quality of water, housing conditions, sanitary facilities etc. explain the reduction in mortality or lead to a decline in mortality caused by certain diseases decrease incidence of many serious diseases, etc.

TABLE: 4.58
Mortality Differential by Types of Residence Among Saharia

Sl. No.	*Types of Residence*	*Child Loss Ratio*	*Child Survival Ratio*
1	Thatched (Very Poor)	0.253	0.747
2	Bamboo Made (Poor)	0.230	0.768
3	Wooden (Medium)	0.194	0.806
4	Cemented (Good)	0.064	0.936

Mortality Differential by Types of Transportation

In the present study among Saharia, there is noted a consistent relation between better transportation and lower child loss ratios as well as higher child survival ratios. Due to undulating hilly foot path, Government transport system is failed to connect all villages (except the village Bijli Ghar and Prem Nagar). Some of the households pertaining to comparatively better financial status, are capable to maintain transportation by two wheeler. In this regard, they are enabled to afford adequate medical facilities, nutritional foods, etc., which influence their low child loss ratio (0.068) as well as high child survival ratio (0.939). In other side, as a reason of extreme poverty, most of the householders transport on foot. Even for their poor financial status, they are not capable to give proper medical facilities, nutritional foods, standard of living, etc. (Table 4.59) to their children which influence their high child loss ratio (0.256) as well as low child survival ratio (0.743). As already stated, the infrastructure facilities available (particularly transportation, medical, standard of living, etc.) have certain bearing on infant and child mortality levels in the region. In the past, the decline in mortality has been attributed to the advances and propagation of medical technology and communication services. Even today, all including both infant mortality and child mortality (and survival) are often linked to the availability of health and communication services (Gwatkin & Brandel, 1981; Mosely, 1985).

TABLE: 4.59
Mortality Differential by Types of Transportation Among Saharia

Sl.No.	*Types of Transportation*	*Child Loss Ratio*	*Child Survival Ratio*
1	Bicycle	0.198	0.811
2	Two Wheeler	0.068	0.939
3	Bullock Cart	0.219	0.764
4	On Foot	0.256	0.743

Mortality Differential by Sources of Water

The child loss and child survival ratios among Saharia are also depended on the quality, cleanness and purification of water. The highest child loss ratio is found to be recorded in those households who collect water from pond (0.302), followed by well (0.220) and well & tube-well (0.144) whereas lowest child loss ratio (Table 4.60) is presented by those households who collect water from tube-well (0.054). In Saharia inhabitat area, the water of pond is not purified and it creates many water born diseases of the children which influence the high child loss whereas the water of tube-well is comparatively better quality and it helps to minimize the child disease as well as child loss.

The child survival ratio is found to be measured as highest in those households who collect water from tube-well (0.855)), followed by well & tube-well (0.780) and well (0.750) whereas lowest child survival ratio (Table 4.60) is depicted by those households who collect water from pond (0.718). Water of tube-well in Saharia inhabitat area is comparatively better (purified) than the water of other sources. As a result, it reduces child diseases which have a positive impact on the high child survival ratio. In other side, the impured water of pond always influences the child diseases which enhance the frequent child deaths so that their child survival ratio is come down.

TABLE: 4.60
Mortality Differential by Sources of Water among Saharia

Sl. No.	*Sources of Water*	*Child Loss Ratio*	*Child Survival Ratio*
1	Well	0.220	0.750
2	Tube-well	0.054	0.855
3	Well & Tube-well	0.144	0.780
4	Pond	0.302	0.718

Mortality Differential by Types of Mass Media Used

The impact of mass media is tremendously incorporated in determining the child loss and child survival. The available data make a depiction that the child loss ratio is found comparatively higher in those households who do not use any mass media (0.263) than those of mass-media users (0.135 at aggregate level). Even news paper readers present comparatively the lower child loss ratio (0.090) than television (0.148) and radio (0.168) users (Table 4.61). By the use of various mass-media, generally they are exposed to outer world and gain the awareness of child caring and rearing and maternal health care. Beside this, educational status and financial position of mass-media users are comparatively better than non-users. So, all these factors are very much helpful to minimize their child loss.

In the present study, it is also noticed that among mass-media users, the child survival ratio (0.868 at aggregate level) is found comparatively higher than (Table 4.61) non-users (0.734). Even news paper readers presents comparatively higher child survival ratio (0.907) than television (0.850) and radio users

(0.849). Generally, the mass-media non-user groups are illiterate and have comparatively lower in financial position. They are also not exposed to be acquainted with the utmost happenings in the context of child caring, rearing, maternal care, etc., which influence their low child survival.

TABLE: 4.61

Mortality Differential by Types of Mess Media Used Among Saharia

Sl. No	Types of Mass Media Used	Child Loss Ratio	Child Survival Ratio
1	Television	0.148	0.850
2	Radio	0.168	0.849
3	News Paper	0.090	0.907
4	Not Used Any	0.263	0.734

Mortality Differential by Types of Watched Movie

The child loss and child survival are sometimes associated with movie viewing. All Saharia people are keenly interested to observe various movies. But their financial constraints usually make an obstacle not to enjoy movie with large extent. However information, collected for the present study imply that the child loss ratio is found to be measured comparatively higher in those heads of the households (Table 4.62) who enjoy various movies (0.254, at aggregate level) as compared to non-movie viewers (0.220). Even specifically war related movie viewers present the high child loss ratio (0.346) as compared to the viewers of violence (0.266), sex (0.253), social (0.216) and romantic (0.188) movies. After completing the routine works, they use to enjoy the various movies mainly in their local video hall and also in cinema hall. Most of them are very poor and illiterate and their limited income does not allow them to observe movie regularly. Due to their poor economy, they are also unable to provide both nutritional foods and proper medical care to their children and women. In this regard, their child loss ratio is recorded comparatively higher than others.

In other side, the child survival ratio is found to be estimated as high in those heads of households who do not watch any movie (0.779) as compared to movie viewers (0.745 at aggregate level). Further, it is a specification that the child survival ratio is presented comparatively higher in romantic movie viewers (0.811) than social (0.782), sex (0.746), violence (0.733) and war (Table 4.62) related movie viewers (0.653). Their poverty and illiteracy always encourage to conduct frequent child births neglecting the nutritional aspects and medical ailments which are very much concerned to be responsible to their low child survival ratio.

TABLE: 4.62

Mortality Differential by Types of Watched Movie Among Saharia

Sl. No	*Types of Watched Movies*	*Child Loss Ratio*	*Child Survival Ratio*
1	Romantic	0.188	0.811
2	Sex	0.253	0.746
3	Social	0.216	0.782
4	War	0.346	0.653
5	Violence	0.266	0.733
6	Not Watched any	0.220	0.779

Mortality Differential by Family Types

As a social unit, the formation of family has a great contribution relating to the child loss and child survival. The collected information for the present study exhibit that among Saharia, the child loss ratio is found to be measured comparatively higher (Table 4.63) in nuclear families (0.224) than joint families (0.204). In most of the nuclear families, the supporting adult children or old persons are far less common. The absence of additional kin seems to be detrimental to child care which becomes the sole responsibility of the mother in a nuclear family. In addition, they are also depressed by other household or outside workload and as a result, their child loss ratio is found comparatively high.

In other side, the child survival is found to be estimated higher (Table 4.63) in joint families (0.795) than nuclear families (0.777). In nuclear families, mothers always have to busy in different activities. So, due to lack of time, child care is almost ignored by them. Even sometimes due to non-availability of supporting persons at home, they carry their child on their back side and keep them in the working place. Cosy life of the child is unable to tolerate this type of physical torture. So, their child survival ratio is come to low. Due to incorporate traditionalism in child care practices, it is often revealed delicious negative effects on child health (Farah & Preston, 1982). But the opinions of Butz, et.al. (1982) define that in case in the member of grand parents and other relatives in the household, substantially reduces infant mortality because of the possibility of getting child care aid from them, incase of mother's inability to provide the same. The statements mention that by the study concerned to rural communities in Punjab and Haryana as well as, inconsistent relation is noted for the case of child survival (Singh, 1986).

TABLE: 4.63
Mortality Differential by Family Types Among Saharia

Sl. No.	Types of Family	Child Loss Ratio	Child Survival Ratio
1	Nuclear	0.224	0.777
2	Joint	0.204	0.795

Mortality Differential by Occupations of Wives

Occupations of Saharia wives play the great role to the child loss and child surviving. The maximum child loss ratios are noticed to be measured in those women who practise begging (0.333), daily labour (0.329), food gathering (0.296) and tribal craft (0.250) whereas lowest child loss ratio (0.135) is presented by those women (Table 4.64) who practise household work (0.135). Due to busy in continuous activities, the working mothers are unable to consume enough time for their child caring and rearing. So, less attention is conferred to child care which reacts negatively on child health. According to a general study, an observation, made by Farah & Preston (1982) focuses that children of working women got higher mortality rate than children of housewives.

The child survival ratios, in other hand are found to be estimated as maximum in those women (Table 4.64) who involve in household work (0.865), animal husbandry (0.808), agriculture (0.790) and tribal craft (0.751) whereas women of begging occupation presents the lowest child survival ratio (0.666). Since occupation is a reflection of a person's economic status. A very noticeable matter is that the women who are in household work, have a comparatively better financial position than others. They not only consume enough time for child caring and rearing but also their family budget is prepared consisting of nutritional foods, medical services, etc. which have a great influence for high child surviving. Mother's occupational status also helps to allot the maternal time for child rearing. And reduction in maternal time, devoted to child care may be directly related to infant and child mortality (Da Vanzo & Lee, 1978; Adak, 1994; Chachra & Bhasin, 1998; Nag, 1998).

TABLE: 4.64

Mortality Differential by Occupations of Wives Among Saharia

Sl. No.	*Types of Occupation*	*Child Loss Ratio*	*Child Survival Ratio*
1	Food Gathering	0.296	0.701
2	Animal Husbandry	0.190	0.808
3	Agriculture	0.210	0.790
4	Daily Labour	0.329	0.747
5	Tribal Craft	0.250	0.751
6	Households Work	0.135	0.865
7	Begging	0.333	0.666

Mortality Differential by Occupations of Husbands

Usually in Saharia tribal community, both husbands and wives participate in various occupations which effectively varies their child loss and child surviving. The maximum child loss ratios among them are projected by those husbands or respondents (Table 4.65) who practise bonded labour (0.267), hunting (0.250), food gathering (0.235) and daily labour (0.232) whereas service holders present the lowest child loss ratio (0.066). The occupational status of husbands serves as an indicator of economic circumstances of households which affect the consumption standards specially among children, quality of shelter, use of medical care, etc. In this study, bonded labour, hunting and food gathering professionals are come under comparatively low income groups whereas service holders and business men are identified under high income groups. The child loss ratio is usually found lower in those professionals whose income is high because they are able to supply the essential needs of their children. So, the child loss ratio is noticed comparatively lower in service holders and business men.

TABLE: 4.65
Mortality Differential by Occupations of Husbands Among Saharia

Sl. No.	*Types of Occupations*	*Child Loss Ratio*	*Child Survival Ratio*
1	Hunting	0.250	0.750
2	Food Gathering	0.235	0.764
3	Animal Husbandry	0.225	0.774
4	Agriculture	0.212	0.787
5	Daily Labour	0.232	0.769
6	Bonded Labour	0.267	0.731
7	Craft	0.220	0.768
8	Business	0.142	0.857
9	Service	0.066	0.933

In other side, the lower child survival ratios are exhibited by those husbands (Table 4.65) who practise bonded labour (0.731), hunting (0.750), food gathering (0.764), craft (0.768) whereas service holders (0.933) and business men (0.857) present the maximum child survival ratios. On the whole, the child survival ratio seems lower when the husbands are economically inactive, than when they are active. Husband's occupations in the service and business sectors appear to be mainly contributing to this trend, while occupations like bonded labour, hunting, food gathering, etc. seem to pose greater risk of the child loss and less chances of child survival. Beside this, comparatively better educational status of service holders also interferes to their high child survival ratio (Adak, 1994; Nag, 1998). The significant effect of father's occupation on child mortality is eliminated when other variables are taken into consideration (Farah & Preston, 1982; Trussel & Preston, 1982).

Mortality Differential by Household Income

Child survival ratio is also depended on the range of household income. The present study expresses that Saharia annual household income is very low and it is varied from below Rs. 3000/- to above Rs. 10000/- (Table 4.66). In this study, income of both husbands and wives is assembled as household income. The maximum child loss ratios are imparted in those households whose income is estimated from below Rs.3000/- (0.333), Rs. 4000/- - 4500/- (0.290) and Rs.4500/- - 5000/- (0.264) whereas the minimum child loss ratios are depicted by the income groups of above Rs.10000/- (0.120), Rs.9000/- - 9500/- (0.142) and Rs.9500/- - 10000/- (0.148). High income serves as an indicator of consumption of better goods and services which make a positive effect to the health of the children. Consumption of nutritional foods, standard of living, sanitary facilities, better medical care, etc., of higher income groups always curtail the child loss. Some of the studies, conducted in different times confer the negative relationship between the child loss ratio and status of income (Frisancho, et.al, 1976; Markides & Barnes 1977; Cochrane, et.al., 1980.

In other side, the maximum child survival ratios are recorded in those house-holds (Table 4.66) who annually earn above Rs.10000/- (0.871), Rs.9000/- - 9500/- (0.857) and Rs.8500/- 9000/- (0.823) whereas the minimum child survival ratios are presented by below Rs.3000/- (0.666), Rs.4000/- - 4500/- (0.741) and Rs.4500/- - 5000/- (0.749) income groups. Due to inadequate supply of essential commodities in those households who are economically not well off , their child survival is much less compared to the more economically well off households. The high income could determine the nutritional levels and access to medical care to the children which in turn are determinants of the high child survival. So, it may be expected a positive relationship between the child survival and income (Anker & Knowles, 1977; Adak, 1994; Chachra & Bhasin, 1998; Nag, 1998; Pandey, et.al. 2001).

TABLE: 4.66
Mortality Differential by Household Income Among Saharia

Income (in Rupees)	*Child Loss Ratio*	*Child Survival Ratio*
< 3000	0.333	0.666
3000 – 3500	0.250	0.750
3500 – 4000	0.230	0.769
4000 – 4500	0.290	0.741
4500 – 5000	0.264	0.749
5000 – 5500	0.243	0.754
5500 – 6000	0.242	0.759
6000 – 6500	0.229	0.814
6500 – 7000	0.237	0.764
7000 – 7500	0.210	0.788
7500 – 8000	0.217	0.781
8000 – 8500	0.244	0.754
8500 – 9000	0.175	0.823
9000 – 9500	0.142	0.857
9500 – 10000	0.148	0.763
10000 >	0.129	0.871

Mortality Differential by Household Clan

The available data for the present study evidence that Sahraia have an existence of 21 exogamous clan units. The maximum child loss ratios are found to be measured in those households (Table 4.67) who belong to Jaborolia clan (0.273). Deboria clan (0.266) and Digoria, Shelia, Norboia & Sholonki clans (0.250 each) whereas minimum child loss ratio is retained in those clans who belong to Negtelia & Ghoria clans (0.166 each) and Paria & Shonoria clans (0.200 each). The child loss r

TABLE: 4.67

Mortality Differential by Household Clan Among Saharia

Sl. No.	*Name of Clans*	*Child Loss Ratio*	*Child Survival Ratio*
1.	Shoria	0.228	0.771
2.	Gobaria	0.220	0.779
3.	Kheria	0.223	0.767
4.	Monia	0.222	0.777
5.	Belhoria	0.241	0.757
6.	Digoria	0.250	0.750
7.	Shelia	0.250	0.751
8.	Deboria	0.266	0.733
9.	Ataria	0.212	0.786
10.	Dhoria	0.237	0.690
11.	Dongia	0.233	0.666
12.	Negtelia	0.166	0.833
13.	Norboia	0.250	0.750
14.	Barodia	0.231	0.760
15.	Badratia	0.206	0.793
16.	Jaborolia	0.273	0.725
17.	Sholonki	0.250	0.750
18.	Paria	0.200	0.798
19.	Ghoria	0.166	0.832
20.	Shonoria	0.200	0.800
21.	Chandia	0.238	0.761

atio is varied in accordance with the traditional rules and regulations of various clans. Most of the illiterate couples in a specific clan are the extreme followers of their traditional orthodox. They are exposed not to violate their rules and norms and even they prefer to tribal doctors and their traditional methods of treatment for their children. In this condition, the unscientific treatment forcefully influences their high child loss as compared to others.

In other side, the maximum child survival ratios are seen to be estimated in those households (Table 4.67) who belong to Negtelia clan (0.833), Ghoria clan (0.832) and Shonoria clan (0.800) whereas minimum child survival ratios are presented by those households who belong to Dongia clan (0.666), Dhoria (0.690) and Jaborolia clan (0.725). It may be attributed that some clan members are literate in various educational levels, financially independent and for treatment of their children and women, they prefer to modern clinical facilities and as a result, their child survival is found comparatively higher than others who are not such type. The studies of Sharma & Sharma (1999), conducted in various tribal groups of Madhya Pradesh report that sometimes child loss as well as child survival is influenced by the rules and regulations of particular clan members.

Mortality Differential by Educational Status of Women

Educational status of women plays a great role in fertility performance. In this regard, the child loss ratio among Saharia is found to be measured as higher in illiterate women (0.223) than the women of literate (Table 4.68) in various educational levels (0.166 at aggregate level). This is very clear that the child loss ratio decreases as mothers' education rises. Educational knowledge of mother always helps to enhance the mothers' ability to provide adequate child care by changing their traditional attitude, belief as well as their role in family decision-making about proper allocation of resources, food, medical care, etc. and as a result, their child loss ratio is imparted comparatively lower (Caldwell, 1979; Caldwell, et.al., 1983).

The child survival ratios tend to be higher in those women who are literate in various educational levels (0.888 at aggregate level) than those (Table 4.68) who are illiterate (0.776). Even among literate women, with the increase of educational level, the child survival ratio also increases. Ignorance of modern health care practices, insanitation, low standard of living, malnutrition, etc., are the attributed reasons of low child survival ratio of illiterate women. In this regard, Kaunstadter's (1972) studies specifically define that for protecting child mortality, the role of educated mothers is very significant as compared to fathers. The mechanisms through educational influences for the child survival are associated with the knowledge of proper utilization of modern health services as well as knowledge of health care, sanitation, personal hygiene and child nutrition (Rosenzweigh & Schultz, 1981; Jain, 1985; Burne & Walker, 1991; Chachra & Bhasin, 1998).

Table: 4.68

Mortality Differential by Educational Level of Women Among Saharia

Sl. No.	*Educational Level of Women*	*Child Loss Ratio*	*Child Survival Ratio*
1.	Illiterate	0.223	0.776
2.	Lower Primary	0.166	0.833
3.	Upper Primary	0.166	0.833
4.	Middle School	0.000	1.000
5.	High School	0.000	0.000

Mortality Differential by Educational Level of Husbands

The educational level of husbands is also incorporately correlated with the child loss and child surviving. Information, collected for the present study record that the child loss ratio among Saharia (Table 4.69) is found to be measured comparatively higher in illiterate husbands (0.223) than the husbands who are literate in various educational levels (0.123 at aggregate level). So, it is a clear statement that child mortality decreases with the increase of educational level. The literate husbands are involved comparatively in better occupation and have a better earning. Most of the husbands of various educational levels prefer to modern medical services for the treatment of their children. Their standard of living, personal hygiene, etc. are comparatively better and all these are attributed as the reasons which reduce their frequent child loss (Adak, 1994; Nag, 1998).

In other side, the child survival ratio of illiterate husbands (Table 4.69) is depicted low (0.765) as compared to literate husbands (0.853, at aggregate level) and even with the increase of educational level, their child survival ratio increases varying to lower primary (0.798), upper primary (0.812), middle school (0.861) and higher school (0.941). Due to better occupation and income, the educated husbands are able to provide the adequate medical facilities, standard of living, nutritional food items, sanitation, etc. which influence their high child survival whereas the illiterate husbands are not financially as well as intellectually capable to facilitate the same and these are the attributed reasons of their low child survival. Child mortality varies inversely with father's education barring a few irregularities. It may also be mentioned here that small amount of education is found to have little effect on child mortality risk and not until primary school is completed does education reduce risks appreciably (Hill, 1991).

TABLE: 4.69
Mortality Differential Educational Level of Husbands Among Saharia

Sl. No	*Educational Levels of Husbands*	*Child Loss Ratio*	*Child Survival Ratio*
1.	Illiterate	0.223	0.765
2.	Lower Primary	0.203	0.798
3.	Upper Primary	0.187	0.812
4.	Middle School	0.064	0.861
5.	High School	0.055	0.941

Mortality Differential by Beneficiary Loan Accepted Families

Beneficiary loan accepted Saharia families are financially advanced and this has an effective inclusion in fertility performance. The child loss ratio is found to be measured as high in those households (Table 4.70) who did not get any loan (0.230) as compared to loan accepted households (0.218 at aggregate level). Further, specifically, the maximum child loss ratios are noticed in those households who accepted fishery loan (0.258), cemented building loan (0.235) and poultry loan (0.231) whereas stone housing loan accepted households do not present any child loss ratio but mat-making loan accepted households have a presentation of lowest child loss ratio (0.164). The loan accepted households are found to have a comparatively better financial position than others. Due to financial improvement, they are able to yield almost all facilities (particularly medical, communication, standard of living, education, etc.) which curtail their child loss.

TABLE: 4.70

Mortality Differential by Beneficiary Loan Accepted Families Among Saharia

Sl. No.	*Name of Various Loan*	*Child Loss Ratio*	*Child Survival Ratio*
1.	Bullock Purchasing Loan	0.209	0.791
2.	Goatery Loan	0.226	0.773
3.	Poultry Loan	0.231	0.765
4.	Fishery Loan	0.258	0.741
5.	Mat-Making Loan	0.164	0.812
6.	Bamboo Work Loan	0.202	0.797
7.	Stone Housing Loan	0.000	1.000
8.	Cemented Building Loan	0.235	0.764
9.	No Any Loans	0.230	0.770

In other side, the child survival ratio is recorded to be low in those households (Table 4.70) who did not get any loan (0.770) as compared to various loan accepted families (0.807, at aggregate level). Even, the maximum child survival ratios are achieved by those households who accepted stone housing loan (1.000), mat-making loan (0.812) and bamboo work loan (0.797) whereas fishery loan accepted households present the lowest child survival ratio (0.741). Their financial problem and socio-cultural disadvantage are mainly indebted to enhance their inability for providing adequate medical care, nutritional foods, standard of living, etc., which influence their low child survival. In the study of Malgavkar & Panandiker (1982), a noticeable point is that the child survival ratio is high in those who are benefited by various development loan schemes. On the other hand, Nag's (1983) comparative study, conducted in West Bengal and Kerala attributes that low infant mortality in Kerala is the effect of better social development.

Mortality Differential by Menarcheal Age of Women

Menarche is a biological phenomenon while its impact is effectively incorporate in fertility performance. The highest child loss ratio among Saharia is found to be accounted in those women who attained menstruation at the age of 15 years (0.271), followed by 14 years (0.227) and 12 years (0.224) whereas lowest child loss ratio is presented by those women (Table 4.71) whose menarche was started at the age of 13 year (0.211). With the increase of menarcheal age, the child loss also increases. Due to maternal diseases, women usually attain menstruation in late. Sometimes children of those mothers are affected by transferring maternal diseases which influence their high child loss.

In other side, the child survival ratios are found to be measured as maximum when women menstruated at the age of 13 years (0.786), 12 years (0.775) and 14 years (0.773) whereas the lowest child survival ratio is presented by those women (Table 4.71) whose menarche was started at the age of 13 years (0.729). So, with the increase of menarcheal age, child survival decreases. Among them, the early age at menarche helps to conduct marriage at early age which influences frequent child births and due to not transmit the maternal diseases, generally their child survival is exhibited high as compared to others. Age at menarche may, in many societies determine the age at marriage because earlier in many societies, a girl was supposed to be married before or immediately after the attainment of menarche (Mandelbaum, 1974). It has many social implications. Indirectly it may determine the age at first birth. Earlier menarche may induce earlier pregnancy and child birth (Freedman, et.al., 1981). Conceive of women in late age usually leads pregnancy wastage and birth of illed child which influence the low child survival.

TABLE: 4.71
Mortality Differential by Menarcheal Age of Women Among Saharia

Age at Menarche (in Years)	*Child Loss Ratio*	*Child Survival Ratio*
12	0.224	0.775
13	0.211	0.786
14	0.227	0.773
15	0.271	0.729
< 13.3 Mean	0.217	0.780
13.3 Mean >	0.249	0.751

Mortality Differential by Age at Marriage of Women

The child loss and child survival are biological events but socially recognized by age at marriage of women. Among Saharia the maximum child loss ratios are expressed by those women (Table 4.72) who were married at the age of 12 years (0.311), 13 years (0.250) and 15 years (0.241) whereas minimum child loss ratios are presented by those women who were married at the age of 17 years (0.199) and 16 years (0.222). The child loss ratio tends to be higher (0.229) when women come in marital alliance before mean age at marriage (<14.0 years) than those (0.221) who come in marital alliance after mean age at marriage (14.0 years >). In the study, an attention is made that their child loss ratio decreases as the age at marriage of women increases. This can be a function of relatively both higher educational attainment and socio-economic advantage. Usually the lower child loss ratio is noticed in those women who are married late because they are not conducive to the child loss (Nag, 1998).

In other side, the maximum child survival ratios are viewed in those women who were married at the age of 17 years (0.801), 16 years (0.777) and 15 years (0.772) whereas minimum child survival ratios are shown by those women (Table 4.72) who were married at the age of 12 years (0.737), 13 years (0.750) and 14 years (0.758). The child survival ratio is comparatively lower (0.748) when women married before mean age at marriage (< 14.0 years) than those (0.783) who were married after mean age at marriage (14.0 years >). Early age at marriage of women indicates low socio-economic status and low educational attainment. Maternal care and child care are usually incorporated in accordance with their traditional rules and regulations. Their traditional way of child care is no more enough and it influences the high child loss. Hill's (1991) studies also elaborate that the children of women who are married before age of 16 years have significantly lower survival risks than the children of women, married at 20 years age or over.

TABLE: 4.72
Mortality Differential by Age at Marriage of Women Among Saharia

Age at Marriage (in Years)	*Child Loss Ratio*	*Child Survival Ratio*
12	0.311	0.737
13	0.250	0.750
14	0.238	0.758
15	0.241	0.772
16	0.222	0.777
17	0.199	0.801
< 14.0 Mean	0.299	0.748
14.0 Mean >	0.221	0.783

Mortality Differential by Settlement Pattern

As the status of stability, settlement pattern sometimes interferes the fertility parameters. In the present study among Saharia, the child loss ratio is found to be comparatively higher in migratory women (0.238) than settled (0.222). It is noticed that occupational status, educational attainment, socio-economic condition, etc. of settled women are relatively better than migrated women. As a result, they can provide the adequate medical facilities, nutritional foods, better standard of living, etc. which are conducive to the child loss. In other side, the child survival ratio (Table 4.73) of migrated women is recorded comparatively lower (0.762) than settled women (0.778). Most of the migrated women are not only illiterate but also they are positioned in socio-economically backward condition. Even they are not aware to sanitation, better standard of living, immunization and medical care for their children which influence their low child survival.

TABLE: 4.73

Mortality Differential by Settlement Pattern of Women Among Saharia

Sl. No.	*Settlement*	*Child Loss Ratio*	*Child Survival Ratio*
1	**Migratory**	0.238	0.762
2	Settled	0.222	0.778

SELECTION INTENSITY

Natural selection is one of the major evolutionary processes which brings changes in the gene frequencies in a population through the differential fertility and mortality. The major components of natural selection (i.e. different fertility & mortality) vary not only due to bio-generic factors but also these are associated with socio-cultural, religions, ethnic and environmental factors. In the present study, an attempt is made to study the index of selection potential 'I', based on differential fertility & differential mortality data, used by the methodology of Crow (1958) and Johnston & Kensinger (1971).

Population components are considered as important not only in studying the population structure and trends but also in measuring micro-evolutionary dynamics. Differential fertility and mortality – the measures of fitness, are the most fundamental events of natural selection – a major process of evolutionary changes in a population. Two major forces of natural selection – differential fertility and differential mortality are responsible for changes in the gene frequencies in a population and selection intensity is a measure of the fitness of population as expressed by the ongoing patterns of differential fertility and differential mortality, combined in a particular manner. The index of opportunity for selection measures the maximum potential rate of changes and in this regard, 'zero' indicates no change (Livingston & Spuhler, 1965). An indirect method for computing the index of total selection, based on the maximum amount of differential fertility and differential mortality in a population was formulated by Crow (1958) and further modified by Johnston & Kensinger (1971) to incorporate the embryonic mortality component.

Indices of Opportunity for Natural Selection

In both the methods (differential fertility & differential mortality), the mortality component is found to be measured as higher (0.389) than fertility component (0.348), hence selection is operating more, through mortality differential than fertility differential (Table 4.74).

In the present study among Saharia, the index of total selection intensity (I_1), calculated according to the formula of Crow (1958) is expressed comparatively lower (0.348) than the index of total selection intensity – I_2 (0.389), calculated according to the formula of Johnston & Kensinger (1971) comprising the reason of inclusion of embryonic deaths in the latter. So it is noticed that differential mortality is found comparatively higher than differential fertility to the total selection intensity. The index of total selection intensity, calculated following the formula of Crow (1958) is found that the value of I_1 (0.348) among Saharia is comparatively higher than Bhotia of Uttar Pradesh (0.330), Swangla (0.339), Ahom of Assam (0.218), Kamati (0.312), Oraon (0.243), Ahom of Manipur (0.218), Hmar (0.340), Koraga (0.340) and others but lower than Bhattra (0.633), Halba (0.388), Madia (0.558), Muria (0.495), Raji (0.862), Shipi (0.482), Bodhs (0.594), Baltis (1.020), Brokpas (0.799), Arghuns (0.828), Singapas (1.070), Manue Kolam (1.012), Apatani Guchi (0.710), Apatani Guth (0.889), Gallinng (1.070), Sonowal Kachari (0.360), Dalu (0.847), Hajoing (0.631), Jaintia (0.635), Pnar (0.401), War Khasi (0.359), Rural Muslim (0.534), Sia Muslim (0.609), Sunni Muslim (0.562), Chenchu (0.810), Hill Kolam (0.728), Sungali (0.606), Yanadi (0.566) and others. The values of I_{mc} and I_f among Saharia are also found to be measured as 0.131 and 0.192 respectively. Among other population of India, these values (I_{mc} & I_f) vary from 0.540 to 0.750 and 0.112 to 0.450 respectively. The I_2 of fertility and mortality components among Saharia, computed according to the formula of Johnston & Kensinger (1971) also tend towards the upper half of the range. The value of I_2 among Saharia is found to be estimated comparatively higher (0.389) than Ahom of Assam (0.308), Kamati (0.319), Oraon (0.369), Ahom of Manipur (0.308), Hmar (0.379) and others but lower than Bhattra (0.637), Halba (0.410), Madia (0.558), Muria (0.514), Bhutia (0.456), Raji (0.979), Bodhs (0.714), Baltis (1.277), Brokpas (0.860), Arghuns (1.048), Dalu (0.897), Hajoing (0.684), War Khasi (0.486), Sia Muslim (0.796), Sunni Muslim (0.668), Jaintia (0.814), Pnar (0.681) and others. The embryonic mortality and childhood mortality among Saharia are depicted as 0.030 and 0.131 respectively. The embryonic mortality among the population of India varies from 0.002 to 0.318 whereas variation of child mortality is also recorded from 0.072 to 0.624.

TABLE: 4.74

Indices of Opportunity for Natural Selection Among Saharia

According to Crow (1958)			*According to Johnston & Kensinger (1971)*			
I_m	I_f	I_1	I_{me}	I_{mc}	I_f	I_2
0.131	0.192	0.348	0.030	0.131	0.192	0.389

In comparison with other population groups of India, it is known that differential mortality is found high among Saharia. Low socio-cultural status, illiteracy, poverty, inadequate medical services, lack of maternal and child care, unscientific delivery, negligence on immunization, malnutrition, impured drinking water, occupational hazards of mothers, various diseases, etc. may be the attributed reasons of high differential mortality (Khongsdier, 1990; Patra & Kapoor, 1997; Langstieh, 2001). Differential fertility and differential mortality are not only varied with bio-genetic factors but also associated with socio-cultural, religious, ethnic and environmental factors. Several studies, conducted in different parts of the world including India clarify that various socio-cultural factors usually influence the total selection intensity and its related components (Spuhler, 1962, 1976, Barrai & Fraccaro, 1964; Cruz Coke, et.al., 1996; Basu, et.al. 1998; Sarkar, 1997).

MIGRATION

In simple words, migration means shifting residence from one place to another. The process of migration usually maintains a balance between population distribution and the supply of natural resources. It is a real fact that migration always increases mobility. Generally, the high degree of mobility is obtained in those people who are civilized. In the context of migration, the terms 'emigration' and 'immigration' are very much required to give acquaintation. Emigration refers to go out of a country, while immigration refers to come in a country. Thus, emigration always decreases the population of a country while increasing is expected by immigration. Further, it is a requirement to understand the terms of 'internal' migration and 'international' migration. Internal migration is confined to perform from one place to another within same country whereas, international migration is occurred crossing one political boundary to another. It is subject to laws regarding migration of the two countries. In the system of immigration, there are two factors in namely the pull factor and the push factor. When people are attracted by the advantages of new place, the benefits are regarded as pull factor. But when people want to save themselves from the restrictions and disadvantages of the existing place of living, then the factor is called as push factor. However, the available information support that in various tribal societies, internal migration is occurred to a large extent. In the present study, all components of Saharia migration are stated in a systematic manner.

Previous Villages and Distance of Migrant's Families

Distance plays an effective role in migratory system. In the present study, it is identified that 26.4 percent families (out of 333) were migrated in different villages. Only 8.0 percent families were migrated from longest distance (150 km.), followed by 112 km. (1.1 percent families), 90 km (9.1 percent families) etc. whereas 21.6 percent families were migrated from shortest distance (4 km.), followed by 5 km. (1.1 percent family), 11 km

(10.3 percent families), etc. (Table 4.75). Distance is thought as a barrier of migratory movement and therefore, an expectation is that the probability of migration between two places diminishes as distance increases. According to the study of Sharma & Sharma (1999), it is clarified that among various tribal villages, a decline in frequency of migration is performed with the increase in distance. In the present study, the collected information illustrate that for the migration, distance is no more a significant matter of fact. Better work opportunity, financial benefit, comfortable environment and others are the attractive reasons which influence

TABLE: 4.75

Name of Previous Villages and Distance of Migrant's Family(s) Among Saharia

Sl. No.	*Name of Previous Village*	*Distance (km.)*	*No. of Family(s)*	*(%)*
1	Naya Gaon	22	20	22.7
2	Jebra	25	6	6.8
3	Sash Ram	90	8	9.1
4	Bish Pai	150	7	8.0
5	Kasher	12	10	11.4
6	Bhatpura	4	19	21.6
7	Ghati Gaon	11	9	10.3
8	Sashai	112	1	1.1
9	Bokar	43	1	1.1
10	Pawa	5	1	1.1
11	Panshi	37	3	3.5
12	Khater	31	1	1.1
13	Gujja	57	1	1.1
14	Sania	35	1	1.1
	Total	**------**	**88(26.4%)**	**100.0**

Saharia people to migrate from one place to another neglecting the longest or shortest distance. But Huff's (1960) studies stress that the migrant's view of remoteness and distance may not be so simple, in fact, his argument is that a migrant tends to regard nearby areas as a strongly differentiated and remote areas as uniform. Similarly, a study of Hagerstrand (1957) suggests that the economic and psychological view of distance may be generalized within a logarithmic transformation of distance.

TABLE: 4.76

Distribution of Migrant's Family Members by Age and Sex, Sex Ratio and Masculinity Proportion Among Saharia

Age Groups (in Years)	*Males*		*Females*		*Total*		*Sex*	*Masculinity Proportion*
	No.	*%*	*No.*	*%*	*No.*	*%*		
0-4	37	16.5	33	16.2	70	16.4	891.89	52.3
5-9	38	17.0	39	19.1	77	18.0	1026.31	
10-14	29	12.9	24	11.8	53	12.4	827.58	
(0-14)	**(104)**	**(46.4)**	**(96)**	**(47.1)**	**(200)**	**(46.7)**	**(923.07)**	
15-19	22	9.8	19	9.3	41	9.6	863.63	
20-24	21	9.4	17	8.3	38	8.9	809.52	
25-29	19	8.5	20	9.8	39	9.1	1052.63	
30-34	12	5.3	13	6.4	25	5.8	900.00	
35-39	10	4.5	9	4.4	19	4.4	846.15	
40-44	13	5.8	11	5.4	24	5.6	800.00	
45-49	10	4.5	8	3.9	18	4.2	932.69	
(15-49)	**(107)**	**(47.8)**	**(97)**	**(47.5)**	**(204)**	**(47.7)**	**(906.54)**	
50-54	3	1.3	4	2.0	7	1.6	133.33	
55-59	2	0.9	3	1.4	5	1.2	1500.00	
60-64	4	1.8	2	1.0	6	1.4	500.00	
65-69	3	1.4	2	1.0	5	1.2	666.66	
70+	1	0.4	0	0.0	1	0.2	000.00	
(50+)	(13)	(5.8)	(11)	(5.4)	(24)	(5.6)	(846.15)	
Total	224 (52.3%)	100.0	204 (47.7%)	100.0	428	100.0	910.71	

Migrant's Population by Age and Sex, Sex Ratio and Masculinity

For preparing a comparative account with the total population, migrant's population are distributed in different groups by age and sex. In the present study among Saharia, migrant's population in 0-14 age group is recorded as 46.7 percent which is comparatively lower than the total population of same age group (47.2 percent). But among migrants, 5.6 percent population is presented above the age of 50 years which is comparatively higher than the total population of the same age group (4.0 percent). After all, it is found a growing population in young generation and high mortality in old generation. Such population distribution are attributed due to high fertility, inadequate old age care, malnutrition, high extent of illiteracy, low level of socio-economic status, etc. Sex ratio of migrant's population is found to be measured as higher (910.71) than total population 863.68) whereas masculinity proportion is lower (52.3) than total population (53.7). Migrant's families are settled in various villages, centre to block area (Table 4.76). Due to such settlement, they get comparatively better opportunity of work than others and for this cause, both males and females involve in various works which tend to reduce discrimination against females. As a result, comparatively their sex ratio and masculinity proportion are found as high and low respectively.

Duration of Migration and Total Population

Duration of migration elaborates the stability of the population who are resettled in the study area. The available information for the present study bestow that the maxin.um families were migrated before 8-9 years (12.3 percent families with 12.2 percent population), followed by 10-11 years (11.8 percent families) and 9-10 years (11.3 percent families) whereas the minimum families (Table 4.77) were migrated before below 2 years (2.0 percent families), 3-4 years (2.0 percent families) and 6-7 years (3.4 percent families). This study also reveals that due to extreme famine, the maximum families were migrated before 8-9 years in the studied area. The minimum families were migrated in various times due to socio-economic and other causes. The evidences illustrating the 'mover-stayer concept' also define that the probability of moving within a specified time .... decreases as the length of maintaining the same residence increases (Rider & Badger, 1943).

TABLE.4.77

Duration of Migration and Total Population Among Saharia

Duration (in Years)	*No. of Families*	*(Percentage)*	*Total Population*	*(Percentage)*
< 2	2	2.3	7	(1.6)
2-3	4	4.5	22	(5.1)
3-4	2	2.3	8	1.0
4-5	5	5.7	25	5.8
5-6	7	8.0	31	7.3
6-7	3	3.4	16	3.7
7-8	6	6.8	31	7.3
8-9	9	10.2	52	12.2
9-10	12	13.6	51	11.9
10-11	10	11.4	45	10.5
11-12	6	6.8	29	6.8
12-13	3	3.4	16	3.7
13-14	8	9.1	39	9.1
14-15	4	4.5	21	4.9
15>	7	8.0	35	8.2
Total	**88**	**100.0**	**428**	**100.0**

Various Reasons of Migration

An exclusive interview elaborates that without having any reasons, nobody is ready to leave his native place. Various reasons are imparted to be incorporated in migratory movement. In the present study among Saharia, it is comprised that the maximum families were migrated in the studied area due to lack of work (54.5 percent), shortage of water (17.0 percent), economic exploitation (10.2 percent), etc. In other side, the minimum families were migrated in this area for the cause of marriage in same clan (1.1 percent), lack of treatment center (3.4 percent), social exploitation (5.7 percent), etc. (Table 4.78). This study also makes an assessment that Saharia have a tendency to migrate from one village to another and even from one area to another. Migration is caused in the Saharia villages either by pressure of economy or by internal conflicts. Natural calamities like - flood, drought, famine, etc. and epidemic diseases are fond to be informed as the responsible factors for their migration. Except economic factor, social factors are also indebted as the causes of their migration. Saharia people leave their place of origin where social barriers are very rigid and they feel isolated from all developmental activities. Similarly when social restriction is rather unbearable, the people leave their society (Raj, 1982; Reddy, 1992; Sharma & Sharma, 1999). According to Thomson & Lewis (1965), it is merely a recognition of the fact that far and away the most important cause of migration during the great emigration from Europe is the desire to improve economic status.

TABLE: 4.78

Various Reasons of Migration Among Saharia

Sl. No.	*Reasons of Migration*	*No. of Families*	*Percentage*
1	Lack of Work	48	54.5
2	Shortage of Water	15	17.0
3	Economic Exploitation	9	10.2
4	Always Indebtedness	7	7.9
5	Marriage in Same Clan	1	1.1
6	Lack of Treatment Centre	3	3.4
7	Social Exploitation	5	5.7
	Total	**88(26.4%)**	**100.0**

Previous and Present Occupations of Migrant's Families

The changing occupational pattern of migrated families

usually indicates the sources of work opportunities and financial development. In comparison between the present and previous occupations, a changing occupational pattern is noticed among migrant's Saharia. In the previous occupation, the maximum families (Table 4.79) practised daily labour (58.0 percent), tribal craft (14.7 percent), agriculture (10.2 percent) whereas minimum families practised hunting (3.4 percent) and food gathering (5.7 percent). Due to non-availability of forest resources and Government restriction on game, hunting and food gathering practices in the present occupation are avoided by most of migrated families. There, large number of families is landless in the present state. So, instead of agriculture, most of them are motivated to practise wage earner (88.6 percent). Only a few families (4.6 0ercent) practise agriculture sharing the land of other landlords.

TABLE: 4.79
Previous and Present Occupations of Migrant's Families Among Saharia

Sl. No.	*Various Occupations*	*Previous Occupation (Percentage)*	*Present Occupation (Percentage)*
1	Labour (Daily & Bonded)	51 (58.0)	78 (88.6)
2	Agriculture	9 (10.2)	4 (4.6)
3	Animal Husbandry	7 (8.0)	2 (2.3)
4	Tribal Craft	13 (14.7)	4 (4.5)
5	Hunting	3 (3.4)	0 (0.0)
6	Food Gathering	5 (5.7)	0 (0.0)
	Total	**88 (100.0)**	**88 (100.0)**

After producing crops, they give fifty percent products to the owners of the land. Due to lack of forest resources, tribal crafts are also far less common and animal husbandry is going to be reduced among them. Various studies report that migration is commonly found among landless people as compared to landlords. Even the availability of cheap rate labour is considered as a reason which tends to influence migration from one to another area (Bhasin, 1990; Pal, 1995; Prasad & Rao, 1996; Sharma & Sharma, 1999).

TABLE: 4.80

Reasons of Pace of Migration Among Saharia

Sl. No. Reasons of Early Migration	*No. of Families*	*Percentage*
1. Urgent Need of Work	34	56.7
2. Lack of Drinking Water	12	20.0
3. Study Purpose (Children)	2	3.3
4. Misfortune in Chait Month	7	11.7
5. Illed Health	5	8.3
Total	**60 (68.2%)**	**100.0**
Sl. No. Reasons of Migration Delayed	*No. of Families*	*Percentage*
1. Tribal Festival	10	35.7
2. Child Birth	8	28.6
3. Pregnant Women	6	21.4
4. Marriage Ceremony	4	14.3
Total	**28 (31.8%)**	**100.0**
Grant Total	88(26.4%)	100.0

Reasons of Pace of Migration

Pace of migration generally indicates the speed of migratory process. In the present study, an attempt is made to findout the various socio-cultural rules and regulations which are very much responsible for early as well as late migration among Sahara. Due to urgent need of work, lack of drinking water, study purpose, misfortune in 'Chait' month and illed health, etc., early migration was performed by 68.2 percent families whereas for the cause of tribal festival, child birth, pregnant women and marriage ceremony, migration was delayed by 31.8 percent families (Table 4.80). Saharia are the members of traditional society. Their society approved traditional rules and regulations are must obeyed by all society members. They believe that if anybody violates these rules, then he may be punished under misfortune circumstance. So, migration is swift or delay, they normally do not care it but in other side, they are very much careful not to violate their socio-cultural rules and regulations.

Demographic Profile of Migrant's

Demographic profile of migrants reviews a comparative account with the demographic situation of total Saharia population. In the present study, it is found that crude birth rate (40.81), general fertility rate (236.82), total fertility rate per women (5.66) and gross reproduction rate per women (2.32) of migrant's Saharia are comparatively lower than total Saharia (Table 4.81). But mortality measures like – crude death rate (28.03), infant mortality rate (166.66), under five mortality rate (85.71) and child mortality rate (57.69) are depicted to be high (except child mortality rate) as compared to total Saharia. At a glimpse of overview observation

TABLE: 4.81

Demographic Variables of Migrant's Saharia

Sl. No.	*Fertility Measures*	*Migrant's Saharia*	*Total Saharia*
1	Crude Birth Rate	40.81	43.76
2	General Fertility Rate	236.82	244.96
3	Total Fertility Rate per Women	5.66	6.70
4	Gross Reproduction Rate per Women	2.32	2.74
Sl. No.	*Mortality Measures*	*Migrant's Saharia*	*Total Saharia*
1	Crude Death Rate	28.03	25.77
2	Infant Mortality Rate	166.66	123.28
3	Under Five Mortality Rate	85.71	82.35
4	Child Mortality Rate	57.69	62.82

reflects that most of the migrated families are settled down arounding the Barai block. Due to such type of settlement, the Government as well as non-Government organizers usually come to the villages and propose them to use the various family planning methods. Even they supply free of cost condom and pills. Free supply of such remedies makes an impact on their fertility performance and as a result, their various fertility measures are recorded comparatively lower than total Saharia. But in the context of mortality measures, migrant's Saharia show comparatively higher than settled Saharia. Poverty, low socio-cultural status, high extent of illiteracy, malnutrition, inadequate medical facility, etc. are the attributed reasons of their high mortality.

Fertility and Mortality Differentials by Occupations of Women

Occupational status is considered to have a great impact for interfering the fertility and mortality differential. In the present study among migrant's Saharia, the maximum mean number of children ever born is exhibited in those women who practise agriculture (4.00), animal husbandry (3.75) and daily labour (3.61) whereas the minimum mean number of children ever born is pertained by those women (Table 4.82) who involve in tribal craft (3.50) and household work (3.60). Their perception is that for better agriculture, adequate man power is required and as a result, generally they are demotivated not to prefer to use the birth control devices. So, their mean number of children ever born is recorded to be high as compared to other professionals. In other side, due to adoption of various family planning methods, comparatively the lower mean number of children ever born is presented by those women who practise tribal craft (3.50). The child loss is also depended on socio-economic and educational status of women. The women of animal husbandry have a poor financial and educational status which effectively enhance their child loss ratio (0.266). Due to comparatively better financial status, the women of household work occupation may devote enough time for child caring and rearing and serve adequate medical facilities and nutritional food items. As an effect, they are enabled to achieve comparatively the low child loss ratio (0.111) and high child survival ratio (0.888).

TABLE: 4.82
Fertility and Mortality Differentials by Occupations of Women Among Migrant's Saharia

Sl. No.	*Various Household Occupations*	*Mean No. of Children Ever Born*	*Child Loss Ratio*	*Child Survival Ratio*
1	Daily Labour	3.61	0.249	0.750
2	Agriculture	4.00	0.125	0.875
3	Animal Husbandry	3.75	0.266	0.733
4	Tribal Craft	3.50	0.238	0.760
5	Household Work	3.60	0.111	0.888

Fertility and Mortality Differentials by Occupations of Migrant's Husbands

Various occupations of husbands also influence the fertility and mortality differentails among migrant's families. Due to high extent of illiteracy and non-adoption of birth control methods, the husbands of animal husbandry occupation present comparatively the higher mean number of children ever born (4.00) than the husbands of labour-daily & bonded labour (3.61) and agriculture (3.33) whereas lower mean number of children ever born is exhibited by those husbands (Table 4.83) who practise tribal craft (3.00). The husbands of tribal craft occupation generally practise their activities staying in their residence. Due to stay at home, the frequent meetings are conducted between those husbands and health workers. Health workers always try to motivate them for using the family planning methods and as a result, their mean number of children ever born is decreased. In other side, due to low socio-economic status, malnutrition, paucity of medical facilities, high extent illiteracy, etc., comparatively the higher child loss ratio is recorded in those husbands who practise animal husbandry (0.250). Comparatively better financial status, adequate modern medical facilities, literacy in various educational levels, etc., are the attributed reasons of low child loss ratio (0.100) as well high child survival ratio (0.900) in those husbands who involve in agriculture.

TABLE: 4.83
Fertility and Mortality Differentials by Occupations of Husbands Among Migrant's Saharia

Sl. No.	*Various Household Occupations*	*Mean No. of Children Ever Born*	*Child Loss Born*	*Child Survival Ratio*
1	Labour(Daily & Bonded)	3.61	0.237	0.761
2	Agriculture	3.33	0.100	0.900
3	Animal Husbandry	4.00	0.250	0.750
4	Tribal Craft	3.00	0.222	0.776

Fertility and Mortality Differentials by Migrant's Household Income

Average live births, the child loss and survival ratios are also varied in accordance with the amount of annual household income. In the present study among migrant's Saharia, it evidences that income and the mean number of children ever born are found in inconsistent relation. It may be attributed that due to better financial status in relation to high income (Rs.9500/- - 10000/-), usually they are encouraged to have more children and for this reason, their mean number of children ever born is found to be measured as high (4.00) and vice-versa (Table 4.84). This study also shows that comparatively lower income groups (Rs.3000/- - 3500/-) present the higher child loss ratio (0.295). Due to financial problem, lower income groups are unable to provide the basic needs like - nutritional foods, better medical facilities, standard of living, etc., which influence their high child loss whereas higher income groups are able to afford the same for their child and as an effect, their child loss is very low and also their child survival is very high as compared to others. Beside this, the higher income groups among migrant's Saharia are literate in various educational levels. The literate householders are more aware to sanitation, standard of living, immunization, etc., which influence their high child survival.

TABLE: 4.84

Fertility and Mortality Differentials by Household Income Among Migrant's Saharia

Income (in Rupees)	*Mean No. of Children Ever Born*	*Children Loss Ratio*	*Child Survival Ratio*
< 3000	0.00	0.000	0.000
3000 – 3500	3.00	0.295	0.666
3500 – 4000	3.50	0.285	0.714
4000 – 4500	0.00	0.000	0.000
4500 – 5000	4.00	0.275	0.625
5000 – 5500	3.76	0.246	0.654
5500 – 6000	3.77	0.294	0.705
6000 – 6500	3.88	0.287	0.711
6500 – 7000	3.42	0.166	0.833
7000 – 7500	3.50	0.178	0.820
7500 – 8000	3.54	0.179	0.819
8000 – 8500	3.40	0.117	0.882
8500 – 9000	3.25	0.076	0.923
9000 – 9500	3.00	0.000	1.000
9500 – 10000	4.00	0.050	0.932
10000 >	0.00	0.000	0.000

Fertility and Mortality Differentials by Educational Status of Migrant's Women

Educational status of women has a great role to influence the mean number of children ever born, child loss and child survival. The available information incurred of migrant's Saharia present (Table 4.85) that the illiterate women comprise comparatively the higher mean number of children ever born (4.00) than the women of lower primary (3.63) and middle school educational levels (2.00). Being influenced to the traditional orthodox, the illiterate women usually neglect to use the family planning methods which are caused as their high mean number of children ever born. But most of the women of literate in various educational levels are very much aware to adopt the various contraceptive devices which decrease their mean number of children ever born. Education of women enhances the ability to provide adequate child caring and rearing, nutritional foods, proper medical services, etc. by changing their traditional attitude and belief and as a result, their child loss ratio (0.239, at aggregate level) is recorded comparatively lower than child loss ratio (0.250) of illiterate women. Due to ignorance to sanitation, health hygiene, immunization, etc., frequent child deaths are taken place and as a reason, the child survival ratio of illiterate women is found to be measured comparatively lower (0.752) than the women of literate in various educational levels (0.875, at aggregate level).

TABLE: 4.85

Fertility and Mortality Differentials by Educational Status of Women Among Migrant's Saharia

Sl. No.	*Educational Status*	*Mean No. of Children Evern Born*	*Child Loss Ratio*	*Child Survival Ratio*
1	Illiterate	4.00	0.250	0.752
2	Lower Primary	3.63	0.239	0.750
3	Upper Primary	0.00	0.000	0.000
4	Middle School	2.00	0.000	1.000
5	High School	0.00	0.000	0.000

Fertility and Mortality Differentials by Educational Status of Migrant's Husbands

Educational status of husbands is also related with the mean number of children ever born, child loss and child survival. In the present study among migrant's Saharia, it is exhibited that with the increase of educational level of husbands, the mean number of children ever born decreases. Most of the illiterate husbands (Table 4.86) are ignorant to use the family planning methods and they are found to have relatively the higher mean number of children ever born (3.65) than the husbands of literate in various educational levels (3.38, at aggregate level). In other side, this study further depicts that comparatively the higher child loss ratio is recorded in the illiterate husbands (0.214, at aggregate level) than the husbands of literate in various educational levels (0.183, at aggregate level). Point is noted that most of the husbands of various educational levels are noticed to have comparatively better financial position and they are enabled to provide adequate medical facilities, nutritional food items, standard of living, etc., which influence their low child loss as well as high child survival than the illiterate husbands.

TABLE: 4.86
Fertility and Mortality Differentials by Educational Status of Husbands Among Migrant's Saharia

Sl. No.	Educational Status	Mean No. of Children Ever Born	Child Loss Ratio	Child Survival Ratio
1	Illiterate	3.65	0.214	0.739
2	Lower Primary	3.55	0.218	0.782
3	Upper Primary	3.50	0.190	0.809
4	Middle School	3.50	0.160	0.785
5	High School	3.00	0.166	0.833

MATERNAL HEALTH CARE

Maternal care is considered as the care which are required for mothers during their pregnancy, at the time of delivery and post delivery period by providing the nutritional foods, proper rest, health services, safe delivery, post-parturient look after, etc. In the context of child bearing, rearing and development, mothers play a crucial role. The prime care-taking role of mothers is acquainted as unique and nobody is capable to continue this. In pre and post-parturient periods, the care of mothers directly influences the growth and development of their children to a large extent. It is ensured that through maternal care, the expectant mothers learn to maintain better health, hope normal delivery, procreate healthy children, acquaint with the artistic methods of proper child care, etc. (Bhuyan, 1999). Under maternal care, the ante natal care is a first relevant stage where the would to be mothers (during pregnancy) are nursed by the direct supervision of doctors (Ahluwalia, 1963; Charles, 1971). In other side, natal care indicates the various health services, required for the women at the time of their delivery. It emphases to provide first priority to safe and clean delivery which are entertained by the women staying at home or admitting in the Hospital (WHO, 1994). In urban area, maternal care is perceived as necessary whereas rural people recognize it as a vogue. But in every urban as well as rural society, maternal care is varied in accordance with their own socio-cultural rules and norms. There are evidences that among most of the deprived tribal cultural societies in rural area, the maternal care is almost neglected. Their socio-cultural orthodox always pressurize them to obey their society approved rules and regulations while loosing maternal care. As belonged to traditional society, maternal care of Saharia tribal groups are not only regulated by their socio-cultural parameters but also concerned with economic status of the members. However, the various stages of maternal care of Saharia tribal community are discussed as follows:

ANTE NATAL CARE

Under maternal care, ante natal care refer to all pregnancy related health services which are required for the women. Staying at home or admitting in Hospital, the pregnant women are rigorously looked after by the direct supervision of doctors (Ghosh, 1983, Bhatnagar, et. al., 1986). In urban belt, ante natal care is acted significantly whereas in rural as well as in tribal area, this has no any serious acceptance. Even, there, the way of ante natal care acceptance is regulated by their socio-cultural rules and norms. The types of ante natal care among Sahara are stated in the following manner:

Cultural Practices - Fetalism

For the present study among Saharia, the gathered information indicates that the special attention to diet was not provided during the pregnancy period of most of the women. They consumed the locally available seasonal vegetables and rarely fruits. To rescue from extreme labour pain, please spiritual power, etc., a major group of expectant mothers observed fast occasionally (90.7 percent). In respecting to social taboo, they did not eat bitter, meat of any animals and birds killed by other predatory animals, etc. Due to their limited income, they were distressed to prefer to the low cost food materials. Most of the pregnant women were very much addicted to the sour and non-vegetable items because these were made easily available under their traditional dietary habit. The present study also focuses that after drinking, some of their husbands pressurized them to perform sexual intercourse (35.7 percent). Among them, the alcoholic drinking and smoking constitute a part of their regular diet (Table 4.87). These beverages are traditionally home brewed for their own consumption as well as entertaining their guests. This study further elaborates that even during pregnancy period, most of the women did not avoid drinking & smoking because of habit, enhancing strength & vigour (62.8 percent). By the evil eyes' effects relating to unborn child to a great extent, health problem, chances of disaster, etc. the maximum pregnant women did not wear costumes and ornaments (70.6 percent). A significant number of expectant mothers carried out certain restrictions in their movement. As their social taboo, they avoided funeral ground, houses of deceased persons, dense forest, barren places, killing the snake and bird, telling lie, etc. during their pregnancy period. Due to inhabit in isolated villages and respect to their socio-cultural norms, the pregnant Saharia women are mostly depended on natural remedies for their body ailments. At initial stage of physical problem, the expectant mothers generally prefer to treat under their traditional healer. But if their diseases are not come under control, then the socio-economically advanced Saharia take the treatment from modern doctors. The available data for the present study confer that due to free checkup, free medicine, doctor always available, etc., a large number of pregnant women were treated under the supervision of modern doctors (64.3 percent). In rarely, the would to be Saharia mothers were immunized (36.3 percent) and in those cases, their child loss and child survival were found to be lower and higher respectively as compared to non-immunized. So, it is assessed that high extent of illiteracy, poverty, low level of socio-cultural status, inhabitation in interior area, etc. are attributed as reasons which regulate the expectant mothers for observing fast, avoiding various food items, practicing sexual intercourse, drinking & smoking, non-wearing costume & ornaments, demarcating on movement, selecting traditional doctors for treatment, etc.

TABLE: 4.87

Observance of Socio-cultural Norms During Pregnancy Period Among Saharia

Sl.No.	*Norms Observance*	*No. of Women*	*Percentage*
1.	Fast Observance	302	90.7
	Non-Observance	31	9.3
2.	Avoidance Food Items	294	88.3
	Non-Avoidance Any Food	39	11.7
3.	Preferable Food Items	312	93.7
	No Preference Any Food	21	6.3
4.	Restriction on Sexual Intercourse	214	64.3
	Non-Restriction on Sexual Intercourse	119	35.7
5.	No Restriction on Drinking/Smoking	209	62.8
	Restriction on Drinking/Smoking	124	37.2
6.	Wearing Costume/Ornaments	98	29.4
	Non-Wearing Costume/Ornaments	235	70.6
7.	Selection of Traditional Doctor	119	35.7
	Selection of Modern Doctor	214	64.3
8.	Immunization of Women	121	36.3
	Non-Immunization of Women	212	63.7

Role of Husbands and Others

As members of nuclear family, husbands require to play a very active role at the time of delivery of their wives. They have to involve in variety of tasks relating to inform local 'Dais' for attending delivery, arrange the needy materials for cutting the navel cords of new born babies, boil the water for bathing both new born babies and mothers, look after other children, etc. In case of delivery in complication, they request the magician to perform worship expecting the minimum labour pain and immediate delivery. But in joint family, all these assigned activities are shared by other members while husbands having a major role.

NATAL CARE

Natal care refer to the care which are provided to the women at the time of their delivery. This is also considered as an important way of nursing for the mothers and new-born children. But different natal care are not equally accepted in every tribal as well as non-tribal society. Even the types of natal care are varied in accordance with the society approved rules and regulations. In various natal care, the first priority is given to safe and clean deliveries which are incorporately related to the survival of the children and better health status of the mothers. The types of natal care among Saharia society are directed by their socio-cultural beliefs, customs and norms and these are stated as follows:

Place of Delivery of Women

In the present study, Table 4.88 depicts that the maximum percentage of deliveries were performed at home (68.3 percent), home of wives' parents (26.9 percent) and Government Hospital (3.7 percent) whereas the clinics of private doctors were chosen for performing the minimum percentage of deliveries (1.1 percent). Saharia are the members of traditional society. Their society approved traditional rules and regulations are extremely followed by them. Being influenced to their unique traditional culture, normally they prefer to conduct delivery at home by the help of their known local 'Dais' (mid-wives). Saharia, in the studied area do not want to avail the facilities, made available to them by the Government either because of unawareness or lack of interest and faith. Despite of the fact, the two villages are situated in close proximity from the Hospital with facilities for delivery, they do not feel it necessary to utilize the services. It is only when the women have some difficulties and local mid-wives and traditional healer are unable to tackle the extremity, then they are facilitated by the doctors in the Hospital or any clinic or nursing home. Their exposures to the outside world and contact with the functionaries are not enabled to change their traditional outlook. Regarding to the child birth, the spiritual and moral needs of the new born are given the highest priority by the villagers who are therefore reluctant to deliver in the Hospital. But the higher proportion of institutional deliveries is an indicator of better health outreach (Mishra, 1993; Adak, 1994; Bhuyan, 1999; Nayak & Babu, 2001; Prasad & Nagaraj, 2001).

Table: 4.88

Place of Delivery of Women Among Saharia

Sl.No.	*Place of Delivery*	*Number of Deliveries*	*Percentage*
1	Home	832	68.3
2	Home of Wife's Parents	328	26.9
3	Clinic of Private Doctors	13	1.1
4	Government Hospital	45	3.7
	Total	**1218**	**100.0**

Delivery Attendants

The collected information exhibit (Table 4.89) that the maximum percentage of deliveries of the respondents or women were performed by the help of local mid-wives (60.7 percent), husbands' relatives (27.6 percent), wives' relatives (7.2 percent) and doctor-nurses in Hospital (3.6 percent) whereas the traditional healer (0.3 percent) and modern private doctor (0.6 percent) assisted to lead the minimum percentage of deliveries. High extent of illiteracy, low socio-economic status and tradition oriented motherhood care are responsible as the tangible factors for such differences. Due to their illiteracy and low socio-cultural status, they are not aware to receive the modern clinical facility from their local Hospital. By the influence of traditional beliefs, they generally depend on their local untrained mid-wives for conducting deliveries. Due to miss operating deliveries by unexperienced mid-wives, still births, neo-natal deaths and infection, tetanus, polio and other diseases are occurred frequently and these components are very much indebted to change their demographic structure. Health culture and health-seeking behaviour among specially the tribal communities are still today not free from superstition, primitivism and localism and all these have a great impact on types of natal care which directly or indirectly influence demographic change (Rajaratnam, et.al., 1997; Sharma, 1998; Nayak & Babu, 2001; Prasad & Nagaraj, 2001). The present study implies that due to low socio-cultural status, high extent of illiteracy and financial problem, the local 'Dais' and traditional healer are obviously requested to perform deliveries and in those cases, comparatively the higher child loss as well as lower child survival are achieved by women.

TABLE: 4.89
Delivery Attendants Among Saharia

Sl. No	*Delivery Attendants*	*Number of Deliveries*	*Percentage*
1	Husband's Relatives	336	27.6
2	Wife's Relatives	88	7.2
3	Mid-Wives ('Dias')	739	60.7
4	Traditional Healers	4	0.3
5	Modern Private Doctors	7	0.6
6	Doctor- Nurses (Hospital)	44	3.6
	Total	**1218**	**100.0**

Naval Cord Cutting Materials

According to the present study (Table 4.90), naval cords of the maximum percentage of new born children were cut by blade (72.1 percent), followed by split (11.5 percent) and scissor (7.2. percent) whereas the naval cords of the minimum percentage of children were cut by knife (3.4 percent) and arrow-head (5.8 percent). Umbilical stump is considered as the main site of tetanus infection for both new born children and mothers. In respecting to their beliefs and norms, the present study expresses that they usually use un-sterilized split, arrow head and knife for cutting the umbilical cords of the new born children. The unsterilized umbilical cords cutting materials may be attributed as the reasons of tetanus infection. But by the positive explanations of health workers and voluntary organizers, most of them were motivated to use sterilized blade and scissor for cutting naval cords and as a result, their infectious diseases were also come under control. Some deliveries were also conducted in Government Hospital and private nursing home and in those cases, naval cords were cut by sterilized scissor and blade which helped to reduce the infectious diseases. The infant deaths are greater among those mothers whose umbilical cords were cut by unsterilized materials (Adak, 1994; Rajaratnam, et.al. 1997).

TABLE: 4.90

Naval Cord Cutting Materials of New Born Children Among Saharia

Sl. No.	*Materials*	*Number of Deliveries*	*Percentage*
1	Split	140	11.5
2	Arrow Head	71	5.8
3	Blade	878	72.1
4	Knife	41	3.4
5	Scissor	88	7.2
	Total	1218	100.00

Sources of Water

Most of the Saharia use water of well and rarely tube-well and pond at the time of delivery. The usable water in Saharia inhabitat area is neither purified nor clean. Even in May and June months, they always face problem due to unavailability of water in well and pond. During this period, tube-well is also failed to get the water layer. So, they collect very less quantity of water from another villages. Water is considered as the essential requirement for all. In this regard, the present study depicts that at the time of delivery, most of the Saharia use water which is available in their locality. Due to use of such impured water, specially their new born babies are suffering from various water borne diseases and infection. Water of tube-well is comparatively better qualitative than the water of well and pond. At the time of delivery, socio-culturally advanced Sahara experincely utilize water of tube-well and as a result, they achieve low child loss as well as high child survival as compared to others.

Food Items and Rest

After delivery, the food items are subjected to a great concern. It is real that any weightage is not given for sanctioning the special foods whereas a wide range of items is prohibited to the mothers. In the opinion of Saharia, vegetables like - pumpkin, bottle gourd, brinjal, etc. get secretion certain more water and therefore, these are late to dry the internal organs. Items containing heavy fat such as oil, mutton, etc. are forbidden in anticipation of digestive problems. Heavy spices are considered as 'hot' and therefore thought as bad. However, improper food items generally make harm for both the mothers and babies by creating various diseases which influence specially the infant deaths. Keeping in view to the health aspect, they recommend rest for the nursing mothers, there is a custom of secluding the women after child-births for certain period of time and this gives them the chance of relaxation to some extent. Rest for the post-parturient mothers is also depended on financial position of the households. The present study expresses that due to financial problem, most of the post-parturient mothers tried to recover their health within short period of time because they were instigated to the responsibility for supporting their husbands in relation to earn. So, it is an assessment that the post-parturient mothers among Saharia entertain shorter rest which influences health problems for both mothers and new born children.

From the forgoing discussion, it is tangible that the modern way of maternal care is almost neglected among Saharia community. As a primitive tribe, the expectant mothers are lagging behind other tribal groups in relation to the utilization of maternal care services. The findings of the study reveal that during pregnancy period, the women are enforced to obey a lot of socio-cultural rules and regulations. Most of the pregnant women are governed by some dietary restrictions. Their traditional customs and norms are very much concerned to the locally available food items which should or should not be eaten by the expectant mothers. Drinking the alcoholic beverage and smoking are considered as the indispensable part of their daily life. Even, a major group of women practise drinking, smoking and sexual intercourse during their pregnancy period. In respecting to their social taboo, they rarely take treatment from modern doctors and practise immunization, avoid funeral grounds and houses of deceased persons, etc. Mostly they prefer to conduct delivery at home, call local 'Dais' for attending delivery, cut naval cord by blade or split, collect usable water from well, restrict various food items and allot very short period of time for post-parturient rest. These wide disparities in maternal care may be attributed due to certain socio-cultural variables like – deplorable low educational status, high extent of poverty, inadequate modern health care facility, inhabiting in remote area, non-admixture with modern society, etc. For their entire upliftment, multi-dimensional development projects should immediately be launched during long time. Under the projects, the first priority should be given on their financial aid and better educational facility. Modern health care system should also be penetrated in an effective way. Then, an exception may be pertained to the advanced socio-cultural aspects as well as maternal status of Saharia.

INFANT AND CHILD HEALTH CARE PRACTICES

The role of mothers is perceived as crucial for child bearing and rearing. Even our ancient history evidences that in every society, the prime care taking role of mothers is appreciated as unique and their position in this regard is not substituted by any body. The growth and development of infant and child are totally depended on pre-parturient and post-parturient care of mothers. Nutritional food intake, proper rest, adequate health care facility, safe delivery, etc. of expectant mothers are directly associated with better health status of infants. So, systematic maternal care is a very significant component which exposed to maintain better health, expect normal delivery, procreate healthy baby and acquaint with the method of proper child care. During a few days after delivery, especially the new born babies are positioned under very vulnerable condition. It is a great challenge for them to adjust with the new victim environment by breathing, accepting of food, etc. The essential requirements of the neo-natal are not only limited in psychological sphere but also these are illustrated in satisfaction of hunger, thirst, sleep, warmth and elimination (Bhuyan, 1999). In every society, there is own maternal as well as infant and child care system which is regulated by their society approved traditional rules and norms. The people of rural area are more efficient to regard their traditional beliefs and customs as compared to the urban settings. As inhabitants in interior area, the indigenous traditional culture of Saharia primitive tribe is still integrated in a great extent. In the context of their entire system of infant and child care, the various components are highlighted under the present study.

As early stage of human beings, the helpless infant and child essentially require various care. Specially neo-natal is considered as the period of delicacy. After birth, the first few days are faced as very critical stage. During this period, they are to tolerate the completely new, strange and victim environment and to adjust with it, the new borns try to get breathing, need food materials and other external components. But sometimes as an effect of crude environment, the new borns are attacked by various diseases which even may loss their survival power. Whereas favourable environment enhances their living quickly with each passing day. However, the needs of babies are not only contained in physical phenomenon but also its adequate expansions are elaborated in psychological aspect. The infant and child care are essential but it's acceptance is varied in accordance with population groups, their place of inhabitation, socio-cultural norms and customs, etc. As interior dwellers, Saharia primitive tribal groups are totally disconnected from national life. In practising infant and child care, they are guided by their society approved traditional socio-cultural rules and regulations which are stated in the following manner:

Bathing and Clothing After Delivery

After delivery, the boiled water mixing with 'Nim Patti'

is kept ready for the bath of new born babies. This substance is believed to purify the new borns and to get free from the infectious diseases. Traditionally, the 'Nim Patti' mixed boiled water is used for bathing both the new born children and also mothers. Socio-economically advanced Saharia use soap and boiled water for bathing purpose after delivery. There is an opinion of the medical expert that giving bath to a baby immediately after birth is not a sound practice. According to them, giving bath means bringing down the baby's body temperature abruptly. Clothing after bath is also related with their socio-cultural tradition. Due to low socio-economic status, illiteracy, etc., generally Saharia use a piece of wasted cloth for wrapping the new borns and in most of the cases, the children are to be come under infectious diseases. For wrapping the new borns, socio-economically advanced Saharia use new, clean and soft cloth which have a chance to avoid the infection.

Initiation of Breast-feeding After Child Birth

The present study depicts that the maximum percentage of women initiated breast-feeding to the children after 12-18 hours (38.8 percent), 8-12 hours (36.9 percent) and 18-24 hours (15.9 percent) of their deliveries whereas the minimum percentage of women initiated breast-feeding to the children after above 30 hours (1.5 percent) and 24-30 hours (6.9 percent) of their deliveries (Table 4.91). Among them, infant feeding practices are closely associated with the culture of their society. Different beliefs, norms, customs, etc. are the responsible factors which determine the duration of initiation of breast-feeding. Socio-economically advanced Saharia usually delay to start breast-feeding to the new born children. Their supporting explanations indicate that after delivery, during some period of time, new mothers are sicken and their milk is thick, indigestible and raw and also not suitable for the infants. But as nutritional food and preventive for new borns, the socio-culturally backward women initiate breast feeding to their children within very short period of time after birth. Postponing suckling is an unnatural practice and not only it does the infants often starve for this period but also makes more difficult to establish lactation later on. Initiation of breast-feeding to the children on the 2nd or 3rd day after birth is the common trend which is uniformly followed by the mothers of each educational class as well as economic strata except the lower groups where the number of mothers initiates breast-feeding on the first day. Breast-feeding immediately after delivery continues to breast-feeding longer usually about twice as long. Immediate breast-feeding provides a measure of immunological protection from diarrhoea and allergy. Even breast-feeding immediately after birth increases the success and duration of the breast-feeding (Rosa, 1978; Salariya, et.al., 1978; Bahl & Singh, 1982; Helsing & King, 1984; Mishra, 1993).

TABLE: 4.91
Initiation of Breast-Feeding After Child Birth Among Saharia

Initiation of Breast Feeding (in Hour)	*Number of Women*	*Percentage*
8-12	123	36.9
12-18	129	38.8
18-24	53	15.9
24-30	23	6.9
30 >	5	1.5
Total	333	100.0

Initiation of Breast-feeding Using Substitute

In the present study, it is observed that the maximum percentage of Saharia women initiated breast-feeding to the children by continuous practicing (18.9 percent), followed by 13.6 percent (spontaneously breast-feeding), 12.9 percent (using honey on nipple), 12.3 percent (practicing with wet cotton), etc. whereas the minimum percentage of Saharia women initiated breast-feeding to the children by practicing with nipple and washing the breast with curd (5.4 percent each), followed by 6.0 percent (practicing with finger), 6.3 percent (using tribal medicine), etc. (Table 4.92). Breast-feeding practice using substitute is depended on socio-economic status and parental education. The women of comparatively lower socio-cultural status apply 'Jhar Fuck', use tribal medicine, curd, etc. before initiation of breast-feeding. Whereas socio-economically advanced Saharia women generally use honey on nipple of the breast for initiation of breast-feeding to the babies. Among them, there is a custom to give some other foods even if breast-feeding is not late. However, from the point of view of nutrition and health, this practice is very unsound. There is a greater risk of adding germs by giving some infected foods. Secondly, by giving other materials like – tribal medicine, curd, etc., one may delay the breast-feeding which is not at all desirable. It is an established fact that for successful breast-feeding, the baby should be put the mother's breast as early as possible. This practice hastens the production of milk and also provides the baby with required nourishment (Mehta, 1975; Katiyer, et.al. 1981; Nalwa, 1981; Mishra, 1993; Bhuyan, 1999).

TABLE: 4.92

Initiation of Breast-Feeding Using Substitute Among Saharia

Sl. No.	*Process of Initiation*	*Number of Women*	*Percentage*
1	By Continuous Practicing	63	18.9
2	By Practicing with Wet Cotton	41	12.3
3	By Using Honey on Nipple	43	12.9
4	Spontaneously Breast Feeding	45	13.6
5	By Practicing with Nipple	18	5.4
6	By Practicing Tribal 'Jhar Fuck'	30	9.0
7	By Using Tribal Medicine	21	6.3
8	By Bringing out Breast Milk	34	10.2
9	By Washing the Breast with Curd	18	5.4
10	By Practicing with Finger	20	6.0
	Total	**333**	**100.0**

Colostrum Feeding of Children

For the first few days, new mothers' breast do not produce very much the ordinary milk. Instead of this, they produce a small quantity of yellow fluid called colostrum which contains less fat and sugar but more protein than ordinary milk. It is very special protective substance for the babies who need most. Protein in colostrum means the availability of immunoglobulin which protects the babies from infection. In older children, the immunoglobulin is secreted by intestine gland but new born babies can not make enough immunoglobulin for themselves. Yet they become exposed to dangerous micro-organisms as soon as they are born. There is 20-40 minutes more immunoglobulin in colostrum than in mothers' blood. When the babies drink the colostrum, the immuniglobulin lies in their intestine and prevents many kinds of infection (Savage, 1983).

TABLE: 4.93

Colostrum Feeding to the New Borns Among Saharia

Sl. No.	*Reasons of Colostrum Feeding*	*Number of Women*	*Percentage*
1	For Nutrition of Child	65	22.6
2	For Healthy Child	41	14.3
3	For Family Rule	14	4.9
4	For Avoiding Disease	31	10.8
5	For Long Age of Child	35	12.2
6	For Strong Child	21	7.3
7	For Brilliant Child	11	3.9
8	For Extra Energy of Child	31	10.8
9	For Fast Growing of Child	38	13.2
	Total	**287 (86.2%)**	**100.0**
Sl. No.	*Reasons of Restriction*	*Number of Women*	*Percentage*
1	For Chances of Dysentery	5	10.9
2	For Chances of Worm Disease	12	26.1
3	For Chances of Abdominal Pain	5	10.9
4	For Chances of Vomiting	6	13.0
5	For Chances of Infection	18	39.1
	Total	**46 (13.8%)**	**100.0**
Grand Total		**333**	**100.0**

Data for the present study exhibit that among Saharia, 86.2 percent women fed colostrum to their borns due to various reasons like – nutrition, long age, extra energy, etc. whereas 13.8 percent women did not feed colostrum for the causes of dysentery, vomiting, etc. (Table 4.93). In the tribal groups, there is existed the different socio-cultural beliefs, customs and norms which determine the colostrum feeding to the new born babies. Comparatively the women of high socio-cultural status are not found to feed colostrum to their children mentioning the various reasons like – chances of dysentery, vomiting, infection, etc. Most of the mothers give colostrum to their babies getting the advices either from the doctor or nurse or from their mothers and mothers-in-law. The practice of discarding colostrum feeding is markedly reduced with the increasing of educated mothers. Unfortunately colostrum feeding is not recommended by our ancient physicians. Colostrum rejection is also a tradition in many Indian communities. Even various studies report that a good percentage of mothers discard colostrum feeding as per the advice of the nursing staff (Rao, et.al., 1972; Singhal & Guru, 1973; Ojha, 1979; Agarwal, et.al., 1986; Pandey & Tiwari, 1993; Basu, 1994; Kshatriya, et.al., 1997).

Frequency of Breast-Feeding

The gathered information imply (Table 4.94) that the maximum percentage of Saharia women fed breast milk to their babies 6-9 times (34.9 percent), 9-12 times (34.5 percent) and 3-6 times (17.7 percent) whereas the minimum percentage of Saharia women (12.9 percent) fed breast milk to their babies above 12 times (in 24 hours). Frequency of breast-feeding is totally depended on the occupational status of women. It is informed that the women who involve specially in household work, have enough time to practise frequently breast-feeding to their children. In other side, due to continuous involvement in work, the women of other occupations do not get any additional time for increasing frequency of breast-feeding. It is also reported that due to poverty, the Saharia women have to involve themselves in various works and as an effect, their breast milk secretion is reducing slowly. So, as a reason of shortage of milk secretion, the required milk for the babies is not stored in the milk glands of women and it naturally influences to high frequency of breast-feeding. Generally mothers feed breast milk to the babies when they are crying demanding it. Breast feeding may be practised either on demand, i.e. whenever a child cries indicating hunger or may be practised on the basis of regular time schedule. But the current advice expresses that breast-feeding is needed on demand (Gopujkar, et.al., 1984). For entertaining the demanded breast-feeding of the babies, sometimes the frequency of breast-feeding is found to be low. There are higher proportion of infants of demand- feeding group, originated from rural area and higher percentage of scheduled (fixed) breast-feeding infants, originated from industrial and urban areas, irrespective of place of delivery. Infants specially in rural area are fed breast milk on demand as expressed by thęir crying (Sharma & Lahoria, 1977; Bahl & Kausal, 1987; Mishra, 1993). Due to low frequency of breast-feeding on demand and shortage of breast milk secretion, Saharia children do not get the required diet and as a result, their health condition is found to be illed which influences high infant deaths.

TABLE: 4.94
Frequency of Breast Feeding Among Saharia

Frequency (in Time)	*Number of Women*	*Percentage*
3-6	59	17.7
6-9	116	34.9
9-12	115	34.5
12>	43	12.9
Total	**333**	**100.0**

Duration of Breast-feeding at a Time

The present study defines that the maximum percentage of Saharia women fed breast milk to their babies during 10-13 minutes (44.8 percent), 7-10 minutes (21.6 percent) and 13-16 minutes (15.3 percent) whereas (Table 4.95) the minimum percentage of women fed breast milk to their babies during above 16 minutes (5.1 percent) and 4-7 minutes (13.2 percent). Socio-cultural interferences and financial problem directly or indirectly regulate the duration of breast-feeding to the babies.

Economically poor Saharia women have to involve themselves in various activities throughout the day and in that condition, they can not consume more time for breast-feeding purpose. Due to lack of supporting persons at home, they generally carry their babies to the working places. During their duty period, occasionally they are allowed to get rest for a certain period of time which they expense for breast-feeding purpose. This shortest duration of breast-feeding is no more enough to supply the required milk to their babies. In other side, it is reported that for involving in heavy work, milk secretion in their breast is slowly come down and for this reason, most of the Saharia mothers are unable to supply the sufficient milk whatever is needed for their offsprings. Breast milk is considered as the only nutritious food for the babies. But due to insufficient breast milk supply, their babies are prostrated containing poor health which influences high infant mortality.

TABLE:4.95

Duration of Breast Feeding at a Time Among Saharia

Duration (in Minute)	*Number of Women*	*Percentage*
4 -7	44	13.2
7-10	72	21.6
10-13	149	44.8
13-16	51	15.3
16>	17	5.1
Total	333	100.0

Methods Used for Increasing Lactation

There is a great emphasis that for increasing lactation, the maximum percentage of Saharia women used sugar (18.6 percent), molasses (17.5 percent), liquid of sweet leaves (9.6 percent), etc.(Table 4.96) whereas the minimum percentage of women sacrificed hen (2.7 percent), used modern medicine (5.1 percent), and others. For increasing lactation, the various usable methods are implemented on the basis of their socio-cultural beliefs, customs and norms. It has a clarification that whenever their babies do not take interest in breast-feeding, then they use mainly sweet tasted materials on nipple of the breast for more lactation. But for the bad effect of evil eyes, sometimes their children are unable to take breast milk and in this condition, the socio-culturally backward Saharia perform hen sacrifice programme, as a cultural activity. Due to heavy work load, generally their breast milk secretion is reduced and in that circumstance, their babies are spontaneously demotivated from breast-feeding practice. But they presume that frequently breast-feedings have a chance to increase more quantity of breast-milk secretion. As a reason, they use another material on breast for increasing frequency of breast-feeding as well as lactation. More lactation always develops the health of babies and reduces the frequent deaths. But any kind of artificial foods for supporting lactation of the babies may be harmful. By the effect of these foods, sometimes babies are suffered from different indigestive and infectious diseases which influence their poor health status (Mishra, 1993).

TABLE: 4.96

Methods Used for Increasing Lactation Among Saharia

Sl. No.	*Methods Used*	*Number of Women*	*Percentage*
1	Honey Used	31	9.3
2	Molasses Used	58	17.5
3	Sugar Used	62	18.6
4	Glucose Powder Used	22	6.6
5	Carefully Feeding	21	6.3
6	Liquid of Sweet Leaves Used	32	9.6
7	'Jhar Fuck' with Water	22	6.6
8	Tribal Medicine Used	28	8.4
9	Hen Sacrificed	9	2.7
10	Modern Medicine Used	17	5.1
11	Lactation Spontaneously	31	9.3
	Total	**333**	**100.0**

Methods Used for Weaning Practice

The present study exhibits that for weaning practice, the maximum percentage of Saharia women used bitter substance (25.9 percent), followed by 23.6 percent (by birth of next child), 23.2 percent (introducing solid food), etc. whereas the minimum percentage of women applied 'Jhar Fuck' (3.2 percent), followed by lack of enough time (3.6 percent) and weaning by force (4.6 percent). Even 33.9 percent women continue breast-feeding to their babies till field study (Table 4.97). Due to respect to their traditional beliefs, norms and customs, the women of lower socio-cultural status usually practise weaning by the use of bitter substance, tribal medicine, 'Jhar Fuck', etc. In other side, comparatively, the women of better socio-economic status practise weaning by birth of next child, introducing solid food and others.

TABLE: 4.97
Methods Used for Weaning Practice Among Saharia

Sl. No.	*Methods Used*	*Number of Women*	*Percentage*
1	Bitter Used	57	25.9
2	By Birth of Next Child	52	23.6
3	Introducing Solid Food	51	23.2
4	Tribal Medicine Used	17	7.7
5	Applying 'Jhar Fuck'	7	3.2
6	Creating Fear of Child Disease	18	8.2
7	Lack of Enough Time	8	3.6
8	Weaning by Force	10	4.6
	Total	**220 (66.1%)**	**100.0**
9	Breast Feeding Continuing	113 (33.9%)	100.0
	Grand Total	**333**	**100.0**

Due to lack of nutritional food and always involvement in heavy work, most of the mothers are unable to feed sufficient breast milk to their babies and in this condition, they generally practise weaning using various methods. The process of weaning may have the grave psychological and physiological consequences. Weaning causes great frustration and sudden weaning is traumatic for the children fróm mothers' breast determental effect on children's personality (Kuppuswamy, 1980). Proper weaning in terms of methods as well as pattern and timing are important for normal development of the children which makes a great effect in demographic situation (Adak, 1994; Bhuyan, 1999).

Children Age of Weaning Practice

It is informed that the maximum percentage of Saharia mothers practised weaning at the age of 2 years of their children (52.3 percent), 3 years (21.8 percent) and 1 year (17.3 percent) whereas the minimum percentage mothers practised weaning at 5 years age (2.7 percent) and 4 years age (5.9 percent) of their children. Only 33.9 percent Saharia mothers practise breast-feeding till field study (Table 4.98). Being influenced by socio-cultural tradition, the illiterate Saharia mothers generally continue breast-feeding during longer period. But due to financial problem, most of the mothers have to involve themselves in heavy work and as an effect, their milk secretion is reduced. So, these mothers are motivated to practise weaning from the early age (below 2 years) of their children. In other side, severe modernization or shifting to the modern economic activities such as service, business, etc. is the attributed reason to have negative impact on longer age of weaning practice. There are two distinct trends in the popular beliefs about long period of breast-feeding of beyond 2-3 years and 'prolonged breast-feeding' which are very beneficial to the children (Helsing & King, 1984). Children who have suckled for a number of years, may become excessive strong, bright or healthy which reduce high infant deaths. The tradition in most parts of the world is to breast feed from 2-3 years and prolonged breast-feeding about 2-3 years is common among lower socio-economic groups in India. Breast-feeding also provides health benefits for the mothers. It accelerates post-parturient recovery and there is also evidence that women who practise breast feeding longer, they have a lower breast cancer rate later in life. (Rao, et.al., 1972; Belavady, 1980; Agarwal, et.al., 1986; Mishra, 1993; Babu, 1996; Bhuyan, 1999). Due to practise weaning at shorter duration (1 year), Saharia children are suffering from various mal-nutritional diseases and comparatively their child loss and their child survival are found to be higher and lower respectively. Infant death is about 1.6 times greater among never breast feed infants than among their breast feed counterparts (Helsing & King, 1984; Mishra, 1993; Bhuyan, 1999).

TABLE: 4.98

Children Age of Weaning Practice Among Saharia

Age of Child (in Year)	*Number of Women*	*Percentage*
1	38	17.3
2	115	52.3
3	48	21.8
4	13	5.9
5	6	2.7
Total	**220 (66.1%)**	**100.0**
Continuing	113 (33.9%)	100.0
Grand Total	**333**	**100.0**

Reasons of Selection of Doctors for Treatment of Children

The collected information comprise that for the treatment of children, 29.1 percent Saharia households selected traditional healer whereas 70.9 percent households selected modern doctors due to various causes like - carefully check up, experienced healer or doctor, free medicine, etc. (Table 4.99). Curative measures or treatments are mainly depended on the economic condition, educational level, accessibility to health care, socio-cultural tradition and so on. Usually Saharia people do not adopt any particular measure immediately after the children become ill. It is only when the ailment persists, they initiate action. Minor ailments like - fever, skin, eye infection, etc. are not taken seriously. It is narrated by many parents that the treatment is depended on the nature of illness. If it is an ordinary one because of some disfunctions of the body, then there is no harm in consulting with the doctors. But if it is caused by some ghosts or spirits and come into complicated nature, then they are to approach their traditional healer. According to Saharia, doctors often in Government Hospital are unavailable. Even the available doctors behave in a very indifferent manner. Again the common medicines are also far less common in the Hospital. The long distance of Hospital from most of the Saharia inhabitat villages is also another obstacle with many in taking the child care. Only when the folk medical care is failed to bring an improvement in the condition of the children, then people tend to think for accepting the benefit of modern medicines from the private doctors or doctors of Government Hospital. It is primarily because the fact

TABLE: 4.99

Reasons of Selection of Doctors for Treatment of Children Among Saharia

Sl. No.	*Reasons of Doctors Selection*	*Traditional Doctor*		*Modern Doctor*		*Total*	
		No.	*%*	*No.*	*%*	*No.*	*%*
1	Carefully Check up	11	11.3	28	11.9	39	11.7
2	Suddenly Treatment	4	4.1	20	8.5	24	7.2
3	Quickly Check up	2	2.1	15	6.4	17	5.1
4	Experienced Doctor	16	16.5	19	8.0	35	10.6
5	Qualified Doctor	0	0.0	16	6.8	16	4.8
6	Medicine Available	6	6.2	14	5.9	20	6.0
7	Free Medicine	6	6.2	32	13.5	38	11.4
8	Always Available (Dr.)	13	13.4	13	5.5	26	7.8
9	Free Check up	5	5.2	12	5.1	17	5.1
10	Faith on Doctor	11	11.3	10	4.2	21	6.3
11	Instrumental Check up	0	0.0	21	8.9	21	6.3
12	Ayurvedic Medicine	15	15.4	0	0.0	15	4.5
13	Better Medicine	5	5.2	11	4.7	16	4.8
14	Easily Feedable	3	3.1	25	10.6	28	8.4
	Total	97 (29.1%)	100.0	236 (70.9%)	100.0	333	100.0

that modern medicines are not readily available and most of the Saharia people do not have much faith on modern clinical system. It may be attributed that better socio-cultural status, higher the literacy rate, etc. are more the reliance on qualified doctors and vice-versa. Science and technology tend to increase rational control over events and thus reduce the need for non-rational technique (Patel, 1991; Bhuyan, 1999). There is a close relationship between the pattern of treatment and death of the children. More the reliance on qualified doctors, the lesser and higher are the number of childhood death and survival respectively. The long distance of primary health centre, poor communication, non-availability of medicines and doctors, indifferent attitude of the health staff to the tribal people, illiteracy, superstition & prejudices and greater faith on traditional health care system, etc. are some of the obstacles which stand between the people and modern health care facility (Adak, 1994; Bhuyan, 1999).

Immunization of Offsprings

Immunity is defined as the ability of the body to recognize, destroy and eliminate ante-genetic material foregone to its own. A person is said to be immuned when he possesses specific protective ante-bodies or cellular immunity as a result of previous infection on immunization (Park & Park, 1985). High extent of illiteracy, low socio-cultural status, etc., may be the attributed reasons which influence not to immunize the Saharia children. It is reported that some of the literate Saharia have little knowledge about the beneficiary aspects of tetanus and polio immunization and for such reasons, their children were permitted to receive immunization (Table 4.100) against different diseases (29.3 percent - tetanus and 25.2 percent - polio). By the positive explanations of various health workers, very less percentage of Saharia were motivated to give permission to their children for receiving immunization against measles (12.5 percent), DPT (9.3 percent) and BCG (8.0 percent). Many collected information react that sometimes due to creative diseases of their children after immunization, they are not interested to receive it. Lack of adequate efforts on the part of ICDS and health functionaries, distrust to the people on this important subject, illiteracy, traditional socio-cultural beliefs, etc., may be transgressed as the reasons of paucity of immunization (Bharadwaj, et.al., 1990; Tandon & Gandhi, 1992; Kshatriya, et.al., 1997; Bhuyan, 1999).

In 1978, the policy of immunization was accepted as a National Health Programme in India. According to this policy, all children under the age of six years are to be immunized against diphtheria, whooping cough, tetanus, poliomyelitis, measles and tuberculosis. From there, all facilities under this programme are available in all Government Hospitals, dispensaries and Primary Health Centres. The process of immunization specifically states that the children below the age of one year are given three doases of DPT (against diphtheria, whooping cough and tetanus), three doases of polio (against poliomyelities) and one doase of measles and B.C.G. each (against measles and T.B.). At the age of 18 to 24 months, booster doses of DPT and polio are given them. These vaccines are supplied with free of cost in all Government Hospitals and Primary Health Centres (PHCs).

TABLE: 4.100
Immunization of Offsprings (After Delivery) Among Saharia

Sl. No.	*Type of Immunization*	*Immunized Offsprings*		*Non-Immunized Offsprings*	
		No.	**%**	**No.**	**%**
1	Measles	152	12.5	1066	87.5
2	DPT	113	9.3	1105	90.7
3	BCG	97	8.0	1121	92.0
4	Polio	307	25.2	911	74.8
5	Tetanus	357	29.3	861	70.7

(Total Ever Born Offsprings =1218)

On the whole, the foregoing discussion assesses that in accordance with the socio-cultural status, Saharia people essentially practise infant and child care. After delivery, the new borns are generally given bath with warm water and wrapped in piece of cloth. In the context of feeding, the nature gifted mothers' breast milk is considered as the most nutritionally balanced diet for the babies. For reluctantly ensuring satisfaction and happy growing of the children, they mostly start breast feeding after almost twelve hours of birth. Among them, there is a custom to give some other substitute food items for initiating breast-feeding. Most of the respondents practise colostrum feeding for conferring immune properties and preventing number of ailments and diseases in the body. Due to continuous involvement in heavy works, the milk secretion in the mothers' breast is slowly come down and as a result, they try to fulfil the demanded milk by enhancing frequency of breast feeding while reducing duration. Sometimes insufficient breast milk secretion is perceived as a reason for refusing breast-feeding of babies. In such situation, they increase lactation by the use of additional food items which sometimes make harmful prostrating to ill-health. Over-loaded work, shortage of milk secretion in the breast and next child birth are the contaminant components which resist them to practise early weaning by using bitter substance on breast, introducing solid food, etc. Weaning practice at early age always confesses the high child loss as well as low child survival. For unavailability of proper modern clinical health services and ancient beliefs, a group of mothers treats their babies under traditional healer and neglect immunization and in those cases, they pertain high child loss as well as low child survival. Lastly, the present study concludes that financial problem, high extent of illiteracy, inadequate health services, traditional socio-cultural beliefs, norms, customs, etc. are attributed as the reasons of their improper infant and child care practices. The real key to successful Saharia infant and child care lies with the improvement of their financial position, educational status, socio-cultural norms, knowledge and competence, practical training and feasible feeding practices, etc.

HEALTH SEEKING BEHAVIOUR

The World Health Organization (WHO, 1971) defines health as "a state of complete physical, mental and social well being and not merely the absence of disease and infirmity". The concept of 'well being' stands for the state of being happy, healthy or prosperous. Well being is further narrated as a harmonious relationship between an individual or a group and its physical, biological and social environment. It also incorporates the feeling of satisfaction which is associated with its outcome. Evidently 'health' includes physical health (healthy), mental health (happy) and social health (prosperous and free from strife). But in common parlance, if one comes acrossing the linguistic variables than there is a chance to fragment the complete meaning of 'health' such as 'good health', 'sound health', 'normal health', ideal health' and the like. This linguistic paradigm is probably inapplicable in the context of Indian tribe. In view of Indian socio-economic constraints, it is desirable to restrict the meaning of the concept of health to the bipolar nexus that is 'health' versus 'disease' with any rider for either.

Disturbance or illed health is a condition that accounts for physical affliction and warrants remedial measures. Health and disease are related to biological and cultural resources of a community in a specific environment. In simple as well as in traditional societies, these phenomena are rooted in social and cultural factors. Man's medical history can only be understood through an analysis of his socio-cultural milieu. In medical matters, man is steadily emerging from the bounds of his traditional cultural matrix. Although the concept of well being and the notion of the disease vary between different tribal groups, yet, in tribal habit, a person is usually considered to be affected with some diseases if the person is incapable of doing the routine work which is usually being expected to be carried out by the individual in the society, i.e. incapacitation from work is the universal index of poor health. Thus the concept of ill health becomes a functional one and not clinical (Bhasin, 1994).

The concept of disease is varied from tribal to non-tribal people. Tribal people believe that the persons who are enabled to do hard work and free from the influence of spirits, they are not come under sickness. Various factors may be attributed as the causes of diseases in tribal society. Due to violation of taboos, the angry deities punish wrongdoers which is expressed as diseases. Beside this, diseases may be affected to those who neglect the ancestors, ghosts, sorceres, witches, spirits, evil eyes, etc. Loss of body equilibrium, the entry of excessive heat or cold into the body, etc. are also the causes of disease. In regarding the curative measures or treatment, tribal people generally prefer to their local traditional healer ('Gunia'). Sometimes, better socio-economic condition, educational status, accessibility to health centre, tradition, etc. influence them for taking the modern health services.

As inhabitants in traditional society, the health seeking behaviour of Saharia is totally depended on social and cultural rules and norms. Their medical history can only be understood through an analysis of their socio-cultural components. Sometimes with the influence of modern culture, they are slowly emerging from socio-cultural boundary and achieving general awareness about health and disease which are going to be regarded as biological event while relating with environment.

Health Condition of Family Members

Most of the Saharia have no any clear knowledge about healthy persons. Their perceptions indicate that healthy persons are called those who are not suffering from any kinds of disease and have some ability to carry on their daily duties properly. Thus, they associate one's ability or disability to do any work with healthy and illed persons respectively. In the present study, the maximum percentage of Saharia are found in the category of very weak (54.7 percent) and weak (37.2 percent) health status whereas healthy (2.2 percent) and normal health (4.9 percent) status are come upon by seeking very rarely (Table 4.101). Most of the Saharia are wage earners. But in their locality, the opportunity of works is not available throughout the year. So, obviously they are facing financial problem and in that condition, they are unable to take adequate medical services specially from private doctors, nutritional food items, etc. Due to their high extent of illiteracy, low socio-cultural status, traditional belief to healer, lack of modern clinical facility, absence of close contact with the advanced people, etc., they are very loose to modern health care practices and sanitation. So, inadequacy of modern medical health care practices, malnutrition, insanitation, etc. are the attributed reasons of their very weak health status (Ghoshmaulik & Karmohapatra, 1995; Pandey, et.al., 2001).

TABLE: 4.101
Health Condition of Family Members Among Saharia

Sl. No.	*Heath Condition of Family Members*	*No. of Males*		*No. of Females*		*Total*	
		No.	*%*	*No.*	*%*	*No.*	*%*
1	Very Weak	494	55.2	419	54.2	913	54.7
2	Weak	327	36.5	294	38.0	621	37.2
3	Normal	54	6.0	44	5.7	98	5.9
4	Healthy	20	2.3	16	2.1	36	2.2
	Total	**895 (53.7%)**	**100.0**	**773 (46.3%)**	**100.0**	**1668**	**100.0**

Age Group-wise Sickness in Last Five Years' Record

Age group-wise sickness yields the hint of disease affected Saharia regarding the different age groups. In the present study, 25.2 percent (out of total population) disease affected Saharia are found to be distributed in different age groups. Among them, below 4 years age group depicts comparatively higher disease affected children (20.3 percent) than others (Table 4.102). Adequate diet is crucial during first five years of the life when rapid growth is occurred and the children are entirely depended on others for their foods. Insufficient food is the result of under-nutrition and stunted growth. Beside body size, nutrition also enhances the one's capacity to learn, to work and to live with a happy life. The Saharia children require adequate and proper nutrition in diet for their subsistence and growth. Of all the stages, childhood specially infancy is perhaps the most critical and vulnerable period. Malnutrition, inadequate medical services, lack of child caring knowledge, insanitation, etc., are the contaminated reasons which influence a high incidence of sickness of children. Immediate separation of new married couples from parents' families, negligence to old age care, poverty, etc. may be mentioned as the reasons for sickness of aged (above 50 years old). Among Saharia, child and old age care, their treatment, etc. are depended on their traditional beliefs, customs and norms. Due to high extent of illiteracy, low level of socio-cultural status, etc., treatment of a major group of Saharia children and old persons is provided by traditional healer. Weak economic condition is one of the important cause which deprives the Saharia from modern private health care. It is also found that the local Hospital is not fully equipped with required medicines, laboratory test and experienced doctors for the general treatment. For their sickness, insufficient treatment is incorporated and the percentage of 'not cured' persons are noticed as high (Ghoshmaulik & Karmohapatra, 1995; Bhuyan, 1999; Misra, 1999).

Table: 4.102

Age Group-wise Sickness in Last Five Years' Record Among Saharia

Age Group of Sickness (in Year)	*No. of Males* No.	%	*No. of Females* No.	%	*Total* No.	%
<4	46	21.3	39	19.2	85	20.3
5-9	29	13.4	21	10.4	50	11.9
10-14	23	10.6	12	5.9	35	8.4
15-19	17	7.9	12	5.9	29	6.9
20-24	12	5.6	20	9.9	32	7.6
25-29	18	8.3	26	12.8	44	10.5
30-34	16	7.4	24	11.8	40	9.5
35-39	12	5.6	10	4.9	22	5.3
40-44	11	5.1	7	3.4	18	4.3
45-49	6	2.8	6	3.0	12	2.9
50-54	3	1.4	7	3.4	10	2.4
55-59	4	1.8	4	2.0	8	1.9
60-64	9	4.2	7	3.4	16	3.8
65-69	7	3.2	6	3.0	13	3.1
70>	3	1.4	2	1.0	5	1.2
Total	**216 (51.6%)**	**100.0**	**203 (48.4%)**	**100.0**	**419 (25.1%)**	**100.0**

Reasons of Sickness (Disease) in Last Five Years' Record

Last five years' record, concerned to the reasons of sickness implies an indication of different diseases which were effective very much. In the present study, it is investigated that a lot of Saharia people is suffering from various diseases like – fever (5.7 percent), pneumonia (6.7 percent), typhoid (6.0 percent), cough (4.5 percent), gastric (6.4 percent), diarrhoea (5.5 percent), tuberculosis (2.9 percent), leucorrhoea (11.2 percent), indigestion (3.3 percent), etc. (Table 4.103). It was also found that out of total (419), disease affected males are high (51.6 percent) as compared to females (48.4 percent). Certain ecological factors and human settlements are paved as the way for the outbreak of some diseases. Socio-cultural and economic factors usually stimulate their incidences and the seasonal factors heighten their incubations and complications which further reinforce their virulence. It may be attributed that rain brings the gastro-intestinal disorders, diarrhoea, dysentery and others. Summer creates cough, fever, etc. whereas winter affects the Saharia with infection of itches, pneumonia, tuberculosis, etc. The largely water-borne diseases bear a close relationship to the hygienic conditions prevailing in a settlement. Due to inhabit on hilly-forest region, streams provide the source of water supply specially in rainy season. The rain water is come down from higher altitudes either by melting snow or from moisture, retained during monsoon. At upper reaches of streams, the water is usually uncontaminated and also when it flows down through various settlements, it looses the quality. The possibility of pollution in drinking water, mixed from human waste is high. In rainy season, the unprotected water sources run from hills to lower belt are also become contaminated by mixing with soil, garbage and other animal waste. The water sources turn into a veritable source of the carrier of good number of diseases like – dysentery, diarrhoea, infection, etc. Most of the diseases are expressed by the effect of poor hygienic conditions and unprotected and ill-kept water which is collected from well, pond and sometimes from stream. Extreme hot weather specially in summer season, impured water, malnutrition, early age at marriage and frequent child birth, etc. are the attributed reasons which influence the high incidence of leucorrhoea disease of women. Saharia are illiterate and living in poor socio-economic conditions. They are superstitious to

Table: 4.103

Reasons of Sickness (Disease) in Last Five Years' Record Among Saharia

Sl. No	*Reasons of Sickness*	*Males*		*Females*		*Total*	
		No.	*%*	*No.*	*%*	*No.*	*%*
1	Fever	15	6.9	9	4.4	24	5.7
2	Pneumonia	16	7.4	12	5.9	28	6.7
3	Malaria	10	4.6	7	3.4	17	4.0
4	Typhoid	14	6.5	11	5.4	25	6.0
5	Cough	11	5.1	8	3.9	19	4.5
6	Abdominal Pain	7	3.2	7	3.4	14	3.3
7	Head Pain	4	1.9	4	2.0	8	1.9
8	Gastric	.15	6.9	12	5.9	27	6.4
9	Anemia	7	3.3	8	3.9	15	3.6
10	Dysentery	12	5.6	10	4.9	22	5.3
11	Diarrhoea	14	6.5	9	4.4	23	5.5
12	Fracture	2	0.9	0	0.0	2	0.5
13	Itch	9	4.1	6	3.0	15	3.6
14	Ringworm	6	2.8	7	3.5	13	3.1
15	Eczema	10	4.6	5	2.5	15	3.6
16	Tuberculosis	8	3.7	4	2.0	12	2.9
17	Burn	3	1.4	1	0.5	4	1.0
18	Polio (Leg)	2	0.9	0	0.0	2	0.5
19	Jaundice	5	2.3	3	1.5	8	1.9
20	Wound	5	2.3	2	1.0	7	1.7
21	Chest Pain	10	4.6	7	3.5	17	4.0
22	Lucoderma	2	0.9	0	0.0	2	0.5
23	Piles	6	2.8	1	0.5	7	1.7
24	Hydrocele	2	0.9	0	0.0	2	0.5
25	Leucorrhoea	0	0.0	47	23.1	47	11.2
26	Over Bleeding	0	0.0	10	4.9	10	2.4
27	Diabetes	9	4.1	2	1.0	11	2.6
28	Indigestion	7	3.3	7	3.5	14	3.3
29	Rheumatic	5	2.3	4	2.0	9	2.1
	Total	**216**	**100.0**	**203**	**100.0**	**419**	**100.0**
		(51.6 %)		(48.4 %)			

some extent and lack of proper knowledge to modern medical facilities. Being influenced to their socio-cultural orthodox, they continue their own traditional perception of health, hygiene, ante-natal, natal and post natal care. There are certain harmful practices like-intake of unhygienic foods (due to poverty), utilization of impured drinking water (not available), use of split, arrow head, knife, etc. for cutting the naval cord of new born, etc. turn into various diseases which confer low health indices as well as unhealthy demographic situation (Bhasin, 1990; Bhagwat & Chirmuly, 1997; Bhuyan, 1999; Pandey, et.al., 2001).

Duration of Sickness in Last Five Years' Record

Very simply, duration of sickness indicates the suffering period of disease. It is usually found that in urban belt, the duration of sickness is decreased by better treatment of experienced doctor whereas rural people are to suffer during long time without having any exposure of modern clinical facility. In this regard, the present study expresses that the duration of sickness among Saharia is varied from below 1 year to above 5 years. The percentage of sick persons (43.9 percent to 6.5 percent respectively) decreases with the increase of duration (Table 4.104). Different traditional beliefs, norms, customs, economic position, educational status, etc. are related with the treatment of sick persons among Saharia. It is reported that illed Saharia who are in comparatively better socio-economic position and educational status, are directly treated under the supervision of modern private doctors or doctors of their local Government Hospital. The modern clinical services are so much effective for yielding the maximum efforts to their complete treatment within very short duration. But when the members of low socio-economic status fall in sick, they generally first contact with the traditional healer. He diagnoses the patients by various indigenous methods and then gives the herbal medicines or in some cases performs 'Jhar Fuck' or applies magico-religious activities or worships and sacrifices the fowel, hen, coconut, locally made wine, etc. regarding the severity of the disease or keeps a watch for long time. In the meantime, if no improvement is taken place, then patients further contact with the modern doctors for getting better treatment. Therefore, it is a clear statement that most of them come for treatment of their diseases under the supervision of traditional healer and then modern doctors. After all, they get loss long time by such types of bilateral way of treatment of their sickness. Some of the diseases like - rheumatic, diabetes, leucorrhoea, fracture, etc. are not cured within short period of time. So, usually longest duration is consumed under the process of such treatment (Tiwari, 1984; Bhasin, 1990; Ghoshmaulik & Karmohapatra, 1995; Bhuyan, 1999; Pandey, et.al., 2001).

TABLE:4.104
Duration of Sickness in Last Five Years' Record Among Saharia

Duration of Sickness (in Years)	*No. of Males*		*No. of Females*		*Total*	
	No.	**%**	**No.**	**%**	**No.**	**%**
<1	96	44.4	88	43.3	184	43.9
1-2	36	16.7	32	15.8	68	16.2
2-3	29	13.4	31	15.3	60	14.3
3-4	27	12.5	24	11.8	51	12.2
4-5	16	7.4	13	6.4	29	6.9
5>	12	5.6	15	7.4	27	6.5
Total	**216 (51.6%)**	**100.0**	**203 (48.4%)**	**100.0**	**419 (25.1%)**	**100.0**

Consultation of Sickness in Last Five Years' Record

The present study imparts a relevant categorization of significant percentage of illed Saharia (20.3 percent) who have consulted with their indigenous healer (tribal doctor) for receiving the traditional culture rooted cures. In supporting this, their statements reflect a number of reasons like – easily feedable medicine, low cost, cultural acceptability, elaborated patient-healer interaction, long time family association, friendly attitude with the healer, etc. Even they usually perceive the traditional medicines for several advantages over the western medicines. Beside this, the location of the Hospital is far away from most of the villages and in that situation, the illed Saharia have a chance to consult frequently with their local traditional medicine man. But a major group of disease affected Saharia (33.4 percent) have consulted with the doctors of Hospital when all other measures, tried earlier failed to bring any improvement in the patients' condition. In sickness condition, some of the socio-economically advanced Saharia (12.6 percent) have directly consulted with the modern private doctors because they are able to afford all expenditure (Table 4.105). By frequent patrolling, generally the mobile doctors try to motivate them for accepting the free of cost modern health care services. In this regard, the available data depict that 21.6 percent Saharia have consulted with the mobile doctors for their sickness. Being disappointed in the earlier cases, only 11.9 percent Saharia have no any desire to consult with any medical personnel. Consultation of sickness to the medical personnel is totally depended on different socio-cultural as well as traditional beliefs, customs, norms, educational status, economic position, etc. Usually low socio-cultural status, illiteracy, poverty, etc. have negative impact which enforces them to consult with traditional healer in sickness and vice-versa. Beside this, medical personnel are also contacted in accordance with the types of disease. Generally ghost, sorcery and evil eye-affected diseases like – cough, abdominal pain,

TABLE: 4.105

Consultation of Sickness in Last Five Years' Record Among Saharia

Sl. No	*Reasons of Sickness*	*Males*		*Females*		*Total*	
		No.	*%*	*No.*	*%*	*No.*	*%*
1	Tribal Doctor	39	18.1	46	22.7	85	20.3
2	Dr. of PHC/Hospital	78	36.1	62	30.5	140	33.4
3	Private Dr. (Modern)	28	13.0	25	12.3	43	12.6
4	Mobile Doctor	48	22.2	43	21.2	91	21.7
5	Not Consulted	23	10.6	27	13.3	50	11.9
	Total	**216** (51.6%)	**100.0**	**203** (48.4%)	**100.0**	**419**	**100.0**

over bleeding, certainly vomiting, etc. are treated by the traditional healer (Duggal, 1990; Pandey & Tiwari, 1993; Lamba & Mehta, 1995; Basu, 1999).

Comments about PHC/Hospital

The present study exhibits that due to various causes like – experienced doctors, careful check up, sudden treatment, etc., 56.5 percent Saharia respondents have furnished their positive comments whereas as the reasons of useless medicine, more time waste, absence of doctors, lack of medicine, etc., 43.5 percent respondents have put up negative comments about Hospital services (Table 4.106). Hospital facilities are not at all satisfactory in the area. Often both doctors and useful medicines are not available in the Hospital. Saharia are very poor and always they are to busy to earn for their livelihood. In that context, they can not afford long time consumption for getting Hospital services. After diagnosis of the sickness, doctors always prescribe the medicines for purchasing from private pharmacist shop. Due to their poverty, they are unable to bear the purchasing cost of medicines which are prescribed by the doctors. It is investigated that due to negligence of responsible authoritative persons, infrastructure facilities of the Hospital are going to be damaged. Even both instrumental diagnosis provision and biochemical laboratory for various tests of sickness are not available in the Hospital. The present study also reports that for getting the services from traditional healer, they neither waste any time nor purchase any medicine from out side medical store and these influence them to prefer to their traditional medicine man ('Gunia'). Actually, the preference of traditional healer as well as doctors of Hospital is depended in accordance with needs of sickness. Usually, the people of lower socio-economic status prefer to traditional healer but after frustration due to non-improvement of patient, they come to take the services from Hospital. The effectiveness of a Hospital in such conditions is reduced in terms of both area and the population covered. If medical facilities are located at fixed places, the efficient doctor or nurse and population ratio would be considerably lower than the accepted international norms (Singh & Kumar, 1988; Bhasin, 1990; Duggal, 1990, Pandev & Tiwari, 1993; Bhuyan, 1999)

TABLE: 4.106
Comments about PHC/Hospital Among Saharia

Sl. No.	Positive Comments	No. of Respondents	Percentage
1	Good Medicine	10	5.3
2	Experienced Doctor	16	8.5
3	Carefully Check up	13	6.9
4	Free Medicine	34	18.1
5	Free Checkup	14	7.5
6	Instrumental Check up	21	11.2
7	Qualified Doctor	22	11.7
8	Quickly Check up	15	8.0
9	Suddenly Treatment	24	12.8
10	Medicine Always Available	7	3.7
11	Doctor Always Available	12	6.4
	Total	**188 (56.5 %)**	**100.0**
Sl. No.	*Negative Comments*	*No. of Respondents*	*Percentage*
1	Useless Medicine	14	9.7
2	No Free Medicine	33	22.8
3	Slowly Treatment	9	6.2
4	More Time Waste	15	10.3
5	Absence of Doctor	17	11.7
6	Lack of Medicine	19	13.1
7	Germful Hospital	5	3.5
8	Inexperienced Doctor	6	4.1
9	No Any Tribal Doctor	9	6.2
10	Hate Them As Tribe	18	12.4
	Total	**145 (43.5%)**	**100.0**
	Grand Total	**333**	**100.0**

The over all discussion discloses that as primitive tribe, Saharia belong to traditional society and their socio-cultural status is very low. Keeping in view of their entire life style, it is proclaimed that they inhabit in remote area, drink impured water, consume the contaminated foods and depend totally on nature. They assure deplorable low literacy rate and bear to have inadequate modern medical facility. Most of them are categorized under very weak health status. Age group-wise sickness measures that by the affect of various diseases, children and old persons are suffering very much as compared to others. It is further clarified that fever, pneumonia, typhoid, gastric, dysentery, lucorrhoea, etc. are highly prevalent diseases among them. For unhealthy treatment of diseases, they are suffering during long time. Even a large number of disease affected persons do not have any intension to consult with the doctors for their treatment. Comprising various comments, they generally make accusation against their local Hospital. Lastly, it is an assessment that the aetiological factors of Saharia are incorporately related with their low socio-cultural milieu. High extent of illiteracy, poverty, malnutrition, lack of purified drinking water, insanitation, inadequate modern medical facility, traditional belief to healer, etc. may be attributed as the reasons of their weak health status. In the present consequence situation, there is an urgent need to implement the financially as well as educationally beneficiary scheme, provide the purified drinking water and adequate modern clinical services, impress then by modern health workers, etc. for the improvement of their health status.

FAMILY PLANNING PRACTICES

Family planning means to have children in a desired number and each child is given birth at a desired time (Matsunaga, 1996). Birth control on the other hand refers to various contraceptive methods which are used to avoid conception. Potts & Selman (1979) stated, "Mostly what family planning programmes do is reduce the number of unwanted births: while this is quite worthwhile in itself, fertility will continue to be high in the absence of any motivation for smaller size". Family planning practices always influence health development and well being family specially for initiating a positive impact to the health of both children and mothers. It is one of the most preventive health care strategy but rarely recognized as such (Jacobson, 1972). The successful limitation of family size by the couples depends not only on their small family ideals but also on their psychological acceptance of family limitation, knowledge of birth control methods, availability of contraceptives, psychological and economic costs and environment favourable to the practice of birth control. Certain motivational aspects, moderated through social and cultural considerations are presumed to curtail fertility. Importancy is concerned among them who have the customary post-partum taboos on inter-course, the custom of delivery at parental homes, social desirability for longer birth interval to protect the health of the mother and child, longer period of lactation, etc. Many Governmental agencies and demographers feel that a rapid increasing of population as well as fertility limiting can be averted only by a greater use of contraceptives by married couples, sexual abstinence and other techniques. A successful family planning programme is enbled to reduce fertility and consequently produce an older population which bear a well-grounded result in stable population theory (Coale, 1972).

However, family planning service for public provision is commonly justified on the grounds of improvement in the health of mothers and children, economic well-being of the couples and the population, status of women, etc. Contraception has an obvious effect on maternal mortality primarily because with fewer pregnancies, each woman is exposed fewer times to the risk of major disability of death that is associated with child bearing particularly in the least of developed countries. The use of contraceptive is increasing gradually over time. India has been specified as the second largest populated country in the world (after China). In 1952, India became the first country of the world for officially adopting family planning programme in order to solve the crucial problem of galloping population. In all the development plans since 1951, family planning has been given a high priority, though greater emphasis is noticed only after the Third Five Year Plan. At first, the programme was adopted as a clinical approach where extension educational approach was introduced in 1963. This motivated educating the population to bring about changes in the knowledge, attitude and behaviour of the people with regard to family planning. In the present study, the various aspects of family planning among Saharia are stated in the following manner:

TABLE: 4.107

View on More or Less Number of Offsprings Among Saharia

Sl. No.	Reasons for More No. of Offsprings	No. of Respondents	Percentage
1	Chances of Child Death	42	23.9
2	Additional Labouring	35	19.9
3	No Preference to Family Planning	24	13.6
4	More Children More Cultivation	17	9.6
5	More Male More Prestige	13	7.4
6	No Limitation as God Gift	19	10.8
7	More Offsprings More Income	26	14.8
	Total	**176 (52.8%)**	**100.0**
Sl. No.	*Reasons for Less No. of Offsprings*	*No. of Respondents*	*Percentage*
1	For Better Accommodation	16	10.2
2	For Better Education	22	14.0
3	No Aged for Supporting Child Care	9	5.7
4	Shortage of Food Material	19	12.1
5	Satisfaction to Child Care	17	10.8
6	For Proper Child Care	15	9.6
7	Control Population Growth	21	13.4
8	For Family Tension	11	7.0
9	For More Weakness	8	5.1
10	No Time for Child Care	13	8.3
11	For Heavy Work Load	6	3.8
	Total	**157 (47.2%)**	**100.0**
	Grand Total	**333**	**100.0**

View on More or Less Number of Offsprings

Traditionally, most of the Saharia are concerned to have many offsprings. In this context the present study exhibits that 52.8 percent of their respondents desired more offsprings due to various reasons like - chances of child death, additional labouring, high income, etc. whereas 47.2 percent respondents preferred to less offsprings for providing better accommodation, education, control population growth, etc. (Table 4.107). This study also reports that usually, Saharia people are directed by their traditional beliefs, customs, norms, etc. which regulate them to make a conscious decision to increase or decrease the family size. High extent of illiteracy, financial problem, low socio-cultural status, etc. (Biswas & Kapoor, 2002) are attributed as the reasons which influence them to have an emotional interest on the view of giving birth to many offsprings. In other side,

TABLE: 4.108

Awareness about Conception among Saharia

Sl. No.	*Symptoms of Awareness*	*No. of Women*	*Percentage*
1	Stop Menstruation Cycle	125	37.5
2	Start Abdominal Growth	19	5.7
3	Start Vomiting	51	15.4
4	Head Pain Feeling	13	3.9
5	No Taste of Any Food	13	3.9
6	Body Pain Feeling	8	2.4
7	Always Weakness	14	4.2
8	Prefer Always Sleeping	12	3.6
9	Prefer Sour Taste Food	26	7.8
10	Abdominal Pain Feeling	9	2.7
11	Always Tiredness Feeling	13	3.9
12	No Interest Work	8	2.4
13	Always Child Related Dreaming	22	6.6
	Total	**333**	**100.0**

a significant number of Saharia women have expressed that due to their extreme poverty, they are being oppressed to involve themselves in heavy work continuing long duration. As a reason, it creates a negative impact for having paucity of time to rear or conceive child frequently. Remote inhabitation, health workers rarely visit in the area, etc. also make a minor scope for convincing them in regarding the less number of offsprings. So, their high extent of illiteracy, limited contact with the people of modern society, etc. are the accused reasons for influencing them not to change their traditional thinking. As a result, a major group of Saharia is not motivated to support less number of offsprings as well as to control frequent child birth by adopting various family planning devices.

Awareness about Conception

Among Saharia, the awareness about conception is varied in accordance with various symptoms. The present study depicts that their all women are aware about conception due to various reasons like – stop menstruation cycle (37.5 percent), start vomiting (15.4 percent), prefer to sour tasted food (7.8 percent), etc. (Table 4.108). In Saharia society, their stated comments about conception are taken as very truthful indicators whereas in modern society, all such are totally baseless (except stop menstruation cycle). Different traditional beliefs, customs, norms, etc. are existed till now in their society. Most of the Saharia women are not only illiterate but also they are ignorant which draw an acquaintation of their insensibility about conception. Even a major group of women reports that they could not understand about the symptoms of their conception. After passing two or three months, generally they felt that they were being conceived and in that condition, they were not permitted (or agree) to perform abortion according to their society approved rules and regulations. Lack of awareness about the symptoms of conception and socio-culturally restriction for conducting abortion are mentioned as the reasons which influence to their frequent child births. In this context, family planning is considered as only one dependable method for saving themselves from frequent conceptions.

Preference of Male to Female Child

Socio-cultural influences play a great role to give preference of male or female child in Saharia Society. The present study shows that among Saharia, male offsprings are preferred to female offsprings due to the reasons of more male more income (26.1 percent), future inheritor (9.6 percent), high chances of male deaths (17.5 percent), etc. (Table 4.109). The effect of sex preference on recent fertility behaviour may be explored by the examine of current contraceptive use. Study of sex preference by this method is not meaningful in where majority of the women are not using family planning. It is also argued that sex composition of the offsprings of family planning users may or may not be same as wanted by acceptors who are highly motivated for limiting their family size. Furthermore, aggregate measures, based on sex composition neutralize important individual differences. The aggregate effect of sex preference is minimized

TABLE: 4.109

Reasons of Preference of Male to Female Child Among Saharia

Sl. No.	*Reasons of Male Preference*	*No. of Respondents*	*Percentage*
1	More Male More Income	87	26.1
2	For Excess Cultivation	18	5.4
3	Long Life Support	18	5.4
4	Traditional Thinking	12	3.6
5	For Maintaining Family Status	10	3.0
6	Future Inheritator	32	9.6
7	More Dominantness in Society	26	7.8
8	Social Prestige	13	3.9
9	Care at Old Age	17	5.1
10	Chances of More Male Death	58	17.5
11	Educated & Service	19	5.7
12	Prefer Equally	23	6.9
	Total	**333**	**100.0**

when the level of eaucation of women or parents is high. The women who are using any family planning method by surviving male children are also considered in this regard. High fertility in developing countries is the result of sex preference. A lot of references implies that the traditional and contemporary societies are attached with strong importance of son. In such societies, religious beliefs are strong and at least one son is required for rituals and continuation of family lineage. To carry the glories of family and to support the familial issues, generally the couples are also instigated to have at least one son. Even male members in the family are also highly treated as sources of power as compared to females (Freedmen, et.al., 1960; Kapadia, 1966; Repetto, 1972; Lahiri, 1974; Sharma & Jain, 1974; McClelland, 1978; Combs & Sun, 1978; Park, 1983; Arnold, 1992; Oldenburg, 1992).

Knowledge and Practice of Family Planning Methods

Knowledge and practice of family planning methods are the two important indicators for measuring the socio-cultural status of the people in a particular community. In the present study, the available data record that among Saharia, 72.1 percent husbands (out of 326) and 60.4 percent wives (out of 333) have achieved more or less knowledge about various family planning methods (Table 4.110). Neighbours, Anganwadi workers, health workers and other family members including early users of birth control devices are the chief sources of disseminating of information. Surprisingly, local media consisting of television, radio, news paper, pamphlets, etc. are also reported to be the sources of information about birth control devices. The practice of contraception depends on the knowledge of contraceptive techniques and the attitudes in the context of their social environment towards birth control. Male-Female differences imply that the burdens of fertility control are borne by women but this is a function of contemporary contraceptive technology where most of the efficient methods are geared to women. The ever married women affirming knowledge of contraceptive methods are quite less in the rural areas. The knowledge of family planning methods has attained the threshold level of social acceptability and that has been disseminated successfully by the Government to meet the needs of eligible women for such methods in both rural and urban areas. The National Family Health Survey, 1992 also conveyed the information about the contraceptive knowledge to be nearly universal in India with 96 percent of currently married women having heard of at least one modern family planning method (Mitra, 1978; Mahadevan, 1989; Chachra & Bhasin, 1998; Veleti, 1998; Mahapatro, et.al., 1999).

Further this study reports that among Saharia, only 15.3 percent husbands (out of 326) and 27.9 percent wives (out of 333) practise birth control devices (Table 4.110). According to the study, it is a highly noticeable point that there is a far difference between knowledge and practice of birth control devices. Saharia are illiterate and positioned in low socio-cultural status. In respecting to their traditional culture, most of the Saharia are not agree to adopt any modern family planning methods. So the practice of birth control devices is reported far less common among them. In the country, particularly in rural and tribal regions, ignorance, tradition, superstitions and lot of cultural repressions of sex feeling are existed and a scheme of family planning is indeed difficult to put through. In spite of their high awareness of birth control measures, the percentage of couples opting for birth control measures is very low. More than 7 or 8 of the couples are not resorted to any birth control device (Mahapatro, et.al., 1999; Maheo & Kalla, 2001; Pandey, et.al., 2001).

TABLE: 4.110

Knowledge and Practice of Family Planning Methods Among Saharia

Sl.No.	*About Family Planning*	*Husbands*		*Wives*	
		Number	*Percentage*	*Number*	*Percentage*
1	Knowledge - Yes	235	72.1	201	60.4
2	Knowledge - No	91	27.9	132	39.6
3	Practice - Yes	50	15.3	93	27.9
4	Practice - No	276	84.7	240	72.1

(Total Husband = 326, Total Wife = 333)

Adoption of Family Planning Methods

Among Saharia, various reasons are concerned to adopt different family planning methods. The present study expresses that generally husbands try to avoid using of contraceptive devices whereas women are enforced because of their low status as compared to husbands. Most of the Saharia are illiterate and

TABLE: 4.111

Adoption of Family Planning Methods Among Saharia

Sl. No.	*Methods*	*No. of Husbands (Percentage)*	*No. of Wives (Percentage)*	*Total (Percentage)*
1	Vasectomy	14 (28.0)	0 (0.0)	14 (9.8)
2	Tubectomy	0 (0.0)	35 (37.6)	35 (24.4)
3	Condom	21 (42.0)	0 (0.0)	21 (14.7)
4	IUD	0 (0.0)	3 (3.2)	3 (2.1)
5	Oral Pills	0 (0.0)	21 (22.6)	21 (14.7)
6	Beverage Food	0 (0.0)	10 (10.7)	10 (7.0)
7	Tribal Medicine	0 (0.0)	9 (9.7)	9 (6.3)
8	Modern Medicine	0 (0.0)	2 (2.2)	2 (1.4)
9	Abstinence	15 (30.0)	13 (14.0)	28 (19.6)
	Total	50 (35.0%) 100.0	93 (65.0%) 100.0	143 100.0

very poor. Due to their poverty, they are unable to manage two square meals regularly and even they occasionally observe hungry during a few days. In this situation, they have adopted sterilization specially tubectomy (24.4 percent) as family planning method for receiving compensation (incentive) both in terms of cash and kinds to compensate for loosing of wages and purchasing medicine. The cash incentive of tubectomy operation ranges higher than the range of vasectomy operation. Generally their received cash is expended for their livelihood instead of medicine purchase. Due to fear of creative pain, very less percentage of Saharia women (2.1 percent) have used intra uterine device (Table 4.111). For maintaining the gap between two frequent births, they use condom, take oral pills, beverage food, tribal medicine and modern medicine and also observe abstinence for birth control. Sometimes, illed health condition is also committed to observe abstinence. Through an exclusive discussion, it is reported that due to fear of wound and unhealthy physique, they do not prefer to vasectomy and tubectomy operations whereas free service of condom, oral pills, beverage food, medicine, etc. influence them to use family planning devices. For their absent mind, sometimes they forget to use the contraceptive devices and as a result, their undesired child birth is performed. The differential performances for the use of particular contraceptive device are attributed as the factors, related to socio-economic diversity, lack of commitment to the programme, inadequate health and infrastructure and insufficient management of the programme (Muthal, 1992; Mutharayappa, 1995; Veleti, 1998; Chachra & Bhasin, 1998; Pandey, et.al., 2001).

Reasons of Adoption of Family Planning Methods

The present study depicts that the maximum percentage of Saharia used family planning devices due to the reasons of long interval between conceptions (28.0 percent), restriction of population growth (20.3 percent), avoidance conception (16.7 percent), etc. (Table 4.112). Economic constraint is found to be the major reason for using birth control devices. In this regard, men and women opt for the birth control devices because of monetary incentives, given by the Government, if they underwent sterilization. These husbands and wives have already got their desired number of children. It is further reported that due to inhabit in nuclear family, they have no any other supporting person for their infants whenever they involve themselves in labouring. In that condition, their adult children sometimes share

TABLE: 4.112

Reasons of Adoption of Family Planning Methods Among Saharia

Sl. No.	*Reasons of Adoption*	*No. of Husbands (Percentage)*	*No. of Wives (Percentage)*	*Total (Percentage)*
1	Restrict Population Growth	17 (34.0)	12 (12.9)	29 (20.3)
2	Avoidance Conception	0 (0.0)	24 (25.8)	24 (16.7)
3	Long Interval Between Conceptions	17 (34.0)	23 (24.7)	40 (28.0)
4	For Accepting Incentives	5 (10.0)	12 (12.9)	17 (11.9)
5	For Enjoyment of Random Sex	8 (16.0)	7 (7.5)	15 (10.5)
6	For Weak Physique	1 (2.0)	9 (9.7)	10 (7.0)
7	For Disease Affected	2 (4.0)	6 (6.5)	8 (5.6)
	Total	50 (35.0%) 100.0	93 (65.0%) 100.0	143 100.0

caring support to their infants and this is resulted by practicing long interval between conceptions through various family planning devices. By the use of contraceptive devices, they also avoid frequent conceptions which influence them to practise daily labour continuously. Beside economic constraint, education is also incorporately related with adoption of family planning methods. Some of the educated Saharia are very much conscious about population growth. For conferring better care and educational facility to their children within their limited income, they restrict a number of child births by adopting various contraceptive devices. Weak or disease affected physique is also not capable to have frequent conceptions. In this condition, conception is avoided or minimized by adopting various birth control devices. For the users of birth control devices, primary health centre or Hospital is found to be the main source to provide birth control services. Close distance of Hospital, better communication system, infrastructural, medicinal and instrumental facilities and availability of qualified doctor-nurses in the Hospital, beneficiary explanation by 'Anganiwadi' workers and health workers, etc. are inadequate and by which most of the couples are not motivated to use the birth control devices. Beside this, a positive relationship between marital communication and fertility regulation is required. Because such marital communication between husband and wife always encourages to use the contraceptives which curtail fertility (Muthal, 1992; Mutharayappa, 1995; Veleti, 1998; Mahapatro, et.al. 1999).

Reasons of Non-Adoption of Family Planning Methods

The present study exhibits that most of the Saharia did not adopt any birth control device due to gift (child birth) of God (35.3 percent), desire of male child (10.0 percent), methods not comfortable (11.6 percent), fear of frequent child deaths (8.4 percent), etc (Table 4.113). They are illiterate and living in poor socio-economic environment. Saharia are superstitious to some extent and do not have any proper knowledge to the modern birth control devices. Their poverty and ignorance are somewhat reasons behind the less unitization of family planning devices. Non-utilization is also come to the notice due to the reasons of misconceptions. In respecting to the socio-cultural tradition, a major fraction of Saharia believe that birth of child is the 'gift of God' and that they should not restrict by the use of birth control devices. Significant percentage of Saharia do not use any contraceptives till date as they want more children in a particular sex (male or female). In other side, usually women presume that sterilization is the reason of ill side effects and as a result, they have a view that who are undergone sterilization, they may not be enabled to do their work properly as they easily get tiredness which demotivates them from the use of such contraceptive devices. They have a disgustion that the use of condom and intra uterine device are not comfortable for random sexual enjoyment. Social hierarchical position also expresses that they are belonging to male dominant society. Usually husbands (elders in supporting husbands) oppose whereas wives are pressurized to adopt the birth control devices. The currently married couples report that they do not use any permanent birth control device till date as they want the desired number of children. Due to high extent of illiteracy, poverty, malnutrition, inadequate medical services, etc., their child mortality is found to be high. In that condition, they are always in suspense to frequent child deaths which influence them not to use birth control devices.

The desireness of many children is defined as the prime reason for non-acceptance of family planning. Son preference is found common among almost all tribes. The reasons for non-acceptance of family planning methods are also poor health status and lack of post operational family support. Since majority of the tribal families are nuclear type and all members in the family including minor children are enforced to work to eke out their living. In such situation, many tribes are not coming forward to accept family planning methods. The other attributed reasons include 'do not know where to get family planning services and lack of proper advice about the method', and so on. Most of the tribal groups are the residents in natural settlements and far away from the health facilities. Even health workers rarely visit in the remote tribal areas. Non-accepter tribes coming under this group are expected the eligible women (health workers) for making a motivational approach to adopt family planning methods

(Mutharayappa, 1995; Chachra & Bhasin, 1998; Mahapatro, et.al. 1999; Maheo & Kalla, 2001).

TABLE: 4.113

Reasons of Non-Adoption of Family Planning Methods Among Saharia

Sl. No.	Reasons of Non-Adoption	No. of Husbands (Percentage)	No. of Wives (Percentage)	Total (Percentage)
1	Gift of God	29 (40.3)	38 (32.2)	67 (35.3)
2	Desire of Male Child	9 (12.5)	10 (8.5)	19 (10.0)
3	Desire of Female Child	4 (5.5)	7 (5.9)	11 (5.8)
4	Health Problem	7 (9.7)	11 (9.3)	18 (9.5)
5	Ill Side Effect	3 (4.2)	6 (5.1)	9 (4.7)
6	Not Comfortable	10 (13.9)	12 (10.2)	22 (11.6)
7	Husband-Elder Opposed	0 (0.0)	21 (17.8)	21 (11.0)
8	For Currently Marriage	3 (4.2)	4 (3.4)	7 (3.7)
9	Fear of Child Death	7 (9.7)	9 (7.6)	16 (8.4)
	Total	72 (37.9%) 100.0	118 (62.1%) 100.0	190 100.0

Reasons of Adoption of Family Planning by Husbands or Wives

The present study expresses that among Saharia, 35.0 percent husbands adopted family planning due to the reasons of external use (30.0 percent), only for husbands use (26.0 percent), doubted on wife's character (14.0 percent) and others whereas 65.0 percent wives adopted family planning mentioning the reasons of only for wives use (24.7 percent), no heavy work load (18.3 percent), husbands' pressure (15.0 percent), etc. (Table 4.114). Saharia are illiterate and bear a low socio-cultural status.

TABLE: 4.114

Reasons of Adoption of Family Planning by Husbands or Wives Among Saharia

Sl. No.	*Adopted by Husbands- Reasons*	*No. of Husbands*	*Percentage*
1	Chances of Infection of Wife	6	12.0
2	Doubted on Wife's Character	7	14.0
3	Only for Husband Use	13	26.0
4	For Weakness of Wife	5	10.0
5	For External Use	15	30.0
6	Chances of Side Effect of Wife	4	8.0
	Total	**50 (35.0%)**	**100.0**
Sl. No.	*Adopted by Wives-Reasons*	*No. of Wives*	*Percentage*
1	Chances of Side Effect of Husband	8	8.6
2	No Heavy Work Load	17	18.3
3	Only for Wife Use	23	24.7
4	For Free Sexual Enjoyment	13	14.0
5	No Work Disturbance	6	6.5
6	For Weakness of Husband	7	7.5
7	By the Pressure of Husband	5	5.4
8	For Mediators' Explanation	14	15.0
	Total	**93 (65.0%)**	**100.0**
	Grand Total	**143**	**100.0**

Due to inhabit in patriarchal society, the male groups are always dominated on females. Decision of male is predominantly incorporated for the use of birth control devices. Usually husbands try to avoid contraceptive practices whereas wives are enforced to adopt and as a result, the female contraceptive acceptors are found to be high as compared to males. Gender relations generally constitute power and dominance especially where the patriarchal society system is existed and in that condition, the life structure of men and women are come in the relation of husbands and wives. In the society, women have little voice in taking decision about any matter of family. In most of the cases, fertility is regulated according to the wish of husbands. Sometimes, due to the effect of various emotional problems, husbands have the chances to forget the use of contraceptives and in that situation, women are better for adopting these. In fact, authority about the

Problems Felt After Adopting Family Planning Methods

In the present study, it is reported that after adopting different family planning methods, most of the Saharia are suffering from various problems like – head pain (8.4 percent), minimum sexual pleasure (10.4 percent), uneasy (11.9 percent), weakness (11,.2 percent), etc. whereas 37.1 percent of them are free from all problems (Table 4.115). Due to illiteracy, socio-cultural backward position, poverty, malnutrition, inadequate medical facility, etc., they are frequently suffering from various physical problems. Their presumption is that all such problems, related to diseases are adopted by acceptance of contraceptives and as an effect, they are gradually demotivated to use any further. The heavy physical work is felt as the burden for the tribal people specially who are inhabiting in the hilly region and in that condition, a recently operated person may develop complications if he would be sent home immediately. However, complaints of acceptors of various contraceptives are dizziness, bleeding, back-pain, body-ache and weakness. Generally most of the acceptors have no any problems whereas in rare cases sufferers are connected with both minor problems like – backache and discomfort and major problems like – acute body-ache, excessive bleeding, swollen uterus, etc. The follow up care, provided by the family planning programme needs improvement. The effective and successful family planning programme requires to be more sensitive to the acceptors rather than just achieving the target (Basu, 1998; Chachra & Bhasin, 1998).

TABLE: 4.115

Problems Felt After Adopting Family Planning Among Saharia

Sl. No.	Various Problems Felt	No. of Husbands (Percentage)	No. of Wives (Percentage)	Total (Percentage)
1	Head Pain	1	11	12
		(2.0)	(11.8)	(8.4)
2	Abdominal Pain	1	7	8
		(2.0)	(7.5)	(5.6)
3	Minimum Sexual Pleasure	12	3	15
		(24.0)	(3.2)	(10.4)
4	Pain of Pelvic Girdle	1	10	11
		(2.0)	(10.8)	(7.7)
5	Uneasy Felt	8	9	17
		(16.0)	(9.7)	(11.9)
6	Infection Followed	2	9	11
		(4.0)	(9.7)	(7.7)
7	Weakness Felt	4	12	16
		(8.0)	(12.9)	(11.2)
8	No Problem Felt	21	32	53
		(42.0)	(34.4)	(37.1)
	Total	**50 (35.0%)**	**93 (65.0%)**	**143**
		100.0	**100.0**	**(100.0)**

Preference for Ideal Number of Offsprings in a Family

The preference for ideal number of offsprings are varied from one family to another among Saharia. The present study illustrates that the maximum percentage of Saharia desire to have two males and one female (37.6 percent), one male and one female (24.3 percent) and three males and one female (22.8 percent) whereas the minimum percentage of them prefer to give birth four males and two females (11.1 percent) and three males and two females (4.2 percent) as the ideal number of offsprings in the family (Table 4.116). This is a clear indication that maximum Saharia people expect more than three children; so even among the users of family planning methods, they limit the family size only after 3 or 4 children because they may be enforced to. The actual awareness of a small family is lacking. High extent of illiteracy, low socio-cultural status, etc. are the attributed reasons which influence them to extend family size. The desired ideal family size is indicative of the women who accept the norm of ideal family size. They may achieve this ideal size or not but it influences the intensity of motivation for adopting family planning devices. Various studies show that there is a wide gap between the preferred family size and the actual family size. In most of the cases, the desired family size can be correlated with the actual family size of the respondents. Usually, the actual family size is found to be lower than desired family size. Generally, the prenatalistic family structure and social values bring pressure on each couple to have at least one son. With high infant and child mortality, nobody is ready to undergo sterilization without having at least two sons and

TABLE: 4.116

Preference for Ideal Number of Offsprings in a Family Among Saharia

Sl. No.	*Ideal No. of Offsprings Preference*	*No. of Parents*	*Percentage*
1	1 Male and 1Female	81	24.3
2	2 Males and 1Female	125	37.6
3	3 Males and 1 Female	76	22.8
4	3 Males and 2 Females	37	11.1
5	4 Males and 2Females	14	4.2
	Total	**333**	**100.0**

therefore sterilization is done at higher priorities. Because of adherence to old culture, the tribal people still take in belonging to a large family, clan, village and for that matter, even they are as a whole irrespective of the quality or the standard of living. Due to poverty, illiteracy, low socio-cultural status, etc., they feel hesitation to come on close contact with outsiders. In this condition, they presume that their traditional culture is far better. So, on behalf of their traditional orthodox, most of them desire more than two children in their family and by which they not only fail to develop their family status but also increase the over all fertility (Bhasin, 1990; Chachra & Bhasin, 1998; Veleti, 1998; Mahapatro, et.al. 1999; Maheo & Kalla, 2001).

Age Group, Occupation, Income and Educational Status and Family Planning Usages

In terms of difference by age of women, experience with having used contraception rises through age group of 20-24 years and decreases thereafter. As middle-aged women, they usually have the desired number of children and then seem to use contraceptives. The older women are more traditional, illiterate and likely to be unaware about contraception or view of the same as appropriate (Muthal, 1992; Veleti, 1998; Maheo & Kalla, 2001). Saharia are poverty stricken and most of them are enforced to practise daily labour. Due to long time regular involvement in duties, their physical condition is not enabled to conceive frequently and as a result, they usually avoid conception by the use of various family planning devices. Several studies also conclude that in most of the cases, female participation in economic activity promotes the performance of family planning programme in India (Jolly, 1986; Nag, 1998). Income is also an important responsible factor for affecting beliefs and usages of contraceptives. Most of the households of comparatively higher income group are literate in various educational levels and they are almost going to be free from socio-cultural barriers which influence them to use various birth control methods. Beside this, the higher income as well as educated group expects to have small size of family for proper child caring and rearing. Even by avoiding frequent conceptions, the healthy mothers are enabled to maintain better health status of their children. So, it is comprehend that there is a positive association between the adoption of contraceptive and economic as well as educational status (Heer, 1966; Coale, 1972; Dixon, 1975; Pakrasi & Haldar, 1980; Singh, 1986; Mahadevan, 1989; Retherford, et.al., 1989; Mutharayappa, 1995; Maheo & Kalla, 2001).

In order to ensure the various components of family planning, the present study has been conducted among Saharia who are constituted as a primitive tribe of Madhya Pradesh as well as India. Most of them are very poor, achieve low literacy rate and inhabit in backward area. They prefer to perform marriage at early age. Among them, the traditional socio-cultural orthodox are respectively inherited by the descendants. Saharia generally prefer to treat under traditional healers whereas modern clinical facilities are existed inadequately. Due to high infant mortality, they appreciate frequently births of offsprings. High extent of illiteracy and backwardness are attributed as the reasons of their unawareness about conception, preference of male child, senselessness of knowledge and practice of family planning, etc. In spite of these, a group of Saharia have adopted various birth control devices because of monetary incentives (specially for sterilization), given by the Government. After adopting family planning, some of them are suffering from various physical problems which are related with irresponsible communication system, long distance of Health Centre, lack of infrastructural, medical and instrumental facilities and unavailability of qualified doctor-nurses in the Health Centres, etc. The women who belong to middle age group, practise household work, earn medium income and achieve literacy in various educational levels, have a positive impact on family planning practice. For increasing the users of contraceptive methods, serious attempts should be made under multi-dimensional tribal development schemes to ensure the programme more effective than just achieving target. The various ways of propagation should also be initiated to motivate them for emerging from their traditional life style, superstitions, cultural repression of male sex feeling existence, economic constrain and illiteracy and to promote them for establishing small family size by accepting modern contraceptive devices with incentives.

CHAPTER - V

SUMMARY, CONCLUSION AND SUGGESTIONS

As representation, this chapter attempts to summarize the descriptive subject matter of introduction, research design and methodology, ethnographic profile of tribes and Saharia as a whole and socio-economic impact on demographic characteristics concerned to the measures of fertility, mortality, migration and maternal and child health care, health seeking behaviour and family planning with a comparative framework of tribal and non-tribal population of India. Lastly, this chapter is enabled to assess the indebted reasons of the vulnerable situation of Saharia and make a lot of suggestions in aetiological sense.

The word 'Tribe' is considered as a social group having specific territory, dialect, cultural homogeneity and unifying social organization. The various Colonial masters for the communities liberally used various terms like – primitive, savage, barbarious, uncivilized, pre-literate, non-literate, little community, aboriginal, native, and others instead of tribe (Kumar, 1998). According to 'Epics' and 'Puranas', it was defined that who dwelt in forest and practised aboriginal folk, they were called as *tribe*. From ancient to the present state, it has been evident that tribal life is very miserable. British Governments in India were not interested to implement any tribal development programme. For only securing the peace, sometimes British Government helped them financially. But after independent, free India has specified the various provisions for the tribal people and those are written in the constitution of this country. Among various tribal groups, different more backward or aboriginal or very old groups have been identified and subsequently they are acquainted as primitive tribes. For small size of community, pre-agricultural stage of economy, high extent of isolation, low level of literacy, etc., these tribal groups have been scheduled for providing them special provisions. Except a few states, tribal people are generally inhabiting all over India. Almost same racial live stock, similar characteristics, better understanding of demographic situation, etc., India has been divided into seven tribal territorial zones (Sinha, 1990; Sharma & Sharma, 1999). In North-Eastern zone, Adi, Khowa, Singpho, Chakma, Moyam, Sema, Hajoing, Naga, Mikir, Bhil, Bhutia, Lepcha, Oraon, Santal, Riang and other tribal groups are inhabiting. Shifting cultivation, agriculture, hunting-gathering, fishing, labouring, basket making, etc. occupations are practised by them. Their physical appearances indicate that they are belonging to Mangaloid racial groups. Baiga, Ho, Lodha, Garo, Kora, Saora, Bhuita and other tribal groups are followed to concentrate throughout the Eastern zone. These tribal groups have also been originated from Mongoloid racial live stocks. At present, these tribal groups are motivated to practise cultivation for their livelihood. Northern zone represents Bhotia, Gaddi, Gujjur, Kinnaura, Swangla, Buksha, Raji, Tharu and other tribal groups. According to their physical appearances, they are grouped under Mongoloid racial live stocks. Hunting, food gathering, herding, various crafting, business, etc. are followed as their main occupations. Central zone is considered as the tribal heart of India. Baiga, Bharia, Bhil, Birhor, Gond, Kamar, Hill Korwa, Halba, Munda, Parja, Saharia and other so many tribal groups are sactterdly dwelling all over every region of this zone. These tribal groups have been categorized as the descendants of Proto-Australoid racial live stocks. They practise hunting, food gathering, fuel selling, labouring, etc. as occupations. They are generally landless. Very less number of tribal groups practise agriculture because they have little size of land. Dhosia, Kokna, Dubla, Gond, Koli, Siddi, Birhul, Oraon, Parja and other tribal groups are at randomly living anywhere throughout the Western zone. It is mentioned that these tribes have also been originated from Proto-Austrloid racial groups. Most of the tribes of this zone traditionally practise hunting and food gathering. But now a days, they are motivated to the profession of cultivation, crafts, local business, animal husbandry, etc. Andh, Bhil, Chenchu, Koya, Kulia, Yanadis, Barda, Irula, Malasar and others are followed as the tribal inhabitants of Southern zone. According to their physical appearances, these tribal groups have been categorized as the descendants of both Caucasoid and Proto-Australoid racial live stocks. Cultivation, collection of honey, roots, tubers, etc. and labouring, milking and churning and other professions are practised by these tribal groups. Island zone is the native place of Andamanase, Jarwas, Nicobarese, Onges, Sentineless and Shompens. These tribal groups are belonging to Negrito and Mongloloid racial live stocks. Hunting and food gathering are considered as their main traditional occupations. But present time, large number of these tribal groups practise fishing, honey collection, basket making, etc.

In the present study, an attempt has been made to assess mainly the demographic aspect of Saharia, a primitive tribe of Madhya Pradesh. Demography indicates the scientific study of human population in regarding their size, structure and development (U.N., 1958). By applying the various statistical methods in demographic study, differential fertility patterns, specific fertility, mortality, migration, etc. are measured in a systematic way. The dispersals of demographic study also focus on population size, territorial distribution, composition of change, social mobility, etc. The present demographic study not only measures the various aspects of population structure but also identifies all the problems and its related components. Further, in accordance with the problems, the various welfare activities are suggested to launch. In continuation with the demographic study, the subject anthropology is concerned very much. Whether, demography and anthropology are the two independent disciplines but in connection with population study, these two disciplines are closely related and formed one subfield, called 'demographic-anthropology'. In the subject of demographic-anthropology, the subject personnel not only cooperate with each other but also share their unique methodology in relation with data collection, data processing and also in report writing.

The tribal and non-tribal population scenario of Madhya

Pradesh as well as India have also been discussed by a brief literature review and these indicate economic characters, income, ownership of land, education, age at menarche, age at menopause, various measures of fertility and mortality rate, selection intensity, migration, maternal and child health care, health seeking behaviour and family planning. For the purpose of this demographic study, the various objectives have been determined in accordance with the different aspects of population groups and these are stated as to study the ethnographic account of Saharia, to study the measures of population by age-sex composition, i.e., age-sex distribution, dependency ratio, index of ageing, sex ratio, masculinity proportion, economic and educational characteristics, martial status, etc., to study the measures of fertility – crude birth rate, general fertility rate, age-specific fertility rate, total fertility rate, mean age at child bearing, general martial fertility rate, age-specific martial rate, child women ratio, etc. and the measures of mortality-crude death rate, age-specific death rate, peri-natal, neo-natal and post-neonatal mortality rates, under-five and child mortality rates, etc., to study the biological determinants like-age at menarche, menopause and the indices of the total natural selection (following Crow, 1958 and Johnston & Kensinger, 1971), to study the maternal & child health care, health seeking behaviour and family planning practices and utilization pattern and to compare the present population with tribal and non-tribal population groups of India.

Materials and methods for collecting different relevant data are discussed in a systematic manner. Before going to the field, the various methods of data collection were decided considering the population group. Literature survey, interview, observation, case study, genealogy schedules, etc. were designed as various data collecting methods considering the aims and the objectives of the study. In the comprehensive schedules, both close ended and open ended questions were arranged including the details about households, age and sex composition, economy, income, education, development schemes, fertility, mortality, migration, maternal and child health care, health seeking behaviour and family planning. For pre-testing the various prepared tools, a pilot study was also conducted among the population. Through this pilot study, the necessary correction, modification and change of research tools were not only incorporated but also acquainted with the over all idea about field situation. During almost eleven months, the present study was conducted among 333 Saharia households. Collecting relevant information, differential fertility, mortality and other demographic variables have been calculated by standard demographic methods and formulae. Methods of Crow (1958) and Johnston & Kensinger (1971) were also used to calculate the data for selection intensity among Saharia.

Out of total number of tribes, 74 groups have been identified as primitive tribes almost all over India and among them, Madhya Pradesh represents 7 tribes. Saharia tribe is one among 7 primitive tribal groups in Madhya Pradesh. These tribal groups have sporadically been concentrated in various districts of this state. For the present study, Banera, Bijli Ghor, Prem Nagar, Bhatpura, Gnadhipura-North and Gandhipura-South - six villages under Barai block (Grid subdivision) in Gwalior district of Madhya Pradesh were selected purposively. The available information hint that Saharia are considered as the member of widespread Kolarian tribe. The history of origination and migration of Saharia tribe are issued as controversial one. It is speculated that due to some sudden natural calamity, the present Saharia perhaps were migrated from Western part, the desecrated area of India. Form etymological point of view, 'SA' means companion and 'HARIA' means tiger. So, the meaning of Saharia is defined as the companion of tiger. However, in the present state, it is known that Saharia tribal groups are not only limited in Madhya Pradesh. Exceeding Madhya Pradesh, their distributions are also followed in Rajasthan, Orissa, Andhra Pradesh and very rarely in Bihar and West Bengal. In various regions, these tribal groups have been acquainted with various names like - Saharia, Sabara, Sora, Sawara, Savar, Saora, Sahariya, etc. In the present study, it is reported that all the Saharia household-members depend on the water of well, tube-well and pond. Most of the time, they face water problem. Due to lack of purified water, they are affected by various water borne diseases. According to the quality, colour, retentive of moisture, etc., their cultivated land is classified as Kala Jamin, Bhokta Jamin, Retile Jamin and

Kakrala Jamin and varieties of crops are produced by land holders. Hamlet is considered as their ecological unit and in every hamlet, more than 25 households are followed to be settled down in a cluster type of arrangement. They construct their huts at randomly within very short space on the top middle portion of a big hill. For constructing their cluster types of rectangular hut, they usually consult with 'Janter' (magician). Village path and drainage facilities are totally absent almost in every hamlet. Very poor medical services are functioned among them. Only a Government Hospital is located on Barai block but there, both experienced medical staff and useful medicines are rarely available. For such problems, most of the Saharia avoid to take medical services at the initial stage of their disease. For their treatment purpose, they initiate first preference to the medicines of their traditional healer. According to the Government rules and regulations, they are restricted not to collect forest products and as a result, most of them have abandoned their traditional hunting, food gathering economy and motivated themselves to practise daily labour, cultivation and others. They eat bread of wheat, maise, millet, etc. as staple food. Non-vegetable food items are much preferred to them. 'Languta' (small cloth) is worn as their males' traditional dress whereas females wear 'Ghaghra' (paticoat), 'Ordi' (bodies), 'Saluka' (blouse), Sharee, etc. Ornaments of silver, zinc, brass, iron, etc. are used mainly by Saharia women. Face, hands and foots of women are tattooed by various colours. They prepare plough, axe, spade, scythe, ladder, iron bars, etc. and use for their own purposes. For the special preparation of hearth, karai, dish vessel, basket, mat, broom, etc., they are highly appreciated by non-Saharia people. Among Saharia, the specific clan members worship the specific deities which indicate them totemic in nature. They are clan exogamous. Saharia are the members of patriarchal tribal group and their properties are transmitted from father to sons. After birth of a child, they observe birth-pollution during six days. Monogamy marriage in negotiation norm is generally conducted among them. Dowry and bride price do not play the important role for the marriage. Divorce and remarriage are rarely practised. Child birth is celebrated as auspicious day. After death, they generally cremate the dead body and on fourth day, they arrange single feast for the purpose of deceased person and then they come on to their daily old routine works. Among them, 'Bhagwan' is respected as the supreme God. For various purposes, they also worship 'Behram, Thakur, Bhumiji', etc. deities, by the help of their traditional religious head. In their traditional political organization 'Sahrama' is respected as the head whereas Patel, Barhai, Pradha, Jankar, etc. are appointed as his subordinates. They mainly regulate their socio-cultural homogeneity and justify the social conflic'ts. Illiteracy rate is very high (76.8 percent) among Saharia.

Saharia are constituted as primitive tribe and their at random dispersions are enumerated in various districts of Madhya Pradesh. In the present study, the maximum efforts are conferred to assess the actual socio-economic aspects, demographic situation and health care of Saharia. Under Barai block of Gwalior district, six Saharia villages including 333 families with 1668 population where 895 males and 773 females have been studied for the present purpose. Among them, the maximum percentage of population are found to be measured in the village Bhatpura (25.8 percent), followed by Bijli Ghor (23.5 percent) and Gandhipura-South (22.5 percent) whereas the village Banera (7.1 percent), Prem Nagar (9.5 percent) and Gandhipura-North (11.6 percent) present to have the minimum percentage of population. Variations of distribution of Saharia population in various villages are mainly depended on their traditional orthodox and work opportunity. In the context of land holding pattern, most of the Saharia families are identified under landless category (88.0 percent) whereas among land ownership group, below one acre to above four acres land are held by 5.1 percent to 0.6 percent Saharia families respectively. Their early history of economy makes a gesture that they were hunters and food gatherers and in regarding land acquiring, they were innocent. Even later on, in one side their acquired land was encroached by dominant groups and in other side, their extreme poverty pressured them to sell their land to the landlords or money lender groups. The present study also depicts that their low socio-cultural status and poor economy motivate themselves to build up their cluster types of residence on the middle-top portion of hill. The purpose of such location are implicated to save them from frequent dismantles by extreme flow of rain especially in rainy season, watch their grazing live-stocks and agricultural land, gain benediction from their primordial God and others. Due to poverty, most of the Saharia inhabit in thatched (34.8 percent) and bamboo (38.1 percent) made residences whereas only 5.7 percent of them dwell in cemented residences which have been constructed by receiving the Government beneficiary loan. For transporting purpose, only 0.6 percent families who live near to Barai block use two wheeler whereas 33.9 percent families maintain communication by bicycle. Due to restrict any conveyance on uneven ridges and undulating hilly foot path, the maximum families (61.6 percent) maintain transpiration depending on foot. As a reason of rarely available of tube-well in the village, the maximum percentage of Saharia collect water from well (40.9 percent) and well & tube-well (38.7 percent) whereas water of pond is used by the minimum percentage (3.6 percent) of them. Whether water of pond is impued but yet they are pressurized to collect its water especially in May-June months when tube-wells don't get water layer. All Saharia are facilitated to consume the free of cost electric power for only lighting purpose. They usually collect the dried wood from their nearest forest and use for fueling. Among them, nuclear families are found to be measured high (91.3 percent) as compared to joint families (8.7 percent). As belonged to traditional society, they are to be married at early age and separated from parents' family which play an important role for the formation of highly nuclear families. Most of the Saharia eat bread of wheat, maize, millet and others as staple foods. They use to prefer to the various non-vegetable food items. Almost all of them are very much addicted to drink their local wine 'Daru'. Only two villages are settled down near to Barai block and they are facilitated by concrete road whereas the other villages are totally isolated without availing such facility. In side the villages, only the uneven hilly footpaths connect all their clusters. It is noticed that due to unavailability, most of the households do not use any mass media (66.7 percent) whereas among user groups, 11.7 percent and 22.7 percent entertain the programmes of television and radio respectively. Only 2.1 percent educated Saharia read news paper occasionally. Their 45.7 percent heads of households do not watch any movies whereas through television and local video hall, the maximum (29.1 percent) and the minimum (3.6 percent) households among all movie viewers prefer to enjoy romantic and violence related movies respectively.

With reference to socio-cultural and demographic parameters, population composition consisting of age, sex, material status, etc. is discussed in a comparative framework of tribal and non-tribal people of India. In this regard, the present study imparts a clear estimation that 47.2 percent, 48.8 percent and 4.0 percent Saharia population are distributed in the age group of 0-14 years, 15-49 years and 50+ years respectively. Higher proportion of people in younger age group indicates the developing status whereas developed status is performed by the presence of higher proportion of population in higher age group. Availability of inadequate population in old age group always guesses low status. Higher fertility and mortality, malnutrition, lack of old age care, inadequate medical facility, low socio-economic status, etc. are attributed as the reasons of higher population in younger age group and lower population in old age group (SRS, 1992). Sex composition of a population is also acquainted to have a great importancy in demographic analysis. It not only makes a balance between sexes but also analyses the socio-economic relationships which are associated with the balance or disparity between the number of males and females. However, sex composition consisting of sex ratio and masculinity proportion of population is varied in accordance with the development activities and socio-cultural status. In the present study, sex ratio of Saharia population is found to be measured as 863.63 which is comparatively lower than Hill Korwa (954.0), Lodha (902.0), Santal (1019.0), people of Madhya Pradesh (985.0), people of India (972.0) and others. Among Saharia, masculinity proportion is estimated as 53.7. In the context of a comparative framework, Saharia masculinity proportion is found higher (53.7) than Bhutia (50.10), Tamang (50.41), Bodh (51.1), Gaddi (53.48), people of India (51.73) and others. Low status of women, early age at marriage of women and frequent child births, male sex preference, achievement of deplorable low literacy rate, etc. are contaminated as the reasons for their low sex ratio and high masculinity proportion. Marital status of Saharia people hints that the percentage of unmarried males (30.2 percent) is found out number as compared to females (26.0 percent). The percentage of married females is comparatively lower (19.6 percent) than males (29.4 percent). Among them, widowers (0.1 percent) and divorces (0.7 percent) are found rarely. Females, married in reproductive age group are high which influence high fertility. Due to lack of old age care, the persons above the age of 50 years are estimated low which indicates higher mortality. In other side, dependency measures the impact of age composition on the livelihood activity of population. Their young age dependency ratio (92.58) and total dependency ratio (96.23) are noticed to be high whereas old age dependency ratio is low (3.65) as compared to Gaddi, Mao, Lepcha, Kandh, Abujhmaria and others. There is a presumption that as the reasons of comparatively higher population growth under the age group of 15 years, Saharia young age dependency ratio is seen high whereas due to lack of old age care, after marriage immediate separation from parents, low socio-economic status, high mortality in senior group, etc., their old age dependency is come to low. High proportion of population under 15 years age group and high mortality in old generation, ageing index of Saharia is calculated as comparatively lower (3.94) than Gaddi (7.95), Lepcha (4.88), Raji (8.53) and others. The number of members in a family varies from 2 to 11 persons but the average number of members in a family is estimated as 5. They are always influenced to give frequent child births which increase the average number of members in a family. The present study provides an existence of 21 clans. Sometimes, their different socio-cultural rules and regulations are varied from one to another clan and in accordance with these, their sex ratio is also varied from 500 (Dongia & Negtelia clan each) to 1500 (Sonoria clan).

Generation-wise occupation among Saharia depicts a variation of changing occupation from grand father to father and then to present generation. As prestigious occupation, major group of people practised hunting (56.4 percent) in grand father generation whereas business and service were practised by nobody. Instead of hunting occupation, daily labour was practised by high extent of households (58.5 percent) in father generation. Due to deforestation, Government ban on hunting operation, unavailability of sizable agricultural land, etc., most of the households (70.2 percent) of present generation are motivated to practise daily labour. Among Saharia community, there is a tradition that both males and females more or less share the economic activity. In this regard, the present study specifies that in primary as well as in secondary occupation, involvement of male workers is found comparatively higher (57.0 percent) than female workers (43.0 percent). Physical problem and frequent conceptions and child births of females are mainly attributed as the reasons which make an obstacle for equal sharing in economic activity. In connection of their economic performance, 54.61 percent and 107.17 percent are found to be calculated as their crude activity rate and general activity rate respectively. As poverty stricken and inhabitant of remote area, most of the Saharia are to be involved in economic activity from their early stage which prostrates to enhance their crude activity rate and general activity rate. Their yearly household income varies from below Rs.3000/- (0.3 percent family) to above Rs.10,000/- (4.5 percent families). Their average income is found to be estimated as very low (Rs.6035/-). Throughout the year, they do not get the continuous work opportunity. Even by the landlords or contractors, they are exploited to pay heavy work and receive very little amount which is not enough for purchasing their necessary commodities and as a result, they are to be incumbered with debt. Educational attainment is far less common and their literacy rate is found to be measured as deplorable low (23.2 percent). High extent illiteracy in parental generation, always involvement in miscellaneous works, poverty, etc. are attributed as the reasons of their low literacy rate (23.2 percent) as compared to Gond (26.4 percent), Abujhmaira (26.9 percent), Raji (33.6 percent) and others. In a specific observation, it is stated that male literacy rate is comparatively higher (28.2 percent) than female literacy rate (17.7 percent). As belonged to matriarchal society, most of the Saharia are entangled to carry on the biasness for male sex preference in a discriminating way which helps to enhance male literacy rate. A very critical analysis exhibits that highest literacy rate is imparted in the age group of 5-9 years

(47.7 percent). As clarification, it may be expressed that in one side, the children of this particular age group are not actively involved in any activity and in other side, attending in school, they are being eligible to receive Government incentives consisting of cash amount, food materials, books, uniforms, etc. So, attraction of incentives makes an impact for enrolment which assists to increase literacy rate. Over all, their motive of educational attainment varies from one to other person in accordance with their difference socio-cultural rules. Some of the Saharia households have been benefited by various loans. There is a focus that the financial position of loan benefited families is comparatively better than others. Their better financial position influences them for educational attainment which plays a great role to increase literacy.

Menarche is a biological phenomenon but it expression is depended on socio-cultural aspects. However, the mean age of menarche of Saharia women is found to be measured as 13.5 years which is comparatively higher than their daughters (13.3 years). Due to severe financial as well as socio-cultural improvement, the descending generation achieves a little augmentation of menarcheal age. But over all socio-cultural development is still remained. They are poverty stricken and facing malnutrition and their literacy rate is very low which make an impact for their low menarcheal age as compared to Hill Korwa (13.67 years), Munda (14.65 years), Abujhmaria (15.0 years) and others. Menopause is also an another biological term which ceases the reproductive function of women by arresting the menstruation flow of blood and ovulation. Genetical factor, lack of nutritional foods, low socio-cultural status, heavy work load, rural setting, etc. may be mentioned as the transgressed reasons for their comparatively lower mean age at menarche (44.6 years) than Ahom (48.0 years), Garo (45.85 years), Thoti (47.35 years) and others. Likewise, marriage is another term and by which the couples are being socially recognized to get the liberties for cohabiting and share the economic and reproductive functions. In the present study, the average age at marriages of Saharia husbands and wives are found to be measured as 17.6 years and 14.0 years respectively which violate the Marriage

Restrain Act, 1976. Poverty, traditional socio-cultural norms, isolation, limited contact with others, etc. are contaminated as the reasons of low age at marriage specially women (14.0 years) as compared to Kamar (14.23 yers), Abujumaria (15.3 years), Hill Korwa (14.9 years), Gond (15.5 years) and others. But by the motivational approaches of various agencies and somewhat socio-economic development, the average age at marriage is lightly improved in descending generation. In this regard, their sons and daughters are found to be attained marriage at the average age of 17.9 years and 14.6 years respectively. Their various norms imply that at the time of marriage, all social activities are not possible to complete. As a result, their sexual intercourse is usually delayed upto the completion of remain social activities. In that context, the specific estimation discloses that after marriage, their sexual intercourse is delayed from below 1 year to 2 years. Due to delay of sexual intercourse and positive explanation of health workers, their first child birth is delayed with having an estimation of 2.4 years as the mean age of interval between marriage and first child birth. Among Saharia community, sometimes the marriage of women is conducted before attaining menarche and even some literates use family planning devices for illustrating a desirable gap between marriage and first child birth. In that context, their mean age difference between marriage and first child birth is found to be measured as 2.9 years. Age difference between husbands and wives is varied from 1 to 7 years whereas the mean age difference is estimated as 2.9 years which is not considered as a significant factor. For the marriage of sons, they usually select their choiceable girls without having any effective manner of the age factor.

Fertility indicates the actual reproductive performance and the number of children, produced by the women. Somewhat similar term - fecundity deals with the capacity to take part in reproduction and produce living offsprings. Both fertility and fecundity are corroborately associated with biological, environmental and socio-cultural factors. In demographic behaviour, fertility is measured but there is no any liability to measure fecundity. However, under various parameters of fertility, child-women ratio is commonly measured from the age and sex distribution of the population group. In the present study, Saharia child-women ratio is found to be estimated as 1238.25 (0-9 years age group) which is comparatively higher than Kamar (1141.31), Dalu (860.80), Jaunsaria (1150.00), Pnar (869.60) and others. Low socio-cultural status, illiteracy, male sex preference and frequent child births, less family planning adoption, etc. are attributed as the reasons of their higher child-women ratio. As an important component in fertility parameter, crude birth rate among Saharia is found to be measured as 43.76. Crude birth rate of Bhil (43.5), Abughmaria (33.9), Jaunsaria (32.0), Santal (37.2) and others are depicted low as compared to Saharia (43.76). Their general fertility rate is also noticed to be accounted as comparatively higher (244.96) than Kamar (177.02), Soliga (188.0), Lodha (133.3), Dudh Khera (164.0) and others. Transitional life from food gathering to food producing stage, early age at marriage, paucity of family planning use, illiteracy, low socio-cultural status, etc. are transgressed as the reasons of their higher crude birth rate and general fertility rate. The maximum and minimum age specific fertility rates are computed in the age group of 20-24 years (328.35) and 40-40 years (125.0) respectively. The women of this particular age group (20-24 years) are more fertile and due to paucity of contraceptive use, they are capable to conceive and give births frequently. By an estimation, total fertility rate per Saharia woman is exhibited to be high (6.70) as compared to Halba (5.89), Madia (6.00), Muria (5.10), Lohar Gadiyas (4.60) and others. The present study also confers an accountation of gross fertility rate per Saharia woman as 2.74 which is found comparatively higher than Kamar (2.36), Bhotia (1.44), Kand (1.44), Thoti (1.84) and others. The mean age at child bearing of women is found to be calculated as 29.30 years. It is revealed high as compared to Dharchulas (24.93 years), Brokpas (25.20 years), Chhetris (23.01 years), Limboos (26.37 years) and others. Likewise various measures of fertility, marital fertility consists of general marital fertility, age specific marital fertility, total marital fertility and gross reproduction in wed-lock. It is observed that general marital fertility rate among Saharia is estimated comparatively higher (248.20) than Kamar (231.41), Marchas (194.44), Kumauni (165.6), Raji (227.64) and others. The estimation of the maximum and the minimum age specific marital fertility rates are found to be concentrated in the age group of 20-24 years (328.35) and 40-44 years (62.50) respectively. In the present study, total marital fertility rate per Saharia woman is found to be measured as 6.41 which is higher as compared to Kamar (6.34), Marchas (5.61), Juhar (4.14), Brokpas (6.0) and others. Another estimation also ensures that gross reproduction rate per Saharia woman in wed-lock is 2.76. High extent of illiteracy, low socio-cultural status, poverty, early age at marriage, non-adoption of contraceptives, inadequate medical facility, etc. are contaminated as the reasons of their higher total fertility rate, gross reproduction rate, general marital fertility rate, age specific martial fertility rate, total martial fertility rate and gross reproduction rate per woman in wed-lock.

It is a study to determine the performance of differential fertility behaviours which are connected with socio-cultural and biological factors. The mean number of children ever born and the mean number of children surviving are separately calculated in accordance with such socio-cultural status and biological perspectives. In this regard, the present study assesses that the fertility differentials among Saharia are pertained with respect to land ownership of households. Both landless and land holder groups require many hands work for labouring and agriculture and these influence them to give births frequently and as a result, their mean number of children ever born is found to be calculated as high. In other side, comparatively better financial status of land holder group supports to increase their mean number of children surviving by initiating all facilities. Illiteracy, low socio-cultural status, poverty, non-utilization of contraceptive devices, inadequacy of medical facility, etc. are incorporately linked with their poor quality of living standard, bad transportation system, impured water sources, non-utilization of mass-media, observing perverted movie, living in nuclear family, traditional system of occupation, low income, harmful norms in particular clan, high extent of illiteracy, mating pattern among high and low educational groups, non-receiving of beneficiary loan, early age at menarche, shorter reproductive span of life, early age at marriage, inexperienced by no any infant death, etc. and these are determinated as the contaminated reasons for tending to increase the mean number of children surviving and vice-versa.

The permanent extinction of all signs of life from living body is meant as dead. In other words, mortality indicates the continuous force of attrition for tending to reduce population as a negative force in the balance of vital processes. However, the measure of mortality level helps to determine the socio-cultural status of the study population. In this regard, the present study measures the various mortality rates and its associated socio-economic components of Saharia primitive tribe and makes a comparative framework with other population groups. By collecting very simplest information related to total population and number of deaths which were occurred in a particular period, crude death rate among Saharia is measured as 25.77. This is found comparatively higher than Gond (23.19), Abujhumaria (14.90), Bhils (15.53), Rang Bhotia (16.11) and others. Inadequate medical facility, deplorable low literacy, poverty, malnutrition, low socio-cultural status, etc. may be mentioned as the contaminated reasons for their higher crude death rate. Due to lack of proper child care, non-immunization, traditional way of treatment, non-availability of nutritional foods, insanitation, negligence to old age care, insecure life of aged, etc., their age specific death rate is come to high (as 329.19 average) below the age of 4 years and above the age of 55 years. There is a depiction that still birth rate among Saharia is calculated as 26.66 and it is found high as compared to Kamar (25.91), Brahmin (10.2), Rajput (11.6), Scheduled Caste (17.8) and others. In other side, peri-natal mortality rate among Saharia is seen to be estimated as 54.79 which is comparatively higher than Brahmin (29.6), Rajput (34.8), Scheduled Caste (25.7), people of Madhya Pradesh (52.9) and others. This is expressed that neo-natal morality rate among them is estimated high (54.79) as compared to Garo (33.9), Khasi (17.2), Machas (14.28), Juhari (40.0) and others. By a calculation, post natal mortality rate among Saharia is conferred as 68.49 which is found comparatively higher than Kamar (53.51), Khasi (24.8), Garo (18.1), Mizo (18.1) and others. For determining the socio-economic development, infant mortality is considered as the highly appreciable method and in this context, infant mortality rate among Saharia is yielded to be measured as 123.28. In a comparative framework, their infant mortality rate is found higher (123.28) than Mirdha (116.0), Hill Kolam (70.59), Zemi

(86.1), Santal (94.8) and others. Their under-five mortality rate is also exhibited to be measured high (82.35) as compared to Khasi (57.96), Garo (79.01), Mizo (31.91), Marchas (42.85) and others. In the present study, child mortality rate is found to be computed as 62.82 which is comparatively higher than Marchas 28.57), Scheduled Caste (46.15), Khasi (15.9), Garo (27.1) and others. Their maximum deaths were taken place by the effect of pneumonia, malaria, tuberculosis and other diseases. Investigation for the present study impart that they are committed to follow their traditional norms. Influencing by their social system, they conduct marriage at early age which prostrates illed health. Frequent child births by untrained delivery attendant, non-immunization, inadequate medical facility, impured drinking water, high extent of illiteracy, poverty, malnutrition, low socio-cultural status, odd environment, etc. are attributed as the reasons of their high mortality.

In demographic study, differential mortality plays a significant role to determine the variation. It is a confession that the differential mortality is varied in accordance with socio-economic condition, biological aspects and maternal factors. In the context of differential mortality, the present study estimates the average child loss ratio and child survival ratio among Saharia on the basis of various variables. In relation to land holding pattern, the landless groups are found to be presented the high child loss ratio and low child survival ratio as compared to land holders. Land less groups are poverty stricken and illiterate. Their inadequate family income is almost failed to provide nutritional foods, standard of living, modern clinical facility, etc. which are enough to enhance child loss as well as curtail child survival. Similarly, the types of residence usually indicate the status of living standard and financial condition. Socio-cultural status and financial condition of most of the Saharia are deplorable low. They usually inhabit in poor quality of residences which are made by thatch and bamboo. Due to inhabit in such residences, their children are frequently affected by various seasonal diseases which tend to increase their child loss. Illiteracy, traditional way of healing practice, financial backwardness, etc. may be attributed as the barriers for their low child survival and vice-versa. Communication by foot, use of impured water from various sources, without any use of mass media, enjoyment of war related movie, living in nuclear family, hard working occupation, low average income, belonging to extremely traditional clan, illiteracy, without having benefit by any loan, high age at menarche of women, low age at marriage, migration, etc. are concerned to the low socio-cultural status, poverty, insanitation, illiteracy, inadequacy of medical service, etc. which influence their high child loss as well as low child survival and vice-versa.

Natural selection is regarded as the evolutionary process which changes the gene frequencies in a population through differential fertility and mortality. The variation of natural selection is contributed by the equal sharing of bio-genetic factors and socio-cultural and environmental aspects. By the methods of Crow (1958) and Johnston & Kensinger (1971), various information related to differential fertility and mortality are found to be computed to analyse the index of selection potential (I). Actually, differential fertility and mortality help to measure the fitness which is considered as most fundamental event of natural selection under the process of evolutionary changes in a population group. As an indirect method, the maximum amount of differential fertility and mortality in a population group was computed by the formula of Crow (1958) but later on, incorporating the embryonic mortality component, formula was modified by Johnston and Kensinger (1971). In the present study, the embryonic mortality is included and then the value of the index of total selection intensity (I_2), computed by the formula of Johnston & Kensinger is found comparatively higher (0.389) than the value of the index of total selection intensity – I_1 (0.348), computed by Crow. Further, in the context of others, the index of total selection intensity (I_1) among Saharia is found high (0.348) as compared to Swangla (0.339), Oraon (0.243), Hmar (0.340), Koraga (0.340) and others. In other side, the total selection intensity (I_2) among Saharia is also noticed as comparatively higher (0.389) than Ahom of Assam (0.308), Kamati (0.319),Oraon (0.369), Hmar (0.379) and others. Low socio-cultural status, illiteracy, early age at marriage, poverty, malnutrition, lack of maternal and child care, traditional way of delivery, non-immunization, etc.

may be attributed as the reasons of their high index of total selection.

In demographic behaviour, migration is entangled to have a great impact for changing the population density. Through the process of migration, people shift their residents from one to another place for various purposes. In the context of migration, the present study confers that 26.4 percent Saharia families (out of 333) are found to be settled down in the study area coming from outside. Distance variation in migrating process is not committed as a matter of fact. However, in regarding the population distribution, sex ratio and masculinity proportion of migrants are found to be measured high (910.71) and low (53.3) as compared to the sex ratio (863.68) and masculinity proportion (53.7) of total Saharia respectively. Due to settlement near to the block area, both males and females migrated Saharia are usually benefited by the assignment of work opportunity which tends to reduce female discrimination. As an effect, their sex ratio and masculinity proportion are come to high and low respectively. Duration of migration is corroborately associated with socio-cultural components. In the present study, the maximum (54.5 percent) and minimum (1.1 percent) percentage of families are found to be migrated due to lack of work opportunity and marriage, conducted in same clan respectively. Most of the migrated Saharia are landless and as a reason, they are motivated to practise daily labour (88.6 percent). Due to deforestation and Government restriction on hunting operation, hunting and food gathering occupations are found to be extinct. For the reason of urgent need of work, lack of drinking water, etc., migration of most of the families (68.2 percent) are noticed to be performed swiftly whereas tribal festival, child birth, etc. are informed as the social barriers for the delay of migration of some families (31.8 percent). Due to new settlement near to block area, they receive work opportunity, increase educational level, practise free of cost birth control devices, etc. which tend to reduce their various measures fertility as compared to the total Saharia. In other side, their provided nutritional foods, medical facility, child care, immunization, etc. curtail various measures of mortality as compared to total Saharia. The present study also discusses that fertility and mortality differentials may be varied in accordance with the occupational, economic and educational status of migrant Saharia. Agriculture based households require adequate manpower for better productivity. For the fulfill of their purpose, they desire to give birth many offsprings without using any birth control devices. As a result, their mean number of children ever born is found to be measured as high. In other side, their comparatively better financial status is enabled to afford the family budget by providing nutritional foods, medical service, standard of living, etc. which play a positive role for their low child loss as well as high child survival. The interfere of financial status makes an aspersion that for increasing man power, they frequently give births without having any use of contraceptives and in this context, their mean number of children ever born is found to estimated as high. As a reason of high income, they can avail to expense amount for better fooding, medical facility, standard of living, etc. which help to decrease their child loss as well as increase child survival as compared to others. In the present study, it is informed that most of the illiterate Saharia are the extreme followers to their traditional socio-cultural orthodox and run under the low category of income. They do not use the modern contraceptives and as an effect, their mean number of children ever born is found to be measured as high. Due to low income, they are failed to provide the essential needs related to nutritional food items, medical service, standard of living, etc. which confer an approach for their high child loss as well as low child survival as compared to others.

Maternal care means the women care which are required during pregnancy, at the time of delivery and post-delivery period by initiating nutritional foods, health services, safe delivery, post-parturient care, proper rest, etc. By the application of maternal care, the would be mothers learn to maintain better health, expect normal delivery, procreate healthy child, acquaint with the methods of proper child care, etc. Maternal care mainly consists of ante natal and natal care. Staying at home or admitting at hospital, ante natal care as well as pregnancy related health care are received by the direct supervision of medical professionals. Whereas, natal care are rigorously activated at the time of delivery and post delivery periods. Ante natal and natal care are varied in accordance with the society approved rules and norms. In the present study, it is followed that Saharia are embarrassed to observe their cultural practices – fatalism as ante natal care. For the rescue from extreme labour pain and avoiding the bad effect of spiritual power, the maximum Saharia women (90.7 percent) observe fast during their pregnancy periods. Being influenced by their traditional norms and taboos, a major group of pregnant women is informed to avoid various food items, practise sexual intercourse, drink & smoke, wear costumes & ornaments, select traditional doctor, neglect immunization, etc. At the time of delivery, the prime care taking role of husbands is prostrated as very crucial. From initial period, concerned to the traditional birth attendance to the final of post parturient stage, all husbands are pressurized to conduct all activities whereas other members of the family just assist them. Under natal care, the place of delivery is totally depended on their socio-economic status. Due to low financial status, illiteracy, follow up traditional norms, etc. their most of the deliveries are performed at home (68.3 percent) by the direct supervision of their local mid-wives (60.7 percent). In respecting to their customs and beliefs, they use split, arrow head and knife for cutting the umbilical cords of the new borns. But by the motivational approaches of various agencies, a major group of Saharia recently uses blade (72.1 percent) for cutting stumps and as a result, they more or less save the new babies and mothers from various infectious diseases. After delivery, usually the new born babies and mothers are washed by locally available impured water which make a disruptive role for creating the water borne diseases and infection. After delivery, they do not give weightage for sanctioning any special food items whereas many prohibitions are concerned to intake foods. Among Saharia, there is a custom of secluding that the new mothers are allowed to take relaxation to some extent. But financial deficiency deprives the long time entertainment of post parturient mothers and as a result, most of them are depressed to resume for continuing the routine work.

With reference to infant and child care practices, the role of mother is perceived as unique. Growth and development of infant and child are directly associated with nutritional food intake, proper rest, medical service, safe delivery, etc. of expectant mothers. Because healthy mother can achieve the priority to bear healthy baby. After birth, the first few days of the infants are considered as critical for tolerating the completely new, strange and victim environment. Through proper nursing and careful observation, they are capable to adjust with breathing, food intake and other external components. However, the infant and child care practices are varied from one to another community in accordance with the variation of their traditional socio-cultural beliefs and norms. In the present study, it is acquainted that after delivery, traditionally Saharia use boiled water mixed with bitter substance for giving bath to both new born babies and mothers. They believe that only bitter substance may contain the capability to vanish infected germs. For socio-economic backward position, most of them use the wasted cloth for wrapping the new born babies. Initiation of breast feeding to the new borns is differed from socio-culturally backward to somewhat advanced Saharia. In respecting to beliefs, customs and norms, the socio-culturally backward groups start breast feeding to their babies as early as possible for nutritional intake and prevention. Their perception is that postponing suckling is an unnatural practice for enhancing the habit of starvation and making difficulty to establish lactation later on. In other side, the advanced groups usually avoid immediate breast feeding bleming thick, indigestible and raw milk of siken mothers. For initiating breast feeding, a major group of women practises feeding frequently (18.9 percent) whereas other groups use substitute like honey, tribal medicine, etc. Generally, the new mothers produce small quantity of yellow milk or fluid called colostrum which contains lesser fat and sugar but heavier protein than ordinary milk. All such substances make immunoglobulin for having a protective capacity from various infections. The women of comparatively low socio-cultural status prefer to initiate immediately breast feeding for various beneficiary purposes (86.2 percent) whereas advanced groups deny to feed mentioning pus like milk secretion of new mothers. Frequency of breast feeding is depended on the occupation of mothers. The mothers who involved in household works get enough time for conducting frequent breast feeding whereas feeding practices are reduced by those mothers who are involved in labouring and other miscellaneous works, performed outside. Due to malnutrition and involvement in heavy works, most of the mothers are become insolvent to secret required milk which is demanded by their infants through crying or other external attitudes. Deficiency of required milk usually shoves to be illed health. Extreme poverty pressurises them to involve in various works and as a result, most of the mothers consume 10-13 minutes (44.8 percent) at a time for breast feeding purpose. Inadequate milk feeding during short period of time may be mentioned as the transgressed reason for poor health status which prostrates to influence high infant mortality. The present study also expresses that for the secretion of insufficient milk, sometimes their babies are not interested to suck and in that condition, mothers use honey, molasses, sugar on the nipple of breast, sacrifice hen, etc. for increasing lactation. Statements, given by the collected information define that the mothers of comparatively better socio-economic status practise weaning by birth of next child (23.6 percent) whereas others, who are illiterate and poverty stricken form this habit by using bitter substance, tribal medicine, etc. on breast. Due to unavailability of milk in the breast and disturbance by work, most of the mothers practise weaning at the age of 2 years (52.3 percent) of their children. For the treatment of their children, doctor selection is concerned as the vital aspect among Saharia. Their poverty, illiteracy, traditional belief, low socio-cultural status, etc. in one side and careful checkup, experienced healer, always available, etc. in other side are assembled to concentrate them for selecting the traditional healer. It is also informed that at initial stage of ailment, they prefer to take treatment under traditional healer. But due to fail in bringing any improvement, they usually turn from traditional to modern doctor for getting treatment. Immunization is still almost unexposed to Saharia offsprings. Very rarely cases, their children are found to be fully or partially immunized by measles, DTP, BCG, polio and tetanus. Their illiteracy, unawareness, suspense of adopted disease, etc. may be attributed as the reasons of non-immunization.

In the context of health seeking behaviour, the updated concept of health indicates a stable situation of physical, mental and social well being. However, health is a relative aspect of disease which afflicts and then requires remedial measures. Concepts of health and diseases and also its curative measures are varied from tribal to non-tribal people in accordance with their socio-economic status. The common perception of tribal people is that before getting bed rest, the person is not called as disease affected. For the ailment of their diseases, they usually prefer to their traditional healer. The collected information in this regard, express that as inhabited in remote area and belonged to traditional society, the Saharia tribal people are still almost unexposed to the modern system of treatment. As poverty stricken, most of them are to be faced the deprivation of malnutrition. Their low standard of living, insanitation, work load, etc. are also embedded as the indebted factors for possessing very weak health status (54.7 percent). Due to financial problem, they are not enabled to provide the adequate nutrients for influencing the rapid growth of the children. As reasons of unawareness, negligence to care and preference of traditional healer, immunization for the children is also affected in a great extent which prostrate high sickness in lower age group. In other side, poverty, malnutrition, negligence to old age care as burden, traditional beliefs, etc. may be attributed as the reasons for high sickness of aged persons. Due to victim environment consisting of heavy cold, hot and rain, impured drinking water, malnutrition, insanitation, low status of living standard and others, most of them are siken by pneumonia, malaria, digestive disorders, water born diseases, etc. At initial stage of their disease, they usually prefer to the treatment of their traditional healer. But due to fail in bringing improvement, they come under the treatment of modern clinical process. So from initial to the final stage of treatment of their disease, they consume enough time which effectively illustrate the duration of sickness from below 1 year to above 5 years. The present study, concerned with the consultation of sickness of last five years' record also comprises that due to poverty, illiteracy and low socio-cultural beliefs, norms and customs, a group of them is entangled to have a motivational approach for consulting with their traditional healer for treatment of their disease. In the context of local Government Hospital services, they are not hagited to confer the negative comments also. Useless medicine, no free medicine, more time waste for treatment, non-availability of both doctor and useful medicine, odd communication system to go Hospital, etc. are accused as the reasons of agitation of unsatisfied attitude to Government Hospital.

Family planning is considered as the significant aspect in population study. Very simply, it indicates the plan for having desired number of children who are given births of a desired time. In other side, birth control is somewhat different terms which prevent conception by adopting various contraceptive methods. However, the purpose of family planning as well as birth control is not only limited in the prevention of conception, its adequate extension is incorporated to develop the health status of family members specially women and children. In this regard, the present study is committed to highlight the various aspects of family planning devices among Saharia tribal community. The available information yield that as the reasons of frequent child deaths, additional labouring, prestigious issue, God gift, etc., the view of a major group of Saharia (52.8 percent) is to have many children. Detachment from the main stream of national life, illiteracy, poverty, low socio-cultural status, paucity of medical facility, etc., may be transgressed as the reasons which make a motivational approach to procreate many offsprings. Most of the Saharia women are regarded as innocent in expressing the symptoms of conception. Their socio-cultural parameters are also corroborately associated with their stated awareness of symptoms which are not scientifically accepted (except menstruational concept). As belonged to traditional society, the socio-economic activities of most of the illiterate Saharia are directed by their strong religious beliefs. In this context, they are instigated to have at least one or more sons on behalf of income benefit, future inheritor, chances of frequently male child deaths and others. In connection with the matter, initially they are not agree to practise family planning methods while they have achieved more or less knowledge. However, socio-economic interferences are also incorporated for adopting various family planning methods. By admixing with other people, a group of literate and poverty stricken Saharia is aware to restrict population growth as well as avoid conception. In this regard, they receive incentives in terms of both cash and kinds by adopting vasectomy or tubectomy family planning method. Others also accept free of cost condom, beverage food, tribal medicine and other contraceptive devices for making interval between conceptions, random sexual enjoyment, etc. As simple mitigation for avoiding frequent child births, the socio-culturally motivated Saharia observe abstinence. The present study also reports that non-adoption of family planning methods of most of the Saharia is also depended on various socio-cultural factors like – God gift (birth), desire of male child, health problem, currently marriage, frequent child deaths and others. For adopting family planning methods adoption, social discrimination and biasness play an important role to vary from husbands (35.0 percent) to wives (65.0 percent). Clarifications incurred of comparatively higher family planning methods adoption by wives are stated as chances of side effect of husbands, no heavy work load (of wives), only for wife use, etc. Over all, after adopting different contraceptive devices, both husbands and wives are more or less suffering from head pain, pain of pelvic girdle, infection and other diseases. For the preference of ideal number of offsprings in a family, opinion is varied from one to another person in accordance with their socio-cultural beliefs, norms and customs. In the present study, it is explained that high extent of illiteracy, poverty, low socio-cultural status, frequent child deaths, etc. are attributed as the reasons which influence the ideal number of family members from 1 male and 1 female to 4 males and 2 females. As the follower of traditional society, their most of the women are married at early age. So, their early age at marriage helps them to give births desired number of offsprings as early as possible. In this regard, most of the family planning methods users are found to be estimated in the age group of 20-24 years. In most of the cases, they practise miscellaneous occupations and their financial and educational status is comparatively better than others.

On the whole, the forgoing discussions recapitulate that as high extent of isolation, small size of community, pre-agricultural stage of economy, low level of literacy and others, Saharia tribal groups are acquainted as primitive tribe. It is substantial that as extreme followers of their socio-cultural orthodox, their almost all activities are regulated by their society approved rules, norms and customs. Any how, they have no any intension to violate their social taboos for the suspense of future inauspicious. Their isolated life in one side, preserves the homogeneity of their unifying social organization and in other side, makes an obstacle to admixture with the main stream of national life. As poverty stricken, they are to face malnutrition and inhabit in cluster types of residence. For the lack of availability of purified water sources, they drink impured water. Being entangled with their traditional culture, they usually conduct marriage at early age neglecting the Marriage Restrain Act. The maximum Saharia are permutated under very weak health status and prostrated to disease. Aetiological aspects of their diseases are conferred by traditional healer whereas the modern clinical facilities are still almost unexposed to them. Beside these, due to illiteracy and traditional beliefs, they prefer to perform delivery at home by the help of their traditional mid-wives and try to avoid immunization. For the reasons of biasness of male sex preference, high infant mortality, traditional thinking, etc., they rarely adopt modern family planning methods. So, on the basis of the over all components, it may be assessed that remote inhabitation, deplorable low literacy, traditional beliefs, early age at marriage, male sex preference, high infant mortality, lack of awareness of birth control devices and others are embarrassed as the possible transgressed reasons for their high fertility. In other side, their financial problem, malnutrition, low standard of living, insanitation, impured drinking water, illiteracy, social taboos, treatment under traditional healer, performation of delivery at home by mid-wives, non-immunization, etc. may be mentioned as the attributed reasons of their high mortality. As mitigation of stated contaminated reasons, the special long time multi-development programmes should be implemented preferably to their financial benefits. Its adequate extension should be made for better educational facility, proper health services, utmost modern family planning devices, availability of nutritional foods and purified water, standard of living, sanitation, etc. In connection with the matter, various agencies should also be deputed to motivate them for emerging from their socio-cultural boundary and mixing with the main stream of national people. Within a stipulated time interval, the progressive stages of various adopted beneficiary programmes should also be monitored for further necessary action. As an effect of such, slowly and gradually they will be exposed not only to acquire the capability for solving their own potential problems but also to acquaint themselves as a socio-economically and demographically advanced Saharia.

BIBLIOGRAPHY

Adak, Dipak Kumar (1994): The Khasi of Shillong (Meghalaya): A Note on Infant and Early Childhood Mortality. *Man In India*, 74 (3): 287-295

Adak, Dipak Kumar and Chaudhuri, Sarit Kumar (1996): Birth Rate and Death Rate of Tripura (1971-1989): A Study of Time Series. *J. Hum. Ecol.*, 7(3): 169-173

Adak, Dipak Kumar (2001): Child Mortality in Three Tribal Population of Shillong. *J. Hum. Ecol.*, 12 (2): 147-152.

Agarwal, Bina (1990): *Social Security and the Family: Croping with Seasonality and Calamity in Rural India.* Peasant Studies, 17:341-412.

Agarwal, D.K., Agarwal, K.N. and Khare, B.B. (1986): *Current Status of Infant and Early Childhood Feeding Practices.* Indian Academy of Paediatrics, Banaras Hindu Uni., Varanasi.

Agarwala, S.N. (1962): *Age at Marriage in India.* Kitab Mahal Pvt. Ltd. , Bombay.

– – –, (1966): *Some Problems of India's Population.* Vora and Co. Publishers,Pvt. Ltd., Bombay.

– – –, (1966): Raising the Marriage Age of Women: A Means to Lower the Birth Rate. *Eco. Pol. Weekly*, 1: 797.

– – –, (1967): *Population.* New Delhi, National Book Trust, India.

Ahluwalia, A.S. (1963): *Cultural Pattern Associated with Child Birth.* Indian J. Public Health, 7: 5.

Aiyappan, A. (1994): "Tribes in South India : 89-97" *Tribal Life in India*, Vol.1. Ed. Devendra Thakur and D.N. Thakur. Deep & Deep Publications, Rajouri Garden, New Delhi

Aiyappan, A. (1994): "Tribes in South India" *Tribal Culture and Identity*. Vol.1. Ed. Devendra Thakur and D.N. Thakur. Deep & Deep Publications, Rajouri Garden, New Delhi.

Amanullah, M. and Naharia, A.L. (1986): "Tribal Development Programmes in Madhya Pradesh: Perspectives and Problems" *Tribal Development-Past Efforts And New Challenges*. Ed. J.P. Singh and N.N. Vyas. The MLV Tribal Research And Training Institute, Tribal Area Development, Rajasthan, Udaipur.

Anker, R. and Knowles, J.C. (1977): *An Empirical Analysis of Mortality Differential in Kenya at the Macro and Micro Levels*. Population and Employment Working Paper No. 60. International Labour Organization, Geneva.

Arnold, F. (1992): Sex Preference and its Demographic and Health Implication. *J. International Family Planning Perspectives*, 18(2): 93-101.

Arora, Sushil (1993): Concept of Ageing and Problems of the Aged: Some Observations. *Man in India*, 73(3): 251-257.

Atkinson, E.T. (1981): *The Himalayan Gazetter*. Vols.II and III, Cosmo Publication, Delhi.

Aurora, G.S. (1972): *Tribe-Caste-Class Encounters: Some Aspects of Folk Urban Relations in Alirajpur Tahsil*, Hydrabad: Administrative College of India.

Awasthi, A.K. (1993): Ethnoecology: An Ecological Strategy for Managing the Ethnoeco System. *Ind. J. App. Pure Biol.*, l8 : 103-106.

Awasthi, Ajay K., Singh R.D. and Pal, Amit (1995): Ethnological Analysis of Gond Tribal System in Sidhi District, Madhya Pradesh. *Ind. J. Hum. Ecol.*, 6(2): 81-88.

Aziz, A.K.M. and Maloney, Clarance (1985): *Life Stages, Gender and Fertility in Bangladesh*, ICDDR, B: Dhaka.

Babu, B.V., Kusuma, Y.S. and Naidu J.M. (1995): Opportunity for Natural Selection Among Four Andhra Caste Populations. *J. Hum. Ecol.*, 6(1): 63-64.

Babu, K.S. (1996): The Influence of Traditional Occupation on Breast-Feeding Pattern. *Man In India*, 76(3): 267-272.

Bagchi, Tilak (1994): *Profiles of Some Indian Tribes*. Purthi Pustak, Calcutta.

Bahl, L. and Kaushal, R.K. (1987): Infant Rearing Practices and Beliefs in Rural Inhabitants of Himachal Pradesh. *J. Ind. Pediatr*, 24: 903-906.

Bahl, L. and Singh, L. (1982): Some Aspects of Infants Rearing Practices and Beliefs in Rural Inhabitants of Himachal Pradesh. *J. Ind. Pediatr*, 10: 921-925.

Bagozzi, Richard P. and Loo, Frances Van (1980): Decision - *Making and Fertility: A Theory of Exchange in the Family*. Ed. Thomas K. Bruch. Westview Press, Central Avenue, Boulder, Colorado.

Bajpai, Harsha Rani and Mitra, Mitashree (1998): Indigenous Medical Practices of Hill Korwas of Madhya Pradesh. *J. Hum. Ecol.*, 9(3): 295.

Balgir, R.S. (1992): Fertility and Mortality Differentials Among the Gujjars of Sub-Himalaya and Himalayan Regions. *J. Hum. Ecol.*, 3(4): 285-290.

– – –, (1993): Sickle Cell Anemia Among the Oilmen of Orissa . *Man and Life*, 14 (1&2): 55-59.

– – –, (1994): Age at Sexual Maturity Among the Eight Endogamous Populations of North-Eastern India. *J. Hum. Ecol.*, 5 (2): 91-96.

Banerjee, A.R., Banerjee, Papia and Das, Geeta (1976): A Study on Still Birth: 363-369 (In) *Biosocial Studies in India*. Ed. Kanti B. Pakrasi, Amulya R. Banerjee and Amal K. Das. Temple Press, Calcutta.

Banerjee, B.G. and Bhatia, K.(1988): *Tribal Demography of Gonds*. Gian Publishing House, Delhi.

Banerjee, D. and Mukherjee, S.P. (1961): The Menarche in Bengali Hindu Girls. *J. Indian Medical Association*, 37: 261-270.

Bardhan, Kalpana (1977): Rural Employment Wages and Labour Markets in India – A Survey of Research III. *Economic and Political Weekly*, xii (28): 1101-1118.

Bardhan, Kalpana (1984): Stratification of Women's Work in Rural India (In) *Social and Economic Development in India*. Ed. Dilip Kr. Basu, New Delhi.

Barrai, I. And Fraccaro, M. (1964): Intensities of Selection in Nomadic and settled Lapps. *Folia Hered Pathal*. 14: 1-6.

Barua, Indira (1992): The Tai Turungs of Assam: A Study of Socio-demographic Profile. *Man in India*, 72(3): 317-329.

Barua, Indira (1996): Menarche in North-East Indian Communities: Some Bio-Social Aspects. *South Asian Anthropologist*, 17(2): 65-72.

Barua, S. (1982): Bio-Demographic Factors Associated with Offspring Mortality among Hajoings of Meghalaya. *J. Ind. Anthrop. Soc.*, 17: 143-146.

Basu, A.M. (1984): Ignorance of Family Planning Methods in India: An Important Constraint on Use. *Studies in Family Planning*, 15: 136-146.

Basu, Debasis (1996): Selection Intensity in the Senowal Kacharis of Assam. *J. Hum. Ecol.*, 7(3): 223-224.

Basu, Minendra Nath and Basu, Malay Nath (1975): *Sociology – An Applied Limb of Cultural Anthropology*. World Press Private Limited, College Street, Calcutta.

Basu, S.K. (1993): Health Scenario and Health Problems: 269-281 (In) *Continuity and Change in Tribal Society*. Ed. Mrinal Miri, Elecgant Printers, Mayapuri, New Delhi.

Basu, S.K. (1994): *Tribal Health in India*. Manak Publication Pvt.Ltd.

Basu, S.K., Jindal, A. and Kshatriya, G.K. (1994): Perception of Health and Pattern of Health Seeking Behaviour among the Selected Tribal Population Groups of Madhya Pradesh and Orissa (In) *Tribal Health in India*. Ed. S.K. Basu. Published by Manak Publication Pvt. Ltd.

Basu, S.K. and Kshatriya, G.K. (1989): Fertility and Mortality in Tribal Populations of Bastar District, Madhya Pradesh. *J. Biol. and Soc.*, 6: 110-112.

Basu, S.K. and Kshatriya, G.K. (1997): Fertility and Mortality Trends in the Kheria Tribals of Orissa. *Social Change*, 27 (1&2): 114-128.

Basu, S.K., Kshatriya, G.K. and Jindal, A. (1988): Fertility and Mortality Differentials among the Tribal Population Groups of Baster District, Madhya Pradesh. *J. Ind. Hum. Biol.*, 30(3): 407-416.

Basu, Sumana (1999): *Health Need Assessment of Tribal Populations of District Midnapur, West Bengal*. Ph.D. Thesis, Unpublished, Delhi Uni., Delhi.

Beall, C.M. (1983): Ages at Menopause and Menarche in a High Altitude Himalayan Population. *Ann. Hum. Biol.*,10: 365.

Bebarta, P.C. (1966): Family Type and Fertility: A Study in Six Delhi Villages. *Economic and Political Weekly*, 1: 633-634.

Becker, G. (1960): An Economic Analysis of Fertility (In) *Demographic and Economic Change in Developing Countries*. Ed. A.J. Coale. Universities National Bureau Committee for Economic Research. Princeton Uni. Press, Princeton.

Becker, G. (1968): An Economic Survey of Fertility. In *Natural Bureau of Economic Research, Demography and Economic Change in Developed Countires*. Prencenton Uni. Press, Precenton.

Behura, N.K. (1991): Anthropology of Disease, Treatment and Cure. *Man and Life*, 17(1&2): 29-39.

Belavady, B. (1980): Breast-Feeding Practices in Andhra Pradesh. *J. Pro. Nutr. Soc. Ind.*, 26: 39-47.

Benjamin, B. (1965): *Social and Economic Factors Affecting Mortality*. Marton Publication, Paris.

Bernard, Catherine (1974): Family Planning: Motivation and Responsibility (In) *Population Growth and Human Development*. Ed. Anthony A.D'Souza and Alfred D'Souza. Indian Social Institute, Indraprastha Press, Bahadur Shah Zafar Marg, New Delhi.

Bhagwat, Sunanda and Chirmuly, Deepti (1997): Traditional Healing Practices in Rural Karnataka. *Man in India*, 77(1): 71-82.

Bhanu, B.A. and Saheb, S.Y. (1983): Tribe in Contemporary India: The Irular of Tamil Nadu, Unpublished, Anthropological Survey of India, Calcutta.

Bharadwaj, A.K., Gupta, B.P., Swain, H.M., Ahuluwalia, S.K. and Vidya, N.K. (1990): Immunization Status of Tribal Children of Himachal Pradesh. *Ind. J. Community Health*, 3(2): 11.

Bhasin, Veena (1990): *Habitat, Habitation and Health in the Himalayas*. Ed. M.K. Bhasin. Published by Kamala-Raj Enterprises, Paharwali, Chawari Bazar, Delhi.

– – –, (1994): *People, Health and Disease: The Indian Scenario*. Kamla Raj Enterprises, Delhi.

Bhatia, P.S. (1990): Health Care Utilisation by the Tribal of Dang District (In) *Demography of Tribal Development*. Ed. A. Bose, V.P. Sinha and R.P. Tyagi. Published by B.R. Publishing Corporation, Shakti Nagar, Delhi.

Bhatnagar, N.K. (1975): Decline in Fertility and Family Planning: An Appraisal in Studies on Fertility in India: 145 (In) *Monographic Series No.7*. Ed. R.S. Kurup. The Gandhigram Institute of Rural Health and Family Planning, Gandhigram.

Bhatnagar, S., Dosajh, V. and Kapoor, S.D. (1986): Maternal and Child Health Status and Pattern of Health Care in Urban Slums of Delhi. *Health and Population Perspectives and Issues*, 11(5): 105

Bhende, A. and Kanitkar, T. (1978): *Principles of Population Studies*. Himalaya Publishing House, Bombay.

– – –, (1991): *Principal of Population Studies*. Himalaya Publishing House, Bombay.

Bhowmick, P.K. (1963): *The Lodhas of West Bengal : A Socio-Economic Study*. Punthi Pustak, Calcutta.

– – –, (1990): *Applied – Action – Development Anthropology*, Calcutta.

Bhuyan, Bandana (1999): *Child Development in Tribal Areas*. Anmol Publications Pvt.Ltd, Darya Ganj, New Delhi.: 1-148.

Biswas, N. (1967): Age at Menarche Among Punjabi Girls of Delhi. *The Anthropologist*, 14:153.

Biswas, Ranjan Kumar (1995): *Demographic Structure of a Tribal Community: The Kamar of Madhya Pradesh*. M. Phil. Dissertation, Unpublished, G.G. Uni., Madhya Pradesh.

Biswas, Ranjan Kumar and Kapoor, A.K. (2003): A Study on Mortality Among Saharia – A Primitive Tribe of Madhya Pradesh. *J. Anthropologist,* 5(4): 282-290.

Biswas, Ranjan Kumar and Kapoor, A.K. (2003): Eucation and its Effect on Fertility and Mortality Differentials Among A Primtive Tribe of Madhya Pradesh. *Indian J. Population Education,* 23 (Dec.): 36-45.

Biswas, Ranjan Kumar and Kapoor, A.K. (2003): Educational Profile of Kamar – A Primitive Tribe of Madhya Pradesh. *Indian J. Adult Education,* 64 (3-4): 35-45.

Biswas, Ranjan Kumar and Kapoor, A.K. (2003): *Ethnographic Study of Saharia – A Primitive Tribe of Madhya Pradesh* (In) Contemporary Studies in Primitive Tribes, Ed. Sarit K. Choudhury and Sucheta Sen Chaudhari.

Biswas, Ranjan Kumar and Kapoor, A.K. (2003): Fertility Prifile of A Primitive Tribe, Madhya Pradesh. *J. Anthropologist,* 5 (3): 161-167.

Biswas, Ranjan Kumar and Kapoor, A.K. (2004): Age at Marriage and Fertiligy and Mortality Differentials Among Saharia Primitive Tribe of Madhya Pradesh. *J. Social Scientist* – Sent for Publication.

Biswas, Ranjan Kumar and Kapoor, A.K. (2004): Infant and Child Health Care Practices Among Saharia – A Primitive Tribe of Madhya Pradesh. (In) *Biosocial Anthropology,* Ed. C.J. Edwin (Sent for Publication).

Biswas, Ranjan Kumar and Kapoor, A.K. (2004): Socio-cultural Impact on Maternal Care Among Saharia Primitive Tribe of Madhya Pradesh. *J. Region, Health and Health Care,* 9 (1 & 2): 1-10.

Biswas, Ranjan Kumar and Kapoor, A.K. (2005): Age at Menarche and Menopause Among Saharia Women – A Primitive Tribe of Madhya Pradesh. *J. Anthropologist,* 7 (2): 105-109.

Biswas, Ranjan Kumar and Kapoor, A.K. (2005): Family Planning Practices Among Saharia Primtive Tribe of Madhya Pradesh. *J. Family Welfare* (Sent for Publication).

Biswas, Ranjan Kumar and Kapoor, A.K. (2005): Health Seeking Behaviour Among Saharia – A Primitive Tribe of Madhya Pradesh. Ind. J. Social Research, 46 (3): 249-260.

Biswas, Ranjan Kumar, Patra, Prasanna Kumar and Kapoor, A.K. (2001): *Demographic Profile of Kamar – A Primitive Tribe of Madhya Pradesh*. Bulletin of the Tribal Research Institute Bhopal, Vol. XXVIII (1 & 2): 67-77.

Bledsoe, Caroline H. and Hirschman, Helen K. (1989): Case Studies of Mortality: Anthropological Contributions: 331-349 (In) Population: Today and Tomorrow – Policies, Theories and Methodologies, Vol. III, Proceedings of the International Population Conference, New Delhi. B.R. Publishing Corporation, New Delhi.

Bleek, W. (1987): Lying Informants: A Field Work Experience from Ghana. *Population and Development Review*, 13.

Bogue, Donald J. (1969): *Principles of Demography*. John Wiley and Sons, New York.

Bongaarts, J.E. (1978): A Frame Work for Analysing the Proximate Determinants of Fertility. *J. Popul. Dev. Rev.*, 4: 105-132.

Bongaarts, J.E. (1980): Does Malnutrition Affect Fecundity: A Summary of Evidence. J. Science, 208: 564-569.

Bongaarts, J. and Potter, P.C. (1983): Fertility, Biology and Behaviour: An Analysis of the Proximate Determinants. Academic Press, New York.

Bose, Ashish, (1991): Demographic Diversity of India, Census-State and District Level Data: A Reference Book. B.R. Publishing Corporation Pvt. Ltd., New Delhi.

Bose, Asish (1996): India's Basic Demographic Statistics. B.R. Publishing Corporation, Ashok Vihar, New Delhi.

Bose, J.K. (1985): Culture Change among the Garos. Institute of Social Research and Applied Anthropology, Calcutta.

Bose, Nirmal Kumar (1994): Tribes in Eastern India: 121-125 (In)

Tribal Life in India, Vol.1. Ed. Devendra Thakur and D.N. Thakur. Deep & Deep Publications, Rajouri Garden, New Dehli.

Bourne, K.L. and Walkar, G.M. (1991): The Differential Effect of Mothers' Education on Mortality of Boys and Girls in India. Pop. Stud., 45:203-219.

Breeks, J.W. (1983): Primitive Tribes and Monuments of the Nilgiris. Cultural Publishing House, Delhi.

Bruch, Thomas K. (1980): Decision – Making Theories in Demography: An Introduction (In) Demographic Behaviour. Ed. Thomas K. Bruch. Westview Press, Central Avenue, Boulder, Colorado.

Bruch, Thomas K. (1980): The Index of Over all Headship: A Sample Measure of Household Complexity Standarized for Age and Sex. Demography,17: 25-36

Busfield, J. (1972): Age at Marriage and Family Size: Social Causation and Social Selection Hypothesis. Biosoc. Science, 4:117.

Butz, W.P., Da, Vanzo. J. and Habicht, J.P. (1982): Biological and Behaviour Influence on the Mortality of Malaysian Infants (In) Soci-Economic Differentials in Child Mortality in Developing Countries. Department of International Economic and Social Affairs. United Nations, New York.

Buvinic, M., Valenzuela, J.P., Molina, T. and Gonzalez, E. (1972): The Fortunes of Adolescent Mothers and Their Children: The Transmission of Poverty in Santiago, Chile. *J. Pupoul. Dev. Rev.* 18(2): 269-297.

Caldwell, John. C. (1979): Education as a Factor in Mortality Decline : An Examination of Nigerian Data. Pop. Stud., 33 (3): 395-413.

Caldwell, John. C., Reddy, P.H. and Caldewell, P. (1983): The Social Component of Mortality Decline: An Investigation in South India Employing Alternative Methodologies. Pop. Stud., 37: 185.

Census of India (1981): Series – II, VII A and B (iii), Household Tables, Office of the Indian Administrative Service, Director of Census Operation, Madhya Pradesh.

Census of India (1981): Series – II, Part IV and B, Fertility Tables, Office of the Indian Administrative Service, Director of Census Operation, Madhya Pradesh.

Census of India (1981): Series – II, Part IX (vi) Special Tables for Scheduled Tribe, Tables – 2, 3,& 4, Office of the Indian Administrative Service, Director of Census Operation, Madhya Pradesh.

Census of India (1981): Series – II, Part - XII – B.Village and Townwise Primary Census Abstract, District Census Handbook of Gowalior, Madhya Pradesh. Office of the Indian Administrative Service, Director of Census Operation, Madhya Pradesh.

Census of India (1981): Series - I, Part IV -A (ii) of 1987, Social Cultural Tables, Office of the Registrar General and Census Commissioner, New Delhi.

Census of India (1981): Series - I, India, Paper–2 of 1984, General Population and Scheduled Castes and Scheduled Tribes. Office of the Registrar General and Census Commissioner, New Delhi.

Census of India (1981): Series - I, India, Paper - 5 of 1984, Age Table Based on 5 Percent Sample Data. Office of the Registrar General and Census Commissioner, New Delhi.

Census of India (1991): Series - I, India, Paper–1 of 1993, Union Primary Census Abstract for Scheduled Castes and Scheduled Tribes. Office of the Registrar General of Census Commissioner, New Delhi.

Census of India (1991): Series - I, India, Paper - 2 of 1993, Housing and Amenities : A Brief Analysis of the Housing Tables of 1991 Census. Office of the Registrar General Census Commissioner, New Delhi.

Census of India (1991): Series - I, India, Paper – 2 of 1992, Final Population Total: Brief Analysis of Primary Census Abstract. Office of the Registrar General of Census Commissioner, New Delhi.

Census of India (1991): Series - I, India, Paper - 1 of 1995, Religion. Office of the Registrar General and Census Commissioner, New Delhi.

Census of India (1991): Series - I, India, Paper - 2 of 1992, Final Population Total, Brief Analysis of Primary Census Abstract. Office of the Registrar General and Census Commissioner, Ministry of Home Affairs, New Delhi.

Chachra, Sushmita Paul and Bhasin, M.K. (1998): Anthropo-Demographic Study among the Caste and Tribal Groups of Central Himalayas: 1. Population Structure. *J. Hum. Ecol.*, 9 (5): 405-416.

Chachra, Sushmita Paul and Bhasin, M.K. (1998): Anthropo-Demographic Study among the Caste and Tribal Groups of Central Himalayas: 2. Fertility Differential and Determinants. *J. Hum. Ecol.*, 9 (5): 417-429.

Chachra, Sushmita Paul and Bhasin, M.K. (1998): Anthropo-Demographic Study among the Caste and Tribal Groups of Central Himalayas: 3. Mortality Differential and Determinants. *J. Hum. Ecol.*, 9 (5): 431-439.

Chachra, Sushmita Paul and Bhasin, M.K. (1998): Anthropo-Demographic Study among the Caste and Tribal Groups of Central Himalayas: 4. Selection Intensities. *J. Hum. Ecol.*, 9 (5): 441-443.

Chachra, Sushmita Paul and Bhasin, M.K. (1998): Anthropo-Demographic Study among the Caste and Tribal Groups of Central Himalayas: 5. Family Planning. *J. Hum. Ecol.*, 9 (5): 445-450.

Chachra, Sushmita Paul and Bhasin, M.K. (1998): Anthropo-Demographic Study among the Caste and Tribal Groups of Central Himalayas: 6. Fertility, Child Mortality & Family Planning. *J. Hum. Ecol.*, 9(5):451-455.

Chagnon, N.A. and Irons, W. (1979): Evolutionary and Human Social Behaviour: The Anthropological Approach. North Scituate, Mass: Duxbury.

Chakraborty, B. and Malakar, C.R. (1980): Fertility Differential, Family Planning and Birth Reduction in Calcutta: 67 (In) *Calcutta Couples: A Bio-Social Profile*. Ed. K.B. Pakrasi, A.R. Banerjee and A.K. Halder.

Chakraborty, D.K. (1990): The Great Andamanese: Struggle for Survival, Calcutta: Seagull Books on Behalf of Anthropological Survey of India.

Chakraborty, S.K. and Ahmed, S.H. (1989): Body Dimensions, Fertility and Selection in a Section of the Galloing with Endemic Hypothyroidism and Congenital Defects of the Central Nervous System: 1-5 (In) General Demography of Indian Population. Anthropological survey of India. Govt. of India, Calcutta.

Chakrapani, C. (1993): Shifting Cultivation and Deforestation: A Socio-Eco System Nexus. J. Hum. Ecol., 4(1): 39-46.

Chakravorti, I and Sinha, A.K. (1991): Declining Age of Menarche in West Bengal. Ind. Med. Assoc., 82: 10.

Chandana, R.C. and Sidhu, Manjit S. (1980): Introduction to Population Geography, Kalyani Publications, New Delhi: 31-81.

Chandrasekar, A., Xaviour and Sirajuddin, S.M. (1998): Opportunity of Natural Selection among the Koraga Tribe of Karanataka. J. Hum. Ecol., 9 (5): 467-469.

Chandrasekhar, S. (1972): Infant Mortality, Population Growth and Family Planning in India. George Allen and Unwin Ltd., London.

Charles, S.K. (1971): Mode of Delivery by Untrained Dais in and around Vellore. Chris. Med., Assoc. of India, 46:82.

Chatterjee, Sikha (1994): Menarche, Menopause and Fertility in the Pachatya Vaidic Brahman Women of West Bengal. Man In India, 74 (3): 271-278.

Chattopadhyay, Madhumala and Prasad, B.V. Ravi (1995): Nutritional Status of the Nicobarese Tribal Children of Harminder Bay, Little Andaman. J. Hum. Ecol., 6 (1): 59-61.

Chattopadhyay, P.K. and Khullar, S. (1969): The Age at Menarche in Indian Girls. Acta Medica Auxologica, 1: 58-62.

Chaturvedi, H.K., Phukan, R.K. and Mahanta, J. (1998): Socio-Economic Factors and Fertility of Rural Women: A Study in Upper Assam. *J. Hum. Ecol.*, 9 (2): 177-180.

Chaudhuri, M. (1996): Sex Ratio of the Scheduled Tribe Population in India. Man And Life, 22 (12): 25-32.

Chaudhuri, M.N. (1994): Health Development among Tribals (In) Tribal Health of India. Ed. S. Basu. Manak Publication Ltd., Laxmi Nagar, Delhi.

Chaudhuri, R.H. (1984): The Influence of Female Education, Labour Force Participation and Age at Marriage on Fertility Behaviour in Bangladesh. *Soc. Biol.*, 31:59.

Chauhan, A.S., Saseendran, P.P. and Singh. K.K. (1991): Demographic profile of Tribal Population of Utter Pradesh (In) Tribal Demography. Ed. R.N. Pati and Lalit Jagatdeb. Ashish Publishing House, New Delhi.

Chetlapalli, S.K., Khan, A.S., Kshatriya, G.K. and Basu, S. (1991): Estimates of Fertility and Mortality in Kuti Kondhs of Phulbani District, Orissa. J. Hum. Ecol., 2:177-180

Choudhury, Bapukan and Devi, Maheswari (1997): Fertility Differentials in Manipur: A Study on the Meiteis and the Muslims. J. Hum. Ecol., 8(1): 51-59.

Choudhury, Jaya (1992): Marriage Conception Interval. Man In India, 72 (1): 91-95.

Choudhury, N.C. (1963): Munda Settlement in Lower Bengal: A Study in Tribal Migration. Bulletin of the Cultural Research Institute, 2: 23-32.

Choudhury, N.C. and Bhowmik, S.K. (1986): Migration of Chotanagpur Tribals of West Bengal (In) Studies in Migration. Ed. M.S.A. Rao. Mohan Publications, Delhi.

Choudhury, Nazneen. (1997): Infant and Child Feeding Practices in Bangladesh, Evidence from Bangladesh Demographic and Health Survey. Demography India, 26: 2.

Choudhury, N.R. and Kumar, R. (1976): Demographic Profile of Bhils. Eastern Anthropologist, 29: 273.

Choudhury, R.K., Naik, Mamatamayee and Mohanty, Manmath Kumar (1994): A Note on Menarcheal Age of Mirdha Women of Orissa. J. Hum. Ecol., 5(2): 123-126.

Choudhury, R.K, Naik, Mamatamayee and Mohanty, Manmath Kumar (1994): Fertility and Mortality among Mirdhas: A Tribal Community of Orrissa. J. Hum. Ecol., 5(3): 191.

Choudhury, Ram Prawesh and Adhikary, Doli (1997): Foetal and Infant Mortality in Two Tribes of Rajmahal Hills, Bihar. J. Hum. Ecol., 2(1): 43-49.

Cliquet, Robert and Thienpont, Kristiaan (1995): Population and Development – A Message from the Cairo Conference. Cluwer Academic Publishers, Dordrecht/Boston/London.

Coale, A.J. (1972): The Growth and Structure of Human Populations. A Mathematical Investigation.Princepton Uni. Press, Princepton.

Coale, A.J., Demeny, P. and Vaughan, B. (1983): Regional Model Life Table and Stable Populations. Academic Press, New York.

Cochrane, S.H., O'Hara, D.J. and Leslie, J. (1980): The Effects of Education on Health. World Bank Working Papers No.405. Washington D.C.

Collier, G.A. (1976): The KINPROGRAM: PUI Programs for the Processing of Genealogical Censuses. Development Anthropology, Stanford University.

Combs, L.C. and Sun, T.H (1978): Family Composition Preferences in Developing Culture: The Case of Taiwan. Popu. Stud., 32: 43-64.

Conde, J. (1978): Rapid Population Growth in Developing Countries: 102 (In) Planning for Growing Populations. Ed. R. Cassen and M. Wolfson. Organization for Economic Co-operation and Development, Paris.

Conrad, Fredrick (1962): Sex Roles as Factors in Longevity. Sociology and Social Research, 7: 195.

Cox, Peter R. (1970): Demography (Fourth Edition), Institute of Actuaries and the Faculty of Actuaries at the Uni. Press, Cambridge.

Crooke, W. (1896): The Tribes and Castes of The North Western India (Calcutta Government Printing Press, Delhi: Cosmo Publications).

Crow, J.F. (1958): Some Possibilities for Measuring Selection Intensities in Man. *J. Hum. Biol.,* 30: 1-13.

Crow, J.F. (1966): The Quality of People: Human Evolutionary Changes. Bioscience, 16: 863-867.

Cruze Coke, R.A.P., Aspillaga, M. Christoffani and Biancani (1996): Evolutionary Forces in Human Populations in Environmental Gradient in Africa. *Chil. Hum. Bio.,* 38: 421-438.

Dandekar, K. (1959): Demographic Survey of Six Rural Communities. Asia Publishing House, Bombay: 53-84.

Dandekar, K. (1975): Why Has the Proportion of Women in India's Population Been Declining? *Eco. Pol.,* Weekly, 10:18.

Dandekar, V.M. and Dandekar, K. (1953): Survey of Fertility and Mortality in Poona District. Gokhale Institute of Politics and Economics, Poona. Publication No. 27.

Das, B. (1985): Fertility and Mortality Differentials among the Khamiyang and Turang Population of Jorhat District, Assam. *J. Assam Sc.Soc.,* 28: 14-19.

Das, F.A. (1992): Trend of Menarcheal Age in the Kaibarta Girls of Dibrugarh, Upper Assam Bull. Deptt. of Anthrop. Dibrugarh Uni., Assam : 113-118.

Das, Farida Ahmed and Saikia, Jukti Ratna (1999): Some Aspects of Fertility of the Garo Women of Pochimbosti Gago Village in Sibsagar District, Assam. *J. Hum. Ecol.,* 10(4): 273-277.

Das Gupta, A. (2000): Kinship Obligation and Fertility Behaviour in Urban India : A Case Study in Patna. South Asian Anthropologist, 21(1): 37-41.

Das Gupta, M. (1990): Death Clustering, Mother's Education and Determinants of Child Mortality in Rural Punjab, India. *Pop. Stud.,* 44: 489.

Das, N.K. and Ghosh, A.K. (1988): Two Muslim Sects. of 24 Paragons, West Bengal – A Study in Selection Intensity. *J. Hum. Sci.,* 37: 237-242.

Das, P.B. (1986): Variation in Age at Menarche of Assamese Girls. Gauhati Uni. Assam. J. Sci., 29: 1-8.

Das, S.K. (1987): A Study of Fertility and Family Planning Practices among the Gonds of Jharsuguda, Unpublished Ph.D. Thesis, Sambalpur Uni., Sambalpur, Orissa.

Das, T.C. (1973): Social Organisation, In the Tribal People of India, Publication Division, Ministry of Information and Broadcasting, Government of India, New Delhi.

Datta, U. (1990): Demographic Investigation among the Koras of Midaapur District, West Bengal, Unpublished Ph.D. Thesis, Ravi Shankar Uni., Raipur.

Dattal, M.S., Sharma, S.S., Verma, J.S. and Kausal, R.K. (1984): Feeding Practices of Infants and Children in Rural and Urban Areas of Himachal Pradesh. J. Indi. Paediatr., 21: 217-222.

Da Vanzo, J. and Lee, D.L.P. (1978): The Comparability of Child Care with Labour Force Participation and Non-Market Activities: Preliminary Evidence from Malaysian Time Budget Data. Rand Paper, 6126.

Davis, K. (1963): The Theory of Change and Response in Modern Demographic History. Population Index, 29: 345.

Davis, K. and Blake, J. (1956): Social Structure and Fertility: An Analytical Framework. Eco. Dev. and Cul. Change, 4 : 211-235.

Day, Lincoln H. (1984): Analysis of Population Trends. St. Martin's Press, New York.

De, P.J. and Sreenath, J. (1983): 'Bharia', in Tribe in Contemporary India, Unpublished Report, Anthropological Survey of India, Calcutta.

Deka, A. (1989): Reproductive Performance and Selection among the Jaintias of the Village Sa-Phai. (In) Genetical Demography of Indian Population. Anthropological Survey of India. Govt. of India.

Deka, R. (1976): Menarcheal Age among the Kachari Women of Upper Assam. Bull., Vo. V., Deptt. of Anthrop., Dibrugarh Uni., Assam, 5: 1-6.

Desai, P.B. (1975): A Survey of Research in Demography, Popular Prakashan, Bombay: 1-25.

Devarapalli (1992): Maternal Care Obstetric Practices among Konda Dora Tribe of Andhra Pradesh. Family Welfare, 38(4): 37.

Devi, P.K. (1979): Peri-natal Mortality and Antepartium Haemorrhage. ICMR Bull., 9:1.

Dixon, R.B. (1975): Women's Right and Fertility. Reports on Population/Family Planning No, 17. The Population Council, New York.

Driver, E.D. (1960): Fertility Differentials among Economic Strata in Central India. Eng. Quart. 7:15.

Driver, E.D. (1963): Fertility Differentials in Central India. Princeton University Press, Princeton.

D'Souza, Anthony A. (1974): India's Population Problem in Perspective (In) Population Growth and Human Development. Ed. Anthony A. D'Souza and Alfred De Souza. Indian Social Institute, Indraprastha Press, Bahadur Shah Zafar Marg, New Delhi.

Duarah, A. (1969): A Study of Certain Aspects of Demography Among the Adis of Mirbuk Villages, Panighat, NEFA. Unpublished Dissertation, Dibrughar Uni., Dibrughar, Assam.

Dubey, Rabindranath (1992): Populations, Enviroment and Regional Planning. Chugh Publications, Allahabad.

Dubey, R.L. and Srivastava, R.P. (1965): Trend of Menarche in 361 Women of Uttar Pradesh. The Anthropologist, X: 7-12.

Duckworth, W.H.L.(1915): Morphology And Anthropology. At the Uni. Press, Cambridge.

Duggal, R. (1990): Health and Population in three Tribal Villages (In) Demography of Tribal Development. Ed. A. Bose, U.P. Sinha and R.D. Tyagi. Published by B.R. Publishing Corporation, Delhi.

Dutta, Bimal Chandra (1999): Some Observations on the Diseases and Traditional Medicine of the Singphos. Man In India, 79(1 & 2): 179-189.

Dutta, D.K. (1983): 'Sayalong': The Ancestor of the Mijis. Resarun, 9:2

Dwivedi, S.N. (2001): Impact of Some Factors on Infant and Child Mortality Rates in Uttar Pradesh: A Component Analysis. South Asian Anthropologist, 1(2): 123-128.

Dyke, B. and Morrill, W.T. (1980): Genealogical Demography, Academic Press, New York.

Dyson, T. and Moore, M. (1983): On Kinship Structure, Female Autonomy and Demographic Behaviour in India. J. Popul. Dev. Rev., 9:35.

Elizabeth, A.M., Saraswathy, K.N. Sachdeva, M.P. Chaudhary, Rewa and Kalla, A.K. (2000): Demographic Profile of Thoti – A Primitive Tribal Population of Andhra Pradesh. Anthropologist, 2(2): 119-122.

Emercy, E., Ault, P.E. and Ager, W.K. (1965): Introduction to Mass Communication. Feffer and Simons Pvt. Ltd., Vakils, Bombay.

Enthoven, R.E. (1975): Tribes And Caste of Bombay. Vol.1. (Bombay: Government Press), Cosmo Publications, Delhi.

Farah, A. and Preston, S.H. (1982): Child Mortality Differentials in Sudan. Pop. Dev. Rev., 8: 365.

Farr, W. (1876): Birth Places of the People and the Laws of Migration, Geographical Magazine, 3.

Fernandes, Walter (1993): Forest and Tribals : Informal Economy, Dependence and Management Traditions: 47-69 (In) Continuity and Change in Tribal Society. Ed. Mrinal Miri. Printed (by) of Elecgant Printers, Maya Puri, New Delhi.

Fisher, R.A. (1930): The Genetic Theory of Natural Selection. Oxford University Press, London.

Flinn, M.V. (1986): Correlates of Reproductive Success in a Carribean Village. J. Hum. Eco., 14:225.

Ford, T.R. and Arcury, T.A. (1984): Population And Health in the Developing World: Research Perspectives for Medical Anthropologists, Soc. Sci. and Medicine, 10.

Freedman, D., Thornton, A. and Wallisch, L.(1981): Age at First Birth and Family Size : Evidence from Longitudinal Study. Soc. Biol., 28: 217.

Freedmen, R., Baumer and Bolte (1960): Expected Family Size and Family Size in West Germany. Pop. Stud., 13: 136-150.

Frisancho, A.R., Klayman, J.E. and Matos, J. (1976): Symbolic Relationship of High Fertility, High Childhood Mortality and Socio-economic Status in an Urban Peruvian Population. Hum. Biol., 48(1): 101-111.

Frisch, R.E. (1974): A Method of Prediction of Age of Menarche from height-weight at Ages 9 through 13 Years. J. Paediatr. 53: 384.

Gandotra, M.M. (1989): Fertility, Mortality and Contraceptive Prevalence in a Tribal Population, Vol. (2): 262 (In) Population Transition in India. Ed. S.N. Singh, M.K.Premi, P.S. Bahtia and Ashish Bose. Published by B.R. Publishing Corporation, Shakti Nagar, New Delhi.

Gayson, Donald K. (1996): Human Mortality in a Natural Disaster: The Willie Handicraft Company. J. Anthropological Research, 52:2.

Gee, E.M. and Veevers, J.E. (1983): Accelerating Sex Differentials in Mortality. An Analysing of Contributing Factors. Soc. Biol., 30:175.

George, M.V. (1970): Demography: A Growing Multidisciplinary Science: 149-156 (In) Studies in Demography. Ed. Asish Bose, P.B. Desai and S.P. Jain. George Allen and Unwin Ltd, Ruskin House, Museum Street, London.

Ghatak, N.K. (1994): Saharia (In) People of India – Rajasthan, Part II. Ed. K.S. Singh. Oxford Uni. Press, Delhi, Bombay, Calcutta, Madras.

Ghosh, A.K. (1970): Selection Intensity in the Kota of Nilgiri Hills, Madras. *Soc. Biol.*, 17: 224-225.

Ghosh, A.K. and Kumari, S. (1973): Effect of Menarcheal Age on Fertility. *J. Ind. Anthrop. Soc.*, 8:165-172.

Ghosh, B.N. (1963): An Exploratory Study on Mid-wifery Practice of Local Indigenous Dias of Pondicherry and Utilization of Automicillary Midwife Services of Health Centre by a Semi-Urban Slum Community. Ind. *J. Public Health*, 7: 5.

Ghosh, B.N. (1985): Scientific Methods and Social Research. Third Edition, Sterling Publishers, Bangalore.

Ghosh Dastidar, Madhusree and Gupta, Ranjan (1993): A Note on Selection Intensity among the Muslims of Calcutta Slum. *J. Hum. Ecol.*, 4(1): 79-80.

Ghosh, S. (1983): Primary Health Care for Developing Countries. J. Ind. Pediatr., 20(4): 235.

Ghoshmaulik, S.K. and Karmohapatra, R.K. (1995): Health Situation of the Juangs of Orissa. South Asian Anthropologist, 16(2): 79-83.

Gogoi, D. (1972): Menarche and Menopause among Women of an Ahom Village in Upper Assam. Bull. 1:18, Deptt. of Anthrop. Dibrugarh Uni., Assam.

Goldberg, D. (1965): Fertility and Fertility Differentials : Some Observations on Recent Changes in the United States: 119-142 (In) Public Health and Population Change. Ed. M.C. Sheps and J.C. Ridley. Uni. of Pittsburg Press, Pittsburg.

Gopujakar, P.V., Chaudhury, S.N., Ramaswami, M.A., Gare, M.S. and Gopalan, C. (1984): Infant-Feeding Practices with Special Reference to the use of Commercial Infant Food. Scientific Report, No.40. Nutrition Foundation of India, New Delhi.

Goswami, L.C. (1988): Child Bearing in Jaintia Tribal Community of Meghalaya; A Study of some of its Beliefs, Customs and Functions, Child Rearing Practices in N.E. Region – A Seminar Report (Mimeo), National Institute of Public Co-operation and Child Development, Guwahati.

Graunt, John (1662): Natural And Political Observations Made Upon the Bills of Mortality.

Greenhalgh, S. (1989): New Directions in Fertility Research: Anthropological Perspectives, Paper Prepared at the General Conference of the IUSSP, New Delhi.

Gregory, Robert J. (1998): An Ecological Educational Opportunity: The Aquarium. *J. Hum. Ecol.*, 9(3): 285-286.

Grount, Captain (1623): Essays on Political Arithmetic (Partially).

Guha, A. and Mukherjee, D.P. (1990): Influence of Cultural Traditions and Social Movements on the Genetic Structure of the Boro Kachari Population. *J. Ind. Anthrop. Soc.*, 25: 73-81.

Guha, P.K. (1997): The Bhotiya of Mana Village: A Study on some aspects of Demography. Man In India, 77(1): 63-70.

Guillard, Achille (1855): Elements de statistique humaine on demographic comparee. France.

Gunasundaramma, Kambham (1980): Fertility and Family Planning Among the Balijas of Tirupati, Andhra Pradesh. Unpublished Ph.D. Thesis. Department of Physical Anthropology and Prehistoric Archaeology.

Gupta, Neena and Jaiswal, I.J.S. (1992): Age at Menarche among three Caste Groups of Jammu City. Man In India, 72(4): 463-467.

Gupta, R. (1980): Selection Intensity in Sherpas. Curr. Anthrop., 21: 136-137.

Gupta, Radhna and Kalita, Manoranjan (1998): Food Habits and Dietary Pattern of Expectant Mothers in the Palampur Sub-division of Himachal Pradesh. *J. Hum. Ecol.*, 9 (2): 163-170.

Gupta, S.P. (1980): Tribal Concept of Health, Disease and Remedy (In) Tribal Health: Socio-cultural Dimensions. Ed. B. Chaudhuri. Inter-India Publications, New Delhi.

Gurumurthy, G. (1986): Culture and Fertility among Yanadis. A Tribal Community in South India. Eastern *Anthropologist*, 39: 35-45.

Gurumurthy, G. (1989): Socio-Cultural Factors Regulating Fertility among Yanadis – a Study of Tribal Communities in Andhra Pradesh (In) Health and Family Welfare Services in India. Ed. B. Jena and R. Pati. Ashish Publishing House, New Delhi.

Gurumurthy, G. (1990): Culture and Fertility Behaviour of Yanadis, Himalaya Publishing House, Bombay.

Gwatkin, D.R. and Brandel, S.K. (1981): Reducing Infant and Child Mortality in the Developiing World, 1980-2000. Overseas Development Council Working Paper, No.2.

Hagerstrand, T. (1957): Migration and the Area : Survey of a Sample of Swedish Migration Fields and Hyphothetical Considerations of Their Genesis, in Hannerberg, D. et.al.(1957): 27-158.

Handwerker, W.P. (1986): Culture and Reproduction (In) An Anthropological Critique of Demographic Transition Theory. Ed. W.P. Handwerker, Boulder, Colorado, Westview Press.

Haque, M. and Samanta, S. (1998): Health and Nutrition among the Kora of Bankura, West Bengal (In) Tribal Culture and Identity. Ed. Chaturbhuj Sahu. Sarup & Sons Publication, Darya Ganj, New Delhi.

Harrison, G.A. and Boyce (1972): The Structure of Human Population (Eds). Oxford, Clarendon.

Hassan, F.A. (1979): Demography and Archaeology. J. Ann. Rev. of Anthrop., 8: 137-160.

Hassan, F.A. (1981): *Demographic Archaeology*. Academic Press, New York.

Hastings, A. (1978): Evolutionarily Stable Strategies and the Evolution of Life Histories. *J. Theor. Biol.*, 75: 527-536.

Hauser, Philip M. and Duncan, Otis Dudley (1959): The Study of Population : An Inventory and Appraisal. The Uni. of Chicago Press, Chicago.

Heer, D. and Smith, D. (1968): Mortality Level Desired Family Size and Polulation Increase. *Journal of Demography*, 5: 104.

Heer,D.M.(1966): Economic Development and Fertility. *Demography*, 3: 423.

Heer, D.M. (1967): Fertility Differences in Andean Countries: A Reply to W.H. Tames. *Popul. Studies*, 21: 21-71.

Helsing, Elisabet and King, F. Savage (1984): Breast-Feeding in Practice. A Manual for Health Workers. Oxford University Press, Delhi: 25-83.

Heman, Natabar Shyam and Reddy, B. Mohan (1999): Opportunity for Natural Selection among the Occupationally Different Groups of Gangte Tribe of Manipur, North-East India. *J. Hum. Ecol.*, 10 (3): 161-166.

Herskovits, M.J. (1952): Man And His Works. Alfred Knopt, New York: 5.

Hill, K. (1991): Child Mortality in Developing Countries: Socio-Economic Differentials, Trends and Implications. Department of International Economic and Social Affairs. United Nations, New York.

Hodson, T.C. (1989): The Naga Tribe of Manipur. Low Price Publication, Ashok Vihar, Phase IV, Delhi.

Howell, Nancy (1986): Demographic Anthropology. J. Ann. Rev. of Anthrop.15:219-247.

Huff, D.L. (1960): A Topographical Model of Consumer Space Preferences. Papers of the Regional Science Association, 6: 159-173.

Hutton, J.H. (1922): Notes on a Type of Snare from the Phom Country. J. Man, 22: 63.

I.C.M.R. (1972): Growth and Physical Development of Indian Infants and Children. Technical Report Series, No.18.

India (1999): A Reference Annual Completed and Ed. Research Reference and Training Division, Publication Division, Ministry of Information and Broadcasting, Government of India.

India (2000): A Reference Annual Completed and Ed. Research Reference and Training Division, Publication Division, Ministry of Information and Broadcasting, Government of India.

Irons, W. (1979): Natural Selection, Adaptation and Human Social Behaviour: 4-38 (In) *Population, Ecology and Social Evolution*. Ed. S. Polger. The Hague, Mouton.

Jacobson, Jodi. L. (1972): Fertility Trends Worldwide. J. Population, 15: 35-45.

Jain, A.K. (1985): Determinants of Regional Variations in Infat Mortality in Rural India. *Pop. Stud.*, 39: 407-424.

Jaiswal, I.J.S. and Jaiswal, Sushma (1981): Age at Menarche among the Aptani of Aurunachal Pradesh. Bull., 10: 50-60. Departt. of Anthrop., Dibrughar Uni., Assam.

Jay, Edward J. (1974): 'A Comparison and Peasent Village in India J. Indian Anthrop. Soc. 9:1.

Jena, Kalendi (1994): Progress of the Educated Tribal Women. Man In India, 74(1): 81-86.

Johnston, F.E. and Kensinger, K.M. (1971): Fertility and Mortality Differentials and Their Implications for Micro Evolutionary Change among the Cashinahua. *J. Hum. Biol.*, 43: 346-356.

Jolly, K.G. (1986): *Family Planning in India*. Hindustan Publishing Corporation, Delhi.

Jones, D.L. (1974): Human Reproduction and Society. Faber and Faber Publication, London.

Jones, Huw (1990): Population Geography, Second Edition, Paul Chapman Publishing Ltd, 144, Liverpool Road, London.

Kagiticibasi, C. (1979): The Value of Children: Some Socio-Psychological Determinants of Fertility in Turkey: 140. (In) Demographic Transition and Socio-Economic Development Proceedings of the UN/UNFPA Expert Group Meeting, Island, 1977. Department of International Economic and Social Affairs. Population Studies, No.5, United Nations, New York.

Kalita, Mondira and Sengupta, Sarthak (1997): Age at Menarche and Menapause Among the Sonowal Women of Dibrugarh, Assam. *J. Hum. Ecol.*, 8(6): 485-486.

Kant (1769): Anthropology. Chicago Uni. Press, Chicago.

Kant, E. (1961): Classification and Problems of Migration: 145 (In) Reading in Cultural Anthropology. Ed. Philips L. Wagner and M. Marvin; Mikesell.

Kantikar, T. (1979): Development of Maternal and Child Health Services in India (In) Child in India. Ed. K. Srinivasan, P.C. Saxena and Tara Kantikar. Published by Himalaya Publishing House, New Delhi.

Kapadia, K.M. (1966): Marriage and Family in India. Oxford Uni. Press : New Delhi.

Kapoor, A.K. (1992): Genetic Diversity among Himalayan Populations. Vinod Publishers and Distributors, Jammu.

Kapoor, A.K. (1993): Ecology and Development in Himalayan (In) *Fragile Environment*. Ed. S.K. Chada. Anmol Publication, New Delhi.

Kapoor, A.K. (1993): The Environmental and Settlement Patterns of the Bhotias in the Central Himalayas : 169-179 (In) *Central Himalayan Panorama*. Ed. S.K. Biswas. Institute of Social Research and Applied Anthropology, Calcutta.

Kapoor, A.K. (1994):Ecology and Tribal in Central Himalayas : 69-90 (In) *Ecology and Man in the Himalayas*. Ed. A.K. Kapoor and Satwanti Kappor. M.D. Publications Pvt. Ltd. New Delhi.

Kapoor, A.K. (1996): Ecology, Demographic Profile and Socio-Economic Development of a Tribe of Central Himalaya: 118-138 (In) *Tribal Development: Options*. Ed. Prasana K. Samal. Published by Gyanodaya Prakashan.

Kapoor, A.K. (2000): Environment, Technology and Development-An Anthropological Study of a Non-Government Organization (NGO) in Himachal Pradesh. Man And Life, 26(3 & 4): 137-159.

Kapoor, A.K. and Kapoor, Satwanti (1985): The Secular Growth Trend among Himalayan Populations. *J. Anthrop. Kozl.*, 29: 85-88.

Kapoor, A.K. and Patra, P.K. (1998): Selection Intensity in a High Altitude Tribe of Central Himalayas. *Ind. Anthrop.*, 28(2) L 81-87.

Kapoor, A.K. and Singh, D. (1997): Rural Development Through NGOs. Rawat Publications, Jaipur.

Kapoor, A.K., Tiwari, S.C. and Prasad, R.P. (1990): *Semi- Nomadism and Transhumance in Central Himalayas: A Pragmatic Perspective. Man In India*, 70 (1): 47-6.

Kapoor, S. (1996): Research, Planning and Development in the Himalayan Region: 197-211 (In): Man and Development in the Himalayan. Ed. A.K. Kapoor and D. Singh Academic Foundation, Delhi.

Kar, R.K. (1994): The Tribes of North – East India: An Overview: 1-13 (In) Tribes of North-East India-Biological and Cultural Perspectives. Ed. Sarthak Sengupta. Gyan Publishing House, Darya Ganj, New Delhi.

Kar. R.K. and Gogoi, Juri (1993): Health Culture and Tribal Life: A Case Study among the Noctes of Aurunachal Pradesh. Man And Life, 19(1 & 2): 29-53.

Kar, R.K. and Mahanta, S. (1975): Menarche and Menopause among the Singhpho Women of Aurunachal Pradesh. *Ind. J. Phys. Anthropo. And Hum. Gen.*, 1: 51-57.

Karmarkar, Tanuja D., Sampathkumar, V., Jeyalakshmi, S. and Abel, R. (1995): *Nutritional Status of Tribal Women in Bihar. Man In India*, 75(2): 209-214.

Katiyar, G.P., Agarwal, D.K., Tripathy, A.M. and Agarwal, K.N. (1981): Feeding Practices in Varanasi District. J. Ind. Pediatr., 18: 65-70.

Kaur, S. and Jaswal, I.J.S. (1998): Child - Rearing Practices in *Urban Middle–Class Families of Jammu. J. Hum. Ecol.*, 9(1): 99-100.

Kautilya (3rd Century B.C.): Arthashastra . At the Ruling Time of Chandragupta Maurya.

Khan, A.S. (1993): Genetic Structure of Dongaria Kondh of Koraput District of Orissa with Special Reference to its Impact on Mortality and Morbidity. Unpublished Ph.D. Thesis.

Khan, M.E. (1987): Infant Mortality in Uttar Pradesh. *J. Soc. Change*, 17(.3): 52-63.

Khan, M.E., Ghosh Dastidar, S.K. and Singh, Ratanjeet (1986): Nutrition and Health Practices among the Rural Women – A Case Study of Uttar Pradesh. Family Welfare, xxxiii: 2.

Khan, N.C. (1976): Some Aspects of Marital Trend Among the Tribals of West Bengal: 143-152 (In) Biosocial Studes in India, Ed. Kanti B. Pakrasi, Amulay R. Banerjee and Amal K. Das. Calcutta Editions Indian.

Khanna, J.K. and Vishisht, K.K. (1985): Landmarks and Research Trends in Humanistic and Social Science. Ess and Ess Publications, New Delhi.

Khongsdier, R. (1990): The Pnar of Sutnga and Moopala Villagers: A Study in Selection Intensity. J. Ind. Anthrop. Soc. 25:182-184.

Khongsdier, R. (1992): Some Demographic Traits among the Pnar of Sutnga and Moopala in Jaintia Hills District of Meghalaya. Man In India, 72(4): 491-495.

Khongsdier, R. (1994): Opportunity for Natural Selection among the War Khasi of Meghalaya, *India. J. Hum. Ecol.*, 5(4): 307-310.

Khongsdier, R. (1995): Prenatal and Postnatal Mortality in the War Khasi of Meghalaya. *J. Hum. Ecol.*, 6(3): 201-204.

Khongsdier, R. and Ghosh, A.K. (1995): Bio-Demographic Study among the War Khasi of Meghalaya. *J. Ind. Anthrop. Soc.*, 29 (1& 2): 195-202.

Kohli, K.L. (1977): Mortality in India. Sterting Publishers Pvt. Ltd, AB/9, Safdarjang Enclave, New Delhi.

Kost, K. and Amin, S. (1992): *Reproduction and Socio-Economic Determinants of Child Survival: Confounded, Interactive and Age Dependent Effects. Soc. Biol.*, 39: 139-150.

Kothari, C.R. (1985): Research Methodology – Methods and Techniques. Wiley Eastern Limited. New Delhi, Bangalore, Bombay, Calcutta, Madras, Hydrabad.

Krishnan, P. and Reddy, P.J. (1994): Demographic Characteristics of Population in India (In) Defferential Development and Demographic Delemma. Ed. Kuttan Mahadevan, Chi-Hsien Tuan, et.al. B.R. Publishing Corporation, Ashok Vihar, Phase IV, Delhi.

Kroeber, A.L. (1948): *Anthropology*. Harcourt Brace, New York.: 1.

Kshatriya, Gautam. K. (1999): Estimate of Fertility and Mortality among the Santals of Mayurbhanj District, Orissa. Under Preparation.

Kshatriya, Gautam. K. (2000): Ecology and Health with Special Reference to Indian Tribes: 229-245 (In) Man-Environment Relationship. Human Ecology (Special Issue). Ed. M.K. Bhasin and Veena Bhasin, No. 9, Kamal Raj Enterprises, New Delhi.

Kshatriya, Gautam. K. and Basu, S. (1993): Fertility and Mortality Trends in Dudh Kharia Tribal Population of Sundergarh District, Orissa. Genetic and Variation and xviii Annual Conference, January. Indian Society of Human Genetic, Hyderbad.

Kshatriya, Gautam K., Singh, Paramjeet and Basu, Salil K. (1993): Fertility and Mortality in Bison Horn Madias of Dantewara Tehsil of Bastar District, Madhya Pradesh. J. Hum. Ecol., 4(2): 93-96.

Kshatriya, Gautam K., Singh, Paramjeet and Basu, S.K. (1997): Anthropo-Demographic Features and Health Care Practices among the Jaunsaris of Jhunser-Bawar, Dehradun, Uttar Pradesh. J. Hum. Ecol., 8(5): 347-354.

Kumar, B.B. (1998): The Tribal Societies of India. Omsons Publication, T-7, Rajouri Garden, New Delhi.

Kumar, P. Vijay and Mitra, Mitashree (1992): Anthropometric Assessment of Nutritional Status of Kamars – A Primitive Tribe of Raipur District, Madhya Pradesh. J. Hum. Ecol., 3(3): 231-233.

Kumar, S. and Chakrapani, C. (1995): Availability, Accessibility and Utilization of Rural Health Service. Family Welfare, 41(3): 52.

Kumari, Indu (1998): Food Habit of Santhal (In) Tribal Culture and Identity. Ed. Chaturbhuj Sahu. Sarup & Sons Publication, Darya Ganj, New Delhi.

Kumari, Parnita K and Kumari, Sulekha (1998): Cultural and Environmental Aspects of Health in Santhal Tribe: 244-255 (In) Tribal Culture and Identity. Ed. Chaturbhuj Sahu. Sarup & Sons Publication. Darya Ganj, New Delhi.

Kumari, Shradha (1998): The Population of Tribes in India with Special Reference of Sex-ratio: 139-145 (In) Tribal Culture and Identify. Ed. Chaturbhuj Sahu. Sarup & Sons Publication, Darya Ganj, New Delhi.

Kunstadter, P. (1972): Demography, Ecology, Social Structure and Settlement Pattern (In) The Structure of Human Populations. Ed. G.A. Harrison, Boyce. Oxford Clarendon.

Kuppuswamy, B. (1980): A Text Book of Child Behaviour and Development. Vikas Publishing House Pvt. Ltd, New Delhi.

Kurup, R.S. (1994): Development of Family Planning Programme in India (In) Differential Development and Demographic Delemma. Ed. Kuttan Mahadevan, Chi-Hsisen, Tuan, et.al. B.R. Publishing Corporation, Ashok Vihar, Phase - IV, Delhi.

Lahiri, S. (1974): Preference for Sons and Ideal Family in Urban India. Ind. J. Soc. work, 34(4): 126-136.

Lamba, R. and Mehta, S. (1995): Priorities in Indian Medicine. A Tribal Perspective. Ind. Anthrop., 25(2): 1-12.

Langstieh, Banrida Theresa (2001): Demographic Structure of the Khasi-Muslims of Shillong, Meghalaya. J. Hum. Ecol., 12(2): 121-125.

Lee, R.B. (1980): Lactation, Ovulation, Infanticide and Women's Work: A Study of Hunter-gatherer Population Regulation (In) Biosocial Mechanisms of Population Regulation. Ed. M.N. Cohen, H.G. Klein. Yale Uni. Press, New Haven.

Lewis, G.J. (1982): Human Migration. Published by Croom Helm, London & Canberra.

Linton, R. (1941): Potential Contributions of Cultural Anthropology to Teacher Education in Culture and Personality. Washington, D.C.

Linton, R. (1945): The Scope and Aims of Anthropology. In the Science of Man in the World Crisis. Columbia Uni. Press, Columbia.

Livingston, F.B. and Spuhler, J.N. (1965): Cultural Determinants of Natural Selection. J. Int. Soc., 17: 118-120.

Lorimer, Frank (1959): The Development of Demography: 124-129 (In) The Study of Population. Ed. Philip M. Hauser and Otis Dudley. The Uni. of Chicago Press, Chicago.

Lyngdoh, S.M. and Verma, Raghu (2001): Malaria in Meghalaya: Socio-demographical and Geographical Problems. J. Hum. Ecol., 12(5): 337-343.

MacIver and Page (1990): Society – an Introductory Analysis. Macmillan India Ltd. (Press), Madras.

Madigam, Farancis (1968): Are Sex Mortality Differentials Biologically Caused? (In) Population and Society Charless Nam. Ed. Haughton, Mifflin Co. Boston.

Mahadevan, K. (1979): Sociology of Fertility: Determinants of Fertility Difference in South India. Sterling Publishers, Delhi.

Mahadevan, K. (1989): Population Dynamics in Indian's States. Fertility and Family Formation and Mortality and Life Affecting Variables. Mittal Publications, New Delhi.

Mahadevan, Kuttan (1994): Demographic Transition and Development Strategies in India (In) Differential Development and Demographic Dilemma. Ed. Kuttan Mahadevan, Chi-Hsien Tuan, et.al. B.R. Publishing Corporation, Delhi.

Mahadevan, Kuttan and Nair, Balakrishnan (1994): Mortality Differentials and Determinants in India (In) Defferential Development and Demographic Dilemma. Ed. Kuttan Mahadevan, Chi-Hsien Tuan, et.al. B.R. Publishing Corporation, Delhi.

Mahajan, Baldev, Tyagi, R.S. and Chaturvedi, U.S. (1994): Educational Administration in Madhya Pradesh. National Institute of Educational Planning and Administration, Sri Aurobindo Marg, New Delhi.

Mahanta, K.C. (1993): Socio-Economic Status of the Aged – A Case Study. Man In India, 73(3): 201-213.

Mahanta, K.C. (1995): A Study of Ethno- Medicines in Assam : A General Perspective. J. Hum. Ecol., 6(2): 105-117.

Mahapatra, Sitakant and Patnaik, N. (1986): Pattern of Tribal Housing. Tribal Dialects and Culture, Bhubaneshwer.

Mahapatro, Meerambika, Sachdeva, M.P. and Kalla, A.K. (1999): Knowledge, Attitude and Practice of Birth Control Devices among Bhattara Tribals of Orissa. J. Hum. Ecol., 10(1): 7-13.

Maharatna, Anup (1996): Fertility, Mortality and Gender Bias among Indian Tribes : What do We Really Know? : 85-118 (In) Tribal Development : Options, Ed. Prasana K. Samal. Gynodaya Prakashan, Nainital.

Maheo, Lorho Mary (1999): A Study of Demographic Dynamics of the Mao Naga Tribe of Senapati District, Manipur with Special Reference to Birth Control Measures. Unpublished Ph.D. Thesis, Uni. of Delhi, Delhi.

Maheo, Lorho Mary and Kalla, A.K. (2000): A Study on Fertility among the Mao Nagas of Senapati District, Manipur. Anthropologist, 2 (2): 123-126.

Maheo, Lorho Mary and Kalla, A.K. (2001): Knowledge, Attitude and Practice (KAP) of Birth Control Measures among the Mao Nagas of Senapati District, Manipur. Anthropologist, 3 (1): 33-42.

Majumdar, D.N. and Madan, T.N. (1986): An Introduction to Social Anthropology. Mayoor Paperbacks, Noida., Uttar Pradesh.

Majumdar (Paul), Gopa (2001): Some Aspects of Fertility of the Mahatos of Midnapore, West Bengal. J. Hum. Ecol., 12 (5): 379-382.

Majumdar, Murari (1962): Vital Rates, National Sample Survey, 54, Government of India. 24.

Majumdar, Murari and Das Gupta, Ajit (1976): Marriage Trends and Their Demographic Implications: 124-135 (In) Biosocial

Studies in India, Ed. Kanti B. Patkrasi, Amulay R. Banerjee and Amal K. Das. Calcutta Editions India.

Majumdar, P.K. and Chaudhuri, A. (1993): Civil Registration of Birth: A Comparison of Four Decades Data. Man And Life, 19 (1 & 2): 97-110.

Malgavakar, P.D. and Panadiker, V.A. Pai (1982): Population and Development. Somaiya Publications Pvt. Ltd, Bombay, Madras, New Delhi.

Malhotra, K.C. (1994): Genetic-Environmental Disorders and Their Impact on Mortality and Morbidity Profile Among the Tribal Populations (In) Tribal Health in India. Ed. S.K. Basu. Manak Publications Pvt. Ltd., Delhi.

Malik, S.L. and Hauspie, R.C. (1986): Age at Menarche Among High Altitude Bodhs of Ladakh (India). Hum. Bio. 58: 541.

Malthus, T.R. (1976): An Essay on the Principle of Population as It Affects the Future Improvement of Society. London: Johnson.

Malthus, Thomas Robert (1798): Principles of Population in An Essay on the Principles of Population. A Summary View of the Principles of Population. Penguin, Harmondsworli, London (J.Johnson).

Mandal, Debabrata (1998): Social and Economic Sensario of A Primitive Tribe in Madhya Pradesh : 236-243 (In) Tribal Culture and Identity. Ed. Chaturbhuj Sahu. Sarup & Sons Publication, Darya Ganj, New Delhi.

Mandelbaum, D.G. (1974): Human Fertility in India: Social Components and Policy Perspectives. Uni. of California Press, Berkeley.

Mann, R.S. (1973): Jarwas of Andaman: An Analysis of Hostility, Man In India, 53 (2): 201-220.

Mann, R.S. (1993): Culture And Integration of Indian Tribes. M.D. Publications Pvt. Ltd., Darya Ganj, Delhi.

Marine–Bettolo, G.B. (1980): Present Aspect of the Uses of Plants in Traditional Medicine. J. Ethnopharm, 2: 5-7.

Markides, K.S. and Barnes, D. (1977): A Methodological Note on the Relationship Between Infant Mortality and Socio-economic Status with Evidence from San Antonio, Texas, Soc. Biol., 24:38.

Marshall, B. John & Steven, Polghr (1976): Culture, Natality and Family Planning (Monograph), Carolina Population Centre, Uni. of North Carolina, Chapel Hill, North Carolina.

Marx, Karl (1933): Wage-Labour and Capital, New York.

Mastana, S.S. (1987): The Genetic Structure and Affinities of the Lobanas of Punjab (India). Dissertation, University of Cambridge, Cambridge.

Mastana, Sarabjit (1996): Age at Menopause among the Lobanas of North-West India. J. Hum. Ecol., 7(2):151-153.

Mathews, C.M.E.(1979): Health and Culture in a South-Indian Village. Published by Sterling Publishers Pvt. Ltd., New Delhi.

Matsunaga, E. (1996): Possible Genetic Consequences of Family Planning. J. Am. Med. Assoc., 198: 533.

Mazumdar (1994): cf. Aiyappan, A. (1994): Tribes in Central India: 113-117 (In) Tribal Life in India, Vol.1. Ed. Devendra Thakur and D.N. Thakur. Deep & Deep Publications, Rajouri Garden, New Delhi.

McClelland, G. H (1978): Determining the Impact of Sex Preference on Fertility: A Consideration of Perity Progression Ratio, Dominance and Stopping Rules Measures Demography, 16: 377-388.

Mead, .M. (1946): Anthropology and Education for the Future (In) Reading in Anthropology. Ed. J.D. Jennings and E.A. Hoebel.

Mehta, R (1975): White Collar and Blue Collar Family Responses of Population Growth in India: 117-161 (In) Response to Capital Growth in India, Ed. M.F. Franda. Frager Publishers.

Miro, C.A. and Potter, J.E. (1980): Population Policy: Research Pointers in the Developing World. Report of the International Review Group of Social Science Research on Population and Development. Frances Printer (Publishers), London.

Mishra, Bani Prasanna (1976): Socio-Economic Adjustments of Tribals. People's Publishing House, New Delhi.

Mishra, Braja Kishori (1993): Feeding Practices of Preschool Children in Western Orissa. I. Demographic Character, Prelacteal Feed and Colostrun Rejection. J. Hum. Ecol., 4 (1): 85-92.

Mishra, Braja Kishori (1993): Feeding Practices of Preschool Children in Western Orissa. II. Breast Feeding. J. Hum. Ecol., 4 (3): 161-170.

Mishra, Braja Kishori (1994): Feeding Practices of Preschool Children in Western Orissa. IV. Nutritional Anthropometry. J. Hum. Ecol., 5(1): 39-48.

Mishra, R.P. (1989): Population and Food Supply in Madhya Pradesh, Northern Book Centre, New Delhi.

Misra, B.D. (1982): An Introduction to the Study of Population. South Asian Publisher Pvt. Ltd., New Delhi.

Misra, Malaya K. (1999): Need for Conservation of Indigenous Medicinal Knowledge and the Herbs. J. Hum. Ecol., 10(5 & 6): 403-406.

Misra, M.K. and Dash, S.S. (2001): Ecological and Socio-economic Profile of Three Kondh Villages of Phulbani District of Orissa, Ind. J. Hum. Ecol. 12 (2): 101-107.

Mitra, Ashok (1978): India's Population: Aspects Quality and Control. Vols. 1 & 2, Abhinav Publications, New Delhi.

Mosley, S.H. (1985): Will Primay Health Care Reduce Infat and Child Mortality. (In) Health Policy, Social Policy and Mortality Prospects. Ed. J. Vallin and A.D. Lopez. Ordina Editions, Liege.

Mosely, W.H. and Chen, L.C. (1984): An Analytical Framework for the Study of Child Survival in Developing Countries: 25 (In) The Child Survival: Strategies for Research. Ed. W.H. Mosely and L.C. Chen. Pop. Dev. Rev., Supplement to Vol. 10.

Mosley, W. H. and Chen, L.C (1984): Child Survival: Strategies for Research, Population and Development Review (eds.), Supplement 1 to 10.

Mukherjee, D.P. (1972): Some Recent Trends in Population Genetics in India. Genetics and Our Health. ICMR Technical Report Series, 20: 234-243.

Mukherjee, D.P. (1974): Fourth Annual Report on the Genetic Studies in Relation to Fertility, an ICMR Project.

Mukherji, R. (1946): Races, Lands and Food, New York.

Mukhopadhyay, B. (1981): A Comparative Micro Demographic Study of two Communities in Coastal Midnapore District, West Bengal. Bio. Soc, 13: 479-490.

Mukhopadhyay, B. (1982): Selection Intensity in the Lepchas of Kalimpong Sub-Division, Curr. Anthrop., 23:577-578.

Mukhopadhyay, D. (1996): Tribals and Forest Development in India: 49-67 (In) Tribal Development: Options. Ed. Prasana K. Samal, Gyanodaya Prakashan, Nainital.

Murthy, G.B. (1987): The Soligas of B.R. Hills: A Demographic Study. Family Welfare, Vol. 34.

Murthy, J.S. and Ramesh, A. (1985): Selection Intensities of Adilabad District, Andhra Pradesh. Ind. Soc. Biol., 25:302-305.

Muthal, Sudha (1992): Attitudes Towards Fertility Control. Man In India, 72 (1): 97-103.

Mutharayappa, R. (1993): Socio-Cultural Factors and Marriage among Jenukuruba and Kadukuruba Tribes of Karnataka. Man In India, 79(1): 17-27.

Mutharayappa, R. (1995): A Study of Acceptors and Non-Acceptors of Family Planning Methods among Three Tribal Communities. Man In India, 75 (1): 11-25.

Mutharayappa, R. (1997): Socio-Cultural Factors and Marriage Among Jenukuruba and Kadukuruba Tribes of Karnataka. Man In India, 77(4): 397-408.

Mutharayappa, R. (1998): Fertility and Family Planning among Jenukuruba and Kadukuruba Tribes of Karnataka. Man In India, 78 (1 & 2): 119-126.

Nachmias, David and Nachmias, Chava (1981): Research Methods in Social Sciences. Second Edition. St. Martin's Press, New Delhi.

Nag, M. (1962): Factors Affecting Human Fertility in Non-Industrial Societies: A Cross Cultural Study. Yale Univ. Publications in Anthropology, No. 66, U.S.A.

Nag, M. (1965): Effect of Christianity on a few Aspects of Khasi Culture. Bulletin, Vol. 14, Department of Anthropology, Government of India.

Nag, M. (1974): Socio-Cultural Pattern, Family Cycle and Fertility: 289 (In) The Population Debate: Dimensions and Perspectives. Paper of the World Population Conference-3. Bruchest (1974), Vol.2, United Nations, New York.

Nag, M. (1983): Impacts of Social Development and Economic Development on Mortality: Comparative Study of Kerala and West Bengal. Econoimc and Political Weekly, 18: 19-21.

Nag, N.G. (1990): Some Demographic Characteristics of Scheduled Tribes with Special Reference to Gujarat, Madhya Pradesh, Rajasthan and Maharashtra: 105-123 (In) *Demography of Tribal Development*. Ed. Asish Bose, U.P. Sinha and R.P. Tyagi. B.R. Publishing Corporation, Shakti Nagar, Delhi.

Nag, Shampa (1998): Anthropo-Demographic Study among the Population Groups of Ladakh in Jammu & Kashmir, India. Unpublished Ph.D. Thesis, Uni. of Delhi, Delhi.

Nagla, B.K. (1986): Tribal Development in India: Problems and Prospects (In) *Tribal Development-Past Efforts and New Challenges*.Ed. J.P. Singh, and N. N. Vyas. The MLV Tribal Research and Training Institute, Tribal Area Development Department,Rajasthan, Udaipur.

Nagraj, K. and Prasad, K. Raghava (1999): Socio-Demographic Factors Influencing Ante-Natal Care-A Community Based Study. *Health and Population Perspectives and Issues*, 22.

Nagraj, K. and Rao, B.V.N. Brahmeswara (1997): Social and Environmental Correlates of Childhood Diarrhoea - A Longitudinal Study. *J. Hum. Ecol.,* 8(4): 255-259.

Nair, K.S. (1979): Intertribal Differences in Educational Achievements. *Ind. Anthrop.* IX.

Nair, N.K. Sukumaran (1987): Tribal Economy in Transition: A Study of Meghalaya. Inter India Publications, New Delhi.

Nair, P.S. (1997): Population Density and Urbanisation in Kerala: Impact on Environment. *J. Hum. Ecol.,* 8 (4): 237-240.

Nair, P.S. and Koteshwar, R. K. (1987): Female Age at Marriage in Northern Karnataka. Soc. Change, 17(3): 65-69.

Nair, V. Balakrishnan (1994): Social Development and Demographic Changes in South India. M.D. Publications Pvt. Ltd, M.D. House, Darya Ganj, New Delhi.

Nair, V. Balakrishnan and Mahadevan, Kuttan (1994): Fertility Behaviour in India and the States (In) Differential Development and Demographic Dilemma. Ed. Kuttan Mehadean, Chi-Hsien Tuan, et. al. B.R. Publishing Corporation, Ashok Vihar, Phase-IV, Delhi.

Nalwa, A.S. (1981): Social Factors Operating in Feeding Practice and Dietary Pattern of Under-Threes. *J. Ind. Prediatr.,* 18: 453-460.

Nanda, Satyajeet and Niranjan, S. (1999): Utilization of Ante Natal Care (ANC) Service by the Scheduled Tribes in India. *J. Hum. Ecol.,* 10 (2): 99-104.

Nandy, Subrata and Sen, Tulika (1993): Menarcheal Age among Some Rural Muslim Women of 24 Paragonas. J. Hum. Ecol., 4 (1): 81-82.

National Family Health Survey of India (1992-93): Published by International Institute for Population Science, Bombay.

Nayak, A.N. and Babu, B.V. (2001): Utilization of Services Related to Safe Motherhood among the Scheduled Caste and Scheduled Tribe Population of Orissa: An Overview. South Asian Anthropologist, 1 (2): 117-122.

Netting, R.M.C., Wilk, R.R. and Amould, E.J. (1983): Household (In) Comparative and Historical Studies of the Domestic Group. Ed. R.M.C. Netting, R.R. Wilk and E.J. Amould. Berkely, Uni.. Calf. Press.

Oberoi, R.C., Sharma, A.K. and Sharma, S.K. (1994): Environmental Limitations, Socio-Economic Status and Constraints of Tribal Economy in outer Himalayas – A Study of Pangi Valley in Himachal Pradesh. J. Hum. Ecol., 5(1): 63-67.

Ojha, K.M. (1979): A Study of Socio-Economic and Cultural Aspects of Infant-Feeding Practices in Rural Gwalior. M.D. Thesis, Jiwaji University, Gwalior, M.P.

Oldenburg, P. (1992): Sex Ratio, Son Preference and Violence in India: A Research Note. J. Economic and Political Weekly, December: 5-12.

Ostergaard, Lise (1992): Gender and Development: A Practice Guide. Routledge: London.

Padmanabham, P.B.S.V. (1981): cf. Reddy, B.M. and Chopra, V.P. (1990): Opportunity for Natural Selection among the Indian Population. Am. J. Phys. Anthrop., 83:281-296.

Padmanabham, P.B.S.V and Jaiswal I.J.S. (1982): A Demographic Study of the Apatanis. Proc. Seminar on Biological and Cultural Variations of the People of North East India. Anthrp. Deptt. Gauhati Uni, Gauhati, Assam.

Pakrasi, K. and Halder, A. (1980): The Calcutta Couples: A Study of the Socio-economic Characteristics, Family Planning and Abortion Behaviour (In) The Calcutta Couples: A Biosocial Profile. Ed. K.B. Pakrasi, A.R. Banarjee and A.K. Halder. Editions Indian, Calcutta.

Pal, Amar Nath (1995): The Political Economy of Migration among the Oraon. J. Man In India, 75(1): 67-77.

Panda, Jayanti (1987): A Study of Fertility and Mortality Patterns among Kondhs of Chakapad, Phulbani. (Unpublished) Sambalpur Uni., Shambalpur, Orissa.

Pandey, G.D. (1989): A Study of Couple Fertility in Tribal Population of Madhya Pradesh. in Singh, et.al. (1989), 2.

Pandey, G.D. (1994): Demographic Characteristics of Tribal and Non-tribal Females – A Comparative Study. Man In India, 74 (1): 39-47.

Pandey, G.D. and Goel, A.K. (1999): Some- Demographic Characteristics of Abujhmaria of Madhya Pradesh. J. Hum. Ecol., 20(2): 85-88.

Pandey, G.D., Roy, J. and Tiwari, R.S. (1996): Socio-cultural Characteristics and Health Seeking Behaviour of the Khairwar of Madhya Pradesh. *J. Fam. Welf.* 42(2): 49.

Pandey, G.D., Roy, J. and Tiwari, R.S. (2001): Socio-Cultural Aspects and Health Care in Pando Tribe of Madhya Pradesh. *J. Hum. Ecol.,* 12 (5): 391-394.

Pandey, G.D. and Saxena, B.N. (1988): District Level Planning for Health and Family Welfare for Tribals. Demography India, 17(2):216.

Pandey, G.D. and Talwar, P.P. (1987): Some Aspects of Marriage and Fertility in Rural Uttar Pradesh. Demography India, 2: 301.

Pandy, G.D. and Tiwari, R.S. (1993): Demographic Characteristics in a Tribal Block of Madhya Pradesh. *Soc. Change,* 23 (3): 124-131.

Pandey, G.D. and Tiwari, R.S. (1993): Socio-Cultural Characteristics and Health Seeking Behaviour of Hill Korwas. Family Welfare, 39(2): 44.

Pandey, G.D. and Tiwari, R.S. (1994): Literacy and Demographic Characteristics: A Study of Association among the Tribals of Madhya Pradesh (In) *Tribal Situation and Development in Central India.* Ed. S.K. Tiwary. M.D. Publication, New Delhi.

Pandey, G.D. and Tiwari, R.S. (1996): Fertility in Hill Korwas – A Primitive Tribe of Madhya Pradesh. Man In India, 76(4): 325-329.

Pandey, G.D., Verma, Arvind and Tiwari, R.S. (2001): Some Correlates of Infant Mortality in a Primitive Tribe of Madhya Pradesh. *South Asian Anthropologist,* 1 (1): 17-20.

Pandit, Apoorva (2001): Indigenous Technological Knowledge and Practices of the Tribal People in Maharashtra. J. Hum. Ecol., 12 (6): 469-472.

Parsuraman, S. and Rajan, S. (1990): On the Estimation of Vital Rates among the Scheduled Tribes of Western India: 131-140 (In) Demography of Tribal Development. Ed. A. Bose, V.P. Sinha and R.P. Tyagi. B.R. Publication, New Delhi.

Park, C.B. (1983): Preference for Sons, Family Size and Sex Ratio: An Empirical Study of Korea. Demography, 20: 333.

Park, J.E. and Park, K. (1985): Text Book of Preventive and Social Medicine, M/s. Banarsidas Bhanot, Jabalpur, M.P.

Parmar, Dinesh and Sengupta, L.K. (1994): Marital Distance and Village Endogamy in Bhilala and Barela Tribes of West Nimar in Central India. J. Hum. Ecol., 5(2): 127-130.

Patel, S. (1991): Tribal Education in India. Mittal Publications, New Delhi.

Patel, Tulsi (1994): Fertility Behaviour: Population and Society in a Rajasthan Village. Oxford Uni. Press. Delhi, Bombay, Calcutta and Madras.

Pathak, Lalit P. (1998): Population Studies – The Descriptive Development Pattern and Information System. Rawat Publication, Jaipur: 1-50.

Pati, Sumana (1982): Fertility and Mortality Rate among the Oraons, Arba-Jharabahal of Sundargarh Distrist, (Unpublished) Sambalpur Uni., Sambalpur, Orissa.

Patnaik, N. (1989): The Saora: Tribal and Harijan Research-Cum-Training Institute, Bhubaneswer.

Patra, Prasanna Kumar and Kapoor, A.K. (1996): Some Demographic Traits among the West Garo Hills, Meghalaya. Man In India, 76(3): 273-278.

Patra, Prasanna K. and Kapoor, A.K. (1997): Opportunity for Natural Selection among the Dalu of West Garo Hills, Meghalaya. J. Hum. Ecol., 8(2):127-129.

Patra, Prasanna Kumar (2001): Demographic Profile with Reference to Development Programmes among the Rajis: A Primitive

Tribe of Uttaranchal. Unpublished Ph.D. Thesis, University of Delhi, Delhi.

Patty, William (1690): Essays on Political Arithmetic.

Pearl, R. (1939): Natural History of Population. Oxford University Press, Oxford.

Pike, K. (1954): Language in Relation to the Unified of Sources of Human Behaviour, Vol.1, Glendale, California: Summer Institute of Linguistics.

Pillai, Mahadevan K. (1971): Study of the Decision Process in Adopting Family Planning Methods. Bulletin of the Gandhigram Institute of Rural Health and Family Planning, VI: 1-56.

Piplai, Chumki (1993): Effects of Family Planning Practices and Income on Fertility and Mortality among two Tea-Garden in the Duars Area of Jalpaiguri District, West Bengal. J. Hum. Ecol., 4 (2): 105-110.

Polgar, S. (1964): Evolution and the Ills of making: 200-211 (In) Horizons of Anthropology. Ed. S. Trx. Aldine, Chicago.

Potts, Malcolm and Selman, Peter (1978): Society And Fertility. Published by Macdonald and Evans Ltd, London.

Potts, M. and Selman, P. (1979): Society and Fertility. Published by Macdonald and Evans Ltd, London.

Prabhakara, N.R. (1986): Internal Migration and Population Redistribution in India. Concept Publishing Company, Bali Nagar, New Delhi.

Prabhu, Pandharinath H. (1991): Hindu Social Organisation. Papular Prakashan Pvt. Ltd., Popular Press Bldg., Tardeo, Bombay.

Prabhu, Pradip (1983): Social Forestry: An Adivasi Viewpoint: 134-143 (In) Towards A New Forest Policy: People's Right and Environmental Needs. Ed. Walter Fernandes and Sharad Kulkarni. Indian Social Institute, New Delhi.

Prakash, S. and Pathmanathan, G. (1992): Age at Menarche and its Prediction in the Welloff North-West Indian Girls. J. Hum. Ecol., 3(2): 133-137.

Prasad, K. Raghava and Nagaraj, K. (2001): Socio-Demographic Correaltes of Place of Delivery and Person Conducting the Delivery in a Rural Community of Andhra Pradesh. J. Hum. Ecol., 12 (5): 357-362.

Prasad, N. Purendra and Rao, P. Venkata (1996): Patterns of Migration from a Drought-Prone Area in Andhra Pradesh: A Case Study. J. Hum. Ecol., 7(3): 135-162.

Premi, M.K., Ramanamma and Bambewale, Usha (1983): An Introduction to Social Demography. Vikas Publishing House Pvt. Ltd, New Delhi.

Preston, S.H. (1975): Introduction Proceeding of Seminar on Infant Mortality in Relation to the Level of Fertility, Bangkok. Committee for International Co-operation of National Research on Demography.

Preston, S.H. (1980): Causes and Consequences of Mortality Declines in Less Developed Countries During the Twentieth Century: 294 (In) Population and Economic Change in Developing Countries. Ed. R.A. Esterlin. University of Chicago Press, Chicago.

Preston, S.H. (1990): Mortality in India: 81 (In) International Population Conference, New Delhi, 1989, Vol.4. IUSSP. Liege.

Price, Richard (1783): Life Table and Rate of Death and Birth Growth of People in Sweden.

Raj, Hans (1982): Population Studies. Surjeet Publication, Kolhapur Boad, Kamla Nagar, Delhi.

Rajaratnam, Abel, Rajaratnam, Jolly and Kamaladoss, Theodore (1997): Maternal and Child Health Practices and Nutritional Status of Malto Tribals in Bihar. Man In India, 77 (1): 29-34.

Rajeeva (1989): An Introduction to the Tribal Development in India. International Book Distributors, Raipur Road, Dehradun.

Rajpramukh, K.E. (1998): Tribal Health in Visakhapatnam District of Andhra Pradesh. J. Hum. Ecol., 9(2): 191-193.

Rajyalakshmi, P. (1991): Tribal Food Habits. Gian Publishing House, New Delhi.

Rajyalakshmi, P. and Geervani, P. (1992): Food Nutrition and Morbidity: Some Observations among Four Tribal Groups of South India. J. Hum. Ecol., 3(2): 115-124.

Raman, G.V. and Naidu, J.M. (1992): Marital Distance in Manne Dora Tribe of Andhra Pradesh. J. Hum. Ecol., 2(3): 59-60.

Rao, B. Dharma and Busi, B.R. (1997): A Study of Physical Growth and Nutritional Status among Savara Tribal Girls of Andhra Pradesh. J. Hum. Ecol., 8(4):249-253.

Rao, B. Dharma and Busi, B.R. (1997): A Study of Physical Growth and Nutritional Status among Jatapu Girls of Andhra Pradesh. J. Hum. Ecol., 8(5): 355-359.

Rao, Dharma, Jaikishan, G. and Busi, B.R. (1998): Growth Progression and Nutritional Status among Some Tribal Children of Visakhapatnam District, Andhra Pradesh. Hum. Ecol., 9(4): 373-378.

Rao, D. Gopal (1974): Population Education. Sterling Publishers Pvt. Ltd., New Delhi.

Rao, D. Hanumantha and Rao, K. Mallikharjuna (1994): Levels of Malnutrition and Socio-Economic Conditions among Maria Gonds. J. Hum. Ecol., 5 (3): 185-190.

Rao, K. Rajendra (1996): Marriage Distance and Pattern of Mate Exchange in two Tribal Groups. Man In India, 76(3):279-285.

Rao, K. Rajendra (1997): Marriage Distance and the Pattern of Mate Exchange Between Clans among the Dhanwar and the Kamar Tribes of Madhya Pradesh. Man In India, 77 (4):381-386.

Rao, M., Rao, N.P. and Mathur, Y.C. (1972): A Survey of Infant-Feeding and Weaning Practices in the Village Fathepur – Hyderabad. J. Ind. Pediatr., 9:480-484.

Rao, V.L.N., Busi, B.R. and Saileela, M. (1995): An Appraisal of the Nutritional Status of Jatapu School Boys of

Vizianagaram District, Andhra Pradesh, Ind. J. Hum. Ecol., 6 (2): 131-133.

Ray, R. and Banerjee, J. (1993): Health Studies among Tribal Women. J. Soc. Change, 23: 209-214.

Reddy, B.M. and Chopra, V.P. (1990): Opportunity for Natural Selection among Indian Populations. Am. J. Phys. Anthrop., 83:281-296.

Reddy, G.P. (1983): Environmental and Ecological Dimensions of Economic Development among the Tribes of Eastern Ghats in Andhra Pradesh: 151-165 (In) Tribal Area Development. Ed. S.N. Mishra and Bhupinder Singh. Society for the Study of Regional Disparities, New Delhi.

Reddy, K.N. (1985): Irulas of Nilgiris : A Study of Anthropological Demography. Research Report. Tamil Nadu Uni., Unpublished. Tamil Nadu, India.

Reddy, N. (1992): Village Economy and the Future Transformation of India: The Circulating Labours of the Village of Andhra Pradesh (In) Images of Rural India. Ed. A. Bhalla and P. Bhumke. Sterling Publishers Pvt. Ltd., New Delhi.

Reddy, R.L. Chandrasekhara, Venkatramana, P. and Reddy, P. Chengal (1992): Nutritional Status of Preschool Children of Chittor District. J. Hum. Ecol., 72(4): 469-473.

Reddy, T.P.K. and Reddy, P.Govinda (1996): Effects of Inbreeding on Morbidity : A Study among Three South Indian Communities . J. Hum. Ecol. , 7(1): 19-23.

Reddy, T. Parvathi Kumar, Reddy, K. Surendranath and Reddy, P. Govinda (1993): Consanguinity and Inbreeding Effects on Fertility and Mortality among Malas of Chittoor District, Andhra Pradesh. J. Hum. Ecol., 4(2): 97-103.

Repetto, R. (1972): Son Preference and Fertility Behaviour in Developing Countries. Studies in Family Planning, 3:70.

Retherford, R.D., Thapa, S. and De Silva, V. (1989): Strength of Fertility Motivation: Its Effects on Contraceptive Use in Rural Sri Lanka. Asia-Pacific Population Journal, 4: 21.

Rider, R.V. and Badger, G.F. (1943): Family Studies in the Eastern

Hill District (Baltimore). A Consideration of Issues Motivated in Determining Migration Rates for Families. Hum. Biol., 15: 101-126.

Ridkar, R. (1969): Desired Family Size and the Efficiency of Current Family Planning Programmes. Pop. Stud., 23: 279.

Rizvi, S.H.M. (1987): Mina: The Ruling Tribe of Rajasthan. Published by B.R. Publishing Corporation, Delhi.

Rob, A.K. Ubaidur (1992): Socio-Economic Determinants of Fertility. What do We Know? Demography India, 21(1): 19.

Roberts, D.F., Chinn, S., Girija,B. and Singh, H.D. (1977): A Study of Menarcheal Age in India. Ann. Hum. Biol. 4:171-177.

Rohini, A. and Reddy, G.Golla .(1985): Some Demographic Tends among the Tribal Women of Andhra Pradesh. Man And Life. 11.

Rohini, A. and Reddy, G. Golla (1989): Fertility Study among the Bagathus – A Tribal Population in V. Panan District of Andhra Pradesh. Man And Life,15.

Rosa, F.W. (1978): Breast Feeding in Family Planning. Protein – Calorie Advisory Group Bulletin, 5.

Rosenzweigh, M.R. and Schultz, T.P. (1981): Child Mortality and Fertility in Colombia: Individual and Community Effects. Centre Discussion Paper No.380. Economic Growth Centre, Yale University, New Haven.

Rosenzweigh, M.R. and Schultz, T.P. (1982): Market Opportunities, Endowments and Intra Family Distribution of Resources: Child Survival in Rural India in American Review, 72.

Roy, Debesh (1995): Marriage Rules and Marriage Rituals among Kokna Tribe of Maharashtra. Man In India, 75(1):25-35.

Roy Burman, B.K. (1961): Ethnographic Study of Soligas, Census of India, Part V-B, No.6, Monograph Series, Karnataka.

Roy Burman, B.K. (1990): Tribal Demography: A Preliminary Appraisal (In) The Tribal Situation in India. Ed. K. Suresh

Singh. Indian Institute of Advanced Study. Saraswati Printing Press, Sector-5, Noida, Uttar Pradesh.

Roy Burman, B.K. (1993): Tribal Population: Interface of Historical Ecology (In) Continuity and Change in Tribal Society. Ed. Mrinal Miri. Printed by Elecgant Printers, Maya Puri, New Delhi.

Roy Burman, S.K. and Bharti, P. (1982): Selection Intensity: Inter and Intra Group Variation. J. Ind. Anthrop. Soc., 17: 289-286.

Roy, T.K. and Rao, G. Rama (1985): Introduction to Evaluation of Demographic Impact of Family Planning Programme. Himalaya Publishing House, Bombay.

Russel, R.V. and Hiralal, Rai Bahadur (1975): The Tribes and Castes of Thee Central Provinces of India (London: Macmillan and Company, Vol. I-IV). Cosmo Publication, New Delhi.

Sabat, Kalpana Rani and Dash, Nirmal Chandra (1996): Socio-Economic and Demographic Profile of A Kandh Village of Eastern Ghats, Orissa. Man In India, 76(2):127-140.

Sabat, Kalpana Rani, Dash Nirmal Chandra and Das, Bijayalaxmi (1997): Habitat and Nutritional Status of A Kandh Village of Eastern Ghats, Orissa. J. Hum. Ecol., 8(1): 13-19.

Sachchidananda and Prasad, R.R. (1996): Encyclopedic Profile of Indian Tribes, Vol.1. (Ed.) Discovery Publishing House, New Delhi.

Sadhu, A.N. and Singh, Amarjit (1985): Research Methodology in Social Science. Himalaya Publishing House, New Delhi.

Saha, D.K. (1986): Communication and Perception of Family Planning among the Santhals (In) Tribal Health: Socio-Cultural Dimensions. Ed. Budhadeb Choudhury. Published by Inter India Publication, New Delhi.

Saha, Kalyan B. and Saha, Uma (1998): An Overview of the Socio-Economic and Demographic Transition among the Santhal: A Census Analysis. Man In India, 78 (1 & 2): 87-101.

Saha , S.S. (1981): Selection Intensity: Inter and Intra Group Variation. J. Anthrop. Soc. 16:185-187.

Saha, S.S. (1982): Opportunity of Selection in the Muria Population of Narayanpur. J. Ind. Anthrop. Soc., 17:283-336.

Sahu, Chaturbhuj (1982): Development of the Birhor Clusters: With Special Reference to the Birhor of Hazaribagh and Giridhi Districts. Ph.D. Thesis Submitted to Ranchi Uni., Ranchi, Bihar.

Sahu, Chaturbhuj, (1995): Birhor Tribe. Sarup & Sons Publication, Darya Ganj, New Delhi.

Sahu, Chaturbhuj (1998): Food and Health Condition of Birhor: A Vanishing Tribe of Bihar: 69-84 (In) Tribal Culture and Identity. Ed. Chaturbhuj Sahu. Sarup & Sons Publication, Darya Ganj, New Delhi.

Sahu, Chaturbhuj (1998)): Some Glimpses of the Tribe: 1-38 (In) Tribal Culture and Identity. Ed. Chaturbhuj Sahu. Sarup & Sons Publication, Darya Ganj, New Delhi.

Sahu, Chaturbhuj (1998): The Birjia: A Primitive Tribe of Bihar: 42-53 (In) Tribal Culture and Identity. Ed. Chaturbhuj Sahu. Sarup & Sons Publication, Darya Ganj, New Delhi.

Sahu, Chaturbhuj and Jha, A.K. (1998): The Lepchas of Darjeeling and Their Language Problem: 84-91 (In) Tribal Culture and Identity. Ed. Chaturbhuj Sahu. Sarup & Sons Publication, Darya Ganj, New Delhi.

Sahu, P.N. (1983): Demographic and Genetic Constitution of A Small Population (The Malia). J. Ind. Anthrop. Soc., 18: 55-59.

Sahu, P.N. (2001): Genetic Demography of Malia: 52-91 (In) Bio-cultural Frontiers of Man. Ed. K.C. Tripathy and N.K. Behura. Published by Department of Anthropology, Utkal University, Bhubaneshwar.

Saikia, Jogamaya K.K. (1994): Religion: A Factor of Culture Change among Angamis in Nagaland: 221-288 (In) Tribes in North-East India - Biological and Cultural Perspectives. Ed. Sarthak Sengupta, Gyan Publishing, Darya Ganj, New Delhi.

Salariya, E.M., Easton, P.M. and Cater, J.L. (1978): Duration of Breast-Feeding after early Initiation and Frequent Feeding. Lancet, 2: 1141-1143.

Salzano, F.M. (1963): Selection Intensity in Brazilian Changing Indians (1998), 199:514.

Samal, Prasana K. (1993): The Status of Women in Central Himalaya: A Cultural Interpretation, 73(1):87-95.

Samal, P.K., Chauhan, M.S. and Fernando, Rajulton (1996): The Functioning and Eco-Cultural Significance of Marriage Type among the Jaunsaries in Central Himalaya. Man In India, 76(3): 199-214.

Sample Registration System (1989): Fertility & Mortality Indicators. Vital Statistic Division, Office of the Registrar General of India. Ministry of Home Affairs, New Delhi.

Sample Registration System (1992): Fertility & Mortality Indicators. Vital Statistics Division, Registrar General of India, Ministry of Home Affairs, New Delhi.

Sample Registration System (1993): Fertility & Mortality Indicators. Vital Statistic Division, Office of the Registrar General of India. Ministry of Home Affairs, New Delhi.

Sarkar, N.C. (1997): Opportunity for Natural Selection among the Muklom of Arunachal Pradesh. Curr. Anthro., 38 (1): 140-143.

Sarkar, N.C., Barua, S. and Varti, R.T. (1994): Opportunity of Selection in the Khamti of Lakhimpur District, Assam, India. J. Hum. Ecol., 5(3): 217-220.

Sarkar, Profulla C. (1992): Problem of Female Literacy in Bangladesh in Socio-Economic and Cultural Perspectives. Paper Presented in the Regional Seminar on Challenges for Change: Literacy for Girls of Today and the Women of Tomorrow, Karachi, Pakistan.

Sarkar, Profulla C. and Banu, Tahmin (1988): Culture, Age at Marriage and Fertility in a Village of Bangladesh. South Asian Anthropologist, 5 (2): 19-29.

Sarkar, Profulla C. (2000): Cultural Parameters of Gender Disparity and Their Impact on the Practice of Contraceptive Devices in Bangladesh. South Asian Anthropologist, 2(1): 43-48.

Sarma, A. Venugopala and Nagraj. K. (1999): A Study on Pattern of Utilization of Health Services in An Integrated Child Development Services Project in Andhra Pradesh. J. Hum. Ecol., 10(1): 1-6.

Sastry, V.N.V.K. (1993): Chenchu Food Gatherers and Hunters of Nallamala Forests – Problems of Transition. Man And Life, 19(1 & 2): 83-96.

Savage, F. (1983): The First Days of Breast Feeding. Afya, 17: 58-68.

Saxena, D.N. (1990): Family Building, Fertility and Family Welfare among Two Tribal Communities of Uttar Pradesh: 249-269. (In) Demography of Development. Ed. A. Bose, V.P. Sinha and R.P. Tyagi.

Saxena, R.N. (1962): Social Economy of A Polyandrous People. London.

Schuler, Sydney, R. Hashemi, S.M. and Jenkins, A.K. (1995): Bangladesh Family Planning Success Story. A Gender Perspective. International Family Planning Perspective, 21(4): 132-137.

Sebastian, A. (1986): Migrants in North-Eastern Region of India: 63-68 (In) The Patterns and Problems of Population in North-East India. Ed. B. Datta Ray. Uppal Publishing House, New Delhi.

Sen, Amartya (1994): Population: Delusion and Reality. New York Review of Books, September, 22.

Sen, Tulika (1994): A Historical Study of Ages at Menarche, Marriage, Menopause and Family Size in High-Caste Bengalees of Calcutta. Man In India, 74 (3): 241-250.

Sengupta, S. (1985): Note Sur L'Age a la Puberte Des Filles. Soc.d' Anthrop.De. Paris,14: 55-58.

Sengupta, Sarthak and Begum, Sabeha (1998): Index of Opportunity for Natural Selection among the Sayed Muslims of Assam J. Hum. Ecol., 9(1): 95-97.

Sengupta, Sarthak and Chakravarty, Kanta (1995): Family Type, Fertility and Mortality: A Study among the Ahoms of Assam. J. Hum. Ecol., 6(3): 197-200.

Sengupta, Sarthak and Chakravarty, Kanta (1998): Effects of Place of Residence on Fertility and Mortality among the Ahoms of Assam. J. Hum. Ecol ., 9(5): 455-461.

Sengupta, Sarthak and Chakravarty, Kanta (1998): Selection Intensity in the Ahoms of Assam. J. Hum. Ecol., 9(1): 83-85.

Sengupta, S. and Gogoi, G. (1993): Menarche and Menopause among the Kaibarta Women of Dibrugarh, Assam. J. Assam Sci.Soc., 35:113-119.

Sengupta, Sarthak and Phukan, Arundhati Gogoi (1997): Socio-Cultural Variation and Selection Intensity among the Oraon of Assam. J. Hum. Ecol., 8(3):153-157.

Sengupta, Sarthak and Rajkhowa, Mina (1996): Menarche and Menopause among the Ahom Women of Dibrugarh, Assam. J. Hum. Ecol., 7(3):211-213.

Shah, A.K. (1958): The Age of Menarche in Gujarati College Girls. J. Ind. Med. Assoc., 30:347.

Shah, U.M. (1999): Cooperative Education for Cooperative Development. Kurukshetra, A J. on Rural Dev., May: 15-18.

Shaikh, Kashem (2000): Impact of Age of Marriage on Fertility in Rural Bangladesh. South Asian Anthropologist, 21(1): 15:22.

Sharma, A.N. (1994): The Bharias of Patalkot. M.K. Offset Printers and Publishers, Bhopal.

Sharma, A.N. (1998): Socio-Cultural and Demographic Profile of Bharias of Patalkot: 146-187 (In) Tribal Culture and Identity. Ed. Chaturbhuj Sahu. Sarup & Sons Publication, Darya Ganj, New Delhi.

Sharma, Anima (2001): Health andHygiene among the Tribals – A Case Study of Gonds. Anthropologist, 3 (3): 191-194.

Sharma, A.N. and Sharma M.N. (1998): Dietary Habits and

Nutrients Intake Pattern among Bharias of Patalkot: 188-203 (In) Tribal Culture and Identity. Ed. Chaturbhuj Sahau. Sarup & Sons Publication, Darya Ganj, New Delhi.

Sharma, D.B. and Lahori, U.C. (1977): Feeding Patterns of Infants and Pre-School Children in Urban and Rural Areas of Jammu. Ind. Pediatr., 14: 247-254.

Sharma, D.V.N. and Jain, A.K. (1974): Preference About Sex of Children and Use of Contraceptive among Women Wanting no more Children in India. J. Demog. In Ind., 3: 81-101.

Sharma, K. (1978): Fertility and Mortality in Khonds: A Tribal Community of Orissa. Man In India, 58(1):77-88.

Sharma, K. (1979): The Kondhs of Orissa, An Anthropometric Study. Concept Publishing Company, New Delhi.

Sharma, K. (1990): Age at Menarche in North-West Indian Females and Review of Indian Data. Ann. Hum. Biol., 17:159.

Sharma, K.K.N. (1992): Assessment of Nutritional Status of the Kairwar Tribal Children of Madhya Pradesh, Ind. J. Hum. Ecol., 3(1): 47-48.

Sharma, K.K.N. (2001): Assessment of Physical Growth among the Hill Korwa Tribal Girls of Madhya Pradesh, India. South Asian Anthropologist, 1 (1): 51-55.

Sharma, M.B. and Chowdhury, Dipesh (1995): Menarche and Fertility: A Correlation Study among the Gond Tribe of Maharashtra. J. Hum. Ecol., 6(3): 209-212.

Sharma, Poonam (1989): Family Welfare Programme in India. Deep and Deep Publications, New Delhi.

Sharma, Ramnath and Sharma, Rajendra K. (1981): Demography and Population Problems. A Rajhan's Publications, Meerut.

Sharma, S.P. and Sharma, J.B. (1999): Tribal Demography. Radha Publications, Darya Ganj, New Delhi.

Sharma, V. and Sharma, A. (1993): The Status of Women, Fertility and Family Planning Tribal of South Rajasthan. Family Welfare, 39(4):20.

Shekar, M. (1984): Health Practice in Relation to Child Birth and

Infant Care. National Institute of Public Cooperation and Child Development, New Delhi.

Shukla, B. R. K. and Rastogi, Sudha (1990): Physical Anthropology and Human Genetics – An Introduction. Palaka Prakashan, S.P. Mukherjee Marg, Delhi.

Shukla, N.B., Sharma, S.S. and Bhushan, Sudha (1994): Age of Menarche of Urban and Rural Sports School Girls. Man In India, 74(3):307-310.

Sidhu, S. and Sidhu, L.S. (1985): Age at Menarche and Menopause in Sansi Female of Punjab. Ind. J. Phy. Anthrop. Hum. Genet., 11: 33-37.

Sikder, M. Abdus Samad (2000): Practice of Contraceptive Devices Associated with Family Structure in Rural Bangladesh. South Asian Anthropologist, 21(1):7-14.

Singh, H.D. and Robert, D.F. (1975): Menarcheal Age in South India. Am.J. Obstet. Gynaecol. 122:537-538.

Singh, Jaspal (1991): Introduction to Methods of Social Research. Sterling Publishers Pvt. Ltd., New Delhi.

Singh, K.P. (1986): Correlates of Fertility Behaviour. Concept Publishing Company, New Delhi.

Singh, K.S. (1994): The Scheduled Tribes, Volume – III. Oxford Uni. Press, Delhi, Bombay, Calcutta, Madras.

Singh, M. Bokul (1989): The Tarao of Manipur: Socio-Demographic Change, Unpublished Ph.D. Thesis, Manipur Uni, Manipur.

Singh, Mutum Bokul (1995): Some Aspects of Socio-Demographic Profile of Tarao. Man In India, 75(1):79-95.

Singh, Nishi (1995): Family and Marriage among Khonds of Koraput District, Orissa – A Comparative Study. Man In India, 75(1):105-110.

Singh, R.A.P. (1990): Methods in Social Research. Printwell Publishers, Jaipur.

Singh, Rita (1996): Equalization of Educational Opportunities – Scheduled Castes and Scheduled Tribes: Problems and Future Strategies. Man In India, 76(2):141-159.

Singh, R. and Kumar, N. (1988): A Qualitative Assessment of the Functioning of PHC in a Tribal Setting – A Case Study. Family Welfare, 35(2):33.

Singh, Udai Pratap and Shukla, R.K. (1992): Trend of Menarche in Five-Endogamous Groups of Tharu Tribal Females of Uttar Pradesh. Man In India, 72(3):343-352.

Singhal, G.D. and Guru, L.V. (1973): Anatomical and Obstetric Considerations in Ancient Indian Surgery. BHU Press, Varanasi, 2:8.

Singhal, Praveen, Gupta, Sagrika and Kaur, Baljinder (1994): Genetic and Socio-Economic Influence on Menarche. J. Hum. Ecol., 5(4):271-275.

Sinha, U.P. (1964): A Comparative Study of the Fertility of the Tribal Labours of Jamashedpur, Buulletin of the Bihar Tribal Research Institute, 6.

Sinha, U.P. (1990): Demographic Profile of Tribal Population in India: 76-104 (In) Demography of Tribal Development. Ed. Asish Bose, U.P. Sinha and R.P. Tyagi. B.R. Publishing Corporation., Shakti Nagar, Delhi.

Sinha, V.C. and Zacharia, E. (1986): Elements of Demography. Allied Publishers Pvt. Ltd.: 1-12.

Sirajuddin, S.M. and Basu, A. (1984): Population Structure, Consanguinity and its Effect on Fertility and Mortality among Chenchu of Andhra Pradesh. Hum. Sci., 33:179-200.

Skinner, G.W. (1975): Change and Persistence in Thai Society (In) Ithaca. Ed. G.W. Skinner. Cornell Uni. Press.

Skinner, G.W. (1977): The City in Late Imperial China. Stanford: Stanford Uni. Press.

Som, Sujit (1993): Demographic Profile of an Orissa Village. Man In India, 73(1): 49-63.

Som, Sujit (1995): The Great Andamanese: An Island Community of Strait Island in Andaman. Man In India, 75(4): 393-399.

Soni, Lok Nath (1985): Agrarian Economy in the Tribal Village.

Case of the Bhilalas: 31-36 (In) Agrarian Situation in India. Ed. S.B. Chakraborty. B.R. Ghosh and Ajit K. Danda. Vol. II, Calcutta: Anthropological Survey of India.

Soni, Lok Nath (1998): Environmental Perspective in Relation to Economy of Some Tribes of Western Madhya Pradesh: 219-228 (In) Tribal Culture and Identity. Ed. Chaturbhuj Sahu. Sarup & Sons Publication, Darya Ganj, New Delhi.

Soni, Lok Nath (1998): The Bhil: 204-218 (In) Tribal Culture and Identity. Ed. Chaturbhuj Sahu. Sarup & Sons Publication, Darya Ganj, New Delhi.

Spuhler, J.N. (1962): Empirical Studies on Quantitative Human Genetics. Proceedings of the UN/WHO Seminar on the Use of Vital Health Statistics for Genetic and Radition Studies. Untied Nations, New York: 241-252.

Spuhler, J.N. (1976): The Maximum Opportunity for Natural Selection in Some Human Populations: 185-226 (In) Demographic Anthropology – Quantitative Approaches. Ed. E.B.W. Zubrow. Albuquerque: University of Mexico Press.

Srikantan, K. Sivaswamy (1989): Family Planning and Fertility Control in India (In) Population: Today and Tomorrow – Policies, Theories and Methodologies. Proceeding of the International Population Conference, New Delhi. Vol. I. B.R. Publishing Corporation, Darya Ganj, New Delhi.

Srinivasan, K. (1988): Some Issues in the Selection and Assessment of the Determinants of Infant Mortality (In) Infant Mortality in India-Differentials and Determinants. Ed. Anrudh K. Jain and Pravin Visaria. Sage Publications, Greater Kailash, New Delhi.

Srivastava, S.C. (1987): Demographic Profile of North-East India. Mittal Publications, New Delhi.

Stockwell, E.G. and Wicks, J.W. (1984): Pattern and Variations in the Relationship Between Infant Mortality and Socio-Economic Status. Soc. Biol., 31:28.

Strassmann, Beverly I. (1997): Polygyny as a Risk Factor for Child Mortality among the Dogon. Curr. Anthrop., 38(4):688-695.

Sudhakar, G., Babu, B.V. and Padma, V. (1997): A Demographic Study of Chakali Caste from Andhra Pradesh. South Asian Anthropologist, 18(1): 37-39.

Sudhakar, G., Padma, V. and Babu, B.V. (1998): Opportunity for Natural Selection in Koppala Velama Caste of West Godavari District, Andhra Pradesh. South Asian Anthropologist, 19(2): 107-109.

Sukhatme, P.V., Edumundson, Wade and Margen, Sheldon (1995): A New Dimension to the Poverty Problem - Education. Hum. Ecol., 6(1): 1-5.

Swedlund, A(1980): Historical Demography: Applications in Anthropological Genetics, Dev. Anthropol, Genet. 1: 17-44.

Swedlund, A and Armelagos, G.T. (1976): Demographic Anthropology. Dubuque: Brown.

Swedlund, A.C. and Armelagos, G.T. (1976): Demographic-Anthropology, W.C. Brown.

Tabah, L. (1980): World Population Trends: A Stocktaking. J. Pop. Dev. Rev., 6: 355.

Talwar, G.P. (1967): A Note on Change in Age at Marriage of Females and Effect on Birth Rates in India. Eug. Quart., 14:291.

Talwar, I., Sharma, K. and Rawat, U. (1987): Socio-Economic Differences in Sexual Maturity in Punjabi Girls: 131 (In) Sports Sciences: Health, Fitness and Performance. Ed. L.A. Siddhu, et.al. IASSPE, Patiala.

Talwar, Prem P. (1988): Infant Mortality-Some Evidences from Rural Madhya Pradesh (In) Infant Mortality in India Differentials and Determinants. Ed. Anirudh K. Jain and Pravin Visaria. Sage Publications, Greater Kailash, New Delhi.

Talwar, P.P. and Bhatia, P.S. (1985): Demographic Situation and Utilization of Health and Family Welfare Services in Rajasthan - A Baseline Survey Report. National Institute of Health and Family Welfare, New Delhi.

Tandon, B. N. and Gandhi, N. (1992): Immunization Coverage in India for Areas Served by the Integrated Child Development Services Programme. The Integrated Child Development Service Consultants. Bulletin of World Health Organisation, 70.

Thakur, Devendra (1993): Research Methodology in Social Science, Deep and Deep Publications, New Delhi.

Thakur, Devendra and Thakur, D.N. (1994): Tribes in Central India: 98-120 (In) Tribal Life in India, Vol. 1. Ed. Devendra Thakur and D.N. Thakur. Deep & Deep Publications, Rajouri Garden, New Delhi.

Thakur, Devendra and Thakur, D.N. (1994): Forest and Tribal Economy: 159-185 (In) Tribal Life in India. Vol.1. Ed. Devendra Thakur and D.N. Thakur, Deep & Deep Publications, Rajouri Garden, New Delhi.

Thakur, Devendra and Thakur, D.N. (1994): Introduction: Tribes in India: 1-38 (In) Tribal Life in India, Vol.4. Ed. Devendra Thakur and D.N. Thakur. Deep & Deep Publications, Rajouri Garden, New Delhi.

Thakur, Devendra and Thakur, D.N. (1994): Scheduled Tribes and Scheduled Areas in India: 39-81 (In) Tribal Life in India, Vol. 1. Ed. Devendra Thakur and D.N. Thakur. Deep & Deep Publications, Rajouri Garden, New Delhi.

Thakur, Devendra and Thakur, D.N. (1994): Socio-Economic Changes of Tribes by Government and Voluntary Agencies (In) Tribal Life in India, Vol. 10. Ed. Devendra Thakur and D.N. Thakur. Deep & Deep Publications, Rajouri Garden, New Delhi.

Thanulingom, N. (1985): Methodology In Social Science, Rainbow Publications, Tamil Nadu.

Thomas, D.S. (1946): The Spoilage,Berkeley, Cal.

Thomas, Mary (1974): Social Dimensions of Rural Population Growth (In) Population Growth and Human Development. Ed. Anthony D'Souza and Alfred De Souza. Indian Social Institute, Indraprastha Press, Bahadur Shah Zafar Marg, New Delhi.

Thomson, W.S. and Lewis, D.T. (1965): Population Problems, McGraw Hill Book Company, New York.

Thukral, A.K. (1996): A Model for Sex Ratio Decline in India. J.Hum. Ecol.,7(2):143-146.

Tiwari, D.N. (1984): Primitive Tribes of Madhya Pradesh. Government of India, Ministry of Home Affairs, Tribal Development Division, New Delhi.

Tiwari, Dinesh Kumar, Sharma, K.K.N. and Dubey, V.S. (2001): Health Profile among Lodha and Munda Tribal Children of Midnapur District, West Bengal. Anthropologist, 3 (3): 189-190.

Tiwari, H.N. and Sinha, Ashok (1997): Incidence of Marriage in Some Population Groups of South Chotanagpur(Bihar). Man In India, 77 (4): 391-396.

Tiwari, Piyush and Sharma, A.N. (2001): An Assessment of Socio-Demographic Correlates Associated with Case of Maternal Malaria. J. Hum. Ecol., 12 (5): 371-373.

Tiwari, R.P. (1998): Level of Literacy among Saur Tribe of Tikamgarh Tahsil of Madhya Pradesh (In) Tribal Culture and Identity. Ed. Chaturbhuj Sahu. Sarup & Sons Publication, Darya Ganj, New Delhi.

Tiwari, R.P. (1998): Tribal Habitat, Economy and Society - A Case Study of Kawar Tribe of Madhya Pradesh (In) Tribal Culture and Identity. Ed. Chaturbhuj Sah. Sarup and Sons Publication, Darya Ganj, New Delhi.

Tiwari, Satish (1999): Indian Population-Today and Tomorrow. Rajat Publications, Geeta Colony, New Delhi.

Tiwari, Satish (2000): Population in South Asia. Rajat Publications, Darya Ganj, New Delhi.

Topal, Y.S., Samal, P.K. and Rawat, D.S (1998): Socio-Economic and Cultural Adaptations in the Sustainable Use and Management of Resources in a High Altitude Village in Central Himalaya. Man In India, 78(1): 9-25.

Trussell, J. and Preston, S.H. (1982): Estimating the Co-variates of Childhood Mortality from Retrospective Reports of Mothers. Health Policy and Education, 3:1.

Turner, H. Jonathan (1994): International Edition-Sociology, Concepts & Uses, Mc. Grow-Hill, Inc.

Udry, R.J. and Cliquet, R.I. (1982): A Cross-Cultural Examination of the Relationship Between Ages at Menarche, Marriage and First Birth. Demography, 19.

U. Ko. Ko. (1987): Children Health: Tomorrow's Wealth. Ind. J. Pediatr., 54(1): 33-34.

Umamani, K.S. and Raju, K.N.M. (1997): Cultural Factors and Pre-Puberty Marriages in Karnataka. Man In India, 74 (4): 363-374.

Unisa, Sayeed (2000): Education and Son Preference in India: A Study Based on NFHS Data. *South Asian Anthropologist*, 21 (1): 23-35.

UNICEF (1991): Children and Women in India: A Situation Analysis, 1990. United Nations Children Fund, New Delhi.

UNICEF (1993): The State of the World's Children, 1990, 1991, 992, 1993. United Nations Children Fund, New Delhi.

U.N. (1958): Determinants and Consequences of Population Trends. Population Studies, No.17, United Nations, New York.

U.N. (1992): World Population Prospectus, Population Division. U.N., New York.

Upreti, R.P. (1969): Bhutias of Uttarkhand: A Study in Cultural Geography. Unpublished Ph.D. Thesis, Agra University: 256-267.

Varte, R. T. (1998): Opportunity for Natural Selection: The Hmar of Manipur, *Ind. J. Hum. Ecol.*, 9(5): 513-514.

Veleti, Kalyani (1998): Patterns of Fertility Control by the Urban Couples: A Socio- Cultural Study in Madras City. *J. Hum. Ecol.*, 9(5): 509-511.

Veleti, Kalyani (2001): Family Structure and its Effective Influence on Fertility. *J. Hum. Ecol.*, 12 (5): 387-390.

Verma, K.K. (1977): *Culture, Ecology and Populations*. Indian National Publishing House, New Delhi.

Verma,S.C. (1978): *The Bhil Kills*. Kunj Publishing House, Delhi.

Vidyarthi, L.P. (1971): The Ranchi Tribals in Andaman and Nicobar Islands. J. Social Research, 14: 50-59.

Vidyarthi, L.P. (1976): Cultural Diversities in the Andaman and Nicobar Islands: A Preliminary Report. *J. Social Research,* 19: 1-15.

Vidyarthi, L.P. and Haldar, A. (1985): Research Methodology in Social Science in India Today and Tomorrow's Printers and Publishers, New Delhi.

Vidyarthi, L.P. and Rai, B.K. (1977): *Tribal Culture of India,* Concept Publishing Company, New Delhi.

Vijayanummi, M. (1995): *Policies, Programme and Population Changes in India.* B.R. Publishing Corporation (P) Ltd., Darya Ganj, New Delhi.

Vithal, C.P. (1992): Socio-Economic Transformation of the Primitive Tribal Group: A Study of Chenchus in Andhra Pradesh, Man In India, 72(2): 189-206.

Ware, H. (1977): Women's Work and Fertility in Africa (In) The Fertility of Working Women: A Synthesis of International Research. Ed. S. Kupinsky. Praeger Publisher, New York.

Ware, H. (1981): Women Demography and Development. Development Study Centre, Australian National University, Canberra.

Weinberg, A.A. (1961): Migration and Belonging: A Study of Mental Health and Personal Adjustment in Israel, Mertinus Nijhoff, The Hague.

Weiss, Kenneth, M. (1976): Demographic Theory and Anthropological Inference. Ann. Rev. Anthrop., 5: 351-381.

Willigan, J. and Lynch K (1982): Sources and Methods of Historical Demography. Academic Press, New York.

Wilson, C. (1985): *Dictionary of Demography.* Basil Blackwell Reference Ltd., London.

Wilson, D.C. and Sutherland, I. (1953): The Age of the Menarche in the Tropics. *J. Brit. Med.,* 2: 607-608.

Wilson, E.O. (1975): *Sociobiology: The New Synthesis*, Cambridge, Belnap.

Wilson, M., Daly, M. and Weghorst, S. (1980): Household Composition and the Risk of Child Abuse and Neglect. *J. Biosocial Science*, 12.

Winick, C. (1957): *Dictionary of Anthropology*.

Wolanski, Nepoleon, Valentin, Graciela, Rojas, Armando and Siniarska, Anna (1998): Age, Season at Menarche, Family Factors and Adult Body Traits in Girls from Yucatan, Mexico (Comparative Study). *J. Hum. Ecol.*, .9(1): 1-17.

World Health Organisation (1970): Technical Report, Series - 442.

World Health Organisation (1971): Planning and Programme for Nursing Series, Public Health Papers, 44.

World Health Organisation (1994): Natal Care Series, 53.

World Health Organisation (1979): *Risk Approach for Maternal and Child Health Care*. WHO Offset Publication, 39.

World Health Organisation (1991): Indicators for Assessing Breast Feeding Practices. Report of an Informal Meeting, 11-12 June, Geneva: WHO.

Wyon, J.B. and Gordon, J.K. (1971): *The Khanna Study: Population Problems in Rural Punjab*. Harvard University Press, Cambridge.

Yadav, Ankur, Sharma, A.N. and Jain, Amita (2001): Socio-Demographic Characteristics of Semi-Nomadic Lohar - Gadiyan of Malthon Town of Sagar District, Madhya Pradesh. *Anthropologist*, 3 (2): 135-137.

Young, P.V. (1960): Scientific Social Survey and Research, 3rd Edition, Prentice Hall, New York.

Young, P. V (1988): *Scientific Social Survey and Research*, Fourth Edition, Prentice Hall of India Pvt. Ltd., New Delhi.

INDEX